D1602263

Poverty and Psychology

From Global Perspective to Local Practice

International and Cultural Psychology Series

Series Editor: **Anthony Marsella**, *University of Hawaii, Honolulu, Hawaii*

ASIAN-AMERICAN MENTAL HEALTH
Assessment Theories and Methods
Edited by Karen S. Kurasaki, Sumie Okazaki, Stanley Sue

THE FIVE-FACTOR MODEL OF PERSONALITY ACROSS CULTURES
Edited by Robert R. McCrae and Juri Allik

POVERTY AND PSYCHOLOGY
From Global Perspective to Local Practice
Edited by Stuart C. Carr and Tod S. Sloan

PSYCHOLOGY AND BUDDHISM
From Individual to Global Community
Edited By Kathleen H. Dockett, G. Rita Dudley-Grant, C. Peter Bankart

TRAUMA INTERVENTIONS IN WAR AND PEACE
Prevention, Practice, and Policy
Edited by Bonnie L. Green, Matthew J. Friedman, Joop de Jong, Susan D. Solomon,
Terence M. Keane, John A. Fairbank, Brigid Donelan, Ellen Frey-Wouters

A Continuation Order Plan is available for this series. A continuation order will bring delivery of each new volume immediately upon publication. Volumes are billed only upon actual shipment. For further information please contact the publisher.

Poverty and Psychology
From Global Perspective to Local Practice

Edited by

Stuart C. Carr
Massey University,
New Zealand/Aotearoa

Tod S. Sloan
Georgetown University,
Washington, D.C.

Kluwer Academic / Plenum Publishers
New York, Boston, Dordrecht, London, Moscow

Library of Congress Cataloging-in-Publication Data

Poverty and psychology: from global perspective to local practice / edited by
 Stuart C. Carr and Tod S. Sloan.
   p.   cm. – (International and cultural psychology)
 Includes bibliographical references and index.
 ISBN 0-306-47764-5
 1. Social psychology.   2. Poverty–Psychological aspects.   I. Carr, Stuart C.   II. Sloan,
Tod Stratton, 1952–   III. International and cultural psychology series.

HM1041.P68 2003
302–dc21   2003051588

ISBN: 0-306-47764-5

© 2003 Kluwer Academic/Plenum Publishers, New York
233 Spring Street, New York, New York 10013

http://www.wkap.nl

10   9   8   7   6   5   4   3   2   1

Acknowledgments

We wish to extend our hearty thanks to Professor Anthony Marsella ('Tony'), for believing in this project throughout. Our sincere appreciation extends to the School of Psychology, Massey University, New Zealand/Aotearoa, for funding the copyediting of the manuscript at a vital stage in its development, and to Georgetown University, Washington DC, for access to library resources. Thank you to the publishing team at Kluwer-Plenum, Christiane Roll in Dordrecht, and Sharon Panulla and Anna Tobias, in New York, for your encouragement and support. Thank you, too, to Kerry Chamberlain, Antonia Lyons, and Darrin Hodgetts, for their generous feedback on Critical Psychology. Last but certainly not least, a big vote for thanks must go to Jude Fredricsen, whose professional copyediting skills and insightful communications helped bring this book to fruition in the proverbial nick of time.

Auckland and Washington,
April 2003

Contents

vii

III. OPPORTUNITY

Chapter 1

Poverty and Psychology
An Introduction

Stuart C. Carr

Poverty is arguably the principal scourge on the planet today. The statistics on it are presented in detail in the next chapter (Prilleltensky, this volume). They are however mind-boggling; almost defying our comprehension. To render them more intelligible therefore, and to paint "the big picture," we need a metaphor, an image. Let us imagine, for instance, that the global village is a community of just 100 persons. In this village, half of the population, or 50 persons, are hungry; 60 live in shanty towns; 70 are illiterate; and just 6 of them control half of the village's total wealth (after Jones, 1999). These are the economics of a grossly distended hourglass (Carr, 1999). They remind us that poverty today is an inherently social as well as economic phenomenon (Marsella, 2003). This book is a response to those reminders. It has been designed to help raise awareness about the behavioral dynamics of poverty, and to suggest ways of redistributing some of the excesses of our age.

Levels of Analysis

Poverty can be understood from a variety of different analytic perspectives, ranging from structural to social, and macro to micro (Müller, 2002). As we might expect in a volume with "psychology" in its title, the contributions in this book are pitched more toward the latter than the former. But they also reflect a raised critical awareness of the limitations in any approach that is overly psychological. In this book, poverty is not pathologized. In fact, the readings derive much of their intellectual and emotional purchase from exploring ways in which poverty *has* been over-psychologized; not only by psychologists themselves, but also by policy makers and the general public alike. Grasping such biases takes us part of the way toward emancipation from them, thus enabling us to reposition ourselves to combat poverty more effectively. To the extent that these goals are shared by all of us, this book and the levels of analysis within it, offer food-for-thought to a range of social scientists, policy makers, and development practitioners.

Those practitioners will be living and working across a swathe of social and community settings. To what extent are our contributions bound by the location of their authors? Firstly, poverty today knows no geographic boundaries (for a hard-hitting example, see http://www.nccbuscc.org/cchd/povertyusa/tour2.htm). Nor does poverty discriminate between sectors urban (http://www.apa.org/pi/urban/povres.html) versus sectors rural (http://www.ezec.gov/About/EmpoweringtheWayOutofPoverty.pdf). Poverty is everywhere. Secondly, the contributors in the book focus more on process than on content per se. They discuss processes of power and prejudice, processes of empowerment and development, and the acquisition of process skills for development out of poverty. Thus, there are at least two major reasons why this book is anchored, but not bounded, by the locale of its contributors.

To see why and how psychology has moved toward these relatively borderless and process-based accounts of the psychology of poverty, we need to trace some of the history in the psychological study of poverty.

A Brief History of Psychology and Poverty

This history can be divided into a series of overlapping layers and phases. If we begin our Cook's tour in the late 1950s, for example, there is a relatively sociological account of poverty. This is best encapsulated in the concept of a "culture of poverty" (Lewis, 1959). During the 1960s, the field moved toward a much more psychological approach, captured most succinctly in the concept of a Need for Achievement (McClelland, 1961). In a similarly psychological way, the 1970s were largely focused on attribution theory, and in particular on how the comparatively wealthy view the causes of poverty amongst the relatively deprived (Feagin, 1972). The 1980s, in turn, witnessed something of a crisis of confidence in this type and level of analysis, culminating in suggestions that psychology may be doing more harm than good (for examples, see Sinha & Holzman, 1984). During the 1990s however, tentative calls that psychology might be able to make a difference began to be appear (e.g., Sloan & Montero, 1990; Carr & MacLachlan, 1998). By the new millennia, we are witnessing a renewed debate about the role of psychology, in fostering critical awareness of the causes of, and solutions to, poverty (Cohen, 2001). This book is situated within, and indeed forms part of, that zeitgeist.

As we briefly review each of the phases below, an attempt will be made to extract the key lessons from each period, with respect to their implications for contemporary understandings and practice. As we do this, it will become apparent that any and every approach is partly a product of its time. This is salutary for us as contemporary readers. It reminds us that the forthcoming readings, too, are a microcosm of their own time. Finally, the historical review will trace the extent to which psychology has moved toward a greater appreciation of the macro, just as the relatively macro disciplines, such as economics, have been moving in the opposite direction (Sen, 1999). In that way, we can appreciate more the broader academic, as well as applied context for the readings that follow.

The Culture of Poverty

In his classic (1959) study *Five Families*, Oscar Lewis argues that people often know less about everyday poverty on their own doorsteps than they do about everyday life in exotic locations in "traditional" societies. Adopting an ethnographic approach, *Five Families* reports a typical day in the life of five Mexican families, whose living conditions and lifestyles vary in their degree of assimilation to "modern" material society of the time. Although Lewis's method was social anthropological, and participant observational (he lived among his subjects over a 15-year period), he also adapted his method specifically to learn more "about the *psychology* of the people . . . how they think and feel" (1959, p. 1; emphasis added). Thus, Lewis's approach to poverty was and is inherently behavioral (see also, Lewis, 1966).

Lewis's message in *Five Families* is that development is often a descent into poverty; that the leaving behind of preliterate cultures gives rise to a "culture of poverty" that is also a "poverty of culture." Over and above the implied romanticism of "traditional" cultures, Lewis believes that the "culture of poverty cuts across regional, rural-urban, and even national boundaries (1959, p. 2). Included in this culture of poverty are factors such as flat affect, family tension, a certain brutality, and generally less space for the "finer," emotions (for additional aspects of the culture of poverty, see Sarbin, 1970). According to Lewis, the road to materialism, despite providing more material goods, is paved with an insidious and ultimately degrading assimilation of materialistic culture, as a generally impoverished existence becomes the norm. One of the most acid features of this sordid form of poverty is a growing disparity between the incomes of poor and rich: Six out of ten of the population are still hungry; six out of ten are ill-housed; and approaching four out of ten are illiterate (1959, p. 9).

As these kinds of figures suggest, the Five Families study can be compared and contrasted with more recent perspectives in several interesting ways. For example, the attempt to study poverty through shared perspectives, and through respecting meaning, is not dissimilar to the kinds of studies about to be reported in this volume,

4 Stuart C. Carr

such as the Voices of the Poor study, which is described in later chapters 2, 6, and 12. At the same time however, the voices of the poor in Lewis's study seem somehow less life-like; less three-dimensional. The reader still feels like an outsider, unable to get in. The tone of the earlier account seems for example to be patronizing – not passing comment directly yet still managing to implicitly position "the poor" well *beneath* the reader: "The smells of unwashed feet, sweat, shoe leather, and fried food, pervaded the room" (1959, p. 64); while, "Their favorite programs are 'El teatro Nescafé,' 'El programa de Max Factor,' 'Pedro Vargas,' and 'El conde de Monte Cristo.' Juanito liked the cartoons" (p. 82).

In the new *Voices of the Poor* (World Bank, 2001), there is more animation: "Poverty is humiliation, the sense of being dependent on them, and of being forced to accept rudeness, insults, and indifference when we seek help" (woman, Latvia, p. 3); "Don't ask me what poverty is because you have met it outside my house. Look at the house and count the number of holes. Look at the utensils and the clothes I am wearing. Look at everything and write what you see. What you see is poverty" (man, Kenya, p. 3). Perhaps this amplified animation is because of today's more constant reminders of wealth and relative deprivation, and a growing awareness of human rights. Perhaps, too, it shines through because our methods are better. I do not know. Either or both ways however, with the passage of time, the "assimilation" into a global community seems to have headed in an opposite, more vociferous and assertive direction to the one originally implied in *Five Families*.

The Behavioral Economics of Poverty

During the 1960s and early 1970s, David McClelland and colleagues articulated what is arguably the most "psychological" of all approaches to-date toward understanding and remedying the state of poverty. The McClelland approach focused on a particular trait, Need for Achievement (NAch). This is now classically defined as 'seeking success in competition with a standard of excellence' (McClelland and Winter, 1971, p. 95). As McClelland and Winter's research showed, the concept of nAch was very much rooted in micro-business, and in particular in the domain of small-medium enterprise (SME) development (McClelland, 1987a, 1987b). Small-medium enterprises are still very much a key concept in development studies generally (World Bank Group, 2001). However, today there is growing recognition that one size does not fit all; that successful small business psychology has to be tailored to fit the local as well as global context (Panda, 2000).

There are a number of reasons for a relative decline of interest in McClelland's own formulation of how Need for Achievement relates to development out of poverty. Firstly, the concept as he defined it has lost its statistical capability to predict economic growth and development (Lewis, 1991). Other values have now repeatedly superseded the relatively individualistic form of competition envisaged by McClelland (e.g., Chinese Culture Connection, 1987; Yu & Yang, 1994; Ornatowski, 1996). Secondly, a reappraisal of some of McClelland et al.'s original data, concerning the impact of training in nAch, reveals that the trainee entrepreneurs who succeeded most also managed to blend what they had learned more effectively with enduring local traditions (McClelland, 1987b; Carr, Mc Auliffe, & MacLachlan, 1998). This same point is suggested too in Panda (2000) and by other commentators (e.g., Lawuyi, 1992). Finally, and most significantly perhaps, the nAch concept has fallen out of use, and usefulness, because of its inherent individualism – and a resultant poor fit to the multicultural and pluralistic realities of the twenty-first century (Hermans & Kempen, 1998).

The Psychologizing of Poverty

The tendency to psychologize poverty that nAch pioneered continued into the 1970s (Feagin, 1972). Feagin's work, and the research it later stimulated, is well reviewed later in this book (Furnham, this volume). Suffice to say, the focus now was on lay attributions for poverty, predominantly attributions being made by the comparatively privileged, i.e., the "non-poor" in the population (for a nice early overview of this lay psychology, see Rainwater, 1970). In a bizarre twist of irony, much of the research failed to appreciate the "fundamental attribution error" (over-blaming the poor for poverty). Thus, although attribution had the potential to be used to *raise* awareness about biases that contribute toward the perpetuation of poverty, it largely failed to do so (Harper, this volume). Instead, as Harper argues, psychology became more a part of the problem than of the solution.

The Poverty of Psychology

This phrase was first used by Pearl (1970), who presaged a growing sentiment that really came to the fore during the 1980s (Sinha & Holtzman, 1984). During this period emerged the sentiment that psychology had had very little impact on poverty levels generally (Melikian, 1984), and was even potentially a negative influence (Mehryar, 1984). Mehryar's critique centered round the idea precisely that "psychologizing" poverty was liable to pathologize the poor rather than the system that constrained them. As such, psychology was playing directly into the hands of those who would wish to keep the wealthy and the poor in their respective places. At the same time however – and this is a theme developed in later chapters in the book – Mehryar also raised the possibility that psychology, and the likes of attribution theory, could be used to sensitize the relatively privileged of the world to appreciate more mindfully their own biases and complicity in keeping the poor "in" poverty. Thus, even during the most difficult of periods for psychology, there was still a glimmer of hope that it could, if applied reasonably mindfully, make a difference.

A Modest Optimism

By the turn of the next decade, the feeling that psychology had a contribution to make was beginning to grow (Sinha, 1990). Sinha's review noted not only potential contributions from attribution theory itself, but also reviewed, for example, design input to interventions for improving health and nutrition among materially impoverished pre-school children. A further review of the role of psychology in helping to reduce poverty concluded that significant contributions could be made in three major life domains, namely (a) health and welfare, (b) social and organizational change, and (c) educational and human development (Carr & MacLachlan, 1998). In order to achieve those improvements, it was argued, greater respect would need to be shown, by psychology and psychologists, toward the interaction between global and local norms (see also, Hermans & Kempen, 1998). For example, Technical Assistance projects, which theoretically consist of expatriates mentoring local replacements for themselves (Chapter 3, this volume), are unlikely to work unless a way is found to remunerate both expatriate "mentor" and local counterpart "mentee" alike, with reasonably equitable, and to that extent just and workable salaries (Carr et al., 1998).

To summarise therefore, during the latter half of the twentieth century, psychology struggled to find a way to make any kind of contribution toward the understanding and reduction of poverty. An initial foray into ethnographic understandings, based on "cultural" rather than "natural" science, soon gave way to increasingly "psychological" approaches (for further evidence of this, see Allen, 1970, especially the Introduction, and Parts 2 and 3 of the book). In that way, Lewis's relatively sociological approach was probably abandoned too early, in favor of an overly psychological tack. Criticism of that direction however then began to rise. The criticism reached its peak during the 1980s. At this point, a reversal of the previous trend began to occur. As a result of that sea change, the new millennium has brought renewed opportunities for psychology to claim a voice. Broadly speaking, this is where the present collection comes in.

A Fresh Start

The collection of readings in this book is designed to reflect a diversity of new approaches to understanding poverty that are being explored, developed, and enacted around the world. These approaches are part of what seems to be a growing response to the criticality of the issue – poverty – that faces the global community. Now is a time when we are witnessing for example the American Psychological Association (or APA) "declare war" on poverty (APA, 2000). As part of this declaration, the APA has become affiliated to the United Nations (Murray, 1998). We are also witnessing entire issues of journals, and books, examining the psychology of poverty, and the poverty of psychology (respectively, for example, Cohen, 2001; and Bullock et al., 2001).

These contributions are part of several wider zeitgeists in psychology. First, there is a growing realization that psychology has over-focused on the "negative" in human behavior, instead of accentuating the positive, and celebrating the various strengths of human spirit (see for example http://www.positivepsychology.org/). Consistent with that growing positive rebound, the second major strand of change is a growing awareness of the situational context in which human behavior occurs. Instead of making "fundamental attribution errors," today's more critical psychology reminds us of the inherent fluidity of people, and their inherent capacity to position themselves to overcome situational constraints (for a lucid example, see Chapter 12, this volume). That ethos, of being inherently capable of change, is where this book is positioned.

Structure of the Book

Just as psychology has been moving again toward a greater appreciation of the role of relatively macro, structural realities in poverty, so, too, the conventionally more macro-level disciplines and agencies, like economics and the World Bank, have been re-integrating "the social" back into their development equations (Sen, 1999; World Bank, 2001). In respect of that zeitgeist, this book contains, for example, many references to Professor Sen's work. Broadly speaking too, we have tried to reflect the shift, and the above convergences, in the *structure* of the book. Specifically, this book utilizes the "three pillars" structure for development out of poverty, identified in the World Development Report for 2000/2001 (World Bank, 2001).

This report is explicitly focused not only on poverty, but also on addressing the needs of poor people on three critical fronts: security; empowerment; and opportunity. Improving security involves reducing, for instance, vulnerability to illness; to natural disasters; and to violence. Empowerment entails according the poor greater "voice" and thereby procedural, distributive, and interactional justice (Ambrose, Seabright, & Schminke, 2002). As one practitioner-manager succinctly puts it, "In the 1970s, development agencies worked for the poor; today they endeavor to work with the poor" (Richards, 2002). Thirdly and finally, the pillar of opportunity involves facilitating greater inclusion of "the poor" in the global economy, whether this occurs through human or material capacity. The latter can include, for example, increasing access to education and training, or to clean land and water (for an earlier discussion of opportunity and poverty, Hunt, 1970). Clean land and water are of course part of security. Thus, whilst being conceptually distinct, the three pillars are functionally linked into one, coherent structure.

Such functional interconnectedness appealed to us as editors. Firstly, it avoids any associations with previous psychological edifices in development work, such as Maslow's ubiquitous and arguably now clichéd linear "hierarchy of needs." Instead, this book recognizes that people can be motivated in parallel, by a diversity of needs. As one Indigenous spokesperson succinctly says, "We want health, housing, and education; but not at the expense of losing our own soul; our own identity; a say in our lives" (Dodson, 1998, p. 8). In other words, without cultural pride, and without all three pillars together, there is no real foundation for concerted development out of poverty. One pillar does not carry the roof. Secondly, the structure was clearly capable of assimilating the contributions that we received for this volume, without any artificial or contrived stretching. Undoubtedly, this was at least partly due to the third and final reason why we chose the structure: The taxonomy of development that it proposes is inherently accommodating toward a psychological perspective. As one earlier writer cogently remarked:

> Too many well-intentioned programs for ameliorating society have ended disastrously, or with unintended and undesirable consequences, because of our insufficient understanding of the psychological characteristics of individuals involved, or because of our inability to predict the psychological impact of programs conspicuously non-psychological in nature. (Allen, 1970, p. 4)

On that suitably mezzanine note, i.e., somewhere in-between the overly micro and the overly macro, let us briefly review the contributions about to follow.

Contents of the Book

Security

The opening chapter, by Isaac Prilleltensky, is perfect for a book of this nature, and for the reader who wishes to grasp "the big picture" on poverty as a basis for the journey to come. In it, Professor Prilleltensky traces the key threads in the fabric of poverty. Links are made for example with the socio-economic perspective articulated by Professor Amartya Sen (1999). Cross-level connections are made between structural and psychological factors, macro- and micro-level processes (see also, Rauch, 2002). Material indices of poverty and deprivation in society are, for example, linked to more micro-level health and well-being indicators. And at the root of these linkages, and at the core of the chapter, Prilleltensky identifies power, and the dynamics of power. Thus, poverty is fundamentally about powerlessness, and the inherent insecurities that this brings.

Those insecurities include for example social injustice, lack of well-being, joblessness, and placelessness. These themes are taken up each, in turn, by the remaining contributions in the section.

Chapter 3 focuses on poverty and injustice, and in particular on how even the best-laid intentions to foster the sense of justice, by aid organizations for instance, can backfire badly. The arenas for such dynamics to unfurl range from charitable fund-raising, to field assignments in expatriate aid, to the very idea of "aiding" others generally. The chapter then focuses on development "from within," as an alternative model for restoring senses of justice. The chapter uses this analysis to synthesize a theory of social justice in the context of poverty. The theory reflects a distillation of several existing principles, ranging from equity, to social identity, to systems archetypes. Its core notion is social equity. In this model, stakeholders in development are motivated to attain and retain a sense of social justice, and power balance, in the transactions between their community and the economy.

This idea of power imbalances, and unfavorable social transactions, is taken further in Chapter 4, on poverty and psychopathology. In the chapter, Fulbright Professor Virginia Moreira describes how political systems and "caring" professions, like psychologists, are still psycho-pathologizing the poor. In that way, a "culture of poverty" is nurtured and sustained by the "medicalization of poverty." A clear example of the interconnectedness between power, and justice, and this positioning of the poor somewhere "beneath" the rest of humanity is found in Professor Moreira's analysis of psychosocial helping professions in Brazil. Even in their supposedly different human service teams, the medical "team" members are still awarded considerably higher salaries than their counterparts from the humanities and social sciences. Medical power still reigns supreme, symbolizing the continuing precedence given to a pathological model of "the poor." Plus ça change...

This idea of the helping professions purporting to aid, but actually contributing toward the problem, is developed further in Chapter 5, on poverty and unemployment. In this chapter, Professors Fryer and Fagan begin by showing how misleading and obscuring official unemployment figures can be in a global economy. More germane, for example, is likely to be the sense of economic insecurity that has accompanied the global trend toward casualized, part-time, and contractual labor. Having made this point, the chapter then takes a masterful turn, illustrating precisely how classical research, "on" the unemployed, conducted of course by researchers who are "employed" to do the research, actually contributes toward the medicalization of poverty. The chapter therefore concludes by articulating a critical community psychological perspective, on the type of employment research that positions the voices of the poor *center*-stage rather than *off*stage; that repositions the poor as interrogating *the system* rather than the other way around.

The concept of community voice is taken to its logical conclusion in the chapter by Peter Spink, which focuses on poverty and sense of place. Like the preceding chapters, Chapter 6 draws much of its inspiration from the works of Professor Sen, and from critical psychology generally. Somewhere between "the community" and "civil society," Spink argues, is the socially constructed "place." The place is a social construction as much as a material one. It is also, more importantly and practically, a conduit for the development of agency. Drawing upon a wide range of community development projects and experiences in the contemporary Brazilian context, Spink illustrates for us the criticality of having a shared nexus of physical and mental spaces; schemata from and around which concerted agency can be orchestrated. In the final analysis therefore, having a sense of place is crucial for counteracting and overcoming insecurity (for an earlier discussion of sense of place, see Kelly & Sewell, 1988).

Empowerment

Having a shared sense of place implies a psychological community, which in turn suggests empowerment. Opening the empowerment section of the book is a chapter by Professors Sánchez, Cronick, and Wiesenfeld, on poverty and community. These authors, who are also leading practitioners, describe how community social psychology (CSP) has taken root in Venezuela. One of the foundations of this paradigm is action research, in which the psychologists becomes part of the process instead of pretending that he or she is somehow 'outside of' (i.e., above) it. Community social psychology is all about agency, and takes as a central goal the promotion of mental health, assertiveness, and, more generally, empowerment. Critical psychology too is part-and-parcel of the CSP movement, notably via its raising of consciousness about the psychology of poverty itself, and via the concerted articulation of human voice. Among those voices, these authors argue, should be heard the political declarations of the psychologist him or her self.

Right at the heart of this political struggle, and at the core of empowerment generally, is the issue of prejudice. In their chapter on poverty and prejudice, Anthony Le Mieux and Felicia Pratto outline an emergent model of prejudice, Social Dominance Theory (or SDT). SDT integrates the concepts of prejudice and power, with one of its central tenets being that power differentials are implicitly internalized into self and role schemata that legitimate and motivate prejudice and discrimination against "the poor." These schemata resemble psychosocial fault-lines that can be activated by the inequities of socio-economic turbulence, and other features of globalization like "free trade." The result is discriminating behavior that opens up the poverty differential still further. In that way, poverty has as much to do with social relationships, and the dynamics of prejudice and empowerment, as it does with the distribution of material resources.

At the core of these social relationships is how each group, relatively poor and prosperous alike, perceive each other. The process of perception is given a scholarly overview in our next chapter, by Professor Adrian Furnham, on poverty and wealth. Himself a leading researcher in the area, Professor Furnham gives us an insightful and lucid commentary on the attribution theory approach to poverty research, that has arguably dominated the psychology of poverty since the early 1970s (Feagin, 1972). After reviewing the chief psychological components of lay theories about poverty, their primary ideological foundations, and their links to charitable behavior, the reader is then given an authoritative analysis of the contemporary relevance of this research to understanding social representations about welfare and homelessness. Furnham's take-home message is that attributions have functions, aiding the comparatively wealthy to "make sense" out of their own position in a society vis-à-vis "the poor." If we want to understand the behavior of the wealthy toward those poor, then we need to understand this "sense-making" function in greater detail.

That task is taken up anew in Chapter 10, written by David Harper. He argues that critical social psychology must take up where attribution theory leaves off. A more discursive approach, Harper argues, would be better positioned to appreciate the fluidity of donor thinking. In addition, critical discursive theory would help to generate more politically aware questions about the role of organizations and systems, rather than individuals and their personal dispositions, in perpetuating and exacerbating poverty. Among the examples that Harper gives are discourses produced and perpetuated within media organizations; within charitable and self-help organizations, both non-governmental and multilateral; within commercial organizations such as multinationals; and within government organizations themselves. Thus, Harper's take-home message is that psychologists can play a part in the amelioration of poverty, by helping to externalize and articulate the discourses around poverty that are created by organizational groups.

This concept is put to the empirical test in the next and final chapter in the section, on poverty and economic crisis. The Aus-Thai Project Team is a multinational and multidisciplinary group of researchers, who decided to apply psychological theory to the Asian economic crisis of the late 1990s. The goal of the project was to chart the rudiments of a process, by which the various stakeholders in economic crisis, including community-based organizations, aid organizations, commercial interests, and the poor and wealthy alike, could attempt to base their discourses about each other on something more solid than mere speculation. To this end, the Aus-Thai Project Team developed a prototype measure of attributions, about both causes of and solutions to economic crisis. That instrument was based on listening to voices from both sides of the development equation, comparatively rich and poor alike. In this way, the Aus-Thai Project chose to respect the value of empowerment.

In addition to this empowerment, there was a second interrelated element in the ethos of the Aus-Thai project. Its ultimate purpose in gathering diverse perceptions on the causes of and solutions to economic crisis was to facilitate the development of confidence and trust in the other party – for example as a future trading partner or as a site for future investment and collaboration. Social capital precedes economic capital. In this way, bursting the bubble of misperception can create opportunities for development that might otherwise not occur. This theme of opportunity is where the remaining readings in the book are focused.

Opportunity

When we think of "opportunity," one of the first words that spring to mind is likely to be "youth." In Chapter 12, Carola Eyber and Alistair Ager focus on this youth demographic, and in particular on the demographic group that today are described as "emerging adults." Amongst the poor, the position of the displaced poor is particularly tenuous, both materially and psychosocially. They often possess no means for communicating or sharing their experiences. Many of them, on the face of it, are particularly vulnerable because they lack access to traditional rites of passage to the adult stage of life. This lack of social "anchorage points" undoubtedly contributes to what many older adults perceive as "unruly" behavior. Yet the chapter prefers instead to accentuate the positive. When the voices of youth are listened to with a more positive attitude, the message we hear is eagerness for education, and for the right conditions to establish a new life. The focus is on the future, not on the past; on agency not dependency or delinquency. Many of the Angolan youths in Eyber and Ager's study are for instance very active in the so-called "informal sector" (Rugimbana, Zeffane, & Carr, 1996). Such resourcefulness, in the face of great resourcelessness, indicates tremendous opportunity for disenfranchised youth to engage in a constructive way with the wider world.

That theme, of an inherent opportunity for participation in the new order, is taken one step further in the next chapter, by Bill Ivory. This author-practitioner looks toward pre-colonial history as a source of inspiration and motivation for economic development. Before colonialization, there was a vibrant economy across the Indigenous Far North of Australia. In his work with the Office of Aboriginal Development, Ivory participates in the resurgence of traditional values, through facilitating the development of small businesses. Most of the world's poor believe that such opportunities are the stuff of development out of poverty (World Bank Group, 2001). Ivory's Indigenous communities are no exceptions to this rule. The chapter illustrates vividly for example how traditional values are a good "fit" to the global economy of the twenty-first century, and how genuine opportunities for business development are adopted readily by the Indigenous communities with whom Ivory works. There is no trace here of so-called "welfare dependency" that has often dominated discourse around Indigenous issues in Australia.

The Office of Aboriginal Development project that Ivory's chapter details, is part of the wider shift away from working *for* the poor to working *with* them (above). This theme is developed further in the chapter by Professors MacLachlan and Mc Auliffe, on poverty and process skills. Consistent with Ivory's project, process skills entail a focus by both community and community aid workers alike on the process of building capacity incrementally, from within the community and upon the community's existing value systems. In MacLachlan and Mc Auliffe's model, aid workers seeking to enjoin this process are encouraged first of all to listen to critical incidents, negative and positive, that the poor have experienced. By listening in this way, it becomes possible for aspiring aid workers to appreciate the value of perspective taking (Nickerson, 1999). They are enabled to critically appraise their own limitations vis-à-vis the community they seek to join. Giving themselves permission to stumble like this gives aid workers a greater appreciation of the realities of poverty, and, in turn, of processes for development out of it.

That message, about *sharing* the perspective of others, through learning by listening, so far has not been very well heeded by social marketing teams in aid organizations. As Chapter 15 points out, many of their advertising campaigns still rely principally on the "hard sell," and on the constraints of manufacturing guilt with no real catharsis to follow. Carr and Atkin's chapter on poverty research analyses the likely sequelae of this approach, from a social psychological point of view. Linking together several apparently diverse lines of enquiry, from management research on organizational learning to laboratory research on backlashes in response to admonishments *not* to stereotype minorities, these authors argue that aid advertisements, as currently structured and designed, are causing more harm than good. By creating implicit backlashes against the poor, these advertisements are fuelling rather than attacking poverty. To combat these deleterious processes, Carr and Atkins outline an action plan for concerted laboratory research, on the psychosocial dynamics of bad and good aid advertisements. Their message, as researchers, is that psychologists can turn their skills for generating economic capital toward generating *social* capital as well.

This point leads us nicely, finally, to an epilogue for the book as a whole. The closing chapter in the volume is an opening. It is an opportune "call to arms" to psychologists the world over, to come out of their proverbial shells; to declare their own interests in the new global order; and to join with others who would seek to eradicate the global scourge that is poverty. We will probably not see this goal realized in our lifetime, but it would be strange indeed if it ever came to pass without at least some contribution from the self-professed students of human behavior.

References

Allen, V. L. (Ed.). (1970). *Psychological factors in poverty*. Chicago, IL: Markham Publishing Company.

Ambrose, M. L., Seabright, M. A., & Schminke, M. (2002). Sabotage in the workplace: The role of organizational injustice. *Organizational & Human Decision Processes, 89*, 947–965.

APA (American Psychological Association). (2000). Resolution on poverty and socio-economic status. http://www.apa.org/pi/urban/povres.html

Bullock, H. E., Wyche, K. F., & Williams, W. R. (Eds.). (2001). Listening to the voices of poor women (special issue). *Journal of Social Issues, 57*, 1–246. [Whole no. 57].

Carr, S. C. (1999). Privilege, privation and proximity: "Eternal triangle" for development? *Psychology and Developing Societies, 12*, 167–176.

Carr, S. C., & MacLachlan, M. (1998). Psychology and developing countries: Reassessing its impact. *Psychology and Developing Societies, 10*, 1–20.

Carr, S. C., Mc Auliffe, E., & MacLachlan, M. (1998). *Psychology of aid*. London: Routledge.

Chinese Culture Connection. (1987). Chinese values and the search for culture-free dimensions of culture. *Journal of Cross-Cultural Psychology, 18*, 143–164.

Cohen, S. (2001). *States of denial: Knowing about atrocities and suffering*. Oxford, UK: Polity.

Dodson, P. (1998). Will the circle be broken? Cycles of survival for Indigenous Australians. North Australia Research Unit Discussion Paper 12. Darwin, Australia: The Australian National University.

Feagin, J. R. (1972). Poverty: We still believe that God helps those who help themselves. *Psychology Today, 6*, 101–129.

Hermans, H. J. M., & Kempen, H. J. G. (1998). Moving cultures: The perilous problems of cultural dichotomies in a globalizing society. *American Psychologist, 53*, 1111–1120.

Hunt, J. M. (1970). Poverty versus equality of opportunity. In V. L. Allen (Ed.), *Psychological factors in poverty* (pp. 47–63). Chicago, IL: Markham Publishing Company.

Jones, M. L. (1999, June). *Development Management and community development*. Darwin, Australia: Northern Territory University.

Kelly, A., & Sewell, S. (1988). *With head, heart, and hand: Dimensions of community building* (2nd ed.). Brisbane, Australia: Boolarong Publishers.

Lawuyi, O. B. (1992). Vehicle slogans as personal and social thought: A perspective on self-development in Nigeria. *New Directions for Educational Reform, 1*, 91–98.

Lewis, J. (1991). Re-evaluating the effect of nAch on economic growth. *World Development, 19*, 1269–1274.

Lewis, O. (1959). *Five families: Mexican case studies in the culture of poverty*. New York, NY: Basic Books.

Lewis, O. (1966). The culture of poverty. *Scientific American, 215*, 19–25.

Marsella, A. J. (2003). Reflections on terrorism: Issues, concepts, and directions. In F. M. Moghaddam & A. J. Marsella (Eds.), *Global community psychology* (in press).

McClelland, D. C. (1961). *The achieving society*. Princeton, NJ: Van Nostrand.

McClelland, D. C. (1987a). Characteristics of successful entrepreneurs. *Journal of Creative, 21*, 219–233.

McClelland, D. C. (1987b). *Human motivation*. Cambridge, UK: Cambridge University Press.

McClelland, D. C., & Winter, D. G. (1971). *Motivating economic achievement*. New York, NY: The Free Press.

Mehryar, A. H. (1984). The role of psychology in national development: Wishful thinking and reality. *International Journal of Psychology, 19*, 59–67.

Melikian, L. H. (1984). The transfer of psychological knowledge to the "Third World" countries and its impact on their development: The case of five Arab Gulf oil-producing states. *International Journal of Psychology, 19*, 65–67.

Müller, G. P. (2002). Explaining poverty: On the structural constraints of income mobility. *Social Indicators Research, 59*, 301–319.

Murray, B. (1998). United Nations needs help from psychology. *APA Monitor, 29, October*, 10.

Nickerson, R. S. (1999). How we know – and *sometimes misjudge* – what others know: Imputing one's own knowledge to others. *Psychological Bulletin, 125*, 737–59.

Ornatowski, G. K. (1996). Confucian ethics and economic development: A study of the adaptation of Confucian values to modern Japanese economic ideology and institutions. *Journal of Socio-Economics, 25*, 571–590.

Panda, N. M. (2000). What brings entrepreneurial success in a developing region? *The Journal of Entrepreneurship, 9*, 199–212.

Pearl, A. (1970). The poverty of psychology – an indictment. In V. L. Allen (Ed.), *Psychological factors in poverty* (pp. 348–364). Chicago, IL: Markham Publishing Company.

Rainwater, L. (1970). Neutralizing the disinherited: Some psychological aspects of understanding the poor. In V. L. Allen (Ed.), *Psychological factors in poverty* (pp. 1–8). Chicago, IL: Markham Publishing Company.

Rauch, J. (2002). Seeing around corners. *The Atlantic Monthly, 4*, 35–48.

Richards, T. (2002). *New Zealand abroad*. Wellington, NZ: Bridget Williams Books.
Rugimbana, R. O., Zeffane, R., & Carr S. C. (1996). Marketing psychology in developing countries. In S. C. Carr & J. F. Schumaker (Eds.), Psychology and the developing world (pp. 140–149). Westport, CT: Praeger.
Sarbin, T. R. (1970). The culture of poverty, social identity, and cognitive outcomes. In V. L. Allen (Ed.), *Psychological factors in poverty* (pp. 29–46). Chicago, IL: Markham Publishing Company.
Sen, A. (1999). *Development as freedom*. Oxford: Oxford University Press.
Sinha, D. (1990). Interventions for development out of poverty. In R. W. Brislin (Ed.), *Applied cross-cultural psychology* (pp. 77–97). Newbury Park, CA: Sage.
Sinha, D., & Holtzman, W. H. (Eds.). (1984). The impact of psychology on "Third World" development [special issue]. *International Journal of Psychology, 19*, 3–192 [Whole issue no. 19].
Sloan, T. S., & Montero, M. (Eds.). (1990). Psychology for the "Third World": A sampler (special issue). *Journal of Social Issues, 46*, 1–151 [Whole issue no. 46]
World Bank. (2001). Attacking poverty: Opportunity, empowerment, and security (World Development Report, 2000/2001). http://www.worldbank.org/
World Bank Group. (2001). Review of small business activities. http://www.ifc.org/smc/html/annual_review.html
Yu, A. B., & Yang, K. S. (1994). The nature of achievement motivation in collectivist societies. *Cross-Cultural research and methodology, 18*, 239–266.

Part I

Insecurity

Chapter 2

Poverty and Power

Isaac Prilleltensky

In the time that it takes you to read this page, approximately 60 children under five will die; most of them from malnutrition and preventable diseases. Hourly, that is about 1,140 children. Annually, that is about 10 million lives. In sub-Saharan Africa, the rate of under-five mortality is 172 per 1,000 live births. In industrialized countries, the rate is 6 per 1,000. While many in the West worry about obesity in children, 149 million children in developing countries experience malnourishment. Some people drink bottled water, others drink only filtered water; 1.1 billion people around the globe have no access to safe water at all (UNICEF, 2001).

But poverty is not something that happens only in remote places to different people. It happens in industrialized countries as well. One in every six children in OECD nations lives in poverty. This equates to about 47 million children. Despite a doubling and redoubling of national income in most (OECD) nations, a significant percentage of their children are still living in families so materially poor that normal health and growth are at risk (UNICEF Innocenti Research Centre, 2000, p. 5). "Relative poverty" is a common term used in industrialized countries. It refers to families with incomes below 50% of the national median. According to that formula, child poverty in OECD countries ranges from 2.8% of all children in Sweden, to 7.9% in France, 12.6% in Australia, 15.5% in Canada and 22.4% in the USA.

Another way to appreciate the toll of poverty is with regard to life expectancy. In 1986, the life expectancy for a Russian male at age 15 was 52 years. In 1994, after the collapse of the economy, males at age 15 could be expected to live only to age 45 (Marmot, 1999). For males, the probability of death between the ages of 15 and 60 in the year 2020 is 32% for the former socialist economies of Europe and sub-Saharan countries, 18% for Latin America, and 12% for most OECD countries (Marmot, 1999). In Britain, life expectancy at age 15 varies considerably among

19

social classes. Data for the period 1987–91 show that women in the bottom two social classes are expected to live 3.4 years less (62.4 years) than those in the top two classes (65.8). For men, the disparity is greater: those in the lower classes will live 4.7 years less (55.8) than those in the upper classes (60.5 years) (Shaw, Dorling, & Smith, 1999).

While shocking, the statistics mask the human face of poverty. A story told by Jean-Bertrand Aristide (2000), child advocate and former president of Haiti, reveals the suffering as well as the resilience and solidarity of the Haitian people. A one-month-old baby was found in a pile of garbage by a poor woman. Part of his hand had been eaten by ants. The poor woman, who already had two children of her own to feed, immediately and without hesitation adopted the baby. Reflecting on the resilience of his people, Aristide (2000, p. 21) invokes wealth of humor, warmth of character, ease of laughter, dignity, and solidarity as building blocks of resistance and strength. In developing countries women sell their own organs to feed their children, while children from young age go to work to support their parents (Feuerstein, 1997). This chapter is about the grim realities of poverty, but also about the struggle to survive it with dignity and solidarity, and about strategies for eliminating poverty. All over the world poor people engage in incredible acts of courage to sustain their families and communities. They do so in the face of adversity, discrimination, exclusion, illness, and forbidding economic crises (Feuerstein, 1997; Lustig, 2001).

The aim of this chapter is to understand the role of power in the following dimensions of poverty: experiences, consequences, sources, and actions. I will explore the implications of these dimensions of poverty for suffering and for wellness. I will do this in three domains: the collective, the relational, and the personal.

Overview

The chapter follows a praxis orientation that combines vision and values, phenomenology and experiential knowledge, social science, health research, and action to overcome oppression (Prilleltensky, 2001). According to this paradigm, the object of committed social science is not only to document but also to transform conditions of suffering and exploitation (Carspecken, 1996; Flyvbjerg, 2001; Goodley & Parker, 2000). This approach amalgamates the voice of the oppressed with critical perspectives on what constitutes the good life, the good society, and what is the role of power in wellness and suffering (Prilleltensky & Nelson, 2002). The application of this orientation to the subject of poverty means that we need to examine experiences, consequences, sources, and actions on poverty from the point of view of poor people and from the perspective of critical social science as well.

Studies dealing with poverty and with well-being rarely combine the psychological and political dimensions of either experience. From a critical and community psychology perspective, there is no experience that is exclusively psychological or political; human phenomena always contain both (Prilleltensky & Nelson, 2002). Power differences exert enormous influence on the human experience. Therefore, in this chapter I will investigate the effects of power on the psychological and political dimensions of poverty. Furthermore, we will explore avenues for gaining power to reduce poverty. We begin this exploration with the four key concepts that concern this topic: power, wellness, experiences of poverty, and suffering.

Power

I begin with power because, in my view, it is the main axis around which oppression and exploitation revolve. Power is multifaceted and ubiquitous. There is physical and psychological power, there is the power of the individual and the power of the corporation, the power of the citizen and the power of the state, the power of the employer and the power of the employee, the power to define poverty and the power to redefine somebody else's identity. Given its cardinal role in social life and social problems, I want to propose a working definition of power I developed with Geoff Nelson:

> Power refers to the capacity and opportunity to fulfil or obstruct personal, relational, or collective needs. We distinguish among power to strive for wellness, power to oppress, and power to resist oppression and strive for liberation. In each instance, the exercise of power can apply to self, others, and collectives; and can reflect varying degrees of awareness with respect to the impact of one's actions. Whereas people may be oppressed in one context, they may act as oppressors in others. Power affords people multiple identities as individuals seeking wellness, engaging in oppression, or resisting domination. Within a particular context, such as the family or work, individuals may exercise power to facilitate the wellness of some people but not of others. Across contexts, actors may engage in contradictory actions that promote personal or collective wellness in one place but that perpetuate oppressive practices in other settings. Due to structural factors such as social class, gender, ability, and race, people may enjoy differential levels of power. Degrees of power are also affected by personal and social constructs such as beauty, intelligence, and assertiveness, constructs that enjoy variable status within different cultures. The exercise of power varies not only across contexts, but also across time. Within a particular setting or relationship, people may occupy different roles at different times, making the exercise of power a very dynamic process. (Prilleltensky & Nelson, 2002, p. 7)

According to this definition, power may be used to strive for wellness, oppress others, and resist exploitation. In the context of poverty, we concern ourselves, respectively, with power to fulfil basic needs, to restrict access to basic needs, and to resist forces of destitution. As power is an amalgam of capacity and opportunity, poor people may experience the former without the latter, in which case the desire to work is insufficient to overcome poverty. Without opportunities and entitlements for employment or without efficient safety nets, no amount of good will can reverse the severe effects of structural poverty (Lustig, 2001; Sen, 1999a, b). This is a point frequently missed by those who blame the poor for their misfortune, ascribing destitution to personality deficiencies and lifestyle choices – myths that easily disintegrate when the context of poverty is taken into account. I provide ample evidence below to refute the theory that anyone with the "right attitude" can overcome poverty.

Power plays a crucial role in experiencing, inflicting, and repulsing poverty. Power's effects can be discerned when we examine the various facets of poverty. While the texture of poverty may be only too obvious to poor people, policy analysts debate its definition and measurement as governments try to manipulate the figures to their own advantage. A recent report of the United Nations Development Programme (May 2001) summarizes the main definitions of poverty. According to the minimal acceptable standard, poverty refers to the "failure of individuals, households or entire communities to command sufficient resources to satisfy their basic needs ... The inability to attain minimal standards of consumption to meet basic physiological criteria is often termed absolute poverty or deprivation" (May, 2001, p. 25). Lack of power to benefit from vital entitlements is at the core of this definition (Sen, 1999b).

Relative notions of poverty refer to the standard of living of a particular group in relation to the standing of less deprived groups. In many OECD countries, household incomes below 50% of the national median constitute relative poverty (UNICEF Innocenti Research Centre, 2001). Associated with relative notions of poverty is the experience of social exclusion and isolation. The poor are often marginalised and deprived of opportunities to participate meaningfully in societal structures. They are often secluded in ghettos, politically disenfranchised, and economically unable to participate in cultural life; they are powerless in the face of ominous barriers to inclusion.

The Human Poverty Index is another common measure of poverty. It uses basic dimensions of deprivation to assess poverty: lack of access to public and private resources, a short life, and lack of basic education (May, 2001). Diverse methods are more suitable to different contexts. Whereas many people in developed countries have access to basic resources such as food and shelter, their life is marred by exclusion and ill health (Shaw, Dorling, & Smith, 1999).

In my view, the plight of the poor is best understood on their own terms. Therefore, I elaborate below on poor people's experiences of deprivation, exclusion, and suffering in their own words. For the time being, suffice it to know that poverty inflicts physical, psychological, and spiritual pain in people of all ages, people who strive for wellness and resist the oppressive burden of destitution.

Wellness

My primary concern is with the effects of poverty on wellness and suffering. I use the term "wellness" as opposed to "well-being" because the former is broader than the latter. Whereas wellness encompasses satisfactory states of affairs at the personal, relational, and collective levels, well-being is typically circumscribed to the personal level alone. Colleagues and I have argued elsewhere that wellness at the personal level is intricately connected to the interpersonal and societal domains (Prilleltensky, Nelson, & Peirson, 2001a, b). We want to distance ourselves from definitions of life satisfaction based primarily on intrapsychic components like beliefs and perceptions. These definitions tend to be psycho-centric because they concentrate on the cognitive and emotional sources and consequences of power-lessness and well-being, to the exclusion of the social, material, and political roots and effects of lack of control and poor quality of life. There is a vast material reality "out there" that impinges on how we feel and how we behave toward each other. While beliefs and perceptions are important, they cannot be treated in iso-lation from the cultural, political, and economic environment (Eckersley, in press; 2000). We require "well-enough" social and political conditions, free of economic exploitation and human rights abuses, to experience quality of life. All the same, we expect interpersonal exchanges based on respect and mutual support to add to our quality of life. Eckersley (2000) has shown that subjective experiences of well-being are heavily dictated by cultural trends such as individualism and con-sumerism; whereas Narayan and colleagues have claimed that the psychological experience of poverty is directly related to political structures of corruption and oppression (Narayan, Chambers, Kaul, Shah, & Petesch, 2000; Narayan, Patel, Schafft, Rademacher, & Kocht-Schulte, 2000).

Much like our definition of power, Sen (1999b) frames poverty in terms of both capabilities and entitlements. Without the latter the former cannot thrive. Both in our definition of power and in Sen's conceptualization of poverty there is a dialec-tical relationship between personal capacities and environmental factors. But our approach to power and Sen's approach to poverty share another dimension. In both cases capacities and resources are at once intrinsically meritorious and extrinsically beneficial. This means that a sense of mastery and control is both an end in itself as well as a means of achieving wellness or reducing poverty. Access to preventive health care and educational opportunities are not only means to human develop-ment but also ends in their own right. Wellness at the collective level is not measured only by the health and educational outcomes of a group of individuals, but also by the presence of enabling institutions and societal infrastructures. Hence, we define wellness in broad terms that encompass social progress and human development.

Our definition of wellness entails personal, relational, and collective wellness to capture precisely the various aspects of a decent and meaningful life; not just

Table 2.1. Synoptic Framework for Understanding, Resisting, and Overcoming Poverty

Wellness	Experiences	Consequences	Sources	Change
Domains and values for progress	Voices of suffering of poor people	Outcomes of health and social science studies	Roots of poverty and suffering	Action needed to promote wellness
Collective Social justice Institutions that support emancipation and human development Peace Protection of environment	Material deprivation and bare subsistence Exploitation Insecurity, chaos and violence *Satisfaction in collective action to help community*	Lack of shelter, malnutrition, vulnerability to illness and disability Lack of trust in, and destruction of, vital community structures Threat to income, safety, education, and growth opportunities *Join others in struggle against poverty*	Economic exploitation and international pressures for structural adjustment Globalization and power differentials Corrupt structures of public protection and inadequate safety nets, primarily in times of crises	Invest in human development and health Resist dominant theory that economic growth is main solution to poverty Join support networks that focus on personal, relational, and collective domains Strive for democracy and freedoms
Relational Social cohesion, diversity Democratic participation	Exclusion based on class, age, gender, education, race and ability *Solidarity and compassion for others who suffer*	Lack of support, competition across social groups, isolation, fragmentation *Acts of solidarity with other oppressed and poor groups*	Dehumanizing Objectification of "other" Competition for scarce resources	Power equalization in personal, relational, and collective domains Prevent exclusion through education
Personal Self-determination, mastery and control Health Personal growth Meaning and spirituality	Multiple restrictions in life Physical weakness Shame Powerlessness *Strength and resilience*	Loss of life opportunities and lack of control Illness, disability and death Lack of dignity Lack of actual and perceived control Hopelessness *Resilience and solidarity*	Insufficient material resources, poor nutrition, and continued exposure to risk Power inequalities Learned helplessness, repeated failure to change living conditions	Join social action groups that work to fight poverty and enhance personal empowerment and solidarity at the same time Educate people to disentangle personal suffering from personal blame

the personal perceptions of individuals, but also the qualities of interpersonal relationships and of the political, cultural and economic structures. Wellness, then, can be defined as a positive state of affairs achieved by the simultaneous and synergistic satisfaction of personal, relational, and collective needs. These needs are met by coherent values, adequate psychological and material resources, and by effective social policies and programs. Personal needs such as control and self-efficacy have to be reflected in social values like self-determination; whereas relational needs such as a sense of community should be met by values and policies fostering social cohesion. In turn, collective needs for fair and equitable distribution of resources and for environmental protection must be upheld in values that foster justice and sustainability (Prilleltensky, 2001; Prilleltensky & Nelson, 1997, 2000; Prilleltensky, Nelson, & Peirson, 2001a, b). The values required to foster wellness, briefly presented in Table 2.1, are mutually reinforcing and fully interdependent. I will provide examples of their interdependence throughout the chapter.

Sen (1999a, b) articulates the complementarity of diverse social structures in fostering what we call wellness and what he calls human development. Sen invokes the interaction of five types of freedoms in the pursuit of human development: (1) political freedoms, (2) economic facilities, (3) social opportunities, (4) transparency guarantee, and (5) protective security.

> Each of these distinct types of rights and opportunities helps to advance the general capability of a person. They may also serve to complement each other...Freedoms are not only the primary ends of development, they are also among its principal means. In addition to acknowledging, foundationally, the evaluative importance of freedom, we also have to understand the remarkable empirical connection that links freedoms of different kinds with one another. Political freedoms (in the form of free speeches and elections) help to promote economic security. Social opportunities (in the form of education and health facilities) facilitate economic participation. Economic facilities (in the form of opportunities for participation in trade and production) can help to generate personal abundance as well as public resources for social facilities. Freedoms of different kinds can strengthen one another. (Sen, 1999b, pp. 10–11)

Our theory of wellness frames human development in terms of the mutually reinforcing properties of personal, relational, and societal qualities. Personal needs such as health, self-determination, and opportunities for growth are intimately tied to the satisfaction of collective needs such as adequate health care, access to safe drinking water, fair and equitable allocation of burdens and resources and economic equality. Citizens require public resources to pursue private aspirations. There cannot be caring without justice, nor can there be justice without caring.

Personal and collective needs represent two faces of wellness. The third aspect, the relational domain, is crucial because individual and group agendas are often in conflict. Indeed, like power, conflict is immanent in relationships. Two sets of needs are primordial in pursuing healthy relationships among individuals

and groups: (1) respect for diversity, and (2) collaboration and democratic participation. Respect for diversity ensures that people's unique identities are affirmed
by others, while democratic participation enables community members to have
a say in decisions affecting their lives (Prilleltensky & Nelson, 2000). Our three
domains of wellness parallel the main freedoms and capabilities required for human development (Sen, 1999a, b). As Sen noted, the main freedoms include "the
development of individual capabilities as well as enhancement of social facilities"
(p. 7). We see below how the three dimensions of wellness correspond to poor people's descriptions of their lives and to Sen's prescriptions for overcoming suffering
and economic disadvantage.

Suffering is the opposite of wellness. It is characterized by unmet needs in the
personal, relational, and collective domains. Suffering comes about by deprivation
of autonomy, human rights, access to food and water, shelter, and protection from
disease and economic crises. At the relational level, suffering occurs when human
interactions are marred by disrespect, shame, exclusion, humiliation, erasure of
identity and repression of diversity. Collectively, suffering is occasioned primarily
by structures of political and economic oppression and exploitation. Table 2.1
shows the main experiences, consequences, and sources of suffering in the lives
of poor people at the collective, relational, and personal domains (Aristide, 2000;
Feuerstein, 1997; Interfaith Social Assistance Reform Coalition, 1998; Lustig,
2001; Narayan, Chambers, et al., 2000; Narayan, Patel, et al., 2000; Parayil, 2000;
Sen, 1999a, b). The table also shows possible actions at the various levels of
analysis to overcome and eliminate the effects of poverty. The synoptic framework
presented in Table 2.1 does not differentiate between developed and developing
countries, nor does it distinguish between rural and urban poverty. A more detailed
discussion of these differences is provided in the next sections. Although most
experiences are negative and related to suffering, I emphasize in italics experiences
related to strength, resilience and solidarity.

Experiences of Poverty

The experience of poverty in developed and developing countries can be
quite different. There is also great variation across urban and rural settings. Indeed, there are thorough reviews of the phenomenology, effects, and political
economy of poverty in developed and developing countries (Chase-Lansdale &
Brooks-Gunn, 1995; Feuerstein, 1997; Interfaith Social Assistance Reform Coalition, 1998; Kawachi, Kennedy, & Wilkinson, 1999; Shaw, Dorling, & Smith, 1999;
Narayan, Patel, et al., 2000; Sen, 1999a). These sources offer in-depth analysis of
poverty in diverse contexts. I will try to reflect here these experiential differences
by quoting from extensive studies conducted with poor people around the world.

In a remarkable study, the Poverty Group of the World Bank conducted participatory poverty assessments with over 60,000 people in over 47 countries (Narayan,

Chambers, et al., 2000; Narayan, Patel, et al., 2000). The two books edited by Narayan and colleagues provide a vivid account of what it is like to live in poverty in urban and rural settings in developing countries. These accounts are supplemented in this chapter by reports on poverty in developed countries like Australia (The Smith Family, 2000), Canada (Interfaith Social Assistance Reform Coalition, 1998), USA (Chase-Lansdale & Brooks-Gunn, 1995), and United Kingdom (Howarth, Kenway, Palmer, & Miorelli, 2000; Maxwell & Kenway, 2000). I will describe experiences of suffering and wellness at the collective, relational, and personal levels. Moreover, I will argue that the role of power in poverty is crucial at all levels of analysis.

Suffering

> On a global scale, absolute poverty is concentrated in the South but relative poverty and real deprivation also exist in the North. In the UK, over a quarter of people live in low-income households, with worse health, lower life expectancy, lower levels of social participation, and worse life chances than those above the poverty line. Children are disproportionately disadvantaged. (Maxwell & Kenway, 2000, p. 1)

At the collective level, people in the South suffer from two sets of devastating experiences: (a) *insecurity, chaos, violence*, and (b) *economic exploitation*. Narayan and colleagues (Narayan, Chambers, et al., 1999; 2000; Narayan, Patel, et al., 2000) interviewed thousands of people who commented on the fear of living with uncertainty and lack of protection. Lack of order and lawlessness exacerbate the plight of the poor and add a dimension of terror to the material deprivation. A poor woman in Brazil pointed out that *there is no control over anything, at any hour a gun could go off, especially at night* (Narayan, Chambers et al., 1999, p. 7). Chaotic environments in politically unstable regimes are fertile grounds for crime and violence. The poor are the most vulnerable of all as they are often homeless and exposed to random acts of violence. Many observed that the police can be quite brutal and heartless in their dealings with the poor. Even more complained about the lack of institutional protection afforded by the State (Narayan, Chambers et al., 2000).

Economic exploitation is felt as a trap without escape. Children and adults working at slavery or near slavery levels have no choice but to relinquish their freedom and abide by rules of despotic employers.

> Officially, slavery no longer exists in Haiti. But through the lives of children in Haiti who live as *restaveks* we see the remnants of slavery. *Restaveks* are children, usually girls, sometimes as young as 3 and 4 years old, who live in the majority of Haitian families as unpaid domestic workers. They are the first to get up in the morning and the last to go to bed at night. They carry water, clean house, do errands and receive no salary ... they eat what is left when the others are finished, and they are extremely vulnerable to verbal, physical and sexual abuse. (Aristide, 2000, p. 27)

Entire communities and entire countries experience economic exploitation. Poor communities working for starvation wages in fields feel trapped (Feuerstein, 1997). Poor countries feel equally trapped by international lending institutions that force governments to drop social services and lift tariffs on imports in the name of efficiency and economic growth. Korten (1995) reviews the cases of Costa Rica and Brazil. In both instances, structural adjustment programs imposed by the International Monetary Fund and the World Bank displaced millions of agricultural workers. Furthermore, many countries have become dependent on imports to meet basic food requirements (Korten, 1995, p. 49). Aristide (2000), in turn, reviews the case of rice production in Haiti. In a matter of ten years, from 1986 to 1996 Haiti increased its import of rice from 7,000 to 196,000 tons per year. During that period Haiti,

> complied with lending agencies and lifted tariffs on rice imports. Cheaper rice immediately flooded in from the USA where the rice industry is subsidized . . . Haiti's peasant farmers could not possible compete . . . Haitian rice production became negligible. Once the dependence on foreign rice was complete, import prices began to rise, leaving Haiti's population, particularly the urban poor, completely at the whim of rising world grain prices. (Aristide, 2000, p. 11–12)

These stories are repeated throughout the entire South (Korten, 1995). The price of structural adjustment policies in countries like Haiti, Brazil and Costa Rica is unemployment and displacement for millions. Measures imposed at the collective level are felt very much at the personal level as well.

Economic policies that result in unemployment affect people in the South and in the North. Based on research in developed countries, Fryer (1998) asserts that "unemployment is centrally involved in the social causation of mental health problems" (p. 78). Furthermore, he claims that unemployment is psychologically debilitating because it "disempowers by impoverishing, restricting, baffling and undermining the agency of the unemployed person . . . Unemployment generally results in psychologically corrosive experienced relative poverty" (Fryer, 1998, p. 83). The impact of recessions can be felt in unemployment and in many other levels as well. Wages go down, health and working conditions deteriorate, and minorities are more visibly excluded from the job market (Fryer, 1998).

Policies and societal practices are very much felt at the individual and interpersonal levels. Just as wellness is brought about by the synergy of personal, relational, and collective needs, so is suffering caused by the synergy of unmet needs at all levels. "Poor people report living with increased crime, corruption, violence, and insecurity amidst declining social cohesion. People feel helpless against forces of change" (Narayan, Patel, et al., 2000, p. 222). We see in this quote the interaction of collective, relational and personal factors in the plight of the poor. Fewer resources at the collective level mean increased competition and exclusion at the interpersonal level. Exclusion, in turn, contributes to isolation and alienation.

In the struggle for survival social relations suffer. Suffering at the relational level is marked by (a) heightened fragmentation and exclusion and by (b) fractious social relations. An Ecuadorian participant in the World Bank study put it succinctly: *What is mine is mine, and what is yours is yours, in this community people are very stingy* (Narayan, Patel, et al., 2000, p. 222).

As noted in Table 2.1, the personal dimension of suffering in poverty is characterized by: (1) powerlessness; (2) limitations and restricted opportunities in life; (3) physical weakness; (4) shame and feelings of inferiority; and (5) gender and age discrimination. Impotence in light of ominous societal forces like crime and economic displacement fuels the sense of powerlessness. Lack of power and sense of control feature prominently in the phenomenology of poverty. People feel they have dreams for their children that will never be fulfilled. Illness and disability were frequently mentioned, not only because of the physical pain endured by malnutrition and harsh labour, but also because a physical disability meant inability to work. With their bodies as their main working tools, an impairment translates into hunger for adults and their children. The body has to endure the lack of shelter, food, water, and clothing. Illnesses and injuries are frequently experienced but infrequently treated. *If you don't have money today, your disease will take you to your grave* (An old man in Ghana, in Narayan, Patel, et al., 2000, p. 218).

Shame was a strong feeling expressed by poor people in the South and in the North. It can be captured by the following quotes from Canadian children:

> *Poverty is . . . pretending that you forgot your lunch, being teased for the way you are dressed, feeling ashamed when my dad can't get a job, not getting a hot dog on hot dog day, being afraid to tell your mom that you need gym shoes, not getting to go to birthday parties, not buying books at the book fair* (Grade 4 & 5 children, North Bay, Ontario, Canada, in Interfaith Social Assistance Reform Coalition, 1998).

Discrimination based on gender and age was a prominent issue in most accounts of poverty. Gender discrimination is strongly felt in the North and Northwest of India and in some parts of East Asia. Studies demonstrate that in these regions there is excess female infant and child mortality. There is also evidence that with the advent of amniocentesis there is selective abortion of female foetuses. In parts of sub-Saharan Africa women have heavier workloads than men and have very little say in private and public decision making (Razavi, 1999).

Reports indicate that poor women are also very often the subject of domestic violence. In 1996 Health Canada produced a report called *Breaking the links between poverty and violence against women*. The authors noted that "many thousands of Canadian women experience poverty and violence every day . . . for many women, poverty adds another dimension to the pain and suffering they experience as a result of violence" (Gurr, Mailloux, Kinnon, & Doerge, 1996, p. 1).

Children and the elderly are also discriminated against. In the USA, for instance, there are approximately three million child abuse reports each year. This is, on average, a report of abuse every ten seconds (US Department of Health and Human Services, 1998). Studies show that a preponderance of child abuse cases take place, in fact, in poor families (Prilleltensky, Nelson, & Peirson, 2001b). Discrimination against the young and the old happens not only in family quarters, but also at state level. The majority of old people in developing countries are uninsured by any type of social security plan. In sub-Saharan Africa less than 10% of the old population is covered. In East Asia less than 30% of old people have any pension or social security. Only the very wealthy can age securely in these countries. In contrast, in most OECD countries between 90% and 100% of old people are covered (James, 2001).

The lived experience of poverty, at all levels of analysis, is characterized by powerlessness. *Poverty is like living in jail, living under bondage, waiting to be free* (A young woman in Jamaica, in Narayan, Chambers, et al., 1999, p. 8). When rice farmers in Haiti work as hard as they can, abide by all the rules, and still cannot compete with American producers, there is a profound sense of powerlessness and lack of control. When little *restavek* girls work day and night and sustain multiple forms of abuse, hopelessness ensues. When poor women are subjected to humiliation, exclusion and violence, powerlessness is the most common outcome. Power differentials sit at the core of suffering for poor people of all ages. The power inequality expressed by poor people is not psychological or political but always both. Material and economic power are intertwined with feelings of shame and inferiority. In the light of so much adversity, it is against the odds that poor people still engage in acts of meaning, solidarity and wellness.

Wellness

Poor people envision a good life based on positive conditions at collective, relational, and personal levels. At the societal level they seek to experience (1) social justice, security and peace; to benefit from (2) material well-being and assets; and to live in places with accessible and responsive (3) community services and organizations. In the South in particular poor people talked at length about the wish to have reliable government agencies. They want to have a police force that will protect them, health professionals that will treat them with respect, and safety nets that will support them in times of crises. Almost uniformly they wish an education for their children. With regards to material well-being, it is worth noting that poor people expect only enough to live. In the South, there were no parallels between wealth and well-being. Material well-being was equated with sufficient nutrition and shelter for a decent life (Aristide, 2000; Feuerstein, 1997; Narayan, Chambers, et al., 1999; 2000; Narayan, Patel, et al., 2000).

These societal resources enable people to participate in society and to develop their potential. The relational domain of wellness, according to poor people, should encompass (a) respect and tolerance for diversity, (b) democratic participation, (c) sense of community, solidarity and (d) social support. At the personal level, poor people expressed a desire for (a) freedom of choice and action, (b) health and physical well-being, and (c) capacity for action. These wishes concur with the wellness model proposed by Prilleltensky and colleagues and briefly summarized in Table 2.1 (Prilleltensky, Nelson, & Peirson, 2001a, b).

In spite of great adversity, many poor people not only wish for but enact many of these qualities; primarily those related to solidarity and support. "Maintaining social traditions, hospitality, reciprocity, rituals, and festivals are central to poor people's defining themselves as humans, despite dehumanizing economic and environmental realities" (Narayan, Patel, et al., 2000, p. 217). A poor woman in Ukraine noted that *without these simple humane signs of solidarity, our lives would be unbearable* (Narayan, Patel, et al., 2000, p. 217).

Table 2.1 reinforces the point that wellness derives from the confluence of collective, relational, and personal factors. In certain contexts some elements would, and should, take precedence. Diverse contexts require unique configurations of wellness-promoting factors and values. At some point in time collective factors may predominate, while in others relational variables would come to the fore. Sen (2001) observed that

> The same values and cultural norms can be extremely successful at one phase of development, but less so at another. What we have to look at is not the general excellence of one set of values over all others, but the specific fit of particular values with the nature of the problems that are faced in a given – but parametrically variable – situation. The contingent nature of the contribution that values make is important to seize (p. 10).

The aim is always to reach a sufficient degree of satisfaction of each dimension of wellness, and to ascertain which dimension requires preference in the present context. Once each domain is sufficiently satisfied and the most pressing one targeted for action, they can all contribute to the whole of wellness for individuals and communities alike. In the absence of any one domain wellness cannot be achieved. And in the absence of power or resources to procure the attainment of collective, relational, or personal needs, wellness remains an illusion. Poor people must have increased access to economic, political, and psychological power to experience wellness.

Consequences of Poverty

There is a negative synergistic effect of the impact of poverty on groups, relationships, and individuals (see Table 2.1). An assault on any one level diminishes the overall wellness of individuals, communities, and nations alike. Let's begin with an examination of poverty on population health.

A woman's lifetime chance of dying in pregnancy or delivery in least developed countries is 1 in 16. In industrialized countries the chances are 1 in 4,085 (UNICEF, 2001). While most poor mothers living in industrialized countries receive much better prenatal care than their counterparts in developing nations, they nevertheless face higher risks than mothers in higher socio-economic groups. Poor mothers in developed countries have greater incidence of premature and low birth weight babies. In general, lower socio-economic groups have greater health risks associated with poor diet, hypertension, physical inactivity, smoking, and lack of breastfeeding (Robertson, Brunner, & Sheiham, 1999).

Life span and the global burden of disease also demonstrate the health effects of poverty. In some regions of Africa life expectancy for women is 35.4 years, whereas in parts of the Western Pacific region it is 80.8 years. Southeast Asia has about 13 times more communicable diseases, maternal, perinatal conditions, and nutritional deficiencies than Europe. The ratio between Europe and Africa is about 1:19 (MacFarlane, Racelis, & Muli-Musiime, 2000).

When probability of death between ages 15 and 60 is compared between richer and poorer countries, the former have outcomes that are about three times better than the latter. Reasons for death include infections, perinatal, nutritional, maternal, cardiovascular, cancer, respiratory disease and other external causes (see Marmot, 1999). Lack of shelter and sanitation are major causes of killing diseases around the world. Feuerstein (1997) reports that between 1988 and 1991, in 34 of the 47 least developed countries, only 46% of the population had access to safe water.

Within countries, the poor, the unemployed, refugees, single parents, ethnic minorities and the homeless have poorer indices of health than more advantaged groups. This applies not only to poor countries, but to rich countries as well. Homeless people in western countries, for example, are 34 times more likely to kill themselves than the general population, 150 times more likely to be fatally assaulted, and 25 times more likely to die in any period of time than the people who ignore them on the streets (Shaw, Dorling, & Smith, 1999).

There is no question that the economic and political environment influences health in potent ways. Consider the following examples provided by Wilkinson (1996). Perhaps contrary to expectations, a child born and raised in Harlem has less chance of living to age 65 than a baby born in Bangladesh. Also in the USA, life expectancy is 7 years longer for whites (76 years) than for African Americans (69 years). In lower social classes, infant mortality in Sweden (500 per 100,000) is less than half the rate in England (1250 per 100,000). Because of more egalitarian income distribution, the life expectancy of Japanese people increased by 7.5 years for men and 8 years for women in 21 years. This dramatic increase took place between the years 1965 and 1986. Japanese people experience the highest life expectancy in the world, near 80 years, in large part because in that period of time they became the advanced society with the narrowest gap in income differences. Communities with higher levels of social cohesion and narrow gaps between rich and poor produce better health and welfare outcomes than wealthier societies with higher levels of social disintegration. Putnam (2000) demonstrated this point with multiple sources of data for the USA throughout the past century.

The data compiled by Marmot and Wilkinson (1999) clearly indicate that, in addition to economic prosperity, equality and social cohesion are also powerful determinants of health. Indeed,

> In the developed world, it is not the richest countries which have the best health, but the most egalitarian... Looking at a number of different examples of healthy egalitarian societies, an important characteristic they all seem to share is their social cohesion... The epidemiological evidence which most clearly suggest the health benefits of social cohesion comes from studies of the beneficial effects of social networks on health. (Wilkinson, 1996, pp. 3–5)

As Wilkinson observed, social cohesion is mediated by commitment to positive social structures, which, in turn, is related to social justice. Individuals contribute to collective well-being when they feel that the collective works for them as well. Social cohesion and coherence are "closely related to social justice" (Wilkinson, 1996, p. 221). Once again we witness the synergistic effects of a collective value such as social justice, with a relational value such as social cohesion. In combination, they produce healthy and engaged individuals that, in turn, contribute to society in terms of productivity and civic engagement (Putnam, 2000; Sen, 1999a, b).

The negative outcomes associated with poverty and inequality are accentuated in times of economic crises or environmental disasters such as earthquakes, floods, and landslides. Lustig (2001) reviews the health and educational effects of recent economic crises in Argentina, Mexico and Indonesia. In Argentina, per capita GDP fell 4.1% and per capita private consumption fell 5.6% in 1995. The same year, per capita daily protein intake fell 3.8%. Growth in primary school enrollment declined from 2.% in 1993 to 0.8 in 1996.

In 1995 Mexico experienced a serious economic crisis. Per capita GDP fell 7.8% and private consumption fell 11.1%. The health repercussions were severe. Among children under age 1, mortality from anemia increased from 6.3 deaths per 100,000 live births in 1993 to 7.9 in 1995. The rate for children age 1–4 rose from 1.7 to 2.2.

Indonesia had a severe economic crisis in 1998. Per capita GDP fell 14.6%. School dropout rates for children 7–12 in the poorest quartile rose from 1.3% in 1997 to 7.5% in 1998. For children age 13–19, the rate rose from 14.2% to 25.5%. The share of children age 7–12 in the poorest quartile not enrolled in school rose from 4.9% in 1997 to 10.7% in 1998. In the age group 13–19, the rate rose from 42.5 to 58.4%.

Inevitably, economic recessions and material deprivation lead to poor outcomes for communities and individuals alike. Mental health deteriorates markedly and symptoms of depression and helplessness ensue (Fryer, 1998). Affected individuals feel disempowered and diminish their contribution to society at large. However, this pattern is not irreversible or overly determined. We will explore later the case of the State of Kerala, India, where human development indicators rise despite poor economic growth (Parayil, 2000). This "negative case" demonstrates that distribution of resources and not necessarily or exclusively economic growth contributes to wellness. In Kerala the population has very high rates of participation in community development, leading not only to social progress but also to personal and collective empowerment (Kannan, 2000). I foreshadow the case of Kerala because it illustrates how relational values of social cohesion and democratic participation, along with collective values of justice and redistribution of resources contribute to improvements in human development indicators. Positive action at the group and collective levels bring about desirable outcomes at the personal level, not the least of which is a sense of power, agency, and control (Franke & Chasin, 2000).

Sources

Despite entrenched ideologies that blame the poor for their misfortune, a cursory analysis reveals that the main sources of poverty are societal and not personal (Leonard, 1997). Rather than provide a comprehensive review of the sources of poverty, which is beyond the scope of this chapter, I will identify key dynamics at the international, national, and community levels (see Table 2.1).

Globalization is colonization by a new name. Whereas in the past powerful countries invaded territories and dispossessed people of their resources by brute force; in the present, international lending agencies pressure poor countries to open their markets to foreign competition. Whereas in the past raw materials and slave labour were extracted from colonies, nowadays economic empires expect the poor to buy their products (Korten, 1995). In many instances, as in the case of Haiti (Aristide, 2000), countries became poor precisely because of a history of colonization, oppression, and dependency (Korten, 1995). Forceful contact with colonizers not only depleted environmental resources but also tarnished social traditions of native groups. In the case of Indigenous Australians this resulted in economic deprivation, psychosocial problems and health outcomes comparable to so-called third world countries (Dudgeon, Garvey, & Pickett, 2000).

Governments create international institutions that serve primarily nations and corporations in the North. As poor countries depend – often because of histories of colonization – on foreign loans, lending institutions like the International Monetary Fund dictate terms and conditions that wipe social services, health care and public education. Economic growth and efficiency, touted as the only way to prosperity,

require the privatization of public utilities and services, resulting in massive unemployment of public sector workers and in restricted access to health, education
(Korten, 1995), and sometimes even water, as is the case in Ghana right now (see
www.africapolicy.org and www.challengeglobalization.org for updates). The case
of rice producers in Haiti illustrated the international dynamics quite well. Governments are forced to open markets and lift restrictions on imports, local producers
have to compete with cheaper foreign products that are either subsidized or produced with more efficient equipment. Once the local competition is eliminated
prices go up and fewer and fewer people have access to them (Aristide, 2000;
Korten, 1995; Weisbrot, 1999).

At the national level, poor countries indebted to the International Monetary
Fund and to the World Bank spend considerable amount of money servicing their
debts. In the case of Mozambique, the country spends 25% of its income from
exports on debt payments. This prevents the country from investing in its own
population. If only half of the debt service payments were spent on health care,
the lives of 115,000 children and of 6,000 mothers who die in childbirth would be
saved (Weisbrot, 1999).

The dominant doctrine that economic growth inflicts short-term pain for long
term gain in poor countries is challenged by Sen (1999a, b; 2001). Sen claims that
investments in education, health and social services in fact contribute to economic
strength. He challenges the received wisdom that "human development is a kind of
luxury that a country can afford only when it grows rich" (Sen, 1999a, p. 10). With
evidence from East Asia, including Japan, Sen demonstrates that policies in favor
of comprehensive human development do not retard but rather enhance economic
prosperity. "These economies went comparatively early for massive expansion of
education, and other ways of broadening the entitlements that allow the bulk of the
people to participate in economic transactions and social change. This happened
well before breaking the restraints of general poverty; indeed, that broad approach
greatly contributed to breaking the restraints of poverty" (Sen, 1999a, pp. 10–11).

Investments in education, health and social facilities enabled East Asian
economies to work on economic deprivation quite successfully. Their major short-
coming, however, was a failure to plan for the possibility of sudden destitution
that comes with economic cycles and recessions. As a result, during the 1997 economic crisis millions of working people became suddenly poor or even destitute
in countries like Indonesia, Thailand and South Korea. "Even though a fall of
5% to 10% of total national income (or of GNP) is comparatively moderate, it can
decimate lives and create misery for millions" (Sen, 1999a, p. 40). According to
Sen, protective security is as important as economic progress. Many of the Tiger
economies of Asia neglected to install safety nets that would catch the victims of
economic downturns. This is when the lack of democracy can be most severely
felt. For recessions hit most harshly the poor, who, without unions or protective institutions, fall rapidly to destitution. "The victims in Indonesia may not have taken

very great interest in democracy when things went up and up. But when things came tumbling down for some parts of the populations, the lack of democratic institutions kept their voices muffled and ineffective" (Sen, 1999a, p. 40).

In Latin America economic crises have had the similar effect of increasing poverty and exacerbating inequality. Based on data from 48 growth and recession periods for 12 Latin American countries, Janvry and Sadoulet (2001) argue that recessions are systematically devastating for the poor. They also note that the gains lost during recessions are not recovered in future spells of growth.

A 1% decline in GDPpc in a recession episode eliminates the gains in urban poverty reduction achieved by 3.7% growth in GDPpc under early growth, the gains in rural poverty reduction achieved by 2% growth under early growth, and the gains in inequality reduction achieved by 9% growth under late growth. Recession has a particularly strong ratchet effect on inequality since subsequent growth is unable to compensate for the higher level of inequality achieved. (Janvry & Sadoulet, 2001, p. 37)

The pressure on poor countries to open their markets, combined with repressive policies of authoritarian regimes conspire to widen the gap between rich and poor. Globalization works for powerful corporations while authoritarian regimes work for the corrupt elites that pillage the nation and its resources. As Sen (1999a, b) has eloquently argued, democracy at the *national* level is a prerequisite for the prevention of destitution. As Aristide (2000) and Korten (1995) have persuasively shown, without *international* justice the downward spiral for the majority of poor countries cannot be averted.

Rural poverty in developing countries is closely connected to environmental degradation and to globalization. Without loans, the rural poor are unable to invest in soil and water conservation. When they are in receipt of loans, they become dependent on lenders and have to use their meager gains to service their debts. Their situation is aggravated by cheap food imports that further depress their returns (Feuerstein, 1997).

The power dynamics operating at the international scene and in developing countries bear resemblance to what happens in developed countries. The same corporations that put pressure on international bodies to open new markets put pressure on domestic governments to reduce public services and cut taxes (Dobbin, 1998). The growing inequality in developed countries is unprecedented. In industrialized countries, economic growth without redistributive policies widens the gap between rich and poor, with adverse health and social effects for the large middle class that is experiencing lower standards of living (Allahar & Cote, 1998; Wilkinson, 1996).

Beyond these power-driven inequalities, poverty is aggravated by cultural factors such as discrimination against women, ethnic minorities, and disabled people. Illness and disability can prove fatal in developing countries and strongly felt in developed countries. Not all rich countries have adequate supports to enable disabled people to work or to provide them with acceptable pensions (Barnes, 1996). The continuing feminization of poverty is a grave concern for women the world over (Razavi, 1999). In all cases, power inequality is at the heart of poverty. Gender inequality, discrimination against disabled people, economic bondage; they all reflect the distinct domination of powerful or culturally privileged people over weaker but not indefensible people. In the next section we explore actions to combat poverty at national, regional, and community levels.

Action

There are few rights more fundamental than the right of people to create caring, sustainable communities and to control their own resources, economies, and means of livelihood. These rights in turn depend on their right to choose what cultural values they will embrace, what values their children will be taught, and with whom they will trade. A globalized economy denies these rights by transferring the power to make the relevant choices to global corporations and financial institutions. Economic globalization is in the corporate interest. It is not in the human interest (Korten, 1995, p. 307).

There is mounting and persuasive evidence concerning the devastating effects of globalization on the already poor and on the rapidly becoming poor (Aristide, 2000; Dobbin, 1998; Korten, 1995). Any action must now take into account that global forces are at play everywhere. Corporations are searching for new markets all over the globe. Their impact in dismantling local economies is felt throughout the world. We should therefore heed Korten's challenge of reclaiming the basic right to make decisions. This means opposing the global trend toward corporate rule. In this section I examine how we might resist global impoverishment; offering avenues for action at the international, national, and community levels.

According to projections of the World Trade Organization, the number of people living on less than US$ 1 per day will grow from 1199 million in 1998 to 1242 million in 2008 (Nordstrom, Ben David, & Winters, 1999). Using a cut-off point of $ 2 per day, the number of poor people in 2008 would be 2722 million. Although the WTO claims that its policies of trade liberalization and rapid economic growth will, in the long term, help the poor, many others contend that current practices exacerbate the plight of the poor living below and above the $ 1-per-day cut-off point (Dobbin, 1998; Korten, 1995). They all agree, however, that most gains are to be made by rich countries. To achieve more equitable trade regulations some authors suggest drastic changes to the policies of the WTO, the IMF, and the World Bank. Korten (1995) recommends the replacement of the last two with UN-based agencies, whereas many activist groups oppose WTO's policies of Trade Related Intellectual Property Rights (TRIPS) and liberalization of trade in basic social services such as health, education and energy (Ransom, 2001). TRIPS promote monopolies by transnational corporations, prevent access to vital medicines, and limit the ability of poor countries to develop their own biotechnology (Ransom, 2001). There are global movements challenging corporate imperialism. Most of these activist groups maintain electronic communication and distribute information on the Internet. The September 2001 issue of the magazine *The New Internationalist*, dedicated to global resistance, contains a useful list of linkages (p. 28).

At the national level, economists and community developers debate the merit of rapid economic growth as a means of overcoming poverty. Sen (1999b) makes the point that "the impact of economic growth depends much on how the *fruits* of economic growth are used" (p. 44, italics in original). He further observes that the positive connection between life expectancy and growth of GNP per head works primarily through investments in health care and poverty removal. In other words, growth per se does not necessarily translate into human development, unless it is properly invested in health, education, social security, social services, and employment programs. Indeed, during the crisis of 1997 the failure of some Asian countries to invest the gains of growth in human development resulted in devastation for millions of people (Sen, 1999a). But there is another route to human development and poverty alleviation that is not linked to rapid or elevated economic growth. "In contrast with the growth-mediated mechanism, the support-led process does not operate through fast economic growth, but works through a program of skillful social support of health care, education, and other relevant social arrangements" (Sen, 1999b, p. 46). The success of this approach is evidenced in countries such as Costa Rica and Sri Lanka and in the State of Kerala in India. These places achieved rapid reductions in mortality rates and marked improvement in living conditions without much economic growth. With a GNP per capita of less than $ 700 per year in 1994, Kerala and Sri Lanka had life expectancy at birth of 73 years. In contrast, with a GNP per capita of $ 4,000, Gabon had a life expectancy of only 54 years. Brazil, with a GNP of nearly $ 3,000, had a life expectancy of 63 years in 1994. Sen concludes from these figures that it is not only growth that will bring prosperity but rather a wise distribution of available resources across the entire population.

The celebrated case of Kerala deserves attention because it reflects vastly different trends than the rest of India and because it demonstrates the power of social policies in poverty alleviation. Parayil (2000), Franke and Chasin (2000), and Kannan (2000) document the success of Kerala in achieving human development rates that are comparable to developed nations. As a percentage of total adult population, Kerala has literacy rates of 94%, compared to 65% in the rest of India and 9% in the USA. Life expectancy for females is 72 in Kerala and 80 in the USA. This is very interesting in light of the fact that Kerala's GNP per capita is $ 324 and the USA's is $ 28,740. Infant mortality per 1,000 in Kerala is 13, compared to 80 in low-income countries, and 65 in the rest of India (Franke & Chasin, 2000). The question is, how did Kerala achieve these positive indices of human development? Through a series of land reforms and redistribution of resources, as well as highly participatory social programs, Kerala managed to invest in social programs dedicated to economic equality and to the improvement of health and education. In the village of Nadur, for instance, the abolition of rice land tenancy contributed dramatically to reductions in inequality. Similarly, the abolition of house compound tenancy had equally positive effects. School and nursery lunches throughout the state improved caloric intake of children in the poorest households by 5%. Provisions made available through ration shops also decreased hunger. Agricultural labor pensions helped a great percentage of the population. "The ration shop, school lunches and agricultural labour pensions benefited female-supported households more than male-supported households. They thus contributed to reductions in one aspect of gender inequality" (Franke & Chasin, 2000, p. 23).

Franke and Chasin (2000) conclude that "Kerala's quality-of-life achievements result from redistribution. But why has redistribution occurred in Kerala?" (p. 24). According to the authors, the answer lies in the century-long history of popular movements in the State. "These movements have gone through many stages, from caste improvement associations to trade unions and peasant associations to Communist parties to the Kerala People's Science Movement" (Franke & Chasin, 2000, p. 24). These social movements have forced the government to listen to the concerns of the poor and have lobbied successfully for the introduction of poverty alleviation measures. The importance of regional, national and global movements to reduce poverty is emphasized by poor people themselves throughout the world. Narayan, Chambers and colleagues (2000) conclude that "coalitions representing poor people's organizations are needed to ensure that the voices of the poor are heard and reflected in decision making at the local, national and global levels" (p. 265).

As noted in Table 2.1, joining strategic social movements is perhaps the most powerful step that citizens can take to eradicate poverty. In some cases these will be global movements, in others they may be regional or community-based coalitions. In North America, community-building efforts have proven useful in bringing people together to fight poverty. Snow (1995) claims that "community-building can enable the underprivileged to create power through collective action" (p. 185), while McNeely (1999) reports that "community building strategies can make a significant difference. There is now evidence of many cases where the residents of poor communities have dramatically changed their circumstances by organizing to assume responsibility for their own destiny" (p. 742). McNeely lists community participation, strategic planning, focused, and local interventions as central to success. Similar initiatives have taken place in Europe to address the multifaceted problems faced by residents in large public housing estates. Community organizing helped many poor neighborhoods throughout the United Kingdom to demand and receive improved social services such as health, policing, and welfare (Power, 1996).

These interventions work at the personal, relational, and collective levels at the same time. By participating in social action groups, citizens feel empowered while they develop bonds of solidarity. The feelings of empowerment and connection contribute to personal and relational wellness; whereas the tangible outcomes in the form of enhanced services and quality of life contribute to collective wellness. Examples of community organizing for health services in developing countries abound (Feuerstein, 1997; MacFarlane, Racelis, & Muli-Musiime, 2000); just as there are multiple cases of resident associations that procure better living conditions in developed countries (McNeely, 1999; Power, 1996; Snow, 1995). The literature on empowerment, community development, and social movements supports the tripartite benefits of participating in social action: enhanced personal, relational, and collective wellness (Faulks, 1999; Nelson, Lord, & Ochoka, 2001; Zimmerman, 2000). The literature on social cohesion and social capital, in turn, supports the claim that higher levels of social participation result in better outcomes for human development (Franke & Chasin, 2000; Putnam, 2000; Sen, 1999b). This is a point made time and again by advocates of higher participation of the poor in programs for the poor (Feuerstein, 1997; Macfarlane, Racelis, & Muli-Musiime, 2000; Narayan, Chambers, et al., 2000).

The ever-present dilemma in community building initiatives is that they work to ameliorate the living conditions of residents without transforming the root causes of the problems (Prilleltensky & Nelson, 1997). Needless to say the roots of poverty are larger than what any one movement can tackle. However, this should not detract activists from devising global strategies that will target the roots and not only the manifestations of poverty. On one hand we need to avoid "paralysis by analysis" in the light of multiple and ominous barriers. On the other hand, we need to remember that community building may be empowering at the personal and local levels, but it may not address the larger causes of endemic poverty, such as globalization, lack of investment in health and education, and corrupt governments. The wisdom in "think globally, act locally" cannot be dismissed. People empower themselves working on local issues while staying tuned to global dynamics.

Nobody can deny that the improvements felt by residents in poor urban estates as a result of community building are meaningful. Tangible outcomes in the form of reduced crime and improved health care do enhance quality of life (McNeely, 1999; Power, 1996). Our challenge, however, is to blend the pursuit for short-term solutions with the pressing need for long-term justice. For it is only when justice prevails that fundamental resources can be distributed fairly, regardless of economic growth. In the absence of justice, the fruits of economic growth and increased riches will continue to go to elites and will only widen the already galactic gap between wealthy and destitute.

Narayan and colleagues summarized the agenda for change proposed by poor people all over the world. In essence,

Poor people call for access to opportunities, decent wages, strong organizations of their own and a better and more active state. They call for systemic change. They want more government, not less government, on which they have influence and with which they can partner in different ways. They look to government to provide services fundamental to their well-being. Poor people's problems cut across sectoral divides. They challenge us to think and plan beyond narrow disciplinary boundaries while still remaining responsive to local realities. (Narayan, Chambers, et al., 2000, p. 266)

These are the expectations of poor people themselves. Based on the study of poor people's realities in 47 countries, Narayan and colleagues identified seven themes that require synergistic attention: (1) from material poverty to adequate assets and livelihoods; (2) from isolation and poor infrastructure to access and services; (3) from illness and incapability to health, information and education; (4) from unequal and troubled gender relations to equity and harmony; (5) from fear and lack of protection to peace and security; (6) from exclusion and impotence to inclusion, organization and empowerment; and (7) from corruption and abuse to honesty and fair treatment.

These themes embody the psychological and political nature of the struggle of the poor. Furthermore, they attend to the synergistic relationship among personal, relational, and collective domains of wellness. In all recommendations, the power to access resources and just treatment is vital. Along with the empowerment of poor people there must be a parallel process of depowerment of rich people (Huygens, 1997).

Conclusion

The presence or absence of wellness-promoting factors at the collective, relational, and personal levels can have, respectively, positive or negative synergistic effects. When collective factors such as social justice and access to valued resources combine with a sense of community and personal empowerment, chances are that psychological and political wellness will ensue. When, on the other hand, injustice and exploitation blend with lack of resources, social fragmentation, illiteracy, and ill-health, suffering is the outcome. Poor people experience the negative synergy of suffering-inducing factors such as these. But whereas poor people may be deprived of material resources, they are not deprived of agency. Even in the light of forbidding forces, they have organized in community groups, coalitions, clinics, and food co-operatives to repel poverty-induced hunger, illness and powerlessness. Inspiring settings combine solidarity with strategy, psychological support with political wisdom, and personal with collective empowerment. Bonding and bridging among and with those who struggle in poverty strengthens the resolve to tackle political and economic exploitation collectively. When amelioration at the local level is paralleled by transformation at the global level, there is hope that poverty may be alleviated, not only here and now, but also tomorrow and wherever there is injustice.

References

Allahar, A., & Cote, J. (1998). *Richer and poorer: The structure of inequality in Canada.* Toronto: Lorimer.

Aristide, J. B. (2000). *Eyes of the heart: Seeking a path for the poor in the age of globalization.* Monroe, ME: Common Courage Press.

Barnes, C. (1996). Institutional discrimination against disabled people and the campaign for anti-discrimination legislation. In D. Taylor (Ed.), *Critical social policy* (pp. 95–112). London: Sage.

Carspecken, P. (1996). *Critical ethnography in educational research.* London: Routledge.

Chase-Lansdale, P., & Brooks-Gunn, J. (Eds.). (1995). *Escape from poverty.* New York, NY: Cambridge University Press.

Dobbin, M. (1998). *The myth of the good corporate citizen: Democracy under the rule of big business.* Toronto: Stoddart.

Dudgeon, P., Garvey, D., & Pickett, H. (Eds.). (2000). *Working with Indigenous Australians: A handbook for psychologists.* Perth, Australia: Gunada Press.

Eckersley, R., (2000). The mixed blessing of material progress: Diminishing returns in the pursuit of progress. *Journal of Happiness Studies, 1,* 267–292.

Eckersley, R. (in press). Culture, health and well-being. In R. Eckersley, J. Dixon, & B. Douglas (Eds.), *The social origins of health and well-being.* New York, NY: Cambridge University Press.

Faulks, K. (1999). *Political sociology: A critical introduction.* Edinburgh: Edinburgh University Press.

Feuerstein, M-T. (1997). *Poverty and health: Reaping a richer harvest.* London: Macmillan.

Flyvbjerg, B. (2001). *Making social science matter: Why social inquiry fails and how it can succeed again.* New York, NY: Cambridge University Press.

Franke, R., & Chasin, B. (2000). Is the Kerala model sustainable? Lessons from the past, prospects for the future. In G. Parayil (Ed.), *Kerala: The development experience* (pp. 16–39). New York, NY: Zed Books.

Fryer, D. (1998). Editor's preface: Special issue on unemployment. *Journal of Community and Applied Social Psychology, 8,* 75–88.

Goodley, D., & Parker, I. (2000). Critical psychology and action research. *Annual Review of Critical Psychology, 2,* 3–18.

Gurr, J., Mailloux, L., Kinnon, D., & Doerge, S. (1996). *Breaking the links between poverty and violence against women.* Ottawa: Ministry of Supply and Services Canada.

Howarth, C., Kenway, P., Palmer, G., & Miorelli, R., (2000). *Monitoring poverty and social exclusion.* York, UK: Joseph Rowntree Foundation.

Huygens, I. (1997, May). *Toward social change partnerships: Responding to empowerment of oppressed groups with voluntary depowerment of dominant groups.* Paper presented at the Biennial Conference of the Society for Community Research and Action, Columbia, South Carolina.

Interfaith Social Assistance Reform Coalition. (1998). *Our neighbours' voices: Will we listen?* Toronto: James Lorimer.

James, E. (2001). Coverage under old-age security programs and protection for the uninsured. In N. Lustig (Ed.), *Shielding the poor: Social protection in the developing world* (pp. 149–174). Washington, DC: Brookings Institution Press/Inter-American Development Bank.

Janvry, A., & Sadoulet, E. (2001). Has aggregate income growth been effective in reducing poverty and inequality in Latin America? In N. Lustig (Ed.), *Shielding the poor: Social protection in the developing world* (pp. 21–39). Washington, DC: Brookings Institution Press/Inter-American Development Bank.

Kannan, K. (2000). Poverty alleviation as advancing basic human capabilities: Kerala's achievements compared. In G. Parayil (Ed.), *Kerala: The development experience* (pp. 40–65). New York, NY: Zed Books.

Kawachi, I., Kennedy, B., Wilkinson, R. (Eds.). (1999). *The society and population health reader: Income inequality and health.* New York, NY: The New Press.

Korten, D. (1995). *When corporations rule the world.* San Francisco: Berrett-Koehler/Kumarian Press.

Leonard, P. (1997). *Postmodern welfare: Reconstructing an emancipatory project.* London: Sage.

Lustig, N. (2001). Introduction. In N. Lustig (Ed.), *Shielding the poor: Social protection in the developing world* (pp. 1–20). Washington, DC: Brookings Institution Press/Inter-American Development Bank.

Macfarlane, S., Racelis, M., & Muli-Musiime, F. (2000). Public health in developing countries. *Lancet, 356,* 841–847.

Marmot, M. (1999). Introduction. In M. Marmot and R. Wilkinson (Eds.). *Social determinants of health* (pp. 1–16). New York, NY: Oxford University Press.

Marmot, M., & Wilkinson, R. (Eds.). (1999). *Social determinants of health.* New York: Oxford University Press.

Maxwell, S., & Kenway, P. (2000). *New thinking on poverty in the UK: Any lessons for the South?* London: Overseas Development Institute.

May, J. (2001). An elusive consensus: Definitions, measurement and analysis of poverty. In United Nations Development Programme (Ed.), *Choices for the poor* (pp. 23–54). New York, NY: United Nations.

McNeely, J. (1999). Community building. *Journal of Community Psychology, 27,* 741–750.

Narayan, D., Chambers, R., Shah, M., & Petesch, P. (1999). *Global synthesis: Consultations with the poor.* Poverty Group, World Bank. www.worldbank.org/poverty/voices/synthes.pdf

Narayan, D., Chambers, R., Shah, M., & Petesch, P. (2000). *Voices of the poor: Crying out for change.* New York, NY: Oxford University Press.

Narayan, D., Patel, R., Schafft, K., Rademacher, A., & Koch-Schulte, S. (2000). *Voices of the poor: Can anyone hear us?* New York, NY: Oxford University Press.

Nelson, G., Lord, J., & Ochoka, J. (2001). *Shifting the paradigm in community mental health: Toward empowerment and community.* Toronto: University of Toronto Press.

Nordstrom, H., Ben David, D., & Winters, L. (1999). *Trade, income disparity and poverty.* Geneva: World Trade Organization.

Parayil, G. (Ed.). (2000). *Kerala: The development experience.* London: Zed Books.

Power, A. (1996). Area-based poverty and resident empowerment. *Urban Studies, 33,* 1535–1565.

Prilleltensky, I. (2001). Value-based praxis in community psychology: Moving toward social justice and social action. *American Journal of Community Psychology.*

Prilleltensky, I., & Nelson, G. (2002). *Doing psychology critically: Making a difference in diverse settings.* New York, NY: London: Macmillan/Palgrave.

Prilleltensky, I., & Nelson, G. (1997). Community Psychology: Reclaiming social justice. In D. Fox & I. Prilleltensky (Eds.), *Critical psychology: An introduction* (pp. 166–184) London: Sage.

Prilleltensky, I., & Nelson, G. (2000). Promoting child and family wellness: Priorities for psychological and social interventions. *Journal of Community and Applied Social Psychology, 10,* 85–105.

Prilleltensky, I., Nelson, G., & Peirson, L. (2001a). The role of power and control in children's lives: an ecological analysis of pathways toward wellness, resilience, and problems. *Journal of Community and Applied Social Psychology, 11,* 143–158.

Prilleltensky, I., Nelson, G., & Peirson, L. (2001b). *Promoting family wellness and preventing child maltreatment.* Toronto: University of Toronto Press.

Putnam, R. (2000). *Bowling alone: The collapse and revival of American community.* New York, NY: Simon & Schuster.

Ransom, D. (May, 2001). The World Trade Organization [Special Issue]. *The New Internationalist, 334.*

Razavi, S. (1999). Seeing poverty through a gender lens. *International Social Science Journal, 51,* 473–482.

Robertson, A., Brunner, E., & Sheiham, A. (1999). Food is a political issue. In M. Marmot & R. Wilkinson (Eds.), *Social determinants of health* (pp. 179–210) Oxford: Oxford University Press.

Sen, A. (1999a). *Beyond the crisis: Development strategies in Asia.* Singapore: Institute of Southeast Asian Studies.

Sen, A. (1999b). *Development as freedom.* New York, NY: Anchor Books.

Sen, A. (2001). *Culture and development.* Paper presented at the World Bank Tokyo Meeting, 13 December. www.worldbank.org/wbi/B-SPAN/sen_tokyo.pdf

Shaw, M., Dorling, D., & Smith, G. D. (1999). Poverty, social exclusion, and minorities. In M. Marmot and R. Wilkinson (Eds.). *Social determinants of health* (pp. 211–239). New York, NY: Oxford University Press.

Snow, L. (1995). Economic development breaks the mold: Community-building, place-targeting, and empowerment zones. *Economic Development Quarterly, 9,* 185–197.

The Smith Family. (2000). *Financial disadvantage in Australia 1999: The unlucky Australians.* Camperdown, NSW: Author.

UNICEF (2001). *The state of the world's children 2002.* New York, NY: Author.

UNICEF Innocenti Research Centre (June 2000). *A league table of child poverty in rich nations: Report card No. 1.* Florence, Italy: Author.

US Department of Health and Human Services. (2000). *Child Maltreatment 1998: Reports from the States to the National Child Abuse and Neglect Data System (NCANDS).* (Washington, DC: U.S. Government Printing Office, 2000). Online statistical fact sheets: www.calib.com/nccanch/pubs/index.htm

Weisbrot, M. (1999). *Globalization: A Primer.* Washington, DC: Center for Economic and Policy Research. Available from http://www.cepr.net/GlobalPrimer.htm

Wilkinson, R. (1996). *Unhealthy societies: The afflictions of inequality.* London: Routledge.

Zimmerman, M. (2000). Empowerment theory: Psychological, organizational and community levels of analysis. In J. Rappaport & E. Seidman (Eds.), *Handbook of Community Psychology* (pp. 43–78). New York, NY: Kluwer Academic/Plenum Publishers.

Chapter 3

Poverty and Justice

Stuart C. Carr

Overview

Psychology needs to make a contribution towards global community development. One domain where it can do that is the field of inter-group relations, which is integral to economic and social change. This chapter first positions development agencies themselves, as groups, inside the overall development process. These groups frequently bring problems of their own to the development equation. Those problems are played out in (1) aid mediascapes, through which aid agencies broadcast disturbing images of the poor to raise funds from donor communities; (2) aid ethnoscapes, where those funds are disbursed by expatriate field workers; and (3) development ideoscapes, where "recipient" communities eschew outside intervention in favor of determination from within. In each case, perceptions of justice are critical to social relations, and this chapter outlines a theory of Social Equity to partially account for, and illuminate, these social influence processes.

Rationale

Through the APA, psychology has been granted special consultative status to the United Nations (Okorodudu, 2000). Psychology has thereby positioned itself to provide behavioral understanding and advice on global challenges such as combating poverty (Marsella, 2000). Poverty-reduction initiatives often take the form of development projects, which range in terms of the level of community participation they afford (O'Gorman, 1992). This level of participation varies from the outside intervention of "band-aid"; to "helping people to help themselves" with

45

Technical Assistance (TA) delivered by expatriate experts; to the dynamics of political struggle for self-determination (Sánchez, 1996). In each of these categories, there are pressing questions about the human factor in development practice (UN Summit for Social Development, 1995). Why for example would UNICEF become concerned that aid agency fund-raising images encourage mass stereotyping of the world's poor (Fountain, 1995)? Why do the people of East Timor wish the UN to leave (ANU/CSEAS, 2000)? Why in the South Pacific did the TA system itself precipitate the closure of an entire National University (ABC, 1998)? These questions make aid organizations as much a part of the problem as part of the solution (Van Brabant, 2000). Recognizing that reality, this paper articulates some foundations for a *psychology of aid organizations* (see also, Anderson, 2002).

Mediascapes That Play to Donor Bias

Many aid organizations rely on public donations to fund their development projects, and a chief source of revenue is the social marketing of images of poverty using television fund-raising advertisements. In a global economy, the mediascape (Appadurai, 1990) where this takes place is just as competitive as anywhere else, with a swathe of aid and welfare agencies jostling for the donor dollar. For viewer consumers of the image, these mediascapes become contact zones where they are exposed daily to graphic images of the deprivation of one very large human group – the world's poor (Marsella, 1998). The barely concealed theory behind these advertisements is that the more pathos their human images manage to convey, the more guilt will be aroused, and the greater will be the felt need to alleviate that guilt by making a dollar donation (Godwin, 1994).

Psychosocial analysis suggests a different outcome. One starting point for that analysis is attribution theory, which research has shown is a better predictor of donation behavior than conventional demographic markers like age and sex (Cheung & Chan, 2000; for alternative and complementary starting points, see Carr, Mc Auliffe, & MacLachlan, 1998). Before they see any aid advertising images of the poor, a vast amount of attribution theory indicates that many donor publics will be habitually inclined, even if they say otherwise, to attribute poverty to dispositions in the poor themselves, such as laziness, listlessness, and a lack of intelligence (Chafel, 1997). This is crucial, because donations are more likely to happen when attributions for poverty are on the contrary situational, for example global climate change (Pawlik & d'Ydewalle, 1996), government corruption (Lea, 1998), and regional economic crisis (Community Aid Abroad/Freedom From Hunger, 1996/7). Viewed in psychosocial terms therefore, one best practice in fund-raising means raising situational awareness to counterbalance relatively habitual dispositional attributions (Carr, 1996). The frame should be more global than local (Hermans & Kempen, 1998). Resulting elevations of consciousness could then help generate social capital rather than depleting it, and to that extent make a more significant contribution towards poverty alleviation than the "band-aid" of throwing money at the problem (Campbell, Carr, & MacLachlan, 2001).

Contemporary Practice

To what extent do aid advertisement theory and practice address these interrelated objectives of raising money and increasing tolerance? Unfortunately, because of the theory that drives them, many aid advertisements deliberately give perceptual "figure" to the human face, whilst the situational causes of poverty, like nature, corruption, and exploitation, are relegated to "ground." The frame is precisely more local than global. Giving perceptual salience to the human figure like this, and especially so in any context of rising individualism (Hofstede & Bond, 1988), is precisely motivational fuel for dispositional attributions, such as laziness, listlessness, and lack of intelligence (Carr, 1996). So too is lack of background information, which aid advertisements must withhold in order to emphasize instead the human image. Decontextualism like this will interact with viewers' value systems (Carr et al., 1998). Specifically, it has now been found that they reinforce perspectives that are fundamentally individualist, and they will deprive perspectives that are relatively collectivist of many of the situational cues to which they are normally sensitive (Choi, Nisbett, & Norenzayan 1999). Thus, aid advertisements are fuelling "fundamental attribution errors" (Krull, Loy, Lin, Wang, Chen, & Zhao, 1999).

Our analysis so far is inter-individual, but its predictions become more disconcerting once we consider dynamics between groups, i.e., a psychology of "the group within the individual" (Reicher, 1996). When individual viewers of aid advertisements are introduced to a figure who is poor and needy, they are explicitly provided with exemplars of an out-group social category, "the poor" (INRA, 1992). Fund-raising advertisements also identify the poor as an out-group economically, geographically, and ethnically, even though any one of these characteristics is normally sufficient in itself to precipitate inter-group prejudice and discrimination (Mamman, 1995). Compared to in-groups ("the viewing public" for instance), out-groups (the poor for instance) tend to be perceived as relatively homogenous. This schematically positions them to be disparagingly stereotyped, for example as a collectively lazy and listless lost cause (Sidanius & Pratto, 1999). Negative stereotypes like this are especially likely when observer groups are invited to attribute their own group's (in-group) successes compared to another group's (out-group) failings, for example being economically prosperous compared to chronically poor (Carr et al., 1998). Such stereotypes also tend to be subconscious (Fazio, Jackson, Dunton, & Williams, 1995), and to that extent relatively mindless (Ajzen & Fishbein, 2000). Adding to this mindlessness, (1) highly visible, (2) vivid, and (3) negatively valenced images of "the poor," like those precisely that define aid advertisements, increase heuristic (a) *discounting* of situational factors, (b) *availability* of stereo-types, and (c) *negativity* in those stereotypes (Carr, 2003). Thus, aid advertisements are fuelling "ultimate attribution errors" (Hewstone, 1990).

Even when these images are of children, aid advertisements are still likely to be fostering donor bias (Carr, 2001). Granted, children are unlikely to be held *individually* responsible or blamed for their own poverty, and they are capable of stirring powerful negative emotions such as guilt, compassion, and empathy, which in reasonable doses do undoubtedly move people to make donations (Thornton, Kirchner, & Jacobs, 1991). The problem however is that fund-raising mediascapes, as we have just seen, invoke a relatively diffused *group* identity ("the poor," whose prototype probably features adults), portrayed in a never-ending *stream* of pathetic images (Carr, 2000). Under such emotionally saturating conditions, clichéd marketing slogans like "All it takes is a dollar a day" rapidly become too much to hear any more (Moeller, 1999). Compassion fatigued viewers may then either dissociate themselves from the poor (Walkup, 1997), or make attributions that fit their negative mood (Forgas, 1995). These reactions can even occur within the same advertisement, such as when images of childhood poverty are *particularly* distressing and guilt inducing (Griffiths, 1999). Thus, high-pressure social marketing, even when it uses children, can backfire.

To sum up, a wide range of theory and research indicates that conventional media depictions of the poor reinforce rather than reduce donor bias among aid advertisement viewers. According to a psychosocial analysis, this will deplete both dollar donations and international social capital.

Raising Consciousness

Conclusions like this lend renewed urgency to calls, made two decades ago, for psychologists to sensitize the "developed" world to some of the realities of life in "developing" economies (Mehryar, 1984). The psychosocial analysis above consistently implies that aid agency advertising is lowering not raising consciousness about the situational causes of poverty (Gergen, 1994). A first step for counteracting that downturn is to start conveying the known situational causes of poverty, as "ballast" for the probably necessary use of human imagery (Godwin, 1994, p. 47). One approach towards achieving this may be to empower aid advertisement audiences to see and hear an empowered poor speak more for themselves (Montero & Dollinger, 1998).

What would these perspectives look like? Although much of this work still remains to be done, a combination of attribution theory and psychometrics can be applied to make some testable estimations. An attribution scale available in Harper (1996) measures both dispositional and situational attributions for poverty, and has shown itself to be reliable for gauging perspectives in both developed and developing areas (Bolitho & Carr, 2001). The scale has for example been applied in Australia and Malaŵi (East Africa), to measure respectively "observer" (outsider) *and* "actor" (insider) perspectives on "Third World" poverty (Campbell et al., 2001). In Campbell et al.'s study, compared to Australian viewer observers, Malaŵian actors living in poverty made more situational attributions for its occurrence (for a recent comparison of actor and observer perspectives within the same country, see for example Morcoel, 1997; or, Abouchedid & Nasser, 2001). So, actors' attributions are liable to look relatively situational to viewer audiences observing those actors – so creating a potential to *raise* the audience's situational consciousness. Among the Australian observers in Campbell et al.'s study, these increases in situational attributions were linked to making heftier donations. Thus, actors' attributions for poverty have the potential to lift how many dollars observers give, as well as elevating their pro-social behavior generally (as politically conscious consumers, campaigners, etc.).

Economic Crisis

An emerging strand of this research consists of applying psychosocial analysis to the "finanscapes" (Appadurai, 1990) of regional economic crisis (Montero, 1996). These crises are creating vast amounts of poverty around the world, and may come to increasingly characterize the global economy for much of this century (Kato, 2000). Recovery *out* of such crises is critically dependent on fostering regional understanding and co-operation (Aus-Thai Project Team, 1998). One way of facilitating these is to measure insiders' attributions about the causes of economic crisis, and to disseminate those messages between groups with a stake in the region's recovery (Aus-Thai Project Team, 1999). A scale recently developed for this purpose measures actors' attributions along three latent dimensions – economic, governance, and human (Aus-Thai Project Team, 2001). Actors' attributions along these dimensions will inform both international and local aid organizations (Teeravekin, 1998), as well as regional business investors (McMichael, 2000), about what kinds of project or program (economic, governmental, human development) best suits the local setting (Aus-Thai Project Team, this volume). Thus, if the predominant attributed cause of crisis is poor economic policy and governance rather than exclusively human factors like those discussed above, then the most sustainable form of intervention is more likely to be fiscal (and relatively macro) than social (and relatively micro).

Social e-marketing

A related seam of psychosocial theory and research is engaging with the "technoscapes" (Appadurai, 1990) of the Internet. Aid and welfare agencies already use Internet advertising extensively for fund-raising purposes. Like their television counterparts however, these advertisements tend to rely on conventional facial imagery. This is despite the fact that Internet technology theoretically allows users time to process information about more abstract, and to that extent potentially *situational* causes of poverty. Such information is moreover presentable dynamically, for example using engagingly interactive visual images and hypertext, which theoretically give the technology an edge over more conventional "snail mail" paper flyers (Carr, 2003). Preliminary tests of such multi-modal reformats, involving both visual photographic and visual textual information, about the *situational* causes of poverty, reflecting perspectives of *poor groups themselves*, have begun to indicate that psychologically appropriate usage of Internet technology may actually increase both situational attributions and donation intentions (Fox & Carr, 2000).

Innovative research like this addresses the concerns that UNICEF has had about international perceptions of poverty. Firstly, it shows that "psychologists from rich industrialized countries can play an immensely valuable role, by trying to sensitize their nations to the . . . real causes and consequences of world poverty and injustice" (Mehryar, 1984, p. 166). Secondly, and just as importantly, it begins to show *how* that sensitization can take place, employing twenty-first-century technology.

Ethnoscapes in Which TA Workers Become Demotivated

What is TA?

At the delivery end of aid projects, of all the monies spent on development assistance, at least one-fifth of it is directed to TA, with much of that being used to pay the salaries of expatriate personnel (Carr et al., 1998). TA projects themselves can be in agriculture, engineering, health, population, management, or education. TA activities in these areas are focused on institutional and human resource development, where they are normally termed "capacity building" (a euphemism for developing the human factor). Thus, TA expatriates can be found conducting the sort of activities with which psychologists are normally very familiar but in aid spheres have been strangely absent, including for instance organizational and curriculum development.

One particular area where psychologists could make a major contribution is in TA project evaluation. Typically, TA projects have either not been evaluated at all, or evaluated in-house (which creates conflicts of interest), or evaluated only in the short term (Picciotto & Rist, 1995). In our experience, a major aspect of TA that urgently requires thorough evaluation, and perhaps considerable "rethinking through," in psychosocial terms, is the widespread social tension that TA experts often create by their mere *presence* in aid field settings (Selby, 1999).

A potent symbol of this tension is the "floating hotel" in Dili East Timor, where many UN TA workers and others have been housed. Until recently, this boat, called "The Olympia," was moored directly in front of local government head offices. Although not terribly comfortable from the inside, from the outside its brightly colored lights and restaurants, as well as security guards, conveyed an impression to the local population of obscene luxury. The extreme affluence and exclusivity The Olympia exuded, not unlike the many other accoutrements of aid projects generally (four-wheel drives, dining facilities, hotel accommodations, served to underscore the social inequities that brought aid in the first place. As well, (and again like those other accoutrements), it saliently reminded the "aided" that "aidiees," as a group, were making a *living* out of them. As one development consultant acerbically remarked about East Timor, the UN there at the time were widely seen as "parasitic" (Martin, 2001).

Less obvious perhaps is that attributions like these, which have been personally witnessed in Africa and other development settings also, are very problematic for many TA expatriates too (Carr, 2000). One domain where those problems are naturally enough most immediate, and therefore most distressing and distracting, is in those expatriates' daily working relationships with their local counterparts within TA projects themselves.

Working Relationships in TA

Typically, these expatriates are hired on contracts of about two years' duration, and the basic goal in that time is to "work their selves out of a job." This is necessary so that their local counterparts can take over once the contract period is up, rendering the technical assistance "sustainable." Clearly, in any such arrangement, the relationship between expatriates and counterparts is going to be critical to the project (World Bank News, 1996). In effect, the technical and the social become inseparable (Gow, 1991). Unfortunately however, like the floating hotel there is a sharp (and this time very concrete and immediate) socio-economic impediment to developing that relationship. TA expatriates are paid from their home country, or by a multilateral agency whose headquarters are located inside an economy that is developed. This typically means that their salaries, which it can be argued have to be competitive in the international market, are far higher than the wages paid to their local counterparts.

The magnitude of difference between these salaries is often mind-boggling. In East Timor for instance, UN administrative staff from overseas, on the lowest level, can earn almost 20 times the pay of local UN administrators, on the highest local rung. Shocking differentials like these commonly create massive human factors obstacles for both local and expatriates alike (MacLachlan, 1993). That is especially so since the local counterparts frequently do much of the same work as their expatriate colleagues, and moreover have more seniority in the kind of job they are doing. Such inequities are partly why perhaps relations between TA expatriates and their local counterparts are sometimes portrayed as "tense," and also perhaps why a significant proportion of TA expatriates never do manage to work themselves out of a job (Fox, 1994). As one major reviewer points out, TA expatriates sometimes leave before the end of their first contract, and so never manage to work themselves *into* the job in the first place (Cassen, 1994). Other expatriates stay for far too long, thus continuing to live a life of luxury they could never imagine or afford at home (Dore, 1994).

A Psychosocial Analysis

A concept that helps to explain each of these failings is equity between groups (Taylor & Moghaddam, 1994). In the context of aid organizations, Social Equity Theory (SET) states that these groups will act in ways to restore a sense of balance between their outcomes-for-inputs, and those of a comparable out-group, such as local counterparts in a TA project (Carr, MacLachlan, & Campbell, 1997). SET thus restates and rejuvenates Adams' (1965) Equity theory, the focus of which is largely inter-individual, by extending it into the domain of this section, whose focus is largely inter-group. Social Equity Theory thus predicts that overpayment, relative to a salient out-group such as Indigenous development workers, will lead many in the overpaid group (TA expatriates) to experience guilt. At least some aid workers (not all of course) join TA projects precisely *because* they are relatively sensitive to social inequity.

Such sensitivities may contribute towards culture shock and thereby to premature exit from TA projects. If expatriates decide to stay with the project however, SET predicts that a substantial proportion of them will collectively, initially, attempt to raise their input to reflect their relatively high outcomes (salaries and other benefits), compared to the salient out-group (local counterparts). In experimental settings, this type of effect has been found to be relatively short-lived (Aamodt, 1999). The problem in development settings like East Timor, however, is that the pay differential – at over twenty times the local salary – simply cannot be made up by extra effort alone. Nor is physically avoiding the source of the discomfort (a classic dissonance-reducing tactic) a practical option, although expatriates and their local counterparts will often practice a form of "social apartheid" outside of work hours (Kealey, 1989). Thus, having failed to restore a sense of balance physically (by working harder), SET predicts that many TA expatriates will restore social equity, between themselves and their local TA counterparts, *psychologically.*

In order to achieve this, TA expatriates must incrementally persuade themselves that their input to the job is superior, and to that extent justifies their comparatively higher pay. Complementing this ultimate attribution error is the concept of inter-group comparison (Hewstone & Greenland, 2000). Social Identity Theory (SIT) proposes that members of groups have a fundamental need to engage in downward comparison, in order to maintain their self-esteem (Aberson, Healy, & Romero, 2000). In TA projects, this theory predicts that expatriate groups drawing salaries that are higher than those drawn by their local counterparts may end up deriving self-esteem from that comparison (Dore, 1994). Inter-group comparison outcomes like this are probably more applicable however to relatively equity *in*sensitive expatriates, and to relatively equity sensitive expatriates only once any psychosocial equity restoration has already taken place.

According to SET therefore, TA expatriate salaries will tend to foster feelings of superiority within TA expatriate groups. To the extent that people who have come to feel superior are less likely to apply themselves as much as before they rationalized their superior pay status with self-acclaimed superior input, TA project pay differentials are predicted to foster progressive expatriate demotivation. The key empirical indicators of this process of demotivation having become engaged, according to both SET and SIT, will be a combination of firstly guilt (about their higher pay), and, secondly, superiority (justifying their higher pay).

An empirical test for these indicators, in TA projects, was conducted recently in the higher education sector where TA projects are relatively common (Carr, Chipande, & MacLachlan, 1998). The study took place at the National University of Malaŵi, in East Africa. There, TA expatriates at the time were drawing approximately between 10 and 20 times the salary paid to their local counterparts. As is common practice in TA projects generally, those TA expatriates were also drawing a local salary, on which many lived whilst banking their TA salary offshore. In other settings, such as the UN operation in East Timor, the local salary is replaced by a relatively generous daily allowance, or per diem, which is paid in the "hard currency" of US dollars.

In the Malaŵian study, an organizational survey asked both TA expatriate and local lecturers to report how each group, foreign expatriate and local counterpart, felt about their comparative levels of pay, performance, and work motivation. Two key findings from this survey bear directly on SET. Firstly, the TA expatriates, as a group, were significantly more likely than their local counterparts to agree with the statement, "Some expatriates on large salaries feel *guilty* because they earn much more than local workers" (emphasis added). Secondly, the TA expatriates, as a group, were more likely than their local counterparts to agree that, "Expatriates are *better employees* than their local counterparts" (emphasis added). Thus, this study found the first empirical signs of precisely the combination of guilt and superiority predicted by inter-group SET.

How do we know that what caused (and causes) demotivation among TA expatriates is actually pay, rather than say unusual characteristics of those who are attracted to overseas development positions? (Littlewood, 1985). Experimental studies of TA salary inequities have adapted a well-known laboratory paradigm for studying the demotivating impact of being paid for a job one would normally do for free (Deci & Ryan, 1999). This adaptation includes overpaying individuals and groups compared to a lower paid individual or group, identifying that overpayment to them along with the magnitude of the differential (twice the pay of their lower paid counterparts, not unlike field settings like Malaŵi), and then denying the higher paid any opportunity to physically increase their input to match their outcome (as in TA projects themselves). The dependent variable in this paradigm, as in Deci and Ryan's model, is the amount of free choice time that the participants subsequently devote to the same task (an operational measure of intrinsic motivation). The less time given over during the free choice period, the more demotivated participants have become on the task.

Using this operational measure of demotivation, overpaid participants typically become demotivated compared to no-payment control groups (Carr, 2001; Carr, McLoughlin, Hodgson, & MacLachlan, 1996). Over and above such demotivation, a significant percentage of the variation in free time devoted to the task is also explained by wide individual differences in equity sensitivity (McLoughlin & Carr, 1997). To the extent that TA expatriates are motivated by Equity Sensitivity, this finding links demotivation directly to equity restoration processes, as well as suggesting various applications to designing expatriate selection and remuneration systems (for details of these, see Carr et al., 1998).

The relevance of this TA research extends well beyond TA projects themselves. Pay diversity is found increasingly throughout the global economy, for example through enterprise bargaining and expatriate business assignments in regions affected by economic crisis (Hermans & Kempen, 1998). So-called "external inequity," or equity between groups, is also a growing concern in industrial and service organizations generally (McShane & Von Glinow, 2000). Thus, the predictions made by SET are becomingly increasingly relevant to organizations across a range of sectors and settings, as indeed are individual differences in equity sensitivity.

To sum up, the research on TA projects, in development settings, has identified a role for psychology in highlighting, empirically and theoretically, the existence of a significant human factors problem in TA remuneration. Problem identification is the first step to problem prevention. That is certainly so for aid organizations, but it is just as true for organizations generally! The research on TA therefore illuminates some of the issues that are germane to organizations worldwide, whether as a result of economic crisis and international assignments, or through the globalization of performance management and pay diversity. If organizational psychology can rise to meet such challenges, it will offer a service to development generally.

Ideoscapes That Mobilize Host Counterparts

For every higher paid person or group there is a lower paid person or group. In TA settings, and individual differences aside, the lower paid group conventionally holds relatively collectivist values, and to that extent will tend to identify itself in any discourse about pay *as* a collective. Collectivist values have in turn been directly linked with increased salience of perceived equity between groups (Smith & Bond, 1999). As well, collectivist values are often linked to belief in distributing rewards on the basis of comparative need, for example to support an extended rather than nuclear family (Carr et al., 1998). Taken together, these factors suggest that SET will apply to local counterparts' perspectives on TA salaries. Specifically, the theory predicts that among local counterparts in TA projects, there will result a combination of (1) perceived injustice and (2) organizational resistance to TA in general, and the dual pay system (above) in particular. As a manifestation of (2), Indigenous employees will tend to withdraw their input in proportion to their reduced outcomes compared to their expatriate counterparts.

The first of these predictions (1) has been tested in the Malaŵian study made by Carr et al. (1998). For instance, Malaŵian lecturers, unlike their TA expatriate counterparts, tended to agree that, "Local people are *de*motivated by the large salaries that some expatriates earn." Similarly, Malaŵian lecturers, unlike their TA expatriate counterparts, also tended to agree that, "Expatriates who work abroad should work under the *same* terms and conditions as local people." Finally, and again unlike their TA expatriate counterparts, Malaŵian lecturers tended to agree significantly more that, "Most companies are *un*fair to their local employees" (emphases added). Each of these findings is indicative of perceptions of injustice, and as such is consistent with SET.

The presence of (2) withdrawal of input is more difficult to establish. In organizational settings generally, this may be quite subtle, for example working a little slower than normal, or not being totally co-operative with expatriate colleagues. Withdrawal can also be more overt and obvious however. In August of 1998, Indigenous academics at the University of Papua New Guinea began an indefinite boycott of classes, in protest at the dual salary system – which the National Academic Staff Association claimed represents group discrimination (ABC, 1998). This industrial action closed the University for some time. Such closure of a key development organization illustrates unambiguously how demotivation can escalate to the point where it has very significant influences, both on organizational behavior and on development itself.

A Startling Conclusion

Given that both TA expatriates and their local counterparts are demotivated by TA expatriate salaries, we could say that pay diversity, in the context of international aid, is creating a double demotivation (Carr & MacLachlan, 1993/4; MacLachlan & Carr, 1993). This double demotivation is the product of an underpaid group seeking social equity and an overpaid group seeking social equity (for a complementary discussion of SIT dynamics in the same social situation, Tajfel, 1978).

A Knotty Problem

Host counterparts are not the only TA employees affected by underpayment. Even amongst TA expatriates themselves, who are working for *different* aid organizations, we have seen that there are wide and essentially irredeemable pay differentials. There are also differentials between expatriates who work for local community-based organizations versus expatriates who work for international aid organizations. Finally, there are differences between local personnel who work for community-based as opposed to international aid organizations (Valdivieso, 2000). Thus, the very way that aid is organized is a Gordian knot of inequitable pay divisions, and to that extent of double demotivation also.

Even beyond relationships involving TA expatriates and local counterparts, within the wider community and its constituent social and community groups, development assistance, like the Olympia did, often creates unwanted and socially divisive tensions (Kohnert, 1996). In West Timor for example, aid given to East Timorese refugees ended up creating social inequities (and very serious tensions) between refugee and local communities (Therrick, 2000). Thus, *aid itself* may be creating a societal form of double demotivation, as each group becomes progressively disengaged and disaffected with the other.

Selecting Regional Expertise

Logically, one way in which many of these problems of social inequity could be avoided altogether is through recruiting expatriates, where local shortfalls genuinely exist, from *within* developing areas (Dore, 1994). As well as these expatriates being more familiar with the realities and terrain of development work, their salaries would be lower, in economic terms, and thus more equitable, in distributive justice terms. Selecting critical personnel from within the *same* developing area would take these benefits even further. It would also be nicely commensurate with the growing emphasis on regional trade blocs as self-sustaining vehicles for development out of poverty (Rugimbana, Carr, Bolitho, & Walkom, 2000).

Psychosocially however, regional initiatives like this may again run up against considerable human factors (Carr, Ehiobuche, Rugimbana, & Munro, 1996). In our studies of expatriate selection within the East African Community bloc for instance, we found significant preferences for expatriates from the "developed" world over expatriates from within the trade bloc itself, even though both groups were equally well qualified and competent (Carr, Rugimbana, Walkom, & Bolitho, 2001). Similar negative (rather than positive) discrimination, against expatriates whose economy-of-origin is within the same region, has been found in West Africa (Eze, 1985), in Eastern Europe (Henderson-King, Henderson-King, Zhermer, Posokhova, & Chiker, 1997), and in Southeast Asia (Lim & Ward, 1999). Thus, the scope for human factors to impede regional development initiatives may have been seriously underestimated by some regional economic planners.

The resultant "inverse resonance" with regional neighboring communities (Carr et al., 1996) may have a psychological basis in regional (and possibly global) schemata. In these schemata, nations and ethnic groups are consensually ranked into a mental hierarchy, which is then applied when making decisions about whether to reject TA personnel from those strata (Sidanius & Pratto, 1999). Thus, African expatriates living and working in Papua New Guinea may find it very hard to become accepted by their Papua New Guinean counterparts (Saffu, 2001; see also, Dore, 1994; for similar schemata operating in the ideoscapes of free trade in goods and services, see Rugimbana et al., 2000).

The general point here is that there may be significant psychological factors that, unless properly managed, are likely to restrict the free flow of human and material resources that trade blocs were set up to promote in the first place. A first step to problem resolution, already taken in the research and theory development outlined above, is problem identification. At that stage, classic I/O psychology initiatives, like structuring selection processes, might reduce these biases. At the same time however, psychology itself is seriously *challenged* by the emerging international research described above. At least one of its sacred cows for instance, namely that "similarity attracts," is put into question when expatriates who originate from cultures- and economies-of-origin that are radically *dis*similar become not less but *more* attractive propositions for selection. Such counterintuitive findings provide what ethnographers call "rich points" for theoretical contemplation, revision, and ultimately perhaps development.

Developing Local Expertise

Given the above human factors issue with raising funds from *outside* of developing regions, and even with disbursing those funds successfully *within* those regions via TA, then it would be reasonable to wonder whether the old paradigm – the very idea of aid and welfare – is truly sustainable beyond providing temporary relief during moments of deep crisis. Instead perhaps, locally anchored projects that *engage* with the wider global economy may offer the best prospect for sustainable growth. For some years for instance, psychology has been involved in the promotion of small businesses, and in particular the motivation to develop them and make them succeed economically (McClelland, 1961). True, McClelland's concept of "Need for Achievement" has been justifiably criticized for its latent individualism, and McClelland himself (1987) found that entrepreneurs who prospered most were those who managed to blend their business acumen with a clear sense of local tradition. Such findings also however indicate that a key to managing small-enterprise development is to turn local traditional values to competitive advantage in a wider economy. This would be part of a developmental process that has been termed "glocalization," as it reflects the joint global and local concerns of people who are normally engaged in development activities (Robertson, 1995).

One region where this idea of fusing regional and local concerns has been gathering momentum is North Australia. There, according to leading Aboriginal advocates, decades of welfare, or domestic aid, has left a psychological legacy of dependence, disease, and deprivation (for an excellent discussion of the behavioral parallels between international aid and welfare in this setting, see Selby, 1999). In his scathing attack on this enculturation of dependence and entitlement, Pearson (1999) has outlined how traditional economies were real, and demanded real responsibility and reciprocity. These traditional economies were and are, according to Pearson, anathema to the disempowerment and "something for nothing" mentality encouraged by welfare. According to Pearson, "we do not have a right to welfare, we have a right to a real economy – we need to wake up to the destructive con that welfare represents" (1999, p. 3).

Similar arguments, based again on the retention of Indigenous values as the platform for economic, community-based development, have been propounded by Dodson, who writes, in direct challenge to one of the "beacons" of much development work (Maslow's hierarchy of need, for example), "We want health, housing, and education. But not at the expense of losing our own soul, our own identity, a say in our lives. We refuse to sacrifice the essence of what makes us Aboriginal people" (1998, p. 8).

A Living Case

Balancing the need for inclusion with respect for tradition is a regional enterprise development program currently being implemented and expanded across Australia's remote Northern Territory. This region of the Australian continent covers an area twice the size of Texas, and is home to the country's highest proportion of Indigenous communities (Ivory, 1999). As Ivory points out, economic activities were thriving in Australia long before Europeans arrived, including regional trade and commerce (1999, p. 62; this volume). In the time since colonization however, pastoralization and other forms of "development," including welfare, have subverted these traditions, communal awareness of which Ivory has helped to rekindle in a growing number of small business development projects. A major impetus to such developments, according to Ivory, has been the old paradigmatic welfare system itself, including a "fund and forget" approach to community development projects that resonates with our analysis of aid above (1999, p. 64).

Working closely within Indigenous communities, and at a pace and scale determined by them throughout, this micro-level program is starting to produce thriving businesses in for example Indigenous cosmetics, packaged water, gravel extraction, trepang harvesting, and ethnic tourism. Out of these relatively successful socio-economic experiences, for which Ivory reports there is much further demand in the bush, has emerged a human factors model of Indigenous Business Development (for details, see Ivory, this volume). In stage one of this model, and facilitated by Ivory (who represents the Office of Aboriginal Development), Indigenous owners take time to appreciate the causes of their poverty, and how to break out of it by engaging with the wider economic system. This includes a review of the perspective of *Balanda*, or non-Aboriginal cultures. In stage two of the model, the prospective entrepreneurs define the cultural objectives for their project. The stakeholders then develop their own business flow chart, which is designed to navigate the bureaucratic maze (Ivory, 1999, p. 65). Overall, and with a minimum of "intervention" by the Office of Aboriginal Development, the meld of local and global in this program has produced business development projects "with a vengeance" (Ivory, 1999, p. 70).

Transcapes and the Meta Process of Equity Escalation

The theme that links together all three previous sections in this chapter is perceived inter-group, or social inequity. We have seen inequity between the poor and the media viewing publics who would give aid to them; between TA experts and their local counterparts; and between Indigenous communities and their non-Indigenous co-nationals. In this final section of the chapter, we outline a common process by which these perceptions of social inequity *interact* with one another, to produce a meta-influence process that appears in all three of the major "scapes" that we have so far considered. The basic template for this process can be found in Open Systems Theory, where it is known as *escalation* (Senge, 2000). In the case of aid and welfare, the bare essence of escalation is that each group's initial tactic for dealing with *its* perception of social inequity will steadily reinforce the other in its *own* perception of social inequity. In this way, social inequity propagates vicious or virtuous circles, depending on whether the initial reactions are socially negative or positive. The subsequent positioning and counter-positioning inherent in such circles, I now contend, can be found across the mediascapes of fund-raising, the ethnoscapes of TA assignments, and the ideoscapes of development projects generally.

The dynamics of these escalating circles is pictorially summarized and depicted in Figure 3.1. In general terms, this model predicts that groups will always compare themselves for social equity. The "have nots" in this comparison (the poor "recipients" in aid projects, the local counterpart in TA) naturally see that (1) their own outcomes are drastically lower than those obtained by their wealthier counterparts (the donor public, the expatriate counterpart in TA). This prompts (2) a reduction of input (e.g., co-operation, goodwill, conscientiousness) in order to raise the value of their social outcome-for-input ratio. The "haves" meanwhile, have been restoring *their* sense of social equity by mentally (3) inflating the sense

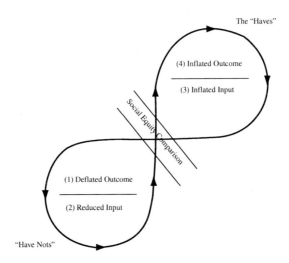

Figure 3.1. Dynamic SET – Double *negative* Pygmalion effects
Source: Adapted from Adams (1965), and Senge (2000).

of their own input, to match their relatively (4) inflated outcomes, so restoring at least some sense of balance with their relatively deprived counterparts. From *this* perspective, reduced input from the out-group (2) merely *reinforces* the inflation-of-input strategy for restoring social equity ("We might be getting more money, but we're *giving* much more too!"). Such "haughty," "self-righteous" attitudes, and the ultimate attribution errors that they leakingly convey then, in turn, reinforce (1) and (2) and, recursively, (3) and (4), and so on. Thus, we witness a doubly negative Pygmalion effect, as each group escalatively conforms to the other's (negative) stereotype of it.

Some Concrete Examples

In the donor mediascape, we have seen how viewers of aid advertisements will derogate the poor in order to assuage any guilt deliberately elicited through steady streams of heart-rending images of suffering and deprivation. Such socially negative maneuvers can be viewed as a form of restoring social equity: What the poor bring to the development equation is reduced to match their acutely deprived outcomes in the new economic order. But we must not forget also that aid mediascapes are portals for the poor as well. Through the global media, they regularly see themselves portrayed as pathetic figures alongside the relative wealth of people living in the "developed" world. Unlike their wealthier counterparts however, their own attributions for the wealth they see are likely to be relatively situational (Hunt, 1996). Each of these factors – being portrayed as pathetic and making situational attributions for wealth – will generate ambivalence towards aid, including indignation and contempt. As a result of this, according to SET, the poor will withdraw their input from aid projects, in proportion to the level to which their input has been implicitly denigrated by fund-raising images. Thus, the wealthy will tend towards despising the poor, while the poor will tend towards despising the wealthy.

Systems theory predicts that these discrepant attributions will eventually interact. The most obvious conduit for this interaction is their shared global mediascape. The poor's growing contempt for aid will filter through for example in media reports of attacks on aid workers (Van Brabant, 2000). These reports will in turn fuel donor bias. The resulting drop in donations will then prompt even more well-meaning, but essentially still derogatory aid advertisements, which in turn will fuel more indignation and contempt. And the cycle continues. Eventually therefore, there will be a double Pygmalion effect, in which each group has *escalatively* conformed to the other's stereotype of itself. Ultimately, and ironically, each group will have done this in the name of social equity.

The same form of analysis can be applied to the ethnoscape of the TA assignment, and the double demotivation created by gross disparities in pay. Equity-sensitive TA expatriates may either find the culture shock of this disparity too difficult to handle, and exit the project prematurely. Or they may start out along the primrose path of developing an inflated sense of input that matches, and to that extent justifies their relatively inflated pay status. And so stay; and stay; and stay. To the extent that these TA expatriates manage to culture an attitude of superiority within and among their selves, whether to assuage guilt or to savor a very favorable inter-group comparison, this will almost certainly be communicated, verbally or non-verbally, to their local counterparts (Robbins, Bergman, Stagg, & Coulter, 2000). That in turn will fuel local indignation, already running high because of traditional values stressing need as a basis for distributing resources. Compounding this, whereas expatriate personnel will learn to exert less of themselves, their local counterparts will expect some justice through expatriate personnel working extra hard to justify their take-home pay. When the opposite in fact happens, SET predicts that local personnel will adjust their input to reflect the magnitude of their disappointment.

The stage is now set, psychologically, for an escalation of double demotivation. Equity-restoring reductions in input from host counterparts will provide reinforcing justifications for expatriates' inflated senses of themselves and their capacities, and for their ultimate attribution errors along that primrose path. These inflated egos will then be recommunicated to host counterparts, in turn reinforcing the latter groups' own equity- restorative withdrawal. Both groups will, once more, progressively conform to the others' stereotype of it. Again there will be not one but two Pygmalion effects, each of which reflects an attempt to restore some sense of social justice. One way of visualizing the tension in this situation

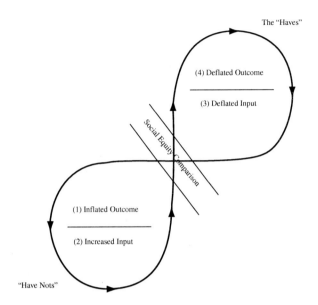

Figure 3.2. Dynamic SET – Double *Positive* Pygmalion effects
Source: Adapted from Adams (1965), and Senge (2000).

is "motivational gravity," by which over-rewarded groups "push down" on under-rewarded groups, while under-rewarded groups "pull down" on their over-rewarded counterparts (Carr & MacLachlan, 1997). Eventually, such tensions may well erupt into the kind of industrial conflict found at the University of Papua New Guinea (above).

If we now re-examine the ideoscapes of small business development, we find the same concept of social equity restoration resulting, this time, in virtuous rather than vicious circles. Prior to programs such as Ivory's, and unfortunately still, the situation clearly resembles negative equity escalation. The indignation and indignity of welfare had been demotivating recipients of state welfare, leading to increasingly disparaging attributions on the part of the wider community, who are tired of observing that welfare has been failing, and that recipient communities are a "lost cause" (Sanson et al., 1996; Sanson & Dudgeon, 2000). Such negative attributions, and related attitudes, can in themselves become a self-fulfilling prophecy, by being communicated to, and feeding into, the desperation and indignity of those very communities living on the margins of "mainstream" society (Steele, 1997).

From Figure 3.2, where Ivory's (1999) work is making a difference is by breaking these cycles at the dependency end, through adopting a "glocal" approach to community development. In this, *local* values are recognized and built upon in order to engage with a *global* economy (Robertson, 1995). Such projects are setting up not the vicious circles of mutual indignation and withdrawal, but rather a series of interlocking circles that are in kind "virtuous" (Dodson, 1998). From Figure 3.2, in these virtuous circles newly garnered collective pride and economic resources are outcomes (1) that motivate (2) increased input. This increased engagement then helps to counteract the impact of negative stereotypes held by sectors of "mainstream" society, possibly encouraging on their part more humility (3) and (4) inter-communal recognition and respect. These replace the guilt, ego-defensive derogation, and ultimate attribution errors depicted in Figure 3.1. Now, the rising social respect implied and conveyed by (4) reinforces the growing sense of Indigenous community pride (1), spurring on still more increased input (2). The result is what Ivory terms, development "with a vengeance" (1999, p. 70). Thus, social equity escalation and double Pygmalion effects are not necessarily negative. According to our analysis, they might well become positive, once aid organizations stop trying so hard to "help the poor," and start listening instead to what the poor themselves have to say about the circumstances of being poor.

Acknowledgments

I gratefully acknowledge the influences in this chapter, of a great friend, mentor, and keeper of the faith, Floyd H. Bolitho. Thanks also to the Psychology staff at Massey University, for their insightful and stimulating questions. This chapter is based on a number of research presentations given in Darwin (Australia), Caracas (Venezuela), and Auckland (New Zealand). Those presentations were funded by the Northern Territory University in Australia, and by Massey University in New Zealand. Thanks to my coauthors in this section, for their insightful comments during various stages of this paper. Thanks also to Harvey Jones, for his generous "e-sculpting" of Figures 3.1 and 3.2. Last but by no means least, thanks also to the many citizens of Africa, Asia, and Oceania, who have contributed so freely to the development of SET.

References

Aamodt, M. G. (1999). *Applied industrial/organizational psychology* (3rd ed.). Belmont, CA: Wadsworth.

ABC (Australian Broadcasting Corporation). (1998). Papua New Guinea academics to take industrial action. *ABC News home page, Monday, August 10*, 4.19 A.E.S.T.

Aberson, C. L., Healy, M., & Romero, V. (2000). In-group bias and self-esteem: A meta-analysis. *Personality and Social Psychology Review, 4*, 157–173.

Abouchedid, K., & Nasser, R. (2001). Poverty attitudes and their determinants in Lebanon's plural society. *Journal of Economic Psychology, 22*, 271–282.

Adams, J. S. (1965). Inequity in social exchange. *Advances in Experimental Social Psychology, 2*, 267–300.

Ajzen, I., & Fishbein, M. (2000). Attitudes and the attitude-behavior relation: Reasoned and automatic processes. In W. Stroebe & M. Hewstone (Eds.), *European Review of Social Psychology, 11*, 1–33. Chichester, UK: Wiley.

Anderson, M. (2002). Reflecting on the practice of outside assistance: Can we know what good we do? In M. Anderson (Ed.), The Berghof Handbook for Conflict Transformation. http://www.berghof-center.org/handbook/anderson/final.pdf

ANU/CSEAS (Australian National University/Center for Southeast Asian Studies). (2000). *Conflict and violence in Indonesia and East Timor: Implications for Australia*. Darwin, North Australia Research Unit.

Appadurai, A. (1990). Disjuncture and difference in the global cultural economy. In M. Featherstone (Ed.), *Global culture: Nationalism, globalization, and modernity* (pp. 295–310). London: Sage.

Aus-Thai Project Team. (1998). Managing economic crisis: A psychosocial approach. *Development Bulletin, 46*, 53–56.

Aus-Thai Project Team. (1999, June). *Complementary perspectives on economic crisis from Bangkok, Thailand, and Darwin, North Australia*. 17th Interamerican Congress of Psychology, Caracas, Venezuela.

Aus-Thai Project Team. (2001, July). *Managing economic crisis: A Human factors approach*. Asian Association of Social Psychology, 4th Annual Conference, Melbourne, Australia.

Bolitho, F. H., & Carr, S. C. (2001). *Measuring attributions for "Third World" poverty: Keeping the baby from the bath-water*. Auckland: Massey University.

Campbell, D. C., Carr, S. C., & MacLachlan, M. (2001). Attributing "Third World" poverty in Australia and Malaŵi: A case of donor bias? *Journal of Applied Social Psychology, 31*, 409–430.

Carr, S. C. (1996). Social psychology and the management of aid. In S. C. Carr & J. F. Schumaker (Eds.), *Psychology and the developing world* (pp. 103–118). Westport, CT: Praeger.

Carr, S. C. (2000). Privilege, privation, and proximity: "Eternal triangle" for development? *Psychology and Developing Societies, 12*, 167–176.

Carr, S. C. (2001, January). *Human factors in service organizations*. Auckland: Massey University.

Carr, S. C. (2003). *Social psychology: Context, communication, and culture*. Sydney: John Wiley & Sons Limited.

Carr, S. C., Chipande, R., & MacLachlan, M. (1998). Expatriate aid salaries in Malaŵi: A doubly demotivating influence? *International Journal of Educational Development, 18*, 133–143.

Carr, S. C., Ehiobuche, I., Rugimbana, R. O., & Munro, D. (1996). Expatriates' ethnicity and their effectiveness: "Similarity-attraction" or "inverse resonance"? *Psychology and Developing Societies, 8*, 265–282.

Carr, S. C., Mc Auliffe, E., & MacLachlan, M. (1998). *Psychology of aid*. London: Routledge.

Carr, S. C., & MacLachlan, M. (1993/4). The social psychology of development work: The double demotivation hypothesis. *Malaŵi Journal of Social Science, 16*, 1–8.

Carr, S. C., & MacLachlan, M. (1997). Motivational gravity. In D. Munro, J. F. Schumaker, & S. C. Carr (Eds.), *Motivation and culture* (pp. 133–155). New York: Routledge.

Carr, S. C., MacLachlan, M., & Campbell, D. C. (1997). Development through educational collaboration: Facilitating Social Equity. *Higher Education Policy, 10*, 81–92.

Carr, S. C., McLoughlin, D., Hodgson, M., & MacLachlan, M. (1996). Effects of unreasonable pay discrepanices for under- and overpayment on double demotivation. *Genetic, Social and General Psychology Monographs, 122*, 477–494.

Carr, S. C., Rugimbana, R. O., Walkom, E., & Bolitho, F. H. (2001). Selecting expatriates in developing areas: "Country-of-origin" effects in Tanzania? *International Journal of Intercutural Relations, 25*, 95–111.

Cassen, R. (1994). *Does aid work?* Oxford, UK: Clarendon Press.

Chafel, J. A. (1997). Societal images of poverty: Child and adult beliefs. *Youth and Society, 28,* 432–463.

Cheung, C. K., & Chan, C. M. (2000). Social-cognitive factors of donating money to charity, with special attention to an international relief organization. *Evaluation and Program Planning, 23,* 241–253.

Choi, I., Nisbett, R. E., & Norenzayan, A. (1999). Causal attribution across cultures: Variation and universality. *Psychological Bulletin, 125,* 47–63.

Community Aid Abroad/Freedom From Hunger. (1996/7). *Why a Third World? Exploring the reasons for poverty in developing countries.* Melbourne: Community Aid Abroad/Freedom From Hunger.

Deci, E. L., & Ryan, R. M. (1999). The undermining effect is a reality after all: Extrinsic rewards, task interest, and self-determination. *Psychological Bulletin, 125,* 692–700.

Dodson, P. (1998). *Will the circle be unbroken? Cycles of survival for Indigenous Australians.* Discussion Paper No. 12. Darwin: North Australia Research Unit/Australian National University. Transcript of the 1998 H. C. (Nugget) Coombs North Australia Lecture.

Dore, R. (1994). Why visiting sociologists fail. *World Development, 22,* 1425–1436.

Eze, N. (1985). Sources of motivation among Nigerian managers. *Journal of Social Psychology, 125,* 341–345.

Fazio, R. H., Jackson, J. R., Dunton, B. C., & Williams, C. J. (1995). Variability in automatic activation as an unobtrusive measure of racial attitudes: A bona fide pipeline? *Journal of Personality and Social Psychology, 69,* 1013–1027.

Forgas, J. P. (1995). Mood and judgment: The Affect Infusion Model (AIM). *Psychological Bulletin, 117,* 39–66.

Fountain, S. (1995). *Education for development.* London: Hodder & Stoughton/UNICEF.

Fox, C. (1994). Educational development cooperation, ethics, and the role of the consultant. *Development Bulletin, 30,* 43–45.

Fox, J., & Carr, S. C. (2000). Internet technology and poverty relief. *South Pacific Journal of Psychology, 12,* 51–56. http://spjp.massey.ac.nz/.

Gergen, K. J. (1994). *Toward transformation in social knowledge.* New Delhi: Sage.

Godwin, N. (1994). A distorted view: Myths and images of developing countries. *Development Bulletin, 30,* 46–48.

Gow, D. D. (1991). Collaboration in development consulting: Stooges, hired guns, or musketeers? *Human Organization, 50,* 1–15.

Griffiths, K. (1999). Aid adverts that juxtapose rich and poor: A preliminary test of their efficacy in North Australia. *South Pacific Journal of Psychology, 11,* 85–88.

Harper, D. J. (1996). Accounting for poverty: From attribution to discourse. *Journal of Community and Applied Social Psychology, 6,* 249–265.

Henderson-King, E., Henderson-King, D., Zhermer, N., & Posokhova, S., & Chuiker, V. (1997). In-group favoritism and perceived similarity: A look at Russians' perceptions in post-Soviet era. *Personality and Social Psychology Bulletin, 23,* 1013–1021.

Hermans, H. J. M., & Kempen, H. J. G. (1998). Moving cultures: The perilous problems of cultural dichotomies in a globalizing society. *American Psychologist, 53,* 1111–1120.

Hewstone, M. (1990). The "ultimate attribution error"? A review of the literature on inter-group causal attribution. *European Journal of Social Psychology, 20,* 311–335.

Hewstone, M., & Greenland, K. (2000). Inter-group conflict. *International Journal of Psychology, 35,* 136–144.

Hofstede, G., & Bond, M. H. (1988). The Confucius connection: From cultural roots to economic growth. *Organizational Dynamics, 16,* 4–21.

Hunt, M. O. (1996). The individual, society, or both? A comparison of Black, Latino, and White beliefs about the causes of poverty. *Social Forces, 75,* 293–322.

INRA. (1992). *The way Europeans perceive the Third World in 1991*. Brussels: Report for the European Community Commission.

Ivory, B. (1999). Enterprise development: A model for Aboriginal entrepreneurs. In S. C. Carr, F. H. Bolitho, & I. P Purcell (Eds.), *Community development in North Australia, South Pacific Journal of Psychology (special issue)* (pp. 62–71).

Kato, T. (2000). Lessons from the Asian crisis. *Journal of Human Development, 1*, 165–168.

Kealey, D. J. (1989). A study of cross-cultural effectiveness: Theoretical issues, practical applications. *International Journal of Intercultural Relations, 13*, 387–428.

Kelley, J. C. (1989). Australian attitudes to overseas aid: Report from the National Social Science Survey. *International Development Issues, 8*, 1–129.

Kohnert, D. (1996). Magic and witchcraft: Implications for democratization and poverty-alleviating aid in Africa. *World Development, 24*, 1347–1355.

Krull, D. S., Loy, M. H. M., Lin, J., Wang, C. F., Chen, S., & Zhao, X. (1999). The fundamental attribution error: Correspondence bias in individualist and collectivist cultures. *Personality and Social Psychology Bulletin, 25*, 1208–1219.

Lea, D. (1998). The ethics of corruption in Papua New Guinea and elsewhere in the developing world. *South Pacific Journal of Philosophy and Culture, 3*, 71–81.

Lim, A., & Ward, C. (1999, August). *The effects of nationality, length of residence, and occupational demand on the perceptions of "foreign talent" in Singapore*. Asian Association of Social Psychology Conference, Taipei, Taiwan.

Littlewood, R. (1985). Jungle madness: Some observations on expatriate psychopathology. *International Journal of Social Psychiatry, 31*, 194–197.

MacLachlan, M. (1993). Splitting the difference: How do refugee workers survive? *Changes: International Journal of Psychology and Psychotherapy, 11*, 155–157.

MacLachlan, M., & Carr, S. C. (1993). De-motivating the doctors: The double demotivation hypothesis in the health services of less-developed countries. *Journal of Management in Medicine, 7*, 6–10.

Mamman, A. (1995). Expatriate adjustment: Dealing with hosts' attitudes in a foreign assignment. *Journal of Transnational Management Development, 1*, 49–70.

Marsella, A. J. (1998). Toward a "global community psychology:" Meeting the needs of a changing world. *American Psychologist, 53*, 1282–1291.

Marsella, A. J. (2000). UN grants American Psychological Association special NGO consultative status. *Psychology International, Summer*, 1–3.

Martin, R. (2001). Personal correspondence, February 28. (citation based on interview about an article written in the East Timorese press).

McClelland, D. C. (1961). *The achieving society*. Princeton, NJ: D. Van Nostrand and Company.

McClelland, D. C. (1987). *Human motivation*. Cambridge, MA: Cambridge University Press.

McLoughlin, D., & Carr, S. C. (1997). Equity sensitivity and double de-motivation. *Journal of Social Psychology, 137*, 668–670.

McMichael, H. (2000, November). *Outlook for business and trade in Eastern Indonesia*. Conflict and Violence in Indonesia and East Timor: Implications for Australia. Darwin, North Australia Research Unit, Australian National University.

McShane, S. L., & Von Glinow, M. A. (2000). *Organizational behavior: Emerging realities for the workplace revolution*. New York, NY: Irwin McGraw-Hill.

Mehryar, A. H. (1984). The role of psychology in national development: Wishful thinking and reality. *International Journal of Psychology, 19*, 159–167.

Moeller, S. (1999). *Compassion fatigue: News-makers bear responsibility*. New York: Routledge.

Montero, M. (1996). Negative social identity and socio-economic crisis: A socio-psychological study. *Revista Interamericana de Psicologia, 30*, 43–58.

Montero, J. M. C., & Dollinger, S. J. (1998). An autographic study of poverty, collective orientation, and identity among street children. *Journal of Social Psychology, 138*, 403–406.

Morcoel, G. (1997). Lay explanations for poverty in Turkey and their determinants. *Journal of Social Psychology, 137*, 728–738.

O'Gorman, F. (1992). *Charity and change: From band-aid to beacon.* Melbourne: World Vision.

Okorodudu, C. (2000). World leaders affirm UN initiatives at historic summit. *Psychology International, Fall*, 9.

Pawlik, K., & d'Ydewalle, G. (1996). Psychology and the global commons. *American Psychologist, 51*, 488–495.

Pearson, N. (1999). *Our right to take responsibility.* Discussion paper for community and regional organizations. Cape York Peninsula: Cape York Land Council.

Picciotto, R., & Rist, R. C. (Eds.). (1995). Evaluation and development. *New Directions for Evaluation, 67* [Whole Issue], 1–175.

Reicher, S. (1996, May). *The group in the individual and the individual in the group.* 25th Meeting of Australasian Social Psychologists, Australian National University, Canberra, Australia.

Robbins, S. P., Bergman, R., Stagg, I., & Coulter, M. (2000). *Management.* French's Forest, New South Wales, Australia: Pearson Education.

Robertson, R. (1995). *Globalization: Social theory and global culture.* London: Sage.

Rugimbana, R. O., Carr, S. C., Bolitho, F. H., & Walkom, E. (2000). The impact of "consumer cringe" on developing regional trade blocks: A Tanzanian case study. *Journal of African Business, 1*, 91–106.

Saffu, K. (2001). Personal correspondence. February 27.

Sánchez, E. (1996). The Latin American experience in community social psychology. In S. C. Carr & J. F. Schumaker (Eds.), *Psychology and the developing world* (pp. 119–129). Westport, CT: Praeger.

Sanson, A., Augoustinos, M., Gridley, H., Kyrios, M., Reser, J., & Turner, C. (1998). Racism and prejudice: An Australian Psychological Society Position Paper. http://www.psychsociety.com.au

Sanson, A., & Dudgeon, P. (Eds.). (2000). Psychology, Indigenous issues, and reconciliation. *Australian Psychologist, 35* [Whole Issue], 79–180.

Selby, J. (1999). Cross-cultural research in health psychology: Illustrations from Australia. In M. Murray & K. Chamberlain (Eds.), *Qualitative health psychology: Theories and methods* (pp. 164–180). Thousand Oaks, CA: Sage.

Senge, P. (2000). *The fifth discipline.* Sydney: Random House.

Sidanius, J., & Pratto, F. (1999). *Social dominance: An inter-group theory of social hierarchy and oppression.* Cambridge, MA: Cambridge University Press.

Smith, P. B., & Bond, M. H. (1999). *Social psychology across cultures.* Boston, MA: Allyn & Bacon.

Steele, C. M. (1997). A threat in the air: How stereotypes shape the intellectual identities and performance of women and African-Americans. *American Psychologist, 52*, 613–629.

Tajfel, H. (1978). *Differentiation between social groups.* London: Academic Press.

Taylor, D. M., & Moghaddam, F. M. (1994). *Theories of inter-group relations: International social perspectives.* Westport, CT: Praeger.

Teeravekin, L. (1998, November). *Decentralization and community development.* Keynote address, National Community Development Policy Conference, Bangkok, Thailand.

Therrick, T. (2000, December). *Past, present, and future: A personal account.* Conflict and Violence in Indonesia and East Timor: Implications for Australia. North Australia Research Unit/Australian National University/Center for South East Asian Studies.

Thornton, B., Kirchner, G., & Jacobs, J. (1991). Influence of a photograph on a charitable appeal: A picture may be worth a thousand words when it has to speak for itself. *Journal of Applied Social Psychology, 21*, 433–445.

UN Summit for Social Development. (1995). Copenhagen, Denmark. http://www.un.org/esa/soicdev/wssd/agreements/

Valdivieso (IMF Head for East Timor). Quoted in Dow Jones Newswires, 21–7–2000.

Van Brabant, K. (2000). *Operational security management in violent environments*. London: Overseas Development Institute.

Walkup, M. (1997). Policy dysfunction in humanitarian organizations: The role of coping strategies, institutions, and organizational culture. *Journal of Refugee Studies, 10*, 37–60.

World Bank News. (1996). Success and failure in Africa: Two case studies in Ghana and Uganda. *Development Bulletin, 37*, 56–57.

Chapter 4

Poverty and Psychopathology

Virginia Moreira

We live in a world in which the indices of poverty and social inequality rise on a daily basis along with the prevalence rates of emotional disorders. This is no mere coincidence. The topics of poverty and psychopathology are often erroneously linked on the basis of two assumptions. The first is the common notion that the poor have no psychological problems. Their problems are seen as material, economic, or physical, and therefore leave no room for psychological concerns. According to this view, it makes no sense to hire psychologists, for example, in hospitals or clinics in poor areas, when there are so many children with bloated tummies full of worms – as if worms were somehow a vaccine against psychological problems. When psychological services are planned for low-income communities, they usually exist only on paper. There is no building, not even a room, where these services can be provided. Hospitals claim they offer psychological services, but when individual attention is needed, the psychologist and patient slip away to find a corner where they can talk, because available rooms are designated for "more important" types of treatment. Privacy, as well as individual space, belongs to the dominant class. The poor are deprived of private space, since their lives are public, and their problems flow into the streets to be witnessed by their neighbors (Guimarães, 1998). Although their lives are exposed to public observation, and a total lack of privacy, their experience of true citizenship is limited, for they feel no power over their public lives.

This first idea has been displaced ever so slowly by a second idea that also links psychopathology to poverty. This second idea holds that "poverty is a disease," the symptoms of which can be treated with medicine. In the poorer regions of northeastern Brazil, for example, the somatization and medicalization of social problems is increasing rapidly and tranquilizers are given to numb the pain, creating the illusion that problems have gone away, but only until the next pill is needed (Guimarães, 1998). The poor are thus transformed into patients. Poverty becomes a mental illness. A problem that is principally social and political is treated as a psychiatric symptom.

These two ideas constitute an ideological process which, on the one hand, is based on Western dualistic thinking that dissociates the body from the mind. This process gives priority to the individual and to biomedical modes for understanding the individual (Marsella & Yamada, 2000; Moreira, 2001). On the other hand, economic development is understood ideologically as a synonym of growth and prosperity, while in reality, current models of development have only generated greater inequality (Lummis, 1991).

In this chapter, I analyze the relationship between psychopathology and poverty on the basis of these two ideas and examine the following:

1. The fabric of psychopathology in the "network society" viewed as a deprivation of power through consumerism and cultural impoverishment.
2. The psychopathological consequences of poverty: low self-esteem, nihilism, and trauma.
3. Ways of intervention, a critique of the medicalization of poverty based on a practical example in the northeast of Brazil, and a new proposal to facilitate citizenship process as prevention and treatment for psychopathology.

The Fabric of Psychopathology

Poverty in the "network society"

The increase of poverty and destitution is a fruit of the globalization of corporate capitalism. The global information society created by globalization provokes the polarization that fuels the growth of poverty. Castells (2000) describes a specific process of inequality which consists of more rapid growth at the top and at the base in the distribution of wealth and income. This causes a shrinking of the middle zone and accentuates social disparities between the populations at the ends of the scale. This shrinking of the already precarious middle class is actually an old process that has become well known to Latin American people in recent years.

Informational capitalism creates deep gulfs between people and locations that are considered "valuable" and those considered "not valuable." Globalization works in a selective fashion, including and excluding segments of economies and societies from the information networks, giving us pockets of rich and poor. According to Castells (2000), the new informational technology is an instrument of the diffusion of poverty, forming "black holes" of informational capitalism, or rather, areas of society in which there is no escape from the pain and destruction. These black holes have all sorts of destructive energy concentrated at their centers.

They are basically characterized by psychological suffering, where emotional disorders, drug addiction, delinquency, imprisonment and lawlessness all have roots in poverty. This "new poverty" of the globalized era also affects working-class families WHO are simply unable to maintain their accustomed standard of living, as well as those, of course, who are part of the traditional below-the-poverty-line group. Once poverty has been transformed into social exclusion and destitution, or rather, as it "goes public," the stigmatizing and the destruction of the personality begin. The social service systems treat poor people as if they are ill and thus only augment their psychological suffering.

Poverty as Deprivation of Power

The concept of poverty as the deprivation of power has been proposed by the economist Amartya Sen (2000) as a more appropriate alternative to the usual economic understanding of the problem of poverty, where the standard criterion is low income. Understanding poverty as a lack of capacity retains low income as an instrumental factor, since it is reflected in significant malnutrition (especially in children), premature death, persistent illness and illiteracy, for example. However, this new concept goes beyond the simple utilitarian, economic understanding, in which attention is drawn away from demands for social justice as well as from the causes of poverty.

Sen (1999) seeks to correct what he identifies as an historical error of economics: the removal of ethics from concepts of human well-being. The deprivation of power and control can be seen as an inability to exercise "freedom." This, in turn, causes poverty. Thus emerges Sen's idea of "development as freedom", which he takes as the title of his book. In other words, simple economic growth does not necessarily mean social development linked to the quality of life and social well-being. Sloan (1993) reminds us of this when he discusses the role of psychology in national development. He cites examples of Latin American countries where higher economic growth rates are rarely reflected in increased opportunities for education, health care, and a better quality of life for the majority.

Sen (2000) proposed a revolutionary vision for economics, redefining economic development as human development for all:

> What does human development do? The creation of social opportunities directly contributes to the expansion of human capabilities and to the quality of life. The expansion of health, educational, and social services contributes directly to the quality of life and its development. There is evidence that even when income is relatively low, a country which guarantees health care and educational services can effectively obtain notable results in the length and quality of life of the entire population. (p. 170)

This perspective on development is a long way from imposing Western capitalism on the world, even though Amarthya Sen was consultant to the United Nations Development Program. Heir of the Smithian tradition, where the concept of freedom has a fundamental role, individual liberty for Sen is essentially a social product, intrinsically linked to social dispositions that aim to expand individual liberty and which are not only concerned with a better life for each person, but also improvement for society as a whole. Sen (2000) puts forth the following types of instrumental freedoms: political freedom, including civic rights and participation in political decisions about who should govern; economic freedom, which refers to the opportunities individuals have to utilize economic resources in order to purchase, produce or trade; social freedom, through opportunities in the areas of education and health, etc., that are made available to the public; guarantees of transparency, which refer to the need for sincerity that preserves trust between people; and finally, security and protection, which provide a network of social (community) security measures that prevent the population in question from going hungry or living in inhumane conditions.

A quick assessment of current Latin American societies with regard to the types of freedom described by Sen shows a negative picture. One finds an absence of civil rights, limited opportunities for citizenship, a mentality of favoritism that distorts elections, and generalized economic difficulties. According to Sen, mental health will be directly affected by the lack of social opportunities as well as by the lack of transparency and protective security. In fact, health and education are not priorities at all. Corruption and deceit are rampant; cynicism is repeatedly kindled. Instead of protective security, social and economic instabilities are created which, without doubt, inspire realistic anxieties and emotional instability. This contributes to the etiology of many psychopathologies. The complaints of patients who suffer from emotional disorders are commonly steeped in this insecurity, in the mistrust of the judicial system, in unemployment, in limited social opportunities, and political manipulation. As Guimarães (1998, p. 1) finds, "many of our clients or patients are among the famished from drought, or scarcity of resources or unemployment in urban life. Some are cared for in psychiatric hospitals, giving thanks to God for having gone mad and for having some food and shelter."

Society is thus organized in exactly the opposite way to that which would provide a base for human development. Liberty is a mirage (Cock, 1996). We live in a culture of human "anti-development". In this sense, the definition of poverty as the privation of power and control can be extremely useful for a reflection on psychopathology, as it deals with a broader concept than "traditional poverty", which is simply the lack of income. However, it is important not to forget that even though poverty and psychopathology are both processes that divest humans of power and capacity, poverty is not a synonym of psychopathology.

Poverty in Consumerism

The current outbreak of mental pathologies has ramifications at the economic level due to the increasing number of people are finding themselves unable to work due to mental illness. There are ramifications at the social level (stigma, social exclusion) and above all, at the psychological level (insecurity, depression, anxiety, and dependency on psycho-pharmaceuticals). All of these are part of a process that divests humans of power. A process of psychosocial impoverishment ensues and constitutes the heart of emotional disorder cases. Consumerist ideology contributes an additional form of impoverishment.

Lummis (1991) proposes a differentiation between four types of poverty. In the first place, there is absolute poverty, or total destitution which is a material poverty involving a lack of food, shelter, hygienic conditions and health. In the second place, there is a situation called poverty by others, but in which those who are called "poor" do not consider themselves poor. A third type is a social poverty, which is controlled by the economic power of the rich, where the poor are kept poor in the service of the rich. A fourth type of poverty is connected to needs created by consumerist ideology. This is the type of poverty I would like to focus on here, since it seems to me that with globalization, this type is an inherent part of any type of poverty, contributing to even deeper impoverishment. I mentioned earlier that absolute poverty, as defined by Lummis, or destitution, increases daily in the current information society, while the second externally-defined type of poverty seems to have been extinguished by globalization, swallowed up by the fourth type that is linked to consumerism. In other words, the notion of having more, always wanting more, is part of consumerist ideology that now reaches the most secluded places on the earth. Thus, it is more probable to find someone who thinks he is poor without really being poor, and who is, in fact, just the opposite, thus perpetuating "social poverty" as well. The fact is that all these types of poverty are sustained by ideological processes, or rather, processes that serve the interests of the powerful by maintaining an unjust system (Sloan, 1997).

The consumerist syndrome is one of the banners of this ideological process and it has serious consequences for mental health. Even the poorest of the poor suffer from this syndrome, as absurd as it may seem, since they cannot afford to consume. Thus, I feel that we could talk of a consumerist poverty that collaborates with the ideological processes of the disempowerment of the individual, an important part of the etiology of various types of psychopathology in the world today. As Lummis (1991) put it, "a society can be organized so that virtually nothing of value can be had in any other way than by exchange for money" (p. 33) and it is exactly in this materialistic way that Western society functions as a whole.

Schumaker (2001) makes reference to the body of research that shows the disastrous consequences of materialism for mental health, including depression, low self-esteem, reduction of satisfaction with one's own life, and general discontent. The effects of materialism via consumerism can be observed in the rural zone of Northeast Brazil, where in the last twenty years there has been a visible trend away from alternative means of survival to purchasing items at the local supermarket. Many people no longer want to plant fruits or vegetables in the backyard or use homemade remedies made from medicinal plants. If something is not from the local store, it has no value. This implies a great loss of the sort of knowledge that has been passed down from generation to generation. In this process, people do not have the resources to buy all they need in stores and as they stop valuing things that are not bought in stores, an extinction of cultural values occurs. As Keys (1985) indicates, the loss of values is an important source of mental pathologies and it is in this way that consumerist poverty collaborates with psychopathology.

Globalization, which is responsible for the "contagion" of this consumerist poverty even among the poorest of the poor, is nothing more than what Paulo Freire called the "cultural invasion," which is non-dialogical and ideological in nature.

Disregarding the potential of the beings it affects, the cultural invasion is the penetration which the invaders make into the contexts of the invaded, imposing on them their own view of the world, stifling creativity . . . In this sense, the cultural invasion, whether done in a "soft" way or in a way which is not directly perceived, is always a violation to the culture being invaded. The invaded culture loses its originality or at least sees itself threatened of losing it. (Freire, 1970/2000, p. 149)

The consumerist perspective of the "invaders" becomes incorporated in the invaded culture, as if it belonged to it, producing an imitation of values. The values of the invaders (in this case, the consumerist values of the Western developed world) become the "agenda" of the invaded: "The more the invasion is accentuated, alienating the 'being' of the culture and the way of life of the invaded, the more they will want to appear to be like those who are invading – walking like they do, dressing like they do, speaking like they do" (Freire, 1970/2000, p. 151). Lacking the economic resources to imitate the invader's level of consumption, the psychological suffering of the poor increases due to the frustration of consumerist desire. They desire things they cannot have and forget or fail to recognize their own genuine needs. This alienation also annihilates a more genuine human desire for citizenship and participation in their own communities.

Cultural Impoverishment

Development linked to globalization can have disastrous consequences for mental health when the values, rituals and behavior of the culture are disrupted. These cultural processes functioned to some extent to protect human beings from various forms of mental pathologies.

A good example of this process is depression, for which loss is one of its traditional causes. In poor regions of the Brazilian Northeast, which go through long periods of uncompromising destitution during years of drought, the infant mortality rate is high. Women who lose their infants traditionally participate in rituals where the community comes together to keep vigil over the body and bury the child, or "angel" as it is called, because of its innocence. This child did not sin during its life and the greatest comfort for the mother is to know that the child certainly went directly to heaven. Another great comfort is the support of the community through the ritual, as death is a significant moment, representing a moment of consolidation of the social fabric. Brazilian culture emphasizes physical proximity and related practices aid the mother and the family at this time. The encounters surrounding the grieving family involve hugs, kisses, and lots of touching. The whole event connects people and functions as a cultural mechanism of protection that has had a preventive effect against depression. It must be remembered that the loss which the mother in poverty experiences is reinforced by the pain of feeling guilty for the relief she feels about the death of her child – "one less mouth to feed"– a feeling that is understood perfectly by those who accompany her in the ritual and in the same painful reality. According to Barreto (1993, p. 13), "the traditional Brazilian culture, through its rituals and beliefs provides compensatory and protective mechanisms against the emotional shock of successive losses of children. With the advent of modernism, these cultural mechanisms are being destroyed and become insufficient to protect the individuals in situations of important losses."

Barreto (1993, p. 14) thus observed some years ago, "if it were not for the cultural mechanisms of protection, we would have epidemics of depression." Now, the rituals are disappearing and a process of cultural impoverishment is taking place. The epidemic of depression has become a source of concern on the part of mental health professionals around the world and has even arrived in the poorest regions of the planet (Schumaker, 1996, 2001; Berlinck, 2000; Morris, 1998; Ehrenberger, 2000). This can be seen in the Central Drylands region of Brazil, where depression is by far the most frequently diagnosed mental illness (Barroso, 2000). This is borne out by the increased use of tranquilizers and anti-depressive medication.

Another important cultural ritual, which is also slowly disappearing in the Northeast of Brazil, is the simple gathering of friends and neighbors to share one another's company. Gradually, the individualist ideology is taking hold (Schumaker & Ward, 2001). As people put aside the ritual of gathering to "shoot the breeze", sitting in the square, waiting for the "Aracatí"[1] to come and chase away the scalding heat, they instead sit in front of the television – a television bought with their "savings," in some cases at the cost of going hungry, or by means of unending installment payments. In the countryside, one does not find the credit-card citizen who would necessarily have to be print literate (Moulian, 1997). However, one can see satellite dishes outside near the *caatinga*[2] (dry lands grass), which are almost larger than the houses of mud and sticks where they are installed. Through these antennas a large part of the attack on traditional cultural values

---

[1] The "Aracatí" is a wind which blows from the coast (city of Aracati) to the drylands through the interior of Ceará, in the Northeast of Brazil, during the periods of long-term drought. There is a set time in which the wind blows in each place.

[2] A type of vegetation in the dry region of Northeast Brazil.

and rituals takes place and "new," "globalized" values are installed. Barreto notes that,

> In this way, cultural mechanisms for the fight against depression are disappearing and psycho-active substances gain power and are embedded. They propose to be the chemical element which can unlock the process of turning back the pages of apathy and suffering. In the same way, "cultural rituals" which awakened the ability of "self-cure" are substituted by "chemical rituals" which are able to intervene very effectively in cellular metabolism, unblocking synapses, and restoring the individual's functional "normalness." (1993, p. 15).

Psychological Consequences

Poverty and Self-esteem

Globalization and the cultural invasion that accompanies it play a role in the etiology of various cases of current psychopathologies. In particular, I will discuss the production of nihilism and the impoverishment of self-esteem. Again, I will describe local manifestations of these problems that certainly exist in various forms around the world.

The poverty of self-esteem (low self-esteem) is a common characteristic in the personality of the Brazilian Northeasterner, a people marked by suffering. This suffering is mainly attributed to the striking climatic situation in the arid region where riverbeds are dry due to the lack of rain, bringing hunger and destitution year after year. Since its colonization, this region has been seen as an "unpleasant land," dry, unproductive, economically backward, with a malnourished population who do not know how to solve their problems alone and are always screaming for new "emergency plans" from the Federal government due to another year of drought (Montenegro, 2000).

The psychological suffering generated by the poverty of self-esteem, inherent to the subjectivity of people in poor regions such as this, is a fundamental piece in the globalization process or the cultural invasion. As Freire (1970/2000, pp. 150–151) reminds us, "a basic condition for the success of the cultural invasion is that those who are being invaded have knowledge of their intrinsic inferiority. Since there is nothing to prove the contrary, as those who are being invaded recognize that they are 'inferior,' they will automatically recognize the superiority of the invaders."

Another manifestation of the feeling of inferiority is reinforced by the ideology that what is "imported" is superior. This is a process that is repeated on different scales. The rural zone dweller feels inferior to the urbanite. For the Brazilian Northeasterner, that which comes from the south is better, because he or she has the idea that the south of the country is economically and politically predominant.

On a larger scale, people in developing societies assume automatically that what is good comes from developed countries, an assumption which of course simply feeds the cycle of economic dependency (Lummis, 1991). Thus, the process of impoverishment of self-esteem occurs in various ways, and is responsible for depression, feelings of anguish, anxiety, and a sense of insecurity. They come from a culture where, as Freire (1980, p. 61) mentioned, "despising one's self is another characteristic of the oppressed which comes from internalizing the opinion of the oppressors about him. These people hear that they are good-for-nothings so often, that they can not learn anything, that they are retarded, lazy and unproductive, that they end up being convinced of their own inability."

Poverty and Nihilism

As the poor lose their values, they no longer believe in themselves or in the world. They go through a process of even more accented divestment of power and citizenship, which could be characterized as nihilism. Nihilism is a psychological state indicated by the lack of meaning or purpose in life, as defined by Nietzsche (1983, p. 384): "the desire to destroy, like the will of an instinct although deeper, the instinct of self-destruction, the will to fall into nothingness." This psychological state is characterized by despair, which is the denial of hope, the abortion of the natural, indispensable impetus to experience life, which would be the active participation as a historical subject. As Freire (1996/2000) has so skillfully articulated, "it needs to be clear that despair is not a natural human way of being human, but a distortion of hope. I am not at first a being of despair, who needs to be converted by hope. I am, on the contrary, a being of hope, who for any number of reasons loses hope and becomes hopeless. This is the source of our struggles as human beings which should be fought with the aim of reducing the objective reasons for hopelessness which immobilize us" (p. 81).

Nihilism contributes to the immobilization of the poor because they feel that nothing can be done, that there is no course of action to take, that nothing is possible. Thus the diagnosis of the "syndrome of nothing" makes sense (Guimarães, 1998). This is the term coined by psychologists who work in health treatment clinics in the countryside of the Northeast of Brazil, to describe the constantly repeated scenario where a patient comes to them saying: The doctor said there's nothing wrong with me! Since there is "nothing wrong," the patient is sent over to the psychologist. In this situation "nothing" has another meaning besides that of the absence of any physical illness which can be objectively treated in the field of medicine. It means nihilism, which characterizes the greatest part of the poor population, and ends up making this diagnosis ironically true. While this is not "natural" to being human, just as hopelessness is not natural, nihilism is taught as part of an ideological system of oppression constituted by the two basic ideas about the relationship between psychopathology and poverty – that the poor have no psychological problems, and that poverty is a disease, so nothing can be done. Nihilism in poverty destroys the human project as a person and as a citizen, and that is why it constitutes psychopathology as it takes place. Through it, the human being, which is non-existent as a project, is transformed into a "passive object," and is thus "ill."

Nihilism in the Brazilian Northeast manifests itself through the heightened passivity of the poor population, which simply submits itself to the destiny that is given, since everything that happens or does not happen is "as God wishes." In the poorest regions this problem is so serious that health professionals consider the fact that a person seeks out help at the local clinic, thus, taking on the role of "patient," an important step. Religion also plays an important role in this process, especially in the zones of religious pilgrimages, where thousands of poor people go to pay their vows and ask the saint to perform a miracle to take away the pain. A second factor, which darkens the picture, is political assistance, which takes place year after year through the "emergency plans" for the drought. Under these plans, people become accustomed to surviving on the little bits the government provides them through the projects, being content with a "food basket."[3] In this manner, the implantation of the "culture of poverty" occurs (Martín-Baró, 1989), where from generation to generation people accept their powerless passivity that, in the next frame, will transform them into "patients", mentally ill persons.

The Trauma of Poverty

The whole process that characterizes poverty as I have been describing it in this chapter is obviously related to the so-called " traumas." The word *trauma* comes from the Greek *tauûma*, meaning "wound" or "contusion"; it refers to *a group of troubles caused somewhat suddenly by a physical agent; a violent shock capable of unlocking somatic and psychic disturbances.* Traumatology [*from traumat(o)* + *log(o)* + *ia*] is the branch of medicine which is concerned with wounds and contusions.

There are so many injuries that lead to psychopathology in its mutual constitution with poverty that professionals in the areas of health and mental health should be given special training as *traumatologists* [specialist in *traumatology*], since they will always face human wounds, bruised lives, and those crippled by globalized poverty, deprived of power and control.

Poverty is in fact a traumatic experience that leaves deep marks. It makes the human being more vulnerable to mental pathologies because it is an experience of social violence against the physical and mental integrity of the person. In India, for example, traumas linked to natural disasters, profound poverty, famine, overcrowding, lack of drinking water, violence between castes, political exploitation,

---

[3] Food baskets with basic foodstuffs given by the government.

endemic corruption, chronic illnesses, child prostitution and high rates of infant mortality are "everyday" traumatic events in the life of the people, with devastating effects (Laungani, 2001). Trauma that arises from such conditions is, at the same time, a cultural and political problem.

Poverty, as the greatest contributor for pathologies, is a form of collective social suffering, a component of the global economic policy where "political and professional processes powerfully shape the responses to types of social suffering. These processes involve both authorized and contested appropriations of collective suffering" (Kleinman, Das & Lock, 1997, p. xii).

It is essential for scholars in psychopathology to take into account the question of power in relation to culture (Kleinman & Good, 1985). What can be observed in the culture of the Brazilian Northeast is the use of psychological and social suffering to maintain the status quo, through the total, improper and inhumane abuse of power, where the trauma of poverty is utilized to silence generation after generation of oppressed people. Mental health professionals end up collaborating with this ideological process when they diagnose post-traumatic disturbances originating from situations of family violence, political oppression or social corruption as if these traumas were individual. They do this from an individual understanding of mental illness, which is a characteristic of the Western world, and part of an ideological process (Schumaker & Ward, 2001; Marsella & Yamada, 2000; Fox & Prilleltensky, 1997; Moreira, 2001; Moreira, in press). In the words of Kleinman (1995),

> the way in which professionals in health institutions think and talk about trauma situates it as an *essential* category of human existence, rooted in individual rather than social dynamics, and reflective more of medical *pathology* than of religious or moral happenings. Psychologists and psychiatrists construct violence as an *event* that can be studied outside of its particular context because of its putative universal effects on individuals. They place it in an overly simple stress model, as the distress produced in a person who has undergone a traumatic episode. Collective trauma is not mentioned. (p. 177)

As you see, poverty is exactly that, a collective trauma, so much so that when mental health professionals treat the effects of poverty as psychopathology originating from an individual trauma, they are working ideologically to perpetuate poverty.

Another aspect that is fundamental to the trauma of poverty is the impact of living in sub-human conditions, which wound individuals in their integrity and human dignity. This is what occurs in the rural zone of the Northeast of Brazil, where we see the break-up of the family (children or parents immigrate to the large cities in search of work), where the land is parched, the cattle are dying for lack of water, and children are crying from hunger. This causes indignation, and imposes emotional problems on the needy population: "Our people succumb to the yoke of illnesses of an under-developed country, such as cholera. They become emotionally ill with low self-esteem, alienation and illiteracy. Divested of humane living conditions, they struggle in the fight for the 'mouthful' of each day. In this way is it difficult not to die of sadness as well" (Guimarães 1998, pp. 1–2). In the same way, even though it is true that sometimes the poor accept humiliating experiences from those upon whom they are economically dependent and from those who have the power to feed their family, it is *not* true that they do not care about this, since "poor people care very much about their pride, and also about justice and decency in human relations" (Lummis, 1991, p. 58). Thus, poverty is a generator of trauma. Mental health cannot exist where there is poverty, not just because this "breeds hopelessness," as Marsella and Yamada (2000) say, but because poverty is part of the unjust, unequal social fabric which hurts, traumatizes and annihilates human dignity.

There is a "black hole" in social justice in the development of psychopathological knowledge due to the famous "scientific neutrality" which has stripped psychology of virtue (Fox & Prilleltensky, 1997). In other words, scientific neutrality impedes an ethical and moral attitude that is committed to human well-being and social justice. Even studies in cross-cultural psychology end up utilizing culture as an independent, worthless variable (Moghaddam & Studer, 1997). I agree with Freire (1996/2000) who said "the position of naïveté or worse, astute neutrality on the part of the one who studies, does not seem to me to be possible, whether he is studying physics, biology, sociology, mathematics, or as an educational thinker [or without a doubt the psychopathologist, the psychologist, the psychiatrist]. No one can be in the world, with the world and with others in the world in a neutral form. I can not be in the world with gloves on my hands only verifying the facts" (p. 86).

Even more serious for the professional or the student of psychopathology is being in the world and yet contributing to ideological strategies which maintain a socially unjust society. This can occur through the application of psychotherapeutic techniques that function as placebos. In other words, when treatment is purely individual and does not incorporate intrinsic socio-political factors in the etiology (Lira, 2000), or when psycho-pharmacological progress is incorrectly used, it merely contributes to the ideological system.

Poverty is a form of socio-political violence that generates traumas. It must be addressed as such. In the words of Kleinman,

Simply put, medicalizing political violence removes the human context of trauma as the chief focus for understanding violence. It treats the person as a patient, the host of a universal disease process, victim of inner pathology. Many persons who experience political violence are the victims of intentional and systematic harm that is motivated by power issues, not pathology. They may develop a post-traumatic disorder syndrome. Do they have a disease? Or are they experiencing a greatly distressing, yet normal, psychobiological reaction? The disease model tends to remove agency. (1995, pp. 182–183)

Ways of Intervention

Medicalization of Poverty

What I am calling medicalization of poverty is part of a growing process of prescribing psycho-pharmaceutical items for mental suffering caused by the situation of poverty. From this comes yet another psychopathology, the increasingly serious problem of "legal" chemical dependency. The exaggerated use of medicine has to do in part with the immediacy and technology aspects of contemporary society which contribute to a situation wherein quick answers are sought for all ailments (Morris, 1998). Beyond this, massive prescriptions of medication have to do with a biomedical ideology (Marsella & Yamada, 2000), where the economic power of the laboratories is prioritized. The complex medical industry is supported in large part by the pharmaceutical industry, which is playing an increasing role in financial markets (Barros, 1995). Thus, a powerful ideological mechanism spreads to the whole world at all social levels, but hits hardest those who are already debilitated. Such is the case in Brazil where health policies are based on a technical, intensely medicalized concept, where the doctor is sought out basically in order to prescribe medicines (Bonfim & Mercuccci, 1997). The powerful pharmaceutical industry with its large promotional investment makes the products appear essential for the maintenance and restoration of health. In the public health system, a large number of people are receiving prescriptions for tranquilizers for the relief of their pain and anxieties, when these symptoms are generally caused by unemployment, hunger, lack of shelter, and the impossibility for improvement in these conditions (Oliveira, 2000).

A study was conducted by Oliveira (2000) with regard to the consumption by poor women patients of the drug benzodiazepines (diazepam). The study concerned both the poor women who consumed the drugs and the doctors who prescribed them. The results showed that prescriptions were frequently inappropriate, with little medical criteria, no follow-up or control, and were used principally to lighten the suffering brought on by the concerns related to caring for a family in poverty. On the one hand, the doctors interviewed claimed that their predecessors had already prescribed diazepam, and that the women arrived requesting the medicine. They say that they do not have an alternative in spite of the fact that it is not always the correct prescription. They understand that diazepam functions as a social shock absorber in a reality where there are no effective policies that provide care for these victims of social injustice. These professionals are aware that they are medicalizing poverty, but they continue to do so. On the other hand, the women who were interviewed clearly stated that when "things get tough" when facing the daily pain of watching their children become ill due to hunger and malnutrition, they take diazepam in order to forget the problems for a while. Thus, diazepam is being prescribed to act, not on a psychological symptom, but rather on a group of social problems.

This leads Oliveira (2000) to conclude that for these women the medical industry and medical professionals make alienation manageable. The medicalization of poverty has also created another psychopathological diagnosis – "legal chemical dependency," that is, addiction that is approved, recommended, and prescribed.

The CAPS in Northeast Brazil

It will be helpful to illustrate this discussion with a brief description of how even de-institutionalized psychiatry services are still dependent on the ideology of the biomedical model and controlled by doctors in poor regions.

The Center for Psycho-Social Assistance (CAPS) is the heir of psychiatric reform in Brazil, which began a process of de-hospitalization. Today, in Ceará, the Psychiatric Reform Movement finds itself on a firm footing, with the operation of nine Centers of Psycho-Social Care (CAPS) in cities located in one of the poorest zones of the world. They provide preventive and alternative mental health care services (public, state or contracted, which vary according to the region and the available resources) in order to avoid hospitalization and stigmatization of the patient. There is a health team formed by psychiatric doctors, nurses, occupational therapists, social workers and psychologists (Sampaio & Barroso, 1994; Sampaio, Santos & Andrade, 1998; Pitta, 1996). The CAPS of the city of Quixadá, which has been operating for eight years, shows that the transfer of patients for hospitalization in psychiatric hospitals in the capital of the state was reduced by nearly 100%; in serious cases of psychotic outbursts hospitalization is done through the regional general hospital and the rate of outbreaks has decreased since the policy of preventative treatment was implanted (Barroso, 2000).

In spite of having reached the forums of discussion of the entire country and despite being significantly present in the policy of various Brazilian states, the Psychiatric Reform Movement and the implementation of new models of administration in caring for the patients with mental disturbances continues to face considerable resistance (Fé, 1995). A study done by Santos (1997) of CAPS in the Northeast of Brazil reveals that although there are some local advances, the services are very unequal and do not show, up to now, the proper capacity to overcome the challenge of transcending its care practices.

One important observation is that, on the one hand, CAPS are characterized by a multi-professional interdisciplinary practice, which seeks the necessary reduction of internal hierarchy. An example of this tactic is the practice of the "emerging therapist," in which any professional from the Center, with whom the patient establishes a link, whether it be a psychiatrist or secretary, is assigned to be the patient's main contact. Another practice involves the rotation of the CAPS Co-ordinator. This position can be occupied by any one of the professionals who works there, independent of their academic level (Sampaio & Barroso, 2001).

On the other hand, concurrent with these democratic measures, is the practice whereby CAPS doctors always receive significantly higher salaries than the other university-degreed professionals, such as occupational therapists, social workers, and psychologists. The topic of salary is never touched on or mentioned in publications about the services that emphasize their multidisciplinary and interdisciplinary ideals. This is an enormous contradiction. It is obvious that the salaries symbolize the value given to each type of work there. Once again we come across the trap of medical power, even in these mental health services which purport to be revolutionary. They recognize that there are many types of psychological suffering that express not only organic or existential problems, but also socio-economic ones caused by alienation of work, unemployment, and oppressive living situations. An extraordinary demand for the services of psychologists and psychiatrists has been identified, because the psychological phenomena are always very complex and require a politically critical and interdisciplinary understanding. However, it is recommended that one of the professionals involved in the selection of the cases treated always be a psychiatrist "due to the organic interfaces and the use of pharmacological items" (Sampaio & Barroso, 2001, p. 6). This psychiatrist always ends up with decision power over the disposition of a case. Thus, the CAPS still find themselves prisoners of the biomedical ideology that is allied with the pharmaceutical industry.

It is not that there are no cases of organic problems; they are as frequent here as in any other place in the world and set in motion by the processes of poverty, which makes treatment with medication necessary in many cases. However, in regions as poor as this one, the symptom frequently is much more social than psychopathological and many times the work of the social worker or policy advocate is much more important than that of the doctor. No medication has the power to cure powerlessness; it functions only as an anaesthetic, a social narcotic, or a shock absorber, as was demonstrated in the study on the dependency of poor women on benzodiazepines (Oliveira, 2000). In contrast to social practice and psychotherapeutic treatments that seek in some way to rescue human potential and enable human beings, psycho-pharmaceutical treatments immobilize and numb the human being. They perpetuate the person's low self-esteem, nihilism and various other characteristics of poverty. Medication should only be utilized as a last resort, when all the other alternatives of treatment have truly run out. Medication impedes any process of social awareness, keeping the person "domesticated" and maintaining naïve awareness, as much as or even more than illiteracy, such as Paulo Freire worked with in the 1970s. More serious yet is what is observed in the rural area of Northeast Brazil, where besides illiteracy, a large part of the population becomes "mentally ill," and as a consequence, become dependent on psycho-pharmaceutical drugs. It is a daily moral and ethical challenge to deal with psychopathology and poverty without confusing the two.

Citizenship: A New Challenge to a Clinical Approach

In order to conclude in a way that opens new pathways, I would like to highlight a common element in both psychopathology and poverty. This element is the unrealized potential for citizenship. Undeveloped citizenship is directly related to the psychological consequences of poverty described in this chapter: deprivation of power, low self-esteem, nihilism, and poor preparation for meaningful participation in the new global economy. Clinical psychology and psychiatry, including the CAPS example, continue to approach problems at the individual level, despite the advances of de-institutionalization. This is an error that becomes even more serious when working at the intersection of poverty and mental illness, where causes and symptoms are easy to confuse. An approach that is simultaneously political and economic, as well as clinical, is needed.

I propose that we reverse our strategy. We should explore working to develop citizenship as a means of therapy. It is not a matter of curing patients in order for them to become citizens, but of facilitating citizenship as an end in itself, which happens to have therapeutic consequences. This process would be similar to the process of conscientization developed by Freire (1980) in his literacy work. Poor people would move from a state of naïve passivity as "patients" toward constructive activity in society. Studies of experimental group treatments, such as those conducted outdoors and in communal living situations, have demonstrated the therapeutic effects of friendships and community projects (Davidson, Haglund, Stayner, Rakfeldt, Chinman & Tebes, 2001). Nevertheless, these tasks are artificially constructed forms of human contact that end up functioning as placebos and do not acquire wider meaning in the life of these patients. The patient continues as a de-institutionalized patient, now with "friends" who are also patients, because in this case friendship is merely a form of occupational therapy.

To address poverty and related mental illness fully, we must go beyond these individualistic interventions. The exercise of citizenship means realizing one's dream of a better life in a just society, at the intersection of public life with private projects. Only in this manner can the genuine human project that is currently blocked within poverty and psychopathology be reinstated.

Acknowledgments

I wish to thank the teams from the CAPS in Quixadá and Canindé in Ceará, Brazil for the information provided and to Coral Calderón, Célio Freire and Francisco Cavalcante Jr. for helpful comments on the first version of this chapter. I would also like to thank Tod Sloan for his important suggestions and comments, and for revising the English of the final version.

References

Barreto, A. (1993). Depressão e cultura no Brasil [Depression and culture in Brazil] *Jornal Brasileiro de Psiquiatria, 42,* 13–16.

Barroso, C. (2000). CAPS: Um novo cenário em Quixadá *Sustentação* [CAPS: a new scene in Quixadá], *2*(3), 36–37.

Barros, J. (1995). *Propaganda de medicamentos: Atentado à saúde* [Medication advertizing: An attack on health]. São Paulo: Hucitec.

Berlinck, M. (2000). *Psicopatologia fundamental* [Fundamental Psychopathology]. São Paulo: Escuta.

Bonfim, J. & Mercuccci, V. (Eds.). (1997). *A construção política dos medicamentos* [The political construction of medications]. São Paulo: Hucitec.

Castells, M. (2000). *Fim de milênio* [The end of the millenium]. São Paulo: Paz e Terra.

Cock, P. (1996). Toward an eco-psychology for sustainable development. In S. Carr & J. Schumaker, *Psychology and developing world* (pp. 191–198). Westport, CT: Praeger.

Davidson, L., Haglund, K., Stayner, D., Rakfeldt, J., Chinman, M. & Tebes, J. (2001). A qualitative study of supported socialization. *Psychiatric Rehabilitation Journal, 24*(3), 275–292.

Ehrenberger, A. (2000). *La fatigue d'être soi. Dépression et societé* [The fatigue of being oneself: Depression and society]. Paris: Odile Jacob.

Fé, N. (1995). *Resistências à reforma psiquiátrica* [Resistance to psychiatric reform] Cascavel: III Jornada Interiorana de Saúde Mental do Ceará e I Jornada de Saúde Mental de Cascavel.

Fox, D., & Prilleltensky, I. (Eds.). (1997). *Critical psychology: An introduction.* Thousand Oaks, CA: Sage.

Freire, P. (1970/2000). *A pedagogia do oprimido.* [The pedagogy of the oppressed] São Paulo: Paz e Terra.

Freire, P. (1980). *Conscientização* [Conscientization]. São Paulo: Moraes.

Freire, P. (1996/2000). *Pedagogia da autonomia* [The pedagogy of autonomy]. São Paulo: Paz e Terra.

Guimarães, A. (1998). A prática psicológica e suas intervenções na promoção da saúde (Psychological practice and its interventions to promote health)*I Simpósio de Psicologia e Saúde em Discussão.* Fortaleza: Centro de Estudos em Psicologia Hospitalar, 23/05/1998.

Keys, C. (1985). The interpretative basis of depression. In A. Kleinman, & B. Good (Eds.), *Culture and depression. studies in the anthropology and cross-cultural psychiatry of the affect and disorder* (pp. 153–174). Berkeley, CA: University of California Press.

Kleinman, A. (1995). *Writing at the margin.* Berkeley: University of California Press.

Kleinman, A., & Good, B. (1985). *Culture and depression: Studies in the anthropology and cross-cultural psychiatry of the affect and disorder.* Berkeley, CA: University of California Press.

Kleinman, A., Das, V., & Lock, M. (Eds.). (1997). *Social suffering.* Berkeley, CA: University of California Press.

Laungani, P. (2001). Culture, cognition and trauma: Cross-cultural evaluations. In J. Schumaker & T. Ward (Eds.), *Cultural cognition and psychopathology* (pp. ????). Westport, CT: Praeger.

Lira, E. (2000). Reflections on critical psychology: Psychology of memory and forgetting. In T. Sloan (Ed.), *Critical psychology: Voices for change* (pp. 82–90). London: Macmillan.

Lummis, C. (1991). Development against democracy. *Alternatives, 16,* 31–66.

Marsella, A., & Yamada, A. M. (2000). Culture and mental health: an introduction and overview of foundations, concepts and issues. In I. Cuéllar & F. Paniagua (Ed.), *Handbook of multicultural mental health* (pp. 3–24). London, UK: Academic Press.

Martín-Baró, I. (1989). *Sistema, grupo y poder: Psicología social desde Centroamérica II* [System, group and power: Social psychology from Central America II]. San Salvador: UCA.

Moghaddam, F., & Studer, C. (1997). Cross-cultural psychology: The frustrated gadfly's promises, potentialities and failures. In D. Fox & I. Prilleltensky (Eds.), *Critical psychology: an introduction* (pp. 185–201). Thousand Oaks, CA: Sage.

Montenegro, A. (2000). *Psicologia do povo Cearense* [The psychology of the people of Ceará]. Fortaleza: Casa José de Alencar Programa Editorial.

Moreira, V. (2001). *Mas allá de la persona: Hacia uma psicoterapia fenomenológica mundana.* [Beyond the person: A "worldly" phenomenological psychotherapy] Santiago: Editorial Universidad de Santiago de Chile.

Moreira, V. (2002). Uma etiologia desideologizadora [A de-ideologizing etiology]. In V. Moreira & T. Sloan, *Personalidade, ideologia e psicopatologia critica* (pp. 157–??). São Paulo: Escuta.

Moreira, V. (in press). The ideological meaning of depression. *International Journal of Clinical Psychology.*

Morris, D. B. (1998). *Illness and culture in the postmodern age.* Berkeley, CA: University of California Press.

Moulian, T. (1997). *Chile actual: Anatomia de un mito* [Chile today: The anatomy of a myth]. Santiago: Arcis.

Pitta, A. (1996). *Reabilitação psicosocial no Brasil* [Psycho-social Rehabilitation in Brazil. São Paulo: Hucitec.

Nietzsche, F. (1983). *Obras completas* [Complete Works]. São Paulo: Abril Cultural.

Oliveira, E. (2000). Saúde mental e mulheres: Sobrevivência, sofrimento psíquico e dependência química lícita. [Mental health and women: Survival, mental suffering and legal chemical dependence]. Sobral: UVA.

Sampaio, J., & Barroso, C. (1994). *Manual de organização do Centro de Atenção Psicossocial de Quixadá* [Organizational manual of the Center for Psycho-social Care in Quixadá]. Quixadá: Secretaria Municipal de Saúde.

Sampaio, J. & Barroso, C. (2001). http://www.discovernet.com.br/saudequixada/producao.html

Sampaio, J., Santos, A., & Andrade, O. (1998). Saúde mental e cidadania: um desafio local. [Mental health and citizenship: a local challenge] In E. Mendes (Ed.). *A organização da saúde no nível local* (pp. 267–280). São Paulo: Hucitec.

Santos, W. (1997). Avaliação crítica dos centros e núcleos de atenção psicossocial no Nordeste [A critical evaluation of the centers and nuclei of psycho-social care in the Northeast]. Dissertação de Mestrado em Saúde Pública: Universidade Estadual do Ceará.

Schumaker, J. (1996). Understanding psychopathology: Lessons from the developing world. In S. Carr & J. Schumaker (Eds.) *Psychology and the developing world* (pp. 180–190), Westport, CT: Praeger.

Schumaker, J. (2001). Cultural cognition and depression. In J. Schumaker & T. Ward (Eds.), *Cultural cognition and psychopathology*, (pp. 53–66). Westport, CT: Praeger.

Schumaker, J., & Ward, T. (Ed.) (2001). *Cultural cognition and psychopathology.* Westport, Connecticut: Praeger.

Sen, A (1999). *Sobre ética e economia* [On ethics and economy]. São Paulo: Companhia das Letras.

Sen, A. (2000). *Desenvolvimento como liberdade* (Development as freedom). São Paulo: Companhia das Letras.

Sloan, T. (1993). Desarrollo nacional o desarrollo humano? Ponencia en el Simposio sobre La Contribución de la Psicolog¡a al Desarrollo Nacional, en el Congreso de la Sociedad Interamericana de Psicologia, Santiago de Chile [National development of human development? Communication presented in the Symposium about psychology's contribution to national development, in the Congress of the Inter-American Society, Santiago, Chile].

Sloan, T. (1997). Theories of personality. Ideology and beyond. In D. Fox & I. Prilleltensky (Eds.), *Critical psychology: An introduction* (pp. 87–103). Thousand Oaks, CA: Sage.

Chapter 5

Poverty and Unemployment

David Fryer and Rose Fagan

In *The World Employment Report 2001* the World Health Organisation (WHO, 2001) estimated that globally "at the end of 2000 some 160 million workers are unemployed, most of them first-time job-seekers," about two-thirds of these in the so-called "developing" world. In addition, the WHO estimated that "about 500 million workers are unable to earn enough to keep their families above the US$ 1-a-day poverty line. These are almost entirely in the developing world. And of the workers who are not among the poor, many lack basic job and income security." The situation appears to be deteriorating.

In the first part of this chapter, we outline the key points of the literatures on unemployment, flexible labor market, poverty and mental health. We then, in the second part, move in closer to describe some specific participatory action research engaging with unemployed poverty in Scotland from a community psychological perspective.

Unemployment: The Nature and Scale of the Problem

Shocking though the above is, the number of people at risk of negative psychological effects of unemployment is usually underestimated. In the UK, for example, though the same point could be made of most countries, unemployment was until recently officially measured in terms of the number of people in receipt of state unemployment benefits, the so-called "claimant count." Counted this way, in March 2002 there were 939,600 unemployed "claimants" in the UK.

However, this way of measuring unemployment is flawed because large numbers of changes in the eligibility criteria for claiming a "job-seeker's allowance" are made by governments for political and administrative reasons. Stricter and stricter criteria have excluded many people from state financial support and also had the politically convenient result of reducing the published headline counts of the number of people "unemployed." However, changes in the number of people who cease to be *recorded* as unemployed are seldom the same as changes in the numbers of people who cease to *be* unemployed.

For these and other reasons, a sample survey definition which counts people as unemployed if they have not undertaken any paid employment in the survey reference period, have looked for a job within the previous four weeks and are available to start one within two weeks, the International Labor Organisation (ILO) definition, is preferred by many. In the period December 2001 to February 2002, 1,520,000 people were unemployed in the UK according to this yardstick.

However, the psychological consequences of unemployment include depression and demoralization and so some unemployed people stop actively looking for employment after a period of time as a result of being unemployed. Using the ILO definition, these people are no longer counted as unemployed.

Accordingly, some prefer another way of indicating how many people are unemployed: the Broad Labor Force Survey. This counts all those who say they want a job and are available to start within two weeks but who have not been actively looking for a job (for all sorts of reasons). This way of counting gives a UK unemployed count of 2,127,000 for the same period.

However, this may still greatly underestimate the number of people looking for employment. If we also count the full-time equivalents of those involuntarily on employment and training schemes, part-time employed, etc., the UK figure climbs to 4,269,500 people, the so-called "slack labor force" (Bivand, 2002).

Most international comparisons of unemployment rates are based on ILO definitions. Just as this is problematic for the UK, so it is problematic for other countries too and thus for global estimates of unemployment.

However we estimate it, the scale of unemployment is vast.

The Relationship Between Unemployment and Mental Health

Concerns have been expressed about the social, physical and mental health consequences of unemployment for at least two hundred years (Burnett, 1994; Garraty, 1978; Keyssar, 1986). However, that unemployment puts mental health at risk has been beyond reasonable doubt since the 1930s (Bakke, 1933; Eisenberg & Lazarsfeld, 1938; Jahoda, 1938/1987; Lazarsfeld-Jahoda & Zeisel, 1933; Pilgrim Trust, 1938). It was reconfirmed by substantial empirical research and scholarship in the 1980s (Warr, 1987) and more recently reiterated by sophisticated reviews and meta-reviews (Murphy & Athanasou, 1999).

Research clarifying the relationship between unemployment and mental health has been carried out in many OECD countries, including: *Australia* (e.g., Feather, 1992); *Austria* (e.g., Kirchler, 1985); *Belgium* (e.g., van Heeringen & Vanderplasschen, 1999); *Canada* (Goldenberg & Kline, 1997); *Finland* (e.g., Virtanen, 1993); *Germany* (e.g., Kronauer, Vogel, & Gerlach, 1993); *Ireland* (e.g., Whelan, 1992); *Italy* (e.g., Pugliese, 1993); *Japan* (Matobe & Ishitake, 1999); *Netherlands* (e.g., Verhaar, de Klauer, de Goede, van Ophem & de Vries, 1996); *New Zealand* (e.g., Barnett, Howden-Chapman, & Smith, 1995; Drewery, 1998); *Norway* (e.g., Claussen & Bertran, 1999; Ytterdahl, 1999); *Spain* (e.g., Varela Novo, 1999); *Sweden* (e.g., Brenner, Petterson, Arnetz, & Levi, 1989; Janlert & Hammarstrom 1992); *USA* (e.g., Dooley, Catalano, & Hough, 1992) as well as the *UK* (see Fryer & Ullah, 1986; Smith, 1987).

There is little published research about the mental health consequences of unemployment outside OECD countries, though research is now coming on-stream from former iron curtain countries in Europe, and the International Commission on Occupational Health (ICOH) Working Group meeting in Paris in September 1998 included a report from India (Joshi, 1999).

The early community-based studies remain exemplars of empirical research excellence with their painstaking attention to detail in context, ingenious triangulation of qualitative and quantitative research, integrity of fieldwork practice and bold conceptualisation (Jahoda, 1938/1987; Lazarsfeld-Jahoda & Zeisel, 1933). Some recent community-based studies bear comparison with these classic studies (Wight, 1993), but, in general, recent research has been dominated by decontextualized quantitative cross-sectional and longitudinal survey research using scales with proven reliability and validity to measure mental health operationalized in a variety of ways.

This research has played an important function in the development of the field. Well-designed, longitudinal studies tracked large, carefully matched, samples of people in and out of paid jobs, from school or employment to unemployment, from unemployment to employment, etc. In study after study, groups that became unemployed during the course of the research exhibited deterioration in mean mental health compared with continuously employed groups. Some of the most persuasive longitudinal quantitative studies were done with young people. Typically these studies measured the mental health of large groups of young people in school and followed them out into the labor market, periodically measuring the mental health of those who got jobs and those who did not and comparing group mean scores cross-sectionally and longitudinally. In study after study, groups of unemployed youngsters were demonstrated to have poorer mental health than their employed peers but statistically significant differences were seldom found between the scores of the same groups when at school (for a relatively rare exception see Hammarstrom, 1994), i.e., overwhelmingly poor mental health was shown to be the *consequence* rather than the *cause* of the labor market transition. In brief, such studies provided powerful evidence that unemployment *causes,* rather than merely *results from,* poor psychological health (Winefield, Tiggemann, & Winefield, 1993).

Recently, sophisticated meta-reviews have emphasized that social causation is involved. To give one example, after a meta-review of sixteen longitudinal studies using valid and reliable measures and published in the last ten years in peer-refereed English language scientific journals, Murphy and Athanasou (1999) concluded that "the results from the 16 longitudinal studies suggest that unemployment has reliable (negative) effects on mental health." They also reported that "effect size information . . . suggests that moving from unemployment to employment not only produces a reliable change to mental health, but a change that is 'practically significant'."

It was never plausible that mass unemployment was caused by mass, sometimes organizationally confined, epidemics of mental illness. Nevertheless, this has not discouraged some politicians and commentators from suggesting that the relationship between unemployment and poor mental health is best explained by people with poorer mental health being more likely to become and remain unemployed ("individual drift" or "selection"). This has the merit, from their perspective, of blaming unemployed people for their own distress and absolving governments and businesses of responsibility for the health consequences of unemployment (see also, Furnham, this volume; Harper, this volume).

The research described here, and elsewhere, has persuaded most researchers in the field that unemployment has mental health consequences that are negative and widespread.

The Flexible Labor Market: The Nature and Scale of the Problem

In many countries, however it is measured, unemployment has been falling in recent years. Unemployment was predicted by the OECD to fall in the 11 countries of the "Eurozone" of the Economic Community, from 10.4% in 1999 to 8.9% in 2001, whilst unemployment in OECD countries was predicted to fall from an average of 9.4% in 1999 to 8.3% by the end of 2001 (Atkinson, 1999). In the UK, even the slack labor force measure fell from 16% of the economically active UK population in June-August 1997 to 13.1% in February 2002 (Bivand, 2002). Given the damaging impact of unemployment on mental health, is this good news?

Taking the 1960s as a reference period, the UK labor market has traditionally been dominated by male employment in permanent, secure, full-time, unionized jobs in large companies in manufacturing industries. However, there has recently been wide agreement that a shift has been underway for some time from male to female, permanent to temporary, full-time to part-time, unionized to deregulated, manufacturing to service employment (Leadbeater & Martin, 1998; RSA, 1997).

Over the last 20 years, millions of full-time jobs have been lost and millions of part-time jobs have been created (Ford, 1995). Moreover, nearly three-quarters of the jobs created since 1992 have been part-time temporary ones; short-term and fixed contract employment is growing (RSA, 1997). In at least some periods, nearly 90% of the overall increase in employment was accounted for by temporary, insecure employment (Trades Union Council, 1995). In 1992, 9.3% of workers in the European Union were on temporary contracts with more than three out of five of such jobs being in low-skilled occupations (De Grip, Hoevenberg & Willems, 1997).

In the decade from 1984 the number of men working part-time in the UK doubled (Cooper, 1998) and about 15% of the European workforce was employed part time in 1991 with the percentage increasing year on year. However, there is massive variation between countries. Over 30% of employment in the Netherlands is part time as opposed to 3.4% in Greece, for example, 56% of part-time work in the European Union is done by low-skilled (and low-paid) workers and twice as many women as men are employed part time (De Grip et al., 1997).

In May 1999, at its annual meeting in Paris, the OECD recommended member countries to make working practices more "flexible": abolishing employment protection policies; ensuring minimum wages for young people are not too high; switching from unemployment to in-work benefits. Part-time work, on-call contracts, fixed-term contracts, seasonal work, agency work, working from home, teleworking, freelancing, self-employment and informal work are all on the increase (Delsen, 1991).

In summary, "the ongoing restructuring and globalization of the economy has changed the nature of work" (Dooley and Catalano, 1999).

The Relationship Between the Flexible Labor Market and Mental Health

What are the psychological consequences of flexible labor market participation and how do they compare with those of unemployment? According to Dooley and Catalano (1999) in the United States "under-employment (involuntary part-time or poverty wage) both appears increasingly common and seems to have health effects more like those of unemployment than adequate employment."

Hartley et al. (1991) explicated the notion of "job insecurity" as the "fundamental and involuntary change from a belief that one's position in the employing organization is safe, to a belief that it is not" (Hartley et al., 1991, p. viii). Studies by the authors in Israel, the Netherlands and the UK showed that job insecurity is associated with experienced powerlessness, impaired mental health (depression and reported psychosomatic symptoms), reduced job satisfaction, reduced organizational commitment, reduced trust in management, resistance to change and poorer industrial relations.

Recently, Burchell et al. (1999) report the results of secondary analysis of data from relevant sources, in-depth interviews and a survey of employees at senior management, line management and shop floor level in 20 UK organizations involved in a wide variety of work: manufacturing, transport, retail, education, health care, etc. The researchers found that job insecurity has gradually increased over the last 30 years for both men and women in both full-time and part-time employment and is now higher than at any time since 1945. The respondents reported that, over the last five years, their working hours had increased, they were having to work more quickly and with less adequate staffing levels. Experienced work pressure, particularly combined with weak supervisory support, was associated with poor psychological well-being and family relations. Whilst job insecurity has traditionally been accepted as a problem for blue-collar workers, professional workers (who in 1987 were the most secure workers) were found to be the most job *in*secure 10 years later. Job insecurity was found to be associated with poorer psychological well-being, poorer family relations and organizational demotivation. Worryingly, both physical and mental well-being was found to continue to deteriorate with continuing job insecurity. (See also Burchell, 1994; Dekker & Schaufeli, 1995.)

Previously unemployed people who have become re-employed are disproportionately at risk of job insecurity since re-employed people are vulnerable to being made unemployed again due to last-in-first-out practices (Daniel, 1974, 1990). However, increasingly researchers are emphasizing that job insecurity is not only, or necessarily, about fear of job loss but also about perceived risk of a deteriorating position within an organization, loss of status within the company; reduced opportunity for promotion, etc. (Burchell et al., 1999).

Evaluation of mental health consequences of participation in employment and training schemes, a vital part of the flexible labor market, reveals a complicated picture. The nature of the labor market context, quality of training and job placement and degree of experienced compulsion are probably critical. Virtanen (1993) found that unemployed people, of any age or sex, who were *forced* into employment through workfare-type programmes used primary health care facilities more frequently, whilst their primary care visits decreased if they became unemployed again.

Re-employment in poor quality jobs can be as, or more, psychologically corrosive than unemployment. It has been shown that re-employment is likely to be at a lower level (Daniel, 1974; 1990). Kaufman (1982) reported that 20% of his re-employed professionals were underemployed (in terms of salary, type of work and skill use) and less than 50% said their lives had returned to normal after re-employment, whilst Fineman (1987, p. 269) found "those re-employed in jobs which they felt to be inadequate were experiencing more stress and even poorer self-esteem, than they had during their period of unemployment". More recently, Graetz (1993) showed that,

> the health consequences of employment and unemployment are directly contingent on the quality of work. This means that the benefits of employment are confined to those, albeit a majority, who manage to find a satisfying job. In contrast, those who do not end up in a satisfying job – approximately one in every five workers – report the highest levels of health disorders.

At the same time, the adverse consequences of job loss are confined to those who were satisfied with their former jobs. (p. 722)

Winefield et al. (1993) followed 3,000 young Australians over an eight-year period and found that those youngsters who had taken jobs with which they were dissatisfied were indistinguishable in terms of mean mental health scores from unemployed youngsters. Both dissatisfied employed and unemployed young people had poorer mean mental health than satisfied employed young people. More recently, Leana and Feldman (1995, p. 1398) report that "unsatisfactorily re-employed workers reported significantly higher levels of anxiety and psychological distress than those who were satisfactorily re-employed; they also reported significantly lower levels of life satisfaction than those who were unemployed."

Finally, there is a vast literature on the impact of organisational/employment stressors on psychological strain (see Fryer & Winefield, 1998; Karasek & Theorell, 1990).

Unemployment, the Flexible Labor Market and Poverty

In Marienthal in the 1930s, families were classified as falling into one of four attitude categories: unbroken, resigned, apathetic, in despair. The connection "between a family's attitude and its economic situation" was so clear that the researchers could predict "at approximately what point the deterioration of income will push a family into the next category" (Jahoda et al., 1933/1972, p. 72). The researchers emphasized that "economic deterioration carries with it an almost calculable change in the prevailing mood" (Jahoda et al., 1933/1972, p. 82).

Lazarsfeld and Zawadski (1935) used personal document analysis to develop a stage account of the impact of unemployment. O'Brien (1986, p. 187) described it as "one of the most detailed" studies noting that it "found that negative feelings were not associated with the loss of a job per se but rather the state of poverty." Jahoda (1938, p. 1987) conducted fieldwork into the impact of unemployment in Wales, UK. The psychological impact was found to be less severe in Wales than Austria. Jahoda commented that this "may have been mainly because of the size and permanence of the unemployment allowance in Wales."

Bakke (1940, p. 17), writing of the decrease in activity of unemployed people, said bluntly "the plain fact is that the decline in recreation results from a decline in income" and O'Brien (1986, p. 196) correctly claimed that although "the literature seems to identify the major stressor as economic deprivation ... the importance of economic factors for the understanding of unemployment effects ... appears to have been underrated by psychological interpreters."

Peter Warr, co-ordinator of a vast body of survey research on unemployment and mental health, acknowledged that unemployed people themselves consistently say that shortage of money is their greatest problem at both personal and family levels. This should not be surprising: Unemployment normally brings a massive reduction in income, the process of claiming state benefits is widely regarded as demeaning, and unemployment often leads to debt.

As long ago as 1938, it was recognized that "just having a job itself is not as important as having a feeling of economic security. Those who are economically insecure, employed or unemployed, have a low morale" (Eisenberg & Lazarsfeld, 1938, p. 361). Echoing this in 1999 Dooley and Catalano wrote: "the ongoing restructuring and globalization of the economy has changed the nature of work. Workers accustomed to well-paid, full-time, secure jobs are increasingly falling not into unemployment but into less desirable forms of work" (Dooley & Catalano, 1999). The flexible labor market is, of course, associated with low and insecure income.

In 1996, the Scottish Low Pay Unit surveyed and analyzed the 6,142 vacancies advertised in 28 job centers. Just over 40% of the jobs were part time, with 20% offering less than 16 hours per week and just over 15% were temporary. Three-quarters of the jobs advertised were low paid and nearly one-third of vacancies actually paid below the UK National Insurance threshold. As the authors of the report commented, in these circumstances "paid work will only move large numbers of people from unwaged poverty to waged poverty" (Unemployment Unit, 1997/1998).

The epidemiological work of Wilkinson has established that whilst there is a "strong international relationship between income distribution and national mortality rates. In the developed world, it is not the richest countries which have the best health, but the most egalitarian" (Wilkinson, 1996, p. 3). This relationship between distribution of income and health is "one of the most powerful influences on the health of whole populations in the developed world to have come to light" (Wilkinson, 1996, p. 4). Wilkinson observes "psychosocial pathways have a central role in linking health to socio-economic circumstances" (Wilkinson, 2000, p. 3). Employment and unemployment are such key pathways.

A Critical Community Psychological Perspective

Although the research reported above has thrown valuable light on a range of important phenomena, it seeks to document distress rather than prevent or reduce it. Moreover, in documenting that distress it colludes with those forces in society for whom unemployment functions effectively as an instrument of social control. If unemployment puts mental as well as physical health at risk, which unemployed person would not want to escape unemployment as soon as possible (thus competing with others for jobs and thus bringing down the cost of labor)? Which employed person would relish risking unemployment by taking industrial action if unemployment courts psychological disaster? Merely to document mental health consequences of unemployment is, ideologically, essentially conservative.

In addition, being quantitative-survey-based in approach, most recent unemployment research has been carried out as an intrusive, bureaucratized, passive processing exercise within a grossly imbalanced power relationship. Ironically, in this it mirrors the way the state processes the unemployed person as a condition of income receipt and which there is reason to think is pathogenic.

Most unemployment research has been carried out within a set of epistemological assumptions derived from positivism. According to this way of thinking any personal relationship or solidarity between the researcher and the "survey respondent" taints the objectivity of the research.

Below we describe an attempt to intentionally reposition research from documenting psychologically distressing aspects of unemployment to intervening to reduce or prevent distress through both the process and outcomes of research. Rather than attempting to minimize the relationship between researchers and participants as a source of potential "information pollution" we sought to maximize the researcher-participant relationship as a source of possible information enrichment. Rather than seeking to minimize the power of the participant and maximize the power of the researcher over the research process, we sought to maximize participant power and minimize researcher power. Rather than seeking to exclude participants' interests from the research design (and thereby exhibiting political bias toward the status quo), we sought to build in participants' interests as central planks of the research design (thereby seeking to reduce participants' disempowerment). We also sought to reposition participants from being answerers of questions and donors of information useful to us as researchers, to being posers of questions and recipients of information (from us) useful to themselves.

Note that whilst most concern with ethical issues in psychological research relates to attempting to ensure that "subjects" are not put at risk or disadvantaged by the research, which aspires to be "value free," our approach was an attempt to be proactively ethical in that it was designed not only to safeguard participants from possible harm but also to actively *promote* the interests of generally disempowered "participants" in research, which aspired to be "value committed."

Whilst this is but a small demonstration project in Scotland, we hope that its core principles might be useful elsewhere.

An Attempt at Community Psychological Engagement
with Unemployed Poverty in Scotland

In the work described below, we sought to: (1) contribute to understanding of the role of psychosocial aspects of income in the experience and mental health of unemployed members of low-income families in community context; (2) expose and examine the "nuts and bolts" of the community-social processes linking inequality at a societal level to physiological processes at the individual level; (3) contribute to the development of innovative participatory methodology; (4) promote the interests of impoverished unemployed people in line with community psychological values; and (5) systematically generate auditable accounts of the experience of income related factors.

We wished to use methods sufficiently sensitive to precisely investigate the phenomena of unemployed poverty in adequate detail yet also sensitive to the needs of participants already at risk of depression, anxiety, humiliation, stigma, lack of support, low self-confidence, invasion of privacy and passive processing. Our methods needed to: (a) facilitate respect, trust and empathy; (b) be non-threatening, non-invasive and transparent in purpose; (c) be individually relevant; (d) facilitate participants' active involvement; (e) empower participants in process and outcome; (f) address subjectivity in context; (g) make it in participants' interests to disclose fully and accurately.

We decided to build the research around the use of a menu-driven interactive program, which allows a person, by keying in their personal circumstances, to work out all the state benefits to which she or he is entitled. In this way, people might become aware of income to which they were entitled but not claiming, or better understand the reasons for non-receipt of income to which they thought they were entitled. Welfare benefit advice was delivered through the Lisson Grove Welfare Benefits Program loaded onto a portable notebook computer.

Around this central core, we carried out and audio-recorded repeated non-directive depth interviewing, observation and document analysis. Field notes were made to keep track of emerging insights. Analysis used a refinement of cognitive mapping, in which emerging themes were mapped through spatial grouping in 2D space of conceptual interdependencies.

Some families we worked with heard of and claimed entitlements to which they did not previously know they were entitled. Most families, however, did not learn of new entitlements but many reported that they were relieved to come to understand why they were (and were not) entitled to certain benefits. The benefit system was widely regarded as arbitrary and unfair. Some family members in our sample used the research intervention to calculate the implications of potential courses of action. Some participants worked out in advance the financial costs and benefits of taking low-paid employment.

Much disclosure occurred relating to: (1) the difficulty of fulfilling not only functional and essential consumption needs but also, crucially, symbolic consumption needs which fuelled social exclusion; (2) the psychological functionality of so-called "irrational" spending and consumption patterns; (3) perceived entitlements and disentitlements; (4) income-source related stigma; (5) negative experience of state agencies and claiming; (6) expenditure planning and prioritization of different family members' needs; (7) the domestic division of financial coping behavior; (8) the use of reciprocal support; and (9) coping strategies the pro-social and mental health promoting nature of participation in informal (black) economic activity.

We worked with 30 families within one deprived community, carrying out multiple advice and interview sessions with different family members. For example, three members of one unemployed family were interviewed repeatedly (three separate interviews were conducted with the father, two separate interviews were conducted with the mother, two separate interviews were conducted with the daughter and one joint interview was conducted with mother and father together). A rich picture was thus built up of how each member conceptualized the major issues facing the family.

Both the mother and the daughter emphasized the *material hardship* being endured. The mother spoke of having to manage with inadequate resources, shopping at second-hand outlets, the inability to afford essentials, living with the responsibility of knowing that her relatives would suffer if she shopped unwisely. She vividly set this current hardship within the context of a life of hardship. The daughter told of no longer getting pocket money from her parents, not being able to earn money because of effectively being imprisoned in her house through fear of violence. She explained how she was excluded through poverty from taking part in school extra-curricular activities and thus isolated from her school friends. The father, on the other hand, despite probing during depth interviews, did not talk of hardship as such.

This way of working gives the lie, if needed, to assumptions of homogeneity in the experiences of differing family members of unemployed poverty. Research on unemployment has often focused by default on the experience of men, who have often themselves focused on their preoccupations of bored work underload, stigma, claiming benefit and job search. Women in unemployed families are more likely, when given the opportunity, to discuss stressful work overload, strenuous efforts to cope with hardship and thus protection of their male partners from associated anxieties.

There was also a "family division of coping labor" with some members trying predominantly to cope by maximizing income and others trying predominantly to limit expenditure and structure it with the least resultant distress.

Some (predominantly women in this research) tended to talk of coping through careful budgeting, economizing and "organized shopping," exploiting special offers wherever they were, reducing expectations of life, creative activities, and cultivating supportive networks within the nuclear and extended family.

Others (predominantly children in this research) tended to cope with unemployed poverty by second-hand shopping, learning when and where to get treats, helping in return for benefits, and making use of free activities.

Others (predominantly men in this research) tended to cope with unemployed poverty by "working on the side" in the black economy. This is seldom explored by social scientists in any detail for the obvious reasons that such work is usually kept secret, not only because it is illegal but because dominant discourses position it as antisocial and immoral. The action research approach adopted here, involving welfare benefit advice, helped build trust and facilitated detailed investigation of all forms of income leading to the uncovering of a very different perspective.

Working on the side whilst claiming unemployment benefits was described as having financial benefits but relatively little was made of these other than that they were often earmarked for particular expensive but necessary items. There was, however, explicit disclosure about the pride obtained through doing good jobs inexpensively with self-taught skills. There was talk of being locally respected for the quality of (black) work. There was evidence of the acquisition of sophisticated understanding of the local (black) labor market. Black economic activity was described in terms of what amounted to self-employment market testing: testing out supply and demand for different skills in differing areas, lowering prices and increasing services to drive competitors out of business, etc.

The receipt of state benefit money is described as redolent with indecency, humiliation, stigma, and depression. The passivity and lack of any reciprocity, of an exchange relationship, with unemployment benefit was especially thoroughly explicated. By contrast, money earned from work on the side was experienced quite differently: there was a reciprocal relationship between the hard work done, the payment received, and the entitlement to spend it as one pleased. Black economic earnings, unlike dole (unemployment benefit) money, was felt legitimately to be one's own. Moreover, receipt of money in exchange for hard physical graft reinforced a sense of masculinity.

Conclusion

The intervention research described above was an attempt to work community psychologically. Community psychology is concerned with understanding socially caused mental health and community problems in the contexts within which they occur and with intervening to prevent or reduce them. Community psychologists assume that many aspects of mental and physical health are strongly shaped by powerful socio-structural and institutional forces, that poor mental health often follows from the disempowerment of those affected, and that many services for people experiencing mental health problems maintain that disempowerment. Community psychologists try to work collaboratively with people in their everyday contexts to shift the balance of power in their direction, believing that the expertise and insight relevant to prevention or reduction of mental health problems are frequently to be found within communities, although the resources required to implement the necessary changes are often to be found outside them. The community psychology approach takes many culturally specific forms but is infinitely malleable as long as the key assumptions and values are not compromised.

Acknowledgment

This paper draws on Fryer, D. (2001). Strukturwandel der Arbeitslosigkeit und psychische Gesundheit. In H. G. Zilian & J. Flecker (Eds.), *Soziale Sicherheit und Strukturwandel der Arbeitslosigkeit (pp.)*. Berlin: Sigma.

References

Bakke, E. W. (1933). *The unemployed man*. London: Nisbet.

Barnett, P., Howden-Chapman. P., & Smith, A. (1995). Unemployment, work and health: Opportunities for healthy public policy. *The New Zealand Medical Journal*, 26 April, *108* (998), 138–140.

Bivand, P. (2002). Tight labor market shows little impact on inflation: Paul Bivand looks at the latest labor market statistics. *Working Brief, 134*, 17–20. May.

Brenner, S-O., Petterson, I-L., Arnetz, B., & Levi, L. (1989). Stress reactions to unemployment among Swedish blue-collar workers. In B. Starrin, P-G Svensson, & Wintersberger, H. (Eds.), *Unemployment, poverty and quality of working life* (pp. ???). Berlin: Sigma.

Burchell, B. J. (1994). Who is affected by unemployment? Job insecurity and labor market influences on psychological health. In D. Gallie, C. Marsh, & C. Vogler, *Social change and the experience of unemployment.* Oxford, UK: Oxford University Press.

Burchell, B. J., Day, D., Hudson, M., Ladipo, D., Mankelow, R. Nolan, J. P., Reed, H., Wichert, I. C., & Wilkinson, F. (1999). *Job insecurity and work intensification: Flexibility and the changing boundaries of work.* York: Joseph Rowntree Foundation (ISBN: 1 902633 41 5).

Burnett, J. (1994). *Idle hands: The experience of unemployment, 1790–1990.* London: Routledge.

Catalano, R., & Kennedy, J. (1998). The effects of unemployment on disability caseloads in California. *Journal of Community and Applied Social Psychology, 8*, 137–144.

Claussen, B., & Bertran, J. (1999). The International Commission on Occupational Health Working Group "Unemployment and Health" 25–26 September, 1998. Paris, France. *In. Arch. Occup. Environ. Health, 72* (Suppl.): S1–S48.

Claussen, B., Bjorndal, A., & Hjort, P. F. (1993). Health and re-employment in a two year follow-up of long-term unemployed. *Journal of Epidemiology and Community Health, 47*(1), 14–18.

Cooper, C. L. (1998). The changing nature of work. *Community, Work and Family, 1*(3).

Daniel, W. W. (1974). *A national survey of the unemployed.* London: Political and Economic Planning Institute.

Daniel, W. W. (1990). *The unemployed flow.* London: PSI.

De Grip, A., Hoevenberg, J., & Willems, E. (1997). Atypical employment in the European Union. *International Labor Review, 136*(1), 49–71.

Dekker, S., & Schaufeli, W. (1995). The effects of job insecurity on psychological health and withdrawal: A longitudinal study. *Australian Psychologist, 30*, 57–63.

Delsen, L. (1991). Atypical employment relations and government policy in Europe. *Labor, 7*(3), 73–91.

Dooley, D., & Catalano, R. (1999). Unemployment, disguised unemployment and health: The US case. *Int. Arch. Occup. Environ. Health, 72* (Suppl.): S16–S19.

Dooley, D., Catalano, R., & Hough, R. (1992). Unemployment and alcohol disorder in 1910 and 1990: Drift versus social causation. *Journal of Occupational and Organisational Psychology, 65*, 4, 277–290.

Drewery, W. (1998). Unemployment: What kind of problem is it? *Journal of Community and Applied Social Psychology, 8*, 101–108.

Eisenberg, P., & Lazarsfeld, P. F (1938). The psychological effects of unemployment. *Psychological Bulletin, 35*, 258–390.

Feather, N. T. (1992). *The psychological impact of unemployment.* New York, NY: Springer Verlag.

Fineman, S. (1987). Back to employment: Wounds and wisdoms. In D. Fryer & P. Ullah (Eds.), *Unemployed people: Social and psychological perspectives.* Milton Keynes, UK: Open University Press.

Ford, J. (1995). Middle England: In debt and insecure. *Poverty, 92*, 11–14.

Fryer, D., & Ullah, P. (1987). *Unemployed people: Social and psychological perspectives.* Milton Keynes, UK: Open University Press.

Fryer, D., & Winefield, A. H. (1998). Employment stress and unemployment distress as two varieties of labor market induced psychological strain: An explanatory framework. *Australian Journal of Social Research, 5*(1), 3–18.

Garraty, J. A. (1978). *Unemployment in history: Economic thought and public Policy.* New York, NY: Harper & Row.

Goldenberg, S., & Kline, T. (1997). Canadian white-collar workers' views of their experience with downsizing or job loss. *Psychological Reports, 80*(3), Pt 1, 707–719.

Graetz, B. (1993). Health consequences of employment and unemployment: Longitudinal evidence for young men and women. *Social Science and Medicine, 35*(6), 715–724.

Hammarstrom, A. (1994). Health consequences of youth unemployment. *Public Health, 108*(6), 403–412.

Hartley, J. F., Jacobson, D., Klandermans, B., & van Vuuren, T. with Greenhalgh, L. & Sutton, R. (1991). *Job insecurity: Coping with jobs at risk.* London: Sage.

Jahoda, M. (1938/1987). Unemployed men at work. In D. Fryer & P. Ullah (Eds.), *Unemployed people: Social and psychological perspectives* (pp.????). Milton Keynes, UK: Open University Press.

Jahoda, M., Lazarsfeld, P. F., & Zeisel, H. (1933/1972). *Marienthal: The sociography of an unemployed community.* New York, NY: Aldine Atherton.

Janlert, U., & Hammarstrom, A. (1992). Alcohol consumption among unemployed youths: Results from a prospective study. *British Journal of Addiction, 87*, 703–714.

Joshi, T. K. (1999). Occupational health and unemployment in India. *Int. Arch. Occup. Health, 72* (Suppl.) S8–S9.

Karasek, R. A., & Theorell, T. (1990). *Healthy work: Stress, productivity and the reconstruction of working life.* New York, NY: Basic Books.

Kaufman, H. G. (1982). *Professionals in search of work: Coping with the stress of job loss and underemployment.* New York, NY: Wiley.

Keyssar, A. (1986). *Out of work: The first century of unemployment in Massachusetts.* Cambridge, MA: Cambridge University Press.

Kirchler, E. (1985). Job loss and mood. *Journal of Economic Psychology, 6*, 9–25.

Kronauer, M., Vogel, B., & Gerlach, F. (1993). *Im Schatten der Arbeitsgesellschaft: Arbeitslose und die Dynamik sozialer Ausgrenzung.* Frankfurt & New York: Campus Verlag.

Lazarsfeld-Jahoda, M., & Zeisel, H. (1933). Die Arbeitslosen von Marienthal. *Psychol. Monographien, 5.* An English language translation appeared in 1971 as Jahoda, M., Lazarsfeld, P. F. & Zeisel, H. (1971). *Marienthal: The sociography of an unemployed community.* Chicago, IL: Aldine Atherton.

Leana, C. R., & Feldman, D. C. (1995). Finding new jobs after a plant closing: antecedents and outcomes of the occurrence and quality of re-employment. *Human Relations, 48,* 12, 1381–1401.

Leadbeater, C., & Martin, S. (1998). *The employee mutual: Combining flexibility with security in the new world of work.* London: Demos/Reed.

Lisson Grove Welfare Benefits Program. Department of General Practice, Community Health Sciences Division, Imperial College School of Medicine, Norfolk Place, London W2 1PG.

Matobe, T., & Ishitake, T. (1999). A strategy for health promotion among unemployed people in Japan. *Int. Arch. Occup. Health, 72* (Suppl.) S31–S33.

Murphy, G. C., & Athanasou, T. A. (1999). The effect of unemployment on mental health. *Journal of Occupational and Organizational Psychology, 72,* 83–99.

O'Brien, G. E. (1986). *Psychology of work and unemployment.* Chichester, UK: John Wiley & Sons.

Pilgrim Trust. (1938). *Men without work.* Cambridge: Cambridge University Press.

Pugliese, E. (1993). The Europe of the unemployed. In M. Kronauer (Guest Editor), Unemployment in Western Europe. *International Journal of Political Economy, 23*(3), 3–120.

RSA. (1997). Key views on the future of work. Redefining Work Discussion Paper, *Royal Society of Arts Journal,* June, 7–13.

Smith, R. (1987). *Unemployment and health: A disaster and a challenge.* Oxford, UK: Oxford University Press.

Trades Union Council. (1995). *Britain divided: Insecurity at work.* London: TUC.

Unemployment Unit (1997/1998). *Working Brief,* 7–8.

van Heeringen, K., & Vanderplasschen, W. (1999). Unemployment and suicidal behaviour in perspective. *Int. Arch. Occup. Environ. Health, 72* (Suppl.), S42–S45.

Varela Novo, M. (1999). Unemployment and mental health in Galicia, Spain. *Int. Arch. Occup. Environ. Health, 72* (Suppl), S14–S15.

Verhaar, C. H. A., de Klauer, P. M., de Goede, M. P. M., van Ophem, J. A. C., & de Vries, A. (Eds.). (1996). *On the challenges of unemployment in a regional Europe.* Aldershot: Avebury.

Virtanen, P. (1993). Unemployment, re-employment and the use of primary health care services. *Scandinavian Journal of Primary Health Care, 11*(4), 228–33.

Warr, P. B. (1987). *Work, unemployment and mental health.* Oxford, UK: Clarendon Press.

Whelan, C. T. (1992). The role of income, life-style deprivation and financial strain in mediating the impact of unemployment on psychological distress: Evidence from the Republic of Ireland, *Journal of Occupational and Organisational Psychology, 65*(4), 331–344.

WHO. (2001): http://www.ilo.org/public/english/support/publ/wer/overview.htm

Wight, D. (1993). *Workers not wasters: Masculine respectability, consumption and employment in Central Scotland.* Edinburgh, UK: Edinburgh University Press.

Wilkinson, R. G. (2000). *Mind the gap: Hierarchies, health and human evolution.* London, UK: Weidenfeld & Nicolson.

Wilkinson, R. G. (1996). *Unhealthy societies: The afflictions of inequality.* London: Routledge.

Winefield, A. H., Tiggemann, M., & Winefield, H. R. (1993). *Growing up with unemployment: A longitudinal study of its psychological impact.* London: Routledge.

Ytterdahl, T. (1999). Routine health check-ups of unemployed in Norway. *Int. Arch. Occup. Environ. Health, 72* (Suppl.)

Zawadski, B., & Lazarsfeld, P. F. (1935). The psychological consequences of unemployment. *Journal of Social Psychology, 6,* 224–251.

Chapter 6

Poverty and Place

Peter Spink

What are we trying to understand? The creation and experience of place. The creation of place is at once so simple – planting a tree in a co-op courtyard – and so complex, as anyone studying the creation of urban space recognizes. Any experience of place weaves together space, built form, behavior, and ideas, at individual and collective levels. And it does so within particular social, economic, political and historical contexts. (Rodman, 1993, p. 123)

Overview and Ethos

In this chapter, poverty is defined socially just as much as economically (Alinsky, 1965, Latouche, 1992). The level of analysis is mezzanine rather than micro or macro, because poverty also takes place midway between the community and the economy. The chapter presents a number of Brazilian case studies and workshop debates on the possibility of mid-range action in poverty reduction. These suggest the criticality of recognizing the *place* as a focus for psychological action. The chapter does not attempt to argue for universal principles. Its conclusions should be seen within the cultural, social, and economic horizons of the Latin American region from where it is being written.

From Poverty to Inequality to Exclusion

It is Western democracy that can be found guiding the many constitutions of Latin America and it is Western democracy that, in most psychological texts, appears as a background taken-for-granted model of political and institutional life.

103

It is also Western democracy that permeates the development debate (Sachs, 1992; Latouche, 1996). In this, to use the arguments of Marshall (1950), equalities in relation to rights and duties are balanced with a minimum tolerance of inequalities in terms of degrees of economic and cultural capital. Western societies are class societies. Rather than giving allegiance to a static hereditary system, they are a result of a constant process of tension, conflict, and negotiation.

The Concept of Rights

The rise of the Western welfare state is part of this process of continued attempts to consolidate and redistribute social guarantees. Part of its slowly negotiated conception involved the interweaving of three different strands of rights (Marshall, 1950). These are the strands of (a) civil rights (freedom of speech, thought, faith, property and the right to justice); (b) political rights (the right to participate in the *polis* both as elector or as elected, as an active and participating voice); and (c) social rights (varying from the right to a modicum of social welfare, to the right to share in the wider social heritage, education, and culture, and to live the life of a civilized being with dignity). Neither of these strands (a) to (c) is pre-existent. They are products of social and political processes. Thus, in many places, including Latin America, even the very basic right to have (a) civil rights is often lacking (Sweden, 1998; Murilo de Carvalho, 2001).

The "neutrality" of Psychology

Whilst many psychologists are politically sensitive and in general progressive, psychology itself has positioned itself as "independent" from everyday life. This can be seen in (1) the support for the neutrality of the scientific method and the logic of knowledge, (2) through the proposition of a real world that exists outside of the person, and (3) through the distinction between pure research (from which *theories* are derived) versus applied *activities* (which relate to a world outside). Psychology has had difficulty accepting the inherent challenge that, with its separation of individual from context, Western psychology's person is far more part of the problem than the solution (Harré, 1998; Farr, 1996; Gergen, 1994; Ibañez, 2001; Rose, 1998; Sampson, 1989; and Shotter, 1993).

Critical Psychology

A major challenge to psychology has been the emergence of a more critical psychology (Ibañez & Íñiguez 1997). Latin America has played its part in this process of shaking psychology's social apathy. It has done this by reconnecting person and context (Lane & Codo, 1985; Martín-Baró, 1983; Montero, 1987; Spink, M.J., 2000). Much of the impetus for this contribution has come from dissatisfaction with social and economic development policies being supported by leading international agencies. Such dissatisfaction is not only present on the streets, it is also a constant feature in the discussions of many applied psychologists.

A Place for Critical Psychology

Let us describe the very high degree of income inequality in Brazil. This is virtually the worst in the world, with the top 10% of the population having 50% of all income, and the bottom 10% having just 1% of it. Expressed in different terms, only 7% of Brazilian families have a joint income of over US$ 1,500 a month; which is the minimum that is sufficient to allow access to the consumer durable goods market. Over 40% of the 150 million population (or 70 million people) are on or below the World Bank's poverty line of US$ 1 per capita a day. In both its developed South East, and its underdeveloped and drought-ridden North East, infant mortality rates for the 20% poorest are over 100 per thousand. This contrasts with just 11 per thousand for the 20% richest in the country. Thus, despite publicity to the contrary, Brazil remains a highly divided country. There is considerable racial intolerance, and widespread social apartheid (Buarque, 1994). Across both urban and rural settings, the new internationalism of "markets" and "opportunities" has actually broken previously stable work relations. It has led to increased use of temporary labor contracts. In fact, over the last 10 years, what was previously a 60:40 relationship between formal and informal work has been completely reversed. Of every ten jobs being created, just two are now salaried positions with proper employment benefits.

Poverty and Social Deprivation

These contradictions between such high degrees of social and economic inequality have inevitably led to the questioning of poverty as an individualized economic problem. It was the economist Sen (1992) who provided the most eloquent break. Sen argued against abstract income levels, in favor of their adequacy for a life lived with dignity. This comes from being well fed, having adequate clothing, shelter, avoiding preventable illness, and assuming an active and upright role in the community. Sen went on to discuss the importance of five fundamental freedoms: political; economic; social; political transparency; and security. According to Sen, poverty and lack of freedoms go together: "Freedoms are not the primary ends of development, they are also amongst its principal means" (1999, p. 10).

Beyond the Local

According to Sen also, in many cases it is not income that will guarantee dignity. In situations of discrimination and exclusion, certain groups are unable to convert income to freedom, and are unable to access minimal social guarantees, because of age, gender, color, ethnic origin, social class, or religion. Many of the elements that go to make up our sense of dignity in everyday life are provided collectively, and no amount of individual income can deal with their absence. Health, education, and transport, are a few examples. Strategies of community health care may use volunteers or small teams working locally, but epidemiological information still has to be processed, and equipment and drugs supplied. An example is the recent action by Brazilian health authorities; who used epidemiological information to argue the international case for a right to use generic, rather than branded medicines to combat HIV/AIDS. In Nicaragua, international aid agencies supported the construction of housing for judges in outlying areas, far away from the main towns and urban centers. Basic civil rights require many things, but a judge and a simple courtroom is certainly part of the process of collective provision. The presence of a live-in judge has proved to be of significant social impact. Whereas previously, the judge would come for the day and hear cases in the corner of the mayor's own office – usually shared by many others – he or she now takes part in the life of the community and in the discussion of social issues.

The Criticality of Access

This idea that poverty is frequently a question of access is further highlighted when it is recognized that whilst 80% of Latin America's population is urban, its surroundings are not. Seventy-one percent of Brazilian municipalities have fewer than 20,000 inhabitants, and 90% have less than 50,000. Many of these have very small urban centers of between 2,000–5,000 people. This pattern of settlement is very different from cities such as São Paulo, set in a conurbation of some 16 million inhabitants. Thus, whilst it is one nightmare to live from hand to mouth in rural areas without services, it is another nightmare to have to get up at four in the morning in a huge metropolis in order to spend up to three hours on many different buses getting to work. Access is about exclusion and about empowerment (Friedmann, 1992). Additional related themes were picked out in the World Bank's *Voices of the Poor* study (Narayan, Chambers, Shah, & Petesch, 1999). In the Brazilian part of the investigation for instance, "security is associated with a variety of factors including employment and regular income, access to food, having good health and access to health services, as well as having a home with property rights" (Melo, 1999).

Beyond the Primary Group

This kind of analysis calls attention to the fact that everyday life is a social process made up of many micro-social events that have considerable consequences for people (Garfinkel, 1976). These take place in a variety of spaces beyond the individual, and beyond the primary group. For example, doctors and judges are present within the daily horizon. Civil society organizations create lines of micro-credit. Local governments paint the municipal budget on the school wall, and call on the community to discuss investment decisions. This is something about which psychologists and psychology ought to have much to say and, equally important within an action research framework, have much to contribute.

Dialogue and Debate: Seeking an Alternative Consensus

Our research group in São Paulo (Spink, 2000) has been looking very closely at practical experiences being developed by municipal governments, non-governmental organizations (NGOs), and community movements that produce a significant impact on poverty. These face head-on questions of social exclusion and extreme inequality, and make significant inroads in terms of effective inclusion. This is being done in two ways: firstly, through identifying cases and describing what is being done; and secondly, through gathering together those involved in the experiences, along with academics, activists, and local government practitioners, to debate the practices, and their results, in order to build guidelines for future action. So far, some 80 different experiences have been studied and discussed in depth. Over 300 different social actors have been involved in the discussions, each of which takes place over two days in a semi-residential format.

The Questions

In the first phase of discussions, held during 1998 and 1999 (Camarotti & Spink, 2000a), the focus was on the possibility of space for action at the municipal level. The questions posed were: What strategies for poverty reduction were possible? What could local governments do? A second phase (1999–2000), arose in part from the conclusions of the first. The focus here has been on the role played by interorganizational alliances in poverty reduction cases. We have concentrated on the presence and effectiveness of links and partnerships between different branches and departments of government; with civil society organizations; with community groups; and with local business firms (Camarotti & Spink, 2000b, 2000c, 2001). The experiences that were presented and debated at the workshops ranged widely. For example, they came from different parts of the country, with different cultural traditions, different political climates and different resources available. These experiences are presented in Table 6.1.

Theme 1: Vicious Circles

A major conclusion emerged from the themes in Table 6.1. Poverty manifests itself in the precarious presence of, and access to, goods and services, and in the absence of effective channels of dialogue between those in power and the demands of the population. These shortfalls result in a vicious circle, in which those interests

Table 6.1. Experiences in Debate

- Joint programs being run by local governments and recyclable materials collectives to organize and utilize the economic potential of waste materials; often including support to co-operatives and the creation of educational opportunities for children.
- Job creation programs linked to environmental preservation.
- Low-cost housing programs being run jointly by municipalities and neighborhood groups which promote community involvement in land title regulation, construction work, income generation and in linked initiatives in areas such as health and education.
- Local health programs, often administered jointly by local governments and community associations, using small mobile health teams and local health centers to reach areas with little access to health resources and promote inclusion of low-income communities within the health service.
- Volunteer health programs focused on prenatal and early infant child care for the most vulnerable sectors and joint church, local government and non-governmental programs working with vulnerable groups such as street children, child prostitutes and victims of family violence.
- Programs being carried out by rural workers and small farmers associations in conjunction with NGOs and development agencies to gain better access to markets through product processing and market-related activities, also creating income and job opportunities for the wider community.
- Creation of market gardening zones around urban areas to provide opportunities for rural workers affected by agricultural transitions.
- Local government involvement in support of more equitable relations between raw material extraction communities and the final purchasers, building up chains of fair trade relations involving workers' associations, NGOs and business firms.
- Self help urban, industrial and small business craft co-operatives.
- Microcredit programs developed by local associations, or through joint partnership with state and local governments.
- Business support for community and local government initiatives.
- Various forms of school grant programs designed to provide a stimulus for parents with low incomes to keep their children in school.
- Various forms of intermunicipal working in joint planning of industrial development, environmental management and food supply.

that are better placed and more capably represented end up being able to claim a more significant part of goods and services than those without such access. This can happen with major government programs of support, for example in agriculture or small business development, where the most disadvantaged are unable to gain access because of a lack of documents, land titles, financial guarantees, or even information. It can also be the case that open planning forums are held at times that are convenient for the government's technical staff, but which make it impossible for disadvantaged communities to attend.

Theme 2: Voice

In addition, the cases and debates summarized in Table 6.1 pointed toward the importance of building citizenship and of democracy, empowerment and emancipation. A key element here is the encouragement and support of autonomous community groups, networks, and social movements, that emerge from, and are sustained by, "the poor." In the 1940s, Alinsky coined the expression *people's organizations* to refer to those organizations that are of, and belong to, the "poor" (Horwitt, 1989). Supporting an autonomous and active voice provides a very different basis from which to discuss alliances and partnerships. Within the local arena, effective local political and social articulation is an important factor.

Theme 3: Process before Plan

A third conclusion from the contents of Table 6.1 is that the experiences, projects, and programs under discussion, many of which were highly successful, were much more processes in action, than coherent and well-designed blueprints. They rarely began in a structured, deductive and preplanned manner, with precise objectives, clear strategies and well-defined procedures and budgets. Rather the opposite was the case. They took shape inductively, in practice and with time, by the integration of diverse and unplanned elements and ideas within a flow of action. These flows were negotiated along the way, taking advantage of openings and possibilities, being influenced by new arguments and contributions. If there was any planning, it was much more adaptive, messy, and incremental, not elegant and concise. Even in so-called "integrated" activities and approaches, it was not possible to identify a programmatic plan that had been previously defined and was capable of guaranteeing results. These were collective and turbulent learning processes, not the technological application of ideal models. They were about innovation not best practices. They used knowledge to get going, but gathered further knowledge, pragmatically and locally relevant, along the road.

This vision of action as a process involves understanding the fight against poverty in terms of access. This access is to a quality of life that brings dignity, equal rights, social inclusion, and citizenship. The experiences discussed in Table 6.1 were all about altering power structures (Prilleltensky, this volume). They were about optimizing alliances between governments and the poor. This was especially so with sub-national governments, who sought greater proximity with excluded groups, through the adoption of participative methods of project administration.

Theme 4: Place as Civil Society

The most important conclusion that emerged from Table 6.1 was a realization about the criticality of what can be termed a mid-range of social action. This is action that goes beyond the many important micro-level actions of individuals and small groups in local solidarity with each other. At the same time however, the front is not so broad as macro-level policy, or related national programs that are often incapable of dealing with the complexity of different demands emerging from variety of different settings. Instead of either of these two "extremes," the mid-range lies between the two. The most adequate expression that emerged to frame the scope of such action is that of *place*. In Portuguese, the word is *lugar*, and its use is virtually identical. This is the place where she lives – *o lugar onde ela mora* – everything in its rightful place – *tudo no seu devido lugar*.

Conceptually, the *place* is wherever we find ourselves. Indeed the *place*, as some participants pointed out, looks like ourselves. It is formed by different and interlocking arenas of demands, conflicts, and claims for improvements in the quality of life. Dense, the *place* is a reference for people's lives in space and time that, depending on circumstances, can be a neighborhood, a municipality, or a region. The *place* is, without doubt, where the simple experiences, tactics, methods, and practices root themselves. The result is an invisible library of poverty reduction solutions. This is illustrated by the following extracts from the consensus conclusions, produced by the 130 participants of the first phase of discussions mentioned above (Camarotti & Spink, 2000a)—see Table 6.2.

The *Place* in Psychology

From Table 6.2, the insistence on *place*, in the discussions, was more than just a "play on words." It was an attempt, by those involved, to construct a practical horizon for action that does not fall into a trap that often befalls the more often used term, *local*. *Local* carries implicitly or explicitly the idea of its counterparts: *national*, or *central*. Thus, *local* government is not *central* or *national* government, and business leaders will refer to questions that can be resolved *locally*; that is to say, that do not require the attention of *top executives*. In the same way that the use of *decentralization* in relation to public policy serves to reinforce the notion of *center*, the emphasis on *local*, portrayed as a smaller folksy version of a whole, duly serves to support the hierarchical segregation of imaginary spaces and powers: the *local*; the *regional*; the *national*; and the *global*. However all of these are not different *places*. They are all the *same place* or, rather, they are ways in which the same *place* has become distorted, segregated, and through which exclusion is reified (Bauman 1998). *Place* and *local* have subtly different meanings, and in Portuguese the word *lugar* is very much linked to social occupation; as in, "the place I call home."

A *Social Construction*

This definition of *place* that emerges from the discussion offers an important alternative perspective for social intervention. It refers to the notion of a collectivity that is possible; of a space and time rooted physically, where the fight for inclusion takes *place* within the conflicts of system and life-world (Habermas,

Table 6.2. Illustrations of the *Place*

- The territorial nature of effective action is also an important element to be taken into consideration. It is fundamental to recognize territoriality in relation to the scope of action. Territoriality is not a synonym for state or municipality, and is frequently related to intermediate spaces such as inter-municipal regions or intra-municipal districts. Territoriality also emerges as an important element for identity: part of the *place* and its historical and cultural roots.
- The path to inter-sectorial working seems to lie in a territorial focus, bringing various elements together in a context where social control is possible. The *place* is thus essential to action, be it sub-municipal, municipal or supra-municipal. The creation of enlarged public spheres where emancipation and empowerment can lead to confrontation and connection between services appears a positive course to follow. There are a large number of actions happening in a bottom-up manner, through which people are managing to develop productive activities. Unfortunately there is a lack of attitudes and actions in the top-down direction; actions that could clear obstacles that reproduce, when not produce, inequality and social exclusion. It was noted that many initiatives do not reach the people who are in the most precarious settings. Again there is the risk of reproducing discrimination and exclusion in the very actions intended to reduce poverty.
- There was consensus about conceiving the local space as a *place*, not translatable as any specific government level, but seen as where the logic of proximity, of encounter and of confrontation becomes possible. The *place* is not given, but is defined and redefined through actions that are themselves linked to a wider context of relations. It is a stimulus for ethical and civic practices on behalf of public agents and also for the development of forms of evaluation that help debate and produce knowledge.
- The different local and sub-national arrangements that are being formed are diverse in nature. They can involve state, municipal and regional organizations, or local agencies of national government, alliances with non-governmental and community organizations, companies and co-operatives, and a large variety of civil institutions and organizations, amongst which the Catholic Church continues to demonstrate a specific and exemplary competence. All have much to contribute and can point to possible courses of action that arise out of simple and concrete solutions. However, it is necessary to reiterate that these cannot be considered as substitutes for a much larger area of responsibility in which the national government's role is central.
- The local arena, as a *place*, is the starting point in the process of confronting poverty and must be given greater priority. The construction of different methods to independently identify and evaluate innovative practices and potential solutions is a service that society needs. Brazil lacks the tradition of the effective evaluation of public policies by governments' own agencies. Information on the heterogeneity of poverty and inequality, as well as on the results and impacts of actions (both positive and negative) is essential to avoid the phenomenon loosing its socio-political shape and becoming a question of individual "misfortune." The creation of indicators for evaluation and of an independent base of socially adequate statistics is extremely important at this moment.
- Lack of income is not synonymous with poverty, but it is an important factor to be considered, calling attention to the consequences of those socio-economic relations that constitute everyday life. However, actions in this area must recognize the importance of political emancipation and the involvement of local players in the discussion of the development of their *place*. Such actions must be initiated from solid, simple and participatory bases that focus concrete and sustainable results.
- The range of actions currently emerging does, without doubt, reposition the role of the state, but does not reduce its central role in combating poverty seen within the framework of exclusion and social inequality. The solutions being developed by the multiple organizations of civil society do point to a wider social responsibility and civic involvement, but they do not, in any way, release public organizations from their obligations to create and sustain equally responsible and committed programs of action.

1984). According to this view, the *moral commonwealth* is in constant negotiation (Selznick, 1992). The concept of *place* brings an added dimension to the grounded and multiple connections between people, institutions, and processes. It adds to the organizational and social practices that form a matrix of links and relationships through which meaning is constantly being produced and negotiated (Hacking 1999). The *place* is an arena of collaboration and solidarity; but it also represents the contradiction and conflict present in social action (Long, 2001).

Linking Psychology and Sociology

Place as a starting point for psychosocial inquiry helps to rebuild many earlier links between psychology and sociology, as for example in Weber's classical discussion of social process and social action. Social processes exist in the social actions of everyday life; friendship is located in the hand shaken on the street corner; solidarity is located in the information shared about opportunities for work.

Environmental Psychology

A move toward the *place* was made in the early days of what would later be called environmental psychology (Craik, 1970). Barker and Wright's work (Barker & Wright, 1955) leading to the concept of *behavior setting*, was fundamental in influencing Goffman's elaboration of *regions* for presenting the self in everyday life (Goffman, 1959). *Place* however, has a certain advantages over behavior setting. It provides more elasticity that enables very different disciplines to share it as a concept. These disciplines range from geographers such as M. Santos (1985, 1996), through to social scientists working in urban studies. For example, the Marxist social theorist H. Lefebvre (1991) produced a milestone contribution to the discussion of *place*, through his systematic analysis of the social construction of space, and his refutation of the common assumption that space is a priori "empty." On the contrary he argued, all space is a social construction, a process of giving meaning that goes beyond mere physical spaces for behavior to occur.

The Place of Land

The concept of *place* is quite close to public space. Any space that we consider as in some way *ours* by *right*, is very much where civil society develops, and around which meaning is built both in terms of spaces and access (Habermas, 1989). Thus public space is the stage on which the drama of communal life is played (Carr, Francis, Rivlin, & Stone, 1992). In Latin America, the single most common cause of all major internal civil wars, revolutions, and military coups, has been and continues to be, in one way or another, land. In many parts of the region, the decision to assume representative leadership on behalf of rural workers

continues to invite constant threats on the person's life, and the same can apply to
the progressive political leadership of rural municipalities, and rural states.

The Place in Organizational Life

In relation to *place*, a business firm is nothing more or less than a contract
between representatives of the State and a set of named others through which the
others may, with limited responsibility, govern a privatized space; a *place* of work.
In doing so, they determine rules and regulations that can considerably restrict
what are taken for granted as collective citizen rights of association and opinion
(Jepperson & Meyer, 1991).

The Place in People's Organizations

Consider in contrast, the many people's organizations and the many practical
everyday responses to living and doing; often referred to – again unfortunately
because how can anything not have form – as informal. In Latin America some
60% at least of all work happens within such arrangements. These, as with the
so-called "formal" arrangements, invoke a whole variety of relationships. Those
relationships range from the instrumental and manipulative, to the substantive and
co-operative. Informal organizations, too, have their bases of legitimacy. These
are derived from family, neighborhood, wider actions of solidarity or, simply,
from survival. However, in many cases, these other arrangements enter into direct
conflict with the state, and their *informality* may become a signal for repression, for
example through fines and taxes, or even through direct violence. Yet why should
those whose shop is nothing more than a trestle table on a street corner be denied
access to a public space that is also occupied – without charge – by advertising, by
privatized utilities, by cars and by the many other bits and pieces of urban life? Here
again, the use of *place* enables psychology to reconnect with the moral questions
of how life is to be lived. Far from being the voluntary occupation of emptiness,
the social construction of *space*, in *place*, is often a question of dispute between
privilege and mechanisms of exclusion. It is in the *place* that civil society grounds
its civic role (Keane, 1998). It is in the place where social capital is collectively
maintained (Putnam, 1993).

Latin American Social Psychology

Especially in its more critical forms of community and political psychology,
Latin American social psychology has moved toward the *place* through the social
framework of the neighborhood or the community group (Sánchez, Cronick, &
Weisenfeld this volume; Montero, 1994; Wiesenfeld & Sanchez, 1995). This is
particularly so amongst those who have drawn together ideas from critical social

psychology and from environmental psychology, and have used these to focus on questions of housing and self-construction (Wiesenfeld 2000, 2001).
Take, for example, Reid and Aguilar (1995), describing their work in Mexico:

> The communities to which the article refers are localities, both urban and rural, undergoing social transformation. The amplitude and extension of the process of urbanization tends to lead to a space oriented by heterogeneity in which forms of solidarity and social grouping are both ruptured and created. Here the original idea of community is transformed into a concept that refers to the collective links produced by psychosocial intervention. The resignification of everyday elements, the revaluing of traditional practices of the locality, just to refer to some parts, signals the emergence of something in common, which is not necessarily encountered explicitly. (p 214 – author's translation)

In an account of community psychology in Venezuela, and the important role being played by the Central University, Wiesenfeld, Sanchéz and Cronick (1995) stress the importance of the *place* seen as a space produced through dispute. Here, the importance of a collective effort (to guarantee and construct paved roads, school buildings, electrification, and health services) is just as much psychology as is the development of counseling services. These are changes that are intimately linked to the everyday construction of the social and civic moral orders. Amongst the examples cited by Wiesenfeld et al. are the technological integration of cement with other, more traditional methods of housing construction, such as clay and organic matter.

> This technology permitted the rural workers, living in precarious conditions, to make their houses immune from insects and parasites and introduce esthetic changes in their environment, which in turn had favorable effects in the community. The project was developed within an overall health program which involved the self-construction of houses using designs that the community developed and the management of a collective loan for the purchase of materials. (p. 259 – author's translation)

A New Role for Channel Theory

A switch to the *place* implies a return to the molar psychology of the everyday, to the intersection of social process and social action. It is in the *place* that the actions that form the processes of social inequality and exclusion can be found. These are practices that could have been different but which, in continuing to be the same, are the constitutive elements of the production of poverty. Take for example the question of documents and forms. It is only necessary to join the queue at the local social security office or similar agency to understand first-hand what it means to wait for hours standing with a small child, only to find that you have brought the wrong document, or completed the form wrongly, and that the person who can speak your language, or understand your problem, is on a coffee break. Queuing in many Latin American countries is far from being the social symbol of equality that some see as marking Anglo-Saxon culture. On the contrary, it is the very opposite. Banks, public agencies, and many different bodies have queues for those that "don't have," and special routes for those that "have."

A Model

An early attempt in psychology to discuss how such patterns of everyday events are built up is Channel Theory (Lewin 1952). Lewin and the Child Welfare Research Station staff at the State University of Iowa had been posed the very appropriate, war-time, question of understanding why people eat what they eat. In his reply, Lewin began by turning the problem around. In most households, he argued, once food is on the table, most – if not all of it – will be eaten. Consequently, the answer to the question why people eat what they eat lies in another question: "How does food come to the table?" Thus, Lewin went on to examine the complex event of *food on the table* by discussing the variety of channels along which potential ingredients flow and pointing to the crucial role of the gatekeepers that open and close the many options that are present.

Social Channels

Food can get on the table because it is produced at home it or it may be bought at a grocery store. There are a variety of ways in which food can be stored, all of which are dependent on other actions, practices and, in some cases access to equipment and services. Food does not move by itself. Somebody buys it, or gathers it, and somebody prepares it. Financial and cultural factors play important parts in determining which gates open and close. As Lewin commented, the cultural availability of food is a very different arena to that of the stock of potentially edible materials. For example, he found that in some parts of the country, peanuts and cottage cheese were considered food for animals, and that nobody would think of eating grasshoppers. Food for children may be different from food for adults, and what the poor should eat different from that the rich should eat. All of these, in turn, will influence what is available, who buys it and makes it, what is grown, and what is offered in what form, and at what price.

Socio-economic Channels

This is precisely the same process that confronts those who work, for example, with microcredit. The question here is not food on the table, but credit for economic activities. What is credit? Who is allowed to have it? And in what circumstances can they have it? The microcredit revolution sparked by the Grameen Bank has shown how with collective action and sums as little as US$ 5, gates can be opened and access to markets achieved (Yunus, 2000). In broader terms, that issue is the backbone that underlies this chapter. How do services get to people and how do people get to services? How are rights exercised, and how are they denied? In Lewinian terms, these questions translate as: "How do we identify the channels along which the construction of citizenship and dignity as social processes flow, along which services are provided and accessed?"; "How do we understand and identify the gatekeepers, and how and where do we intervene?" These are all concepts of *place.*

Educational Channels

Take the example of children in school. The event that can be called "children in school" involves at least two different channels of activities: (1) Getting education and schools to children; and (2) getting children to education and schools. In each channel, there are multiple interfaces and obstacles; different patterns of social meanings; common sense that isn't common sense; and multiple prejudices that are in play. But they are all identifiable through the psychology of the everyday, through a psychology that takes the *place* seriously as a starting point. Thus the channel that takes education to children involves activities such as building schools, training teachers, organizing the school curriculum, and supplying material, books and school meals. The channel that takes the children to education is built up of laws, transportation services, incentives, and approaches.

Examples from Schools

One such approach began life in the 1930s in rural France and is currently being applied with considerable success by progressive mayors and agricultural workers' community organizations in various parts of Brazil. It involves providing intensive residential school study in alternating two- or three-week periods for rural children. This enables the children to move comfortably between school and the farm within a pedagogical framework that values agricultural activities and community values, rather than devaluing them in favor of a dominant urban discourse. Another very effective idea was developed during the progressive government of the economist and social development theorist, C. Buarque in the Federal District of Brasília. This has since been exported to various Latin American countries, as well as to part of Africa. A school grant (*bolsa escola*) of an equivalent value to a minimum salary (US$ 70 a month) is offered to very low-income families with school-age children. These children would normally be sent on to the streets to raise money by begging, or placed within the informal labor market. The rules are simple, "children in school" and "no skipping classes." The monthly grant is handed over to the children's mother, through a special bank account accessed by a magnetic card – itself a major social intervention in gender politics. The costs of the program are considerably less than would be the social costs, over the long term, of thousands of illiterate and unschooled adults, for example on trajectories toward living by crime. But getting the children into school is only the start of the solution. What kind of schooling will they find? Will it too be accessible? Again channel theory can help to build up in a step-by-step manner a view of the many doors that are present in the subtle processes whereby exclusion is produced and reproduced.

Examples from Health

Take, for example, HIV/Aids. For life to be lived with dignity and citizenship by those who are affected by HIV/Aids, it is important to build up the multiple channels of activity to improve public policies in the health delivery field, and to maintain test equipment, medicines, and support services for those who might need them. Yet it is also important to get people to the services. As those involved in educational programs have commented, the most elegant school buildings are useless if there are no children. During the initial period of the HIV/Aids epidemic in Brazil, the principle groups at risk were relatively clearly bounded, and so the second of the channels – even though complex – was less difficult. The problems were with the first channel. Here, the work of the NGOs, many of which were also HIV/Aids support groups, was essential. It meant seeking out ways of mobilizing resources, and pressurizing governments to adopt policies and set-up services. Today in Brazil, the pattern has changed, and the boundaries are considerably more blurred. The epidemic is moving out from the main urban centers, and crossing different "at-risk" populations. It is becoming ever present as a further addition to the range of problems being faced by communities in situations of poverty and social exclusion. The challenge is now placed more within the second channel, and the enormous difficulties of practical prevention in settings of heterogeneity, poverty, and exclusion. It is one thing for health workers to advocate the importance of prenatal attention to avoid vertical transmission. It is something else for pregnant women to find and get to a prenatal care center.

Conclusion

Lewin's channel theory provides an important analytical instrument for think-ing about and acting upon the complex chains of activity that are present in everyday events by which inequality, exclusion, and poverty are produced and reproduced. Channel theory offers a different starting point, for a non-reductionist psychology committed both morally and practically, to the *place*. This means a commitment to the mid-range horizons of action possibilities. It is in the practice of the *place*,

as our many different examples have illustrated, that theory-as-knowledge is to be found. It is in the politics of the *place* that an action-research approach to poverty is both possible and urgently required.

References

Alinsky, S. D. (1965). The war on poverty: Political pornography. *The Journal of Social Issues, 21*, 1, 41–48.

Barker, R. G., & Wright, H. F. (1955). *Midwest and its children.* Evanston, IL: Row Peterson.

Bauman, Z. (1998). *Globalization: The Human Consequences.* Cambridge: Polity Press.

Buarque, C. (1994). *A revolução nas prioridades: Da modernização técnica à modernidade ética.* São Paulo: Paz e Terra.

Camarotti, I., & Spink, P. (2000a). *Estratégias locais para redução da pobreza: Construindo a cidadania.* São Paolo: Escola de Administração de Empresas da Fundação Getulio Vargas.

Camarotti, I., & Spink, P. (Eds.). (2000b). *Parcerias e pobreza: Soluções locais na implantação de políticas sociais.* Rio de Janeiro: Editora da Fundação Getulio Vargas.

Camarotti, I., & Spink, P. (Eds.). (2000c). *Parcerias e Pobreza: soluções locais na construção de relações sócio-econômicas.* Rio de Janeiro: Editora da Fundação Getulio Vargas.

Camarotti, I., & Spink, P. (Eds). (2001). *Redução da pobreza e dinâmicas locais.* Rio de Janeiro: Editora da Fundação Getulio Vargas.

Carr, S. Francis, M. Rivlin, L. G., & Stone, A. M. (1992). *Public space.* New York, NY: Cambridge University Press.

Castel, R. (1995). Y a-t-il des exclus? L'éxclusion en débate. *Lien Social et Politiques – RIAC, 34*, Paris, Montreal, Autumn. In L. Bógus, M. C. Yazbeck, & M. Belfiore-Wanderley (Eds.). (1997). *Desigualdade e a questão social* (pp. 15–48). São Paolo: EDUC.

Craik, K. (1970). Environmental psychology. *New Directions in Psychology, 4.* New York, NY: Holt, Rinehart & Winston.

Farr, R. M. (1996). *The roots of modern social psychology.* Oxford: Blackwell.

Friedmann, J. (1992). *Empowerment: The politics of alternative development.* Oxford: Blackwell.

Garfinkel, H. (1976). *Studies in ethnomethodology.* New York, NY: Prentice Hall.

Gergen K. J. (1994). *Realities and relationships: Soundings in social construction.* Cambridge, MA: Harvard University Press.

Goffman, E. (1959). *The presentation of self in everyday life.* New York, NY: Doubleday.

Habermas, J. (1984). *The theory of communicative action.* Boston, MA: Beacon Press.

Habermas, J. (1989). *The structural transformations of the public sphere.* Cambridge, MA: MIT Press.

Hacking, I. (1999). *The social construction of what?* Cambridge, MA: Harvard University Press.

Harré, R. (1998). *The singular self: An introduction to the psychology of personhood.* Thousand Oaks, CA: Sage.

Horwitt, S. D. (1989). *Let them call me rebel: Saul Alinsky, his life and legacy.* New York, NY: Alfred A. Knopf.

Ibáñez, T., & Íñiguez, L. (Eds.). (1997). *Critical social psychology.* London: Sage.

Ibañez, T. (2001). *Municiones para disidentes: Realidad – verdad – política.* Barcelona: Editorial Gedisa.

Jepperson, R. L., & Meyer, J. W. (1991). The public order and the construction of formal organizations. In W. W. Powell & P. J. DiMaggio (Eds.), *The new institutionalism in organizational analysis* (pp. 204–231). Chicago, IL: Chicago University Press.

Keane, J. (1998). *Civil society: Old images, new visions.* Cambridge: Polity Press.

Lane, S. T. M., & Codo, W. (Eds.). (1985). *Psicologia social: O homem em movimento.* São Paulo: Brasiliense.

Latouche, S. (1992). Standard of living. In W. Sachs (Ed.), *The development dictionary* (pp. 250–263). London: Zed Books.

Latouche, S. (1996). *The Westernization of the world.* Cambridge: Polity Press.

Lefebvre, H. (1991). *The production of space.* Oxford : Blackwell.

Lenoir, R. (1974). *Les exclus.* Paris: Seuil.

Lewin, K. (1952). *Field Theory in social science.* London: Tavistock Publications.

Long, N. (2001). *Development sociology: Actor perspectives.* London: Routledge.

Marshall, T. H. (1950). *Citizenship and social class and other essays.* Cambridge: London University Press.

Martín-Baró, I. (1983). *Acción y ideología: Psicología social desde Centro América.* El Salvador: UCA Editores.

Melo, M. (1999). *Consultations with the poor. Brazil National Synthesis Report.* Washington, DC: World Bank Poverty Reduction and Economic Management Network.

Montero, M. (Ed.). (1987). *Psicología política latinoamericana.* Caracas: Editorial Panapo.

Montero, M. (Ed.). (1994). *Psicología social comunitaria.* Guadalajara: Universidade de Guadalajara.

Murilo de Carvalho, J. (2001). *Cidadania no Brasil: O longo caminho.* Rio de Janeiro: Civilização Brasileira.

Narayan, D., Chambers, R., Shah, M., & Petesch, P. (1999). *Global synthesis: Consultations with the poor.* Washington, DC: Poverty Group, World Bank.

Putnam, R. D. (1993). *Making democracy work: Civic traditions in modern Italy.* Princeton: Princeton University Press.

Reid, A., & Aguilar, M. A. (1995). Mexico: La construcción de una psicologia social comunitaria. In E. Wiesenfeld & E. Sanchez. (Eds.), *Psicologia social comunitaria: Contribuciones latinoamericanas* (pp. 189–218). Caracas: Fondo Editorial Tropykos.

Rodman, M. (1993). Beyond built form and culture in the anthropological study of residential community spaces. In R. Rotenberg & G. McDonogh (Eds.), *The cultural meaning of urban space* (pp. 123–138). Westport, CT: Bergin & Garvey

Rose, N. (1998). *Inventing our selves: Psychology, Power and Personhood.* Cambridge: Cambridge University Press.

Sachs, W. (Ed). (1992). *The development dictionary.* London: Zed Books.

Sampson, E. E. (1989). The deconstruction of self. In J. Shotter & J. Gergen, (Eds.), *Texts of identity* (pp. 1–19). London: Sage.

Santos, M. (1985). *Espaço e método.* São Paulo: Nobel.

Santos, M. (1996). *A natureza do espaço.* São Paulo: Hucitec.

Selznick, P. (1992). *The moral commonwealth: Social theory and the promise of community.* Berkeley, CA: University of California Press.

Sen, A. (1992). *Inequality reexamined.* Cambridge, MA: Harvard University Press.

Sen, A. (1999). *Development as freedom.* Oxford: Oxford University Press.

Shotter, J. (1993). *Cultural politics of everyday life.* Buckingham: Open University Press.

Spink, M. J. (Ed.). (2000). *Práticas discursivas e produções de sentidos no cotidiano.* São Paulo: Cortez.

Spink, P. K. (2000). The rights approach to local public management: Experiences from Brasil. *Revista de Administração de Empresas, 40,* 3, 45–65.

Sweden, Ministry for Foreign Affairs. (1998). *A human rights message.* Stockholm: The Swedish Institute.

Wiesenfeld, E. (2000). Praticas sociales y politicas publicas: Aportes de la psicologia social a la problematica residencial. *Psicologia e Sociedade, 12,* 1–2, 194–220.

Wiesenfeld, E. (2001). *La autoconstrucción: Um estudio psicosocial del significado de la vivienda.* Caracas: Universidad Central de Venezuela.

Wiesenfeld, E., & Sanchez, E. (Co-ord.). (1995). *Psicologia social comunitária: Contribuciones latinoamericanas.* Caracas: Fondo Editorial Tropykos.

Wiesenfeld, E., Sanchez, E., & Cronick, K. (1995). La psicologia social comunitaria en Venezuela. In E. Wiesenfel & E. Sanchez (Co-ord.). *Psicologia social comunitária: Contribuciones latinoamericanas.* Caracas: Fondo Editorial Tropykos.

Yunus, M. (2000). *O banqueiro dos pobres.* São Paulo: Editora Ática.

Part II

Empowerment

Chapter 7

Poverty and Community

Euclides Sánchez, Karen Cronick, and Esther Wiesenfeld

This chapter defines a position vis-à-vis poverty from the standpoint of Community Social Psychology (CSP). It first reviews some conceptions of poverty and then briefly describes the emergence of CSP in Latin America. This provides a context for the chapter, as well as theoretical and methodological foundations for studying poverty. To illustrate those foundations, we detail two case examples. These are a housing loan purchase program and the creation of a power and water system. Based on these cases, and a CSP analysis of them, the chapter concludes by synthesizing a range of social psychological suggestions for reducing poverty.

Psychology and Poverty

Psychology

In the social sciences, poverty has been associated more with sociology than with psychology. This is so because sociology has traditionally dealt with issues of collective concern, whereas psychology, in general, has been more oriented towards dealing with individual behavior, cognition, and emotion. However, social psychology, and more recently CSP, has addressed topics such as migration, exclusion, racial and gender discrimination, unemployment, and homelessness. Community psychology took up the cause of poverty in the late 1960s by stressing the importance of the ecology of a person-environment interaction, particularly in economically deprived sectors of society. This reorientation began with the recognition by clinical psychologists of the importance of community environment in

123

the prevention and cure of psychological disorders. In that context, poverty was seen as an important condition that affected the community at large.

Poverty

Poverty burdens the lives of most people on Earth. Some data that illustrate this affirmation are the following: 800 million people suffer from malnutrition and 4 billion live in poverty; the wealth of the 225 richest individuals in the world is equal to the income of the poorest 47% of the world's population. This means that 225 people earn the same as 2.5 billion others. As regards Latin America, Boltvinik (1995) estimated that in the year 2000, 44% of the population would live under the poverty line, and that projection coincides with data provided by the Executive Secretary of the Economic Commission for Latin America (ECLA). According to ECLA, this 44% figure represents 211 million people who lived in poverty at the end of the 1990s, while 18.5% (89 million) lived under conditions of extreme poverty. This last percentage constitutes an increase of 7.8% (0.6 million people) when compared with 1997 data.

Meanings of Poverty

The attempt to understand poverty, given its complexity, has included the analysis of related concepts such as wealth, inequality, social justice, cultural poverty, and social exclusion.

Poverty and Wealth

Poverty and wealth can be conceived as the opposite ends of a continuum, depending on the absence or presence of well-being, quality of life, exchange, accumulation of capital, and access to goods and services. Poverty is related to the insufficiency of these commodities (Sen, this volume). In general, the wealth or poverty of a given group or nation is determined statistically in terms of some measure of central tendency. However, these measures may be misleading. As Andrew Lang once said, statistics can be used the way a drunken man uses lampposts, for support rather than illumination (Furman University Mathematical Quotation Server). It is important for analysts to examine the complete distribution of economic data before employing a given measure, such as average figures. Even the richest country in the world by average standards has large pockets of poverty that are not apparent in many central tendency measures. As Derber (2000, p. 12) said,

With the 1990s came the revelation that the USA had become the most unequal country in the developed world – with the gap between rich and poor growing disturbingly
vast. By the mid-1990s, not only was the gap the largest in 50 years, but also as the
United Nations reported, "the USA is slipping into a category of countries – among
them Brazil, Britain, and Guatemala – where the gap between rich and poor is the
worst around the globe."

Even these observations may be misleading. For a country in which the "gap"
between the rich and the poor is relatively small, but where monetary incomes are
very low or almost nonexistent, the gap will seem very small. It may be that the
poor in the country with the large gap are better off than those in the one where it is
small. Thus, the wealthy of the world are concentrated in Europe and the USA, but
as Fernie (2000) has pointed out, the income of 358 of the world's richest people
is equal to that of 2.3 billion other people on earth. The incomes of these very,
very rich people will increase the central tendency measures and the "gap" in most
statistical measures.

Hence it is necessary to distinguish between "relative poverty," in the sense
of Runciman (1966), and "absolute poverty." Absolute measures of the difference
between well-being and poverty are aimed at determining the precise cut-off point
that defines the difference between "the poor" and the "non-poor." For some authors (Sen, 1978, in Altimir, 1992), there is a "core" of absolute poverty, in which
destitution, malnutrition, and hardship are present in tangible form. Relative measures, on the other hand, suggest that poverty is at least in part a state of mind. That
is, people are poor if they feel themselves to be so in relation to some sort of standard. Thus, the urban poor in New York may be better off than refugees in Uganda,
but because they compare themselves to the relatively affluent lower-middle class
in the USA; that is, their access to resources is so limited that they find themselves
excluded from the way of life enjoyed by those around them (Townsend, 1979).

Rawls (1999) suggests that the least advantaged sectors of a social group
might be those who must live with less than the median income of that group. This
is a relative measure of wealth and poverty because the median changes in each
population that is surveyed. This designation falls apart, however, when almost all
its members are destitute because the statistical range is reduced. Thus, whichever
way we turn, it is difficult to avoid defining poverty by reference to a social point
of view.

Poverty and Inequality

Integral to that social point of view is inequity. Poverty and inequality are
also two separate notions. In this distinction, poverty is often interpreted as a state
that should inspire the compassion or charity of the more advantaged members,
and not as a structural characteristic of society. Inequality on the other hand,

though related to poverty, is a structural concept that refers to the injustice of class, economic, gender, race, and other differences. It has been considered such an important dimension that it presently seems to be one of the main reasons for worldwide instability (Bessis, 1995).

When conceived as a structural characteristic like this, poverty has been explained by diverse theoretical rationales (Rawls, Keynes, Friedman, and Marx). How one conceives the macroeconomic structure will determine how one explains poverty, and what one is prepared to do about it. Different theories give birth to different economic strategies for producing given economic change. Thus, the tactics employed, such as tax rebates, the imposition (or removal) of customs duties, or foreign-debt payments, the granting of tenure in squatter neighborhoods, urban renewal, the establishment of institutions such as the World Bank or agencies such as UNICEF, and the development of welfare benefits, represent different ideas about how poverty happens, and what can be done about it. "Welfare" supposes the development of a "safety net," which places a limit on how much "want" a society will tolerate. The same concept also supposes an obligation on the part of the more economically able to support those "in need." Overall therefore, how we socially construct inequity determines what we will try to do about it.

Poverty and Social Justice

The whole idea of social inequity is related to the concept of social justice. This is conceived as more than just the need for economic equality. It involves more than a duty of compassion on the part of those who are "better off." There must be some consideration of the economic and social "rights" that human beings have. The idea of universal rights was developed in the USA in the first 10 amendments to its Constitution, and in the Universal Declaration of Human Rights after the French Revolution. On December 10, 1948, the concept of such rights was formalized in an international agreement at the United Nations. This began with recognition of all people's legitimate and lawful claim to life, liberty, and security. Other rights have been elaborated since then, in various national constitutions and international agreements. These include the satisfaction of basic material needs such as adequate nourishment, access to dignified working conditions, health care, decent shelter, and the reduction of avoidable, premature mortality. We might add to these rights those of culturally appropriate education and literacy, safe and sustainable neighborhoods, and environments, the possibility of having a satisfying family life, using one's own language, and participating in the culture and the political structure of an own social group.

This elaboration of rights may seem to have branched off from our initial discussion of poverty. However, severe poverty and destitution impose disempowerment and disenfranchisement on the economically disadvantaged in terms of their possible social and political participation in their culture. This is so because lack of respect for their basic rights frustrates people's ability to solve their problems through reflection and common deliberation. In the publication entitled *Social Reform and Poverty*, (BID & PNUD, 1993) it is pointed out that both low income and lack of satisfaction of basic needs are related to individuals' and families' exclusion from the complex of productive processes, social integration, and access to opportunities. Hence, "universal" human rights also become *relative* in underprivileged conditions.

Poverty and Culture

Poverty is often measured in terms "economic" and "material," but there are always cultural overtones to these labels. For example, the more affluent sectors of the economy believe the poor are in this condition because their lack of skills, knowledge, competence, or lack of talents, condemn them to penury. In short, they are supposed to belong to a "culture of poverty" (Lewis, 1979). Central to this perceived culture of poverty are "social exclusion," and "lack of social adaptation" (Amorós & Ayerbe, 2000). Thus, "culture" works against a group of people because their values, beliefs and practices, isolate them from the possibility of economic advancement or development. Children grow up socialized to live in poverty. The old idea of "achievement motivation" in psychology is related to this position. It was felt that achievement is a Western value, related to a competitive approach toward life that can be taught. According to this view, achievement motivation is at odds with tradition, family-centered values of affiliation, and hierarchic power relations. People from traditional cultures could not "develop" because they spent their time in interpersonal interchange rather than goal-oriented activities.

Valentine (1991) describes two other ways of portraying poverty and culture.

Beliefs about Control. One is that the poor suffer from external oppression, and an imposed value system. An important point to consider here is power relationships. Among the theoretical orientations used in psychology to explain this relationship, we can mention Seligman's (1975) *learned helplessness* theory. In this, people learn that they do not have the means to control what happens to them, and so stop trying to do so. In the relationship between culture and poverty, this would mean that the poor become "conditioned" to the fact that they cannot change their plight. They accept a "helpless" posture vis-à-vis their capacity for producing change.

The Roles of Adaptiveness. The second of Valentine's (1991) models describes cultures as heterogeneous and adaptive. In this sense, cultural elements that have been developed to make poverty more endurable function also to perpetuate it. For example, poor children drop out of school in order to "help out" in the family. These children then beg or work at menial jobs, and never return to school, thus increasing the ranks of the underskilled. From a community psychology point of view however, these local cultural values are taken as important resources for producing change. The solidarity shown by these children could therefore be harnessed for other purposes.

Poverty and Social Exclusion

Poverty contributes to exclusion in a number of ways, for example by exclusion from work and production and by exclusion from opportunity (BID & PNUD, 1993; Spink, this volume). Nonetheless, in a number of countries the poor remain incorporated into networks of social protection and mutual assistance. This fosters integration not exclusion. The disruption of these solidarity networks is an important factor pushing individuals below the poverty line. This is the case in the USA, and in a number of Latin American countries where single-parent families headed by women are among the poorest. Similarly, discrimination based on gender or membership in a minority group increases the risk of destitution (Bessis, 1995).

Summary

The ideas expressed above illustrate the fact that poverty cannot be conceived as an absolute, defined exclusively by objective indicators such as income, consumption, and/or access to goods and services. Rather, poverty is a relative phenomenon. This relativity springs from its variability in terms of the context, the time, and the circumstances in which it occurs; its plurality, harboring multiple interpretations, some of which are mutually inconsistent; its complexity, since it includes psychological, social, cultural, political, economic, and legal dimensions at the local, regional, and global levels; and its multisectoriality, since a variety of actors participate in the work of understanding and addressing it.

The interaction of this diverse set of aspects renders poverty into a social construction. As such, understandings of, and responses to, poverty will be influenced by the different versions elaborated by different agents. Each of these represents one facet that, in the course of interaction and confrontation with the others, engenders more relevant and heuristic approaches than any of the partial versions offered by any single sector. Thus, one size does not fit all. As España (2001, p. 8) points out, "... strategies for overcoming poverty in Malaysia should be different from those used in Vanuatu or Venezuela."

Nonetheless, solutions to the problem are frequently limited to macropolitical policies that originate with transnational agencies or government offices. Without disparaging the importance of those measures and even from within the relativistic, multidimensional, complex, and multisectorial conception of poverty, the joint efforts of the experts in all disciplines cannot succeed in putting those actions into effect unless they incorporate the knowledge, experience, needs, feelings, expectations, resources, and proposals, of the main players, the poor themselves. Their perspectives have generally been ignored in formulating conceptions of poverty, and actions to address it. Their initiatives, efforts, and strategies to improve their living conditions, have likewise been ignored. This omission reveals a skew toward the conceptualization of poverty as a deficit, ruling out the contribution poor people could make on the basis of the resources, capacities, and potential they develop in their own struggle against poverty.

Along these lines, we believe that poverty must be approached collectively. However, we also believe that this collective response must include the poor. Such an approach will ensure the incorporation of their points of view. Hence, the definition of poverty will reflect the multiple versions of its nature. It is from this standpoint that CSP, with given its characteristics, objectives, and theoretical and methodological grounding, makes a particular contribution to the problem of poverty.

Community Social Psychology (CSP)

The Origin of Community Social Psychology (CSP)

CSP is one of the few fields of psychology to have emerged and taken shape on the basis of a commitment to the transformation of living conditions for the poor, within a community context. It is also one of the few fields of psychology that has generated any theoretical and methodological production of its own in Latin America. This is mainly because those productions are closely linked to the region's particular characteristics and requirements. Unlike other areas of psychology and other social sciences, in which theories, methods, and models are applied regardless of context, CSP recognizes context as a relevant dimension whose particularities are not unrelated to the experiences that take place therein. Its origins go back to the late 1970s, when some Latin American social psychologists who rejected experimental social psychology as a way to approach social problems began to participate in communities, mainly low-income urban ones, on the basis of a new epistemological and methodological paradigm.

The Foundations of Community Social Psychology

At the outset CSP drew on the contributions of such disciplines as philosophy, social planning, and sociology, as well as psychology itself. In the latter case, it focused on behavioral base theories and attribution theories (Montero, 1983; Serrano-García, López & Rivera Medina, 1987). But the contributions which most strongly influenced CSP's own evolution came from popular education, and especially ideas on the processes of problematization and consciousness raising introduced by Paulo Freire and militant sociology. These included Orlando Fals Borda's proposal for Action Research (AR). More recently, this has been complemented and enriched by qualitative research concepts, and from the theoretical viewpoint by such approaches as social constructionism and critical theory (Wiesenfeld, 1994).

Consciousness-raising and Problematization. It was Freire (1972, 1976) who, based on his educational experience with illiterate populations, developed these two closely intertwined ideas. Freire defined consciousness-raising as the transformation of the naïve or transitive consciousness, characterized "... by simplicity in the interpretation of problem" (Freire, 1976, p. 54). Consciousness-raising travels from a pessimistic view of their solution, into a critical consciousness (critical transitivity) which is "... oriented toward social and political responsibility [and] is characterized by a profound interpretation of problems" (Freire, 1976, p. 55, parenthesis added). The latter is a consciousness that fosters in the subject the responsibility to participate in the transformation of situations.

Transitive consciousness is expressed in language, and its transformation relies on language. It is pursued through a dialogue-based education between the educator and the person being educated, in which knowledge is not imposed on the subject, but is the outcome of their communication with the educator. In this respect, for Freire, dialogue has a deconstructive function (problematization). It fosters the development of an awareness of the self's social situation, and effective action thereon.

Action Research. Action research (AR) is a theoretical and methodological proposal for the production of knowledge and promotion of social change. It owes much of its development, in Latin America, to the extensive work of Orlando Fals Borda (1959, 1978). Since at least 1950, he has made highly important contributions to what he has termed AR. AR, or participatory action research (PAR), as Rahman (1989) prefers to call it, is according to his view, "... an action-oriented research which is participatory and a participatory research which is united to action" (p. 129). The aim of PAR is to foster the transformation of reality with the participation of the social actors involved in the research process. For Rahman, however, social transformation is not limited to possession of the means of material production that generate unjust structures. It extends also to possession of the means of production of knowledge, which can also provoke dependence in the subject of research – in this case, dependence on the researcher.

A more recent definition of AR is provided by Greenwood and Levin (2000). For them, AR is "... research in which the validity and value of the results obtained are tested and proven through the processes of cooperation, between researchers and research subjects for purposes of the production and application of knowledge in social change projects intended to increase equity, well-being, and self-determination" (p. 94). These authors agree with Rahman, that research and action are inseparable in AR; and that knowledge should be produced and action generated, in support of social change. In other words, AR is vindicated to the extent that it provides effective support for the participants' action.

Integration of theory and practice, according to Greenwood and Levin (2000), is ensured by three characteristics of AR:

1. It is co-generative. The professional researcher works with the local participants to define the local problems experienced by the latter, to collect and organize the information, to analyze it, and to design and implement the action to be taken in pursuit of social change. The professional researcher-participant relationship is thus one of mutual influence, in which both parties' perspectives on action are changed in the course of the research.
2. It links professional knowledge with popular knowledge. AR is grounded in the interaction of these two sets of knowledge. It recognizes the value of popular knowledge for understanding problems, and for designing a social change process.
3. It redefines the validity or credibility and confidence of the research. Its success stems from the parties' will to act on the findings, and the degree to which its products meet the expectations of the local participants.

Characteristics of CSP

The foundations of CSP discussed above give it a set of characteristics whose fulfillment is largely visible in practice:

- Its field of action is the community, understood as a structured social grouping based on the feeling of community, i.e., meeting the requirements of membership, mutual influence, integration, need satisfaction, and shared emotional bonds (McMillan & Chavis, 1986).
- The community's world is one in which its members are active in the production of the meanings that comprise it. CSP values these interactions as a source of understanding of the community's problems and management of the desired transformation.
- The production of meanings in the community is culturally and historically conditioned. The community's particular understanding of its world is impregnated with the cultural productions prevailing in its environment at a given time. But those understandings also change to reflect the new meanings produced by the community.
- It is participatory, being promoted by the community on the basis of a dialogue-based relationship with the researcher. It is based on a questioning of its interpretation of reality, and the consequences of the latter.

- It is open to the contribution of other interpretative perspectives, which may pave the way for new understandings of the community's world.
- It is transformative, because it pursues a change of the established order in conjunction with the community. This is a change undertaken to increase the community's degree of satisfaction and self-determination. In the words of Serrano García et al. (1987), it is a change of form, of values, and of structure.

Social Constructionism

Having characterized CSP, we can now go on to examine constructionism. This is a term we will use to refer to the proposals of Guba and Lincoln (1994), and Gergen (1999), stressing the role of social exchange in the construction of reality.

An Iterative Cycle

According to Guba and Lincoln (1994), constructionism can be viewed as a 3D paradigm structured on the basis of a relativistic ontology. Reality is not simple, but multiple and plural – because it is socially constructed. Hence, it reflects the diversity of points of view circulating in its context. The construction of reality springs from a foundation of transactional and subjective epistemology. In this, the researcher and the research subject interact in the production and negotiation of knowledge. The construction of reality springs also from a hermeneutic and dialectic methodology in which the point is to know the individual actors' interpretations or meanings. This works in an iterative cycle of analysis; critique; reiteration; and reanalysis, which leads to a joint construction or co-construction (Guba & Lincoln, 1994).

Gergen's Views

There is a certain similarity between the preceding statements and those made by Gergen (1999). Gergen is a major advocate of socio-constructionist psychology. In the first place, for Gergen, language is the medium for construction of reality. This language is not a function of the properties of reality, but of the group or communal interactions out of which texts are constructed. As well, by drawing their meaning from social relations, the media for describing or explaining reality are conditioned by the culture and history in which those relations take place. Constructionism poses the creation of new forms of language (oral, written), and new forms of interpretation (generative discourse is Gergen's term). These challenge traditional understanding, and suggest new forms of action. Finally, reflection on the forms of understanding reality is vital to the consideration of other understandings of people's well-being.

A Socio-constructionist Community Social Psychology

Based on Freire's ideas, CSP recognizes the role of language in effecting the construction of reality, its resignification or assignment of new meanings, and the actions required to transform it. These processes of deconstruction and reconstruction do not usually occur in the absence of community social psychologists. Rather, they occur inside the dialogue-based relations built up between them and the other members of the community. With AR or PAR, we stress that community social psychologists and the community advance together in a process of reflection, research, and change. This co-management relationship between the two parties, is present in socio-constructionism. This speaks of an epistemology of intersubjective transactions between researchers and participants, and a methodology oriented toward understanding and change in these constructions.

Overall therefore, we conclude that CSP can be defined as a CSP with a socio-constructionist base. This brings us close to what López Sánchez and Serrano Garcia (1995) mean, when they state that Berger and Luckman's theory of social construction of reality is one of the basic foundations of CSP in Puerto Rico. We can summarize all of this by saying that CSP is a psychological discipline that conceives reality in the community as an outcome of social construction processes. Relying on the perspectives of the community members, CSP co-manages with them the research, as well as critical reflection on the conditions that comprise that reality, and the production of knowledge aimed at achieving effective actions of social transformation.

Examples of Community Social Psychology

A Housing-purchase Loan Program

The first such example we wish to describe is an experience jointly promoted by an international organization and a government agency. This project was assisted by input from a range of professional disciplines. Advisers were included from architecture, economics, engineering, geography, sociology, and community social psychology. The overall aim was to implement a housing-purchase loan program for low-income families. Before funds could be disbursed, it was necessary to make sure these loans were appropriate for the residents of four pilot communities, located in four cities of Venezuela that were chosen for the program's opening phase. The fit between the program's requirements and the beneficiaries' characteristics would be determined by the results of a survey, previously designed and applied in other Latin American countries.

The principal requirements for receiving credit were: (1) to have a stable income equivalent to a specified multiple of the monthly minimum wage; (2) to have an ability to save; (3) to be the owner of the housing unit in which the applicant lived; and (4) to be competitive with other families in the low-income neighborhood in question.

Wiesenfeld, one of this chapter's authors, and other social psychologists, provided advice regarding the project's psychosocial and community dimensions. In disagreement with the methodology proposed by the international organization, and in accordance with certain principles of CSP, the team of psychologists proposed a methodological strategy not limited to collecting data (the survey). They recommended including the facilitation of problematizing processes, relating to the residential conditions then prevailing in the communities involved. A focus group technique was judged appropriate to this end. This is because it encourages group interaction and critical reflection by the participants. It also stimulates them to express multiple points of view on the issue under discussion, in this case the housing issue. Nonetheless, the focus group procedure was adopted only after it had been explained to the groups and they had chosen to accept it.

The focus group sessions were used to explore the meaning of housing for the participants as well as their criteria of habitability. They also served to specify the forms of occupation or acquisition of housing; the types of financing and saving to which the families resorted; their current housing conditions; the chances for the transformation thereof; and finally, the participants' expectations, possibilities, and constraints, for achievement of that transformation.

Six focus groups were organized in each city, each one with six to eight participants who represented the chosen communities and voluntarily agreed to participate when they were informed of the purpose. Participation in this group activity brought to light, among other things, a set of contradictions implicit in the international organization's criteria. For example, the family income and housing ownership requirements limited access to the program's benefits exclusively to families whose income was high enough to ensure repayment of the loans. It was limited to those having an ability to save from a stable salary that exceeded the multiple of the minimum wage deemed sufficient to enable repayment. This criterion also required ownership of the land on which the new housing units would be built.

Among the results of the focus group activities was the conclusion that no distinction should be made between owners and non-owners. Nor should there be any distinction among people with different levels of purchasing power and saving ability. The reason for this was that the appropriation of space – formally or informally – in many Venezuelan low-income neighborhoods, and prolonged residence in those neighborhoods, tends to generate feelings of appropriation vis-à-vis the location, and of attachment toward the neighbors. These feelings are valued and defended by the residents, and stimulate them to seek the legalization of their property.

As regards the family income criterion, the economic crisis, growing unemployment, instability of employment, and other problems generate mobility on the salary scale. This ranges from total absence of income for periods of time, to receipt of income during other periods. Regarding the competitiveness criterion, families were expected to compete with each other in terms of purchasing power and ability to save, in order to qualify for credit. The participants disliked this requirement, since communities pursue the satisfaction of their needs and goals collectively. In other words, this kind of community is characterized by a co-operative organization of actions, and by bonds of solidarity that guide those actions. These in fact bear no resemblance to the assumptions – such as competitiveness – which often orient official housing programs.

In a word, the results of the focus group activities revealed the differences between the program's criteria and the users' points of view. Hence, where the organization expected competitiveness, the prospective users proposed "...doing the work in conjunction with the local residents, encouraging each one of them with assistance." Where the organization demanded an ability to save at a bank, the prospective users conceived saving as "something that can't be done because there is no way to do it; one's entire salary goes to buy food, and when one has a little extra it goes for some emergency" (generally to treat a health problem). And as regards recovery of the investment, the alternatives for people were congruent with their precarious circumstances. In this regard, the prospective users were willing to repay the loan "by working and refraining from buying things," and at best, to self-manage in order not to go into debt, to buy materials in groups in order to lower their cost, to use natural materials or local resources (e.g., sand from the river), and to rely on the human resources present in the community (carpenters, electricians, masons, etc.), also with a view to cutting costs. Where the organization demanded land ownership, the users reported a history of illegal occupations and loans from relatives and friends (repaid over very long periods of time), as well as a gradual, step-by-step construction process that begins with a plot of land and a wood and zinc shack, which is then steadily improved until it turns into a substantial structure. They also reflected a different view of what property consists of. When a person buys land and a house, these become theirs, even if there are no property deeds. Fundamentally therefore, something belongs to a person because it has been paid for with money.

To sum up, the activity performed was an exercise that strengthened the participants as regards the importance the group attributes to intracommunity relations. It acknowledged the value of the users' points of view for the implementation of housing programs. It also shed light on an ethic of relations, the preservation of which was more important to the participants than improvement of their housing conditions: "What am I going to do with a good house, if I don't have my neighbors, who have laughed and cried with me, who have held my hand and I have held theirs?" This ethic orients community psychosocial processes, and helps reaffirm the psychosocial dimension of housing. As well, it provides a basis for questioning official programs and criteria that would otherwise have undermined the conceptions arising from people's own self-knowledge.

These recommendations created some issues for the representatives of the government agency and international organization. When confronted with these issues however, they engaged in a critical reflection on the need to incorporate a number of aspects into the housing policy framework. In this regard, the promotion of self-reflective and problematizing processes, as well as the incorporation of the poor people's points of view, made it possible to restructure the meanings that guided the design of the official programs. In that way, the process facilitated and optimized the program's implementation.

Creating a Power and Water System

The second illustrative case is based on the work of Bermúdez (2002). This consisted of an intervention in the El Caruto peasant community in central Venezuela. That community is comprised of over 200 inhabitants, with an average age of 27 years and a 70% illiteracy rate. About 20% are agricultural workers, who earn the rural minimum wage. This is equivalent to US$ 190 per month or less. The other 80% are self-sufficient farmers working small plots of land that they possess. The community has no potable water supply. Its members take water from a nearby river. Nor does it have electricity. Houses have *bahareque* (mud) walls, and are mostly in a poor condition. The intervention in question was intended to determine why the inhabitants had taken no collective action to satisfy their most serious needs, especially water supply and electricity. To this end the researcher – who is known in the area because of her religious preaching as a member of a missionary group – organized meetings with the population over several weekends. These inquired into the feasibility of doing a study on their conception of community participation (CP), and the conditions they believed might facilitate a community participation project.

Once the study's utility for the community had been agreed upon, she used a set of drawings to explain to the community members the principal concepts of qualitative research being proposed. In addition, agreement was reached on the possibility of involvement in the different stages of the research process. Since the researcher could only go to El Caruto on certain weekends, during which time the resident families often had occupations to carry out, this participation was limited to certain phases of the research. Those phases included description of the topic-problem to be addressed; selection of the data collection method; identification of the families to be interviewed; checking of the results thereof; analysis of the implications of those results for participation; and the drafting of a work plan.

The information was collected through semi-structured interviews with families in their homes. The interviews focused on the following topics: top-priority needs; ways to satisfy them; the meaning of community participation; community organization; leadership; experience in participation; organization and leadership of the community; and conditions that stimulate participation.

The results were analyzed by the researcher, according to qualitative data analysis procedures in Strauss and Corbin (1990). This yielded a preliminary version of analysis that was presented to the community for its consideration at a meeting. After the community made its own judgment (generally consistent with the conclusions presented), the final version of the analysis of the information was drawn up. Thereafter, at another meeting, the researcher proposed to examine the responses given by the community to each of the issues covered in the interviews. This examination was based on the following scheme: (1) a critical analysis of the constructions expressed on these issues, such as the meaning of need or participation, with a focus on these constructions' implications for pursuing or inhibiting change actions; (2) an analysis of discrepancies between the population's current situation and the social constructions identified in the interviews; (3) identification of new alternatives for construction and action, including the potential constraints on implementation; (4) the formulation of recommendations for enhancing the community's organization, fostering participation, and taking other actions to improve the quality of life for El Caruto's inhabitants. This last working meeting, whose goal was to stimulate the deconstruction of the prevailing versions and the formulation of new construction, was based on the suggestions of Willig (1999) regarding socio-constructionist research.

The work done with the El Caruto community led to several accomplishments.

In the first place, the community formulated a work plan. This began by addressing the water supply problem through community construction of small dams on the river, to store water for the dry season. This was to be complemented by the installation of pumps to send water from the dams to a storage tank, located in the village. The community wanted to take advantage of these construction demands, to enhance its organization, develop new leadership, and train itself to subsequently generate solutions to other problems it may face.

In the second place, the inhabitants moved away from the idea that their basic needs could satisfied only by their internal leader, the Commissioner. This person was a public authority figure, who is basically responsible for law enforcement in the village, fostering harmony among the residents, resolving conflicts that occur among them, pursuing solutions to social problems, etc.). The incumbent is usually imposed by the political parties, or by a political leader external to the community, such as the mayor of the municipality of which it is a part, who in turn has been chosen by the political organizations. Alternatively, the Commissioner is picked by the missionaries; who voluntarily co-operate with the community in certain development activities. Having changed from relying on these sources, the community now perceives that it has more autonomy in addressing its problems. It has become more proactive in launching actions for change, such as forming an intention to elect its own Commissioner.

In the third place, the community modified its conception of community participation. In the past, participation had been viewed as "activist" in nature, as the performance of activities by one or more community members to achieve the satisfaction of small-scale demands. Now, it has come to be understood as collective action to achieve important goals that will enhance their quality of life. As well, it has become a form of social interaction for critical reflection about action, and a way to learn how to build self as individual and as part of a group.

In the fourth place, and also as a product of the dialogues facilitated by the researcher, the community members gained a conscious awareness of the relations between their context of poverty and their history of dependence on leadership imposed by the political parties. They became aware of the constructions in which they had viewed themselves as passive and individualist objects of external action. The deconstruction of these versions led them to conceive of themselves as active subjects in a collective sense.

Community Social Psychology and Poverty

We believe the background, characteristics, theoretical foundations, and methodological strategies of CSP are compatible with the concept of poverty as a socially constructed process. Poverty is temporary and changeable. This contrasts with a hegemonic understanding of poverty, which universalizes and/or fragments, and in which the poor have no role to play. From the CSP standpoint by contrast, the definition of, and action against, poverty cannot occur in the absence of recognition of the particular context of the community with which one is working, or from outside of the group's own experience. The context has ecological conditioning factors that differentiate particular situations of poverty. Accordingly, instead of poverty, what we find are poverties. Moreover, the poor take an active part in the struggle against poverty, developing strategies of coping which, when shared with all the members of the community, comprise a valuable collective knowledge for the formulation of any plan.

Community Social Psychology values the specificity of the community context, and in this respect it fosters, together with the members of the community, an understanding of poverty's multiple social, political, economic, and psychological components. At the same time, it fosters (also in conjunction with the community members) an identification of the different resources and potentials found in it. These can nourish the activities undertaken in connection with the projects to be developed.

As well, by stimulating community organization and participation in actions to relieve poverty, CSP generates an additional effect. It facilitates the construction of the individual and the community, to develop a different vision of themselves, that of a proactive individual and collectivity. Put in terms of empowerment theory, CSP acts as a mechanism that facilitates the "... process ... by which people, organization, and communities gain mastery over their affairs" (Rappaport, 1987, p.112). To sum up, with its focus on the community, CSP is capable of contributing to the struggle against poverty. It does this by incorporating the community members' own perspectives on poverty, and on what can be done to reduce poverty. It achieves this primarily by facilitating the community's participation in these actions. CSP is also interested in the production of a kind of knowledge that, from the epistemological standpoint outlined above, integrates the conceptualizations elaborated by the discipline in interaction with the community members. This is done in such a way that the resulting knowledge generates the drive for new actions the community will take.

Psychology and the Reduction of Poverty

In this section, we develop a very brief series of references to activities that professional psychologists can develop in order to both reduce poverty and increase well-being.

The Promotion of Mental Health, Assertiveness and General Empowerment

This is one of the most traditional of psychological endeavors. However, we would like to recast this task. We do not believe that the psychologist's job is to define mental health. This is something that local neighborhoods and cultures must do. What psychologists can do, however, is help people achieve the conditions that promote well-being, in local terms. This may produce cultural conflict among some professionals, who feel perhaps that certain cultural practices are "unhealthy" (compare the views of many Western cultures on the isolation of women and overly stern disciplinary customs or legal procedures). What the psychologists or other social promoters can do, however, is to problematize these practices. That is, they can enter into a sustained dialogue with all the stakeholders involved, in order to question the justice, advisability, benevolence, and the possible benefits and difficulties associated with the policies and practices under consideration.

In this, it may well happen too that the facilitators end up being convinced by the local way of doing things. For example, health promotion has changed radically in recent decades, due to the influence of acupuncture, herbal medicines, yoga, and other formerly "primitive" methods of avoiding and curing illness and

promoting health. It may also happen that local values that are associated with traditional cultural solutions are redeemed, with new awareness. In certain cultures
(e.g., the Otavalo of Ecuador) the isolation of women has been a key to the preservation of Indigenous cultures that have faced centuries of colonial and neocolonial
challenges. This has been an important achievement for these people, although at
an evident cost for the women themselves. Nevertheless, women's cultural isolation may be reshaped in terms that promote local language enrichment, family
protection and child-care activities, while at the same time allowing women more
individual freedom. This cannot be achieved by a "missionary" attitude, nor by
the imposition of external values. It must be a decision made by the community
members themselves.

The Creation of Social Networks and the Promotion of Institutional Structures

This is also a well-used technique in CSP. It involves promoting the association of people with like interests, and needs, in groups of varied structures, such
as encounters for families that must deal with a member's Down syndrome, working mothers' day-care centers, and parent-teacher associations. Other alliances
can be imagined, such as non-governmental organizations (NGO), co-operatives,
trade unions, pressure groups, and extended family structures. In so-called "Third
World" countries, these organizations can be critical to the survival of the poor.
Community promoters can strengthen all these relationships.

Facilitation of these networks can be seen in two different ways: (a) individual empowerment; and (b), group empowerment. At an individual level, this
kind of intervention strategy is related to the notion of "perceived participatory
competence" (McMillan, Florin, Stevenson, Kerman, & Mitchell, 1995). This has
to do with personal empowerment tactics. Thus people develop their ability to
participate by honing interpersonal, management, and practical skills while acting
collectively. We can mention two examples. Firstly, when the garbage collectors
in San Antonio de los Altos in Venezuela formed a co-operative, they had to learn
leadership skills, accounting and even, in some cases, to read and write (Cronick,
1992; Cronick, 2000); secondly, in a self-help building project community members needed to learn basic architectural principles, soldering, and day-care and
teaching skills (Sánchez, Cronick & Wiesenfeld, 1988). This learning was then
useful in other contexts. In addition, other personal characteristics, such as self-
esteem and the ability to speak in public, became enhanced.

At a group level, networking increases individuals' relative power to get
things done. The promotion of formal, legally structured organizations can be an
important social tool for distressed communities (Cronick, 1998). This has to do
with the definition of what communities are. They have often been defined as having
a sense of community (Sarason, 1974; Sarason, 1986; Miller, 1986; McMillan &

Chavis, 1986; McMillan, 1996; Wiesenfeld, 1997). Yet this notion often has to be further elaborated, by the formation of mediating institutions such as community associations. These provide roles and procedural rules for group interaction and for inter-group transactions. Thus, a president can lead meetings and represent the group; a treasurer keeps the accounts; a secretary keeps the minutes. And these can be powerful figures in enhancing people's capacity to get things done. When an organization "speaks out," it has more clout than an individual does. For example, when dialysis patients pool their separate voices they may have more influence. They can confront hospital practices and even influence legislation on organ transplants (Torres, 1997).

Links to Poverty Reduction

This idea is related to poverty reduction in two senses. Firstly, it reduces exclusion effects. The impoverished renal patients described by Torres were clients of a free medical service, and were not respected by the hospital medical and administrative staff. When the community organized the Renal Patients' Association, the staff had to pay attention to them. Secondly, it promotes economic stability and improves people's quality of life. This can be appreciated in the results of group efforts to set up an economic enterprise, such as a co-operative; to build suitable housing, or to solve other problems such as environmental deficiencies (the purification of fresh water supplies), legal difficulties (land tenure), educational shortcomings (adequate schooling for children rejected by the public school system).

Poverty, Teaching, and CSP

Perhaps the best way to broach this topic is through a description of how the authors of this paper handle the teaching of social intervention in the graduate program of the same name at the Central University of Venezuela. This is a four-semester series of courses, the first of which is theoretical. The subsequent courses are theoretical and practical. In these, teaching follows a plan largely based on the principles of Participatory-Action-Research. We will describe how we apply the model to teaching. Firstly, however, we will briefly review its use in community settings. This model proposes the following sequential steps: (1) community or group members (C/GMs) discuss and identify their problems and aspirations with the facilitators, and then look for possible solutions, in view of the resources they have with which to achieve these solutions; (2) all the participants work on the solution – this is the "practice" phase; (3) the C/GMs and the facilitators discuss the usefulness and benefits of the results of this practice; (4) problems are identified and, when the participants are not satisfied, new solutions are proposed. This may be the beginning of a new string of practical activity.

This sequential relationship between (theoretical) reflection and (practical) activity is designed to respond to the vital and changing needs of the C/GMs. It also supposes a critical interaction between scientific knowledge and the commonsensical notions brought to the process by the C/GMs. The members learn new ways of handling things (e.g., mud walls can be reinforced with plastering). But they also add to and modify this understanding, by incorporating their own observations and ideas (e.g., it is important to leave a space at the top for air circulation). In this way, new comprehension is produced.

In teaching, similar steps are followed. Theoretical problems, such as "social exclusion," are presented and discussed in class among all the participants. At the same time, the students begin to work in a community or group to determine the community or group members' felt needs. Problematizing techniques are used, and time is spent relating the theoretical considerations to practical experience.

The notion of problematization originated in Paulo Freire's work. It consists of an almost Socratic process of questioning and answering, in which a facilitator leads the other participants to an awareness of "what they always knew" – an awareness which may have been previously ideologically hidden. Freire (1972, 1976), in his adult literacy teaching helped the C/GMs to place their new learning in the context of past experience. In this way they not only learned to read and write. They also became aware, for example, that the system of absentee landlords, in which they worked on land belonging to someone else, was a kind of exploitation. They began to question whether this was the only way of doing things.

In our teaching, collective reflection produces new awareness in the students. For instance, they become aware of how they have "decided for" the C/GMs what their problems are, instead of letting them "work things out for themselves." They may have decided, for example, that the problem is the number of school dropouts. After collective reflection however, it may become clear that the school system, the curriculum, or the transportation service, is inadequate for these students. It may be that the students are undernourished, and so cannot concentrate in class; or, that they must go out to earn money for the family by street vending.

In this way, the students become aware of the C/GMs' problems. And at the same time, they become aware of what it means to facilitate in poverty-stricken areas. Perhaps we can say that one of the most important aspects of this process is the need to put aside previous notions about what it means to be poor, and what can be done about it. Also, the students become aware that there are no isolated problems. People's lives are a whole fabric, so to speak. For example, the problem of uncontrolled birth rates in the "Third World" is sometimes related to people's need to have surviving children when they are elderly. In areas where there is no social security, the childless old are often abandoned and homeless. Students become aware of this by letting people describe how they live, what they want in life, and what their difficulties are. When students think they can descend from the comfort of their offices and offer contraceptive pills to solve the problem, they are missing the point. Thus, they will probably face a major intervention failure.

This briefly summarizes our teaching posture. It has less to do with a mechanical selection of appropriate themes for study than with creating the opportunity for increased awareness. It involves reflection and observation about particular communities and their problems. But perhaps more importantly, it promotes a process of self-reflection, in which students are led to question their own ideologically colored omniscience, with regard to the causes of, and solutions to, poverty.

The Systematic Study of the Conditions that Produce or Alleviate Poverty, and Interdisciplinary Activities. There are many social, political, and environmental problems related to poverty that require urgent study. The choice of a discipline, or of a paradigm within a given discipline, for research related to these issues, is based, at least in part, on the particular way the researcher approaches them. Thus a biologist, a chemist, and a social psychologist, may see the same problem of desertification in different ways. The first two professionals will appreciate the kinds of plant and animal life, the tendency to overgrazing, and land acidity or salinity. The social psychologist will identify social constructions, social organizations and networks, the need for competence building, levels of self esteem, and the like. The problem, however, goes beyond, and encompasses, each of these factors. It is only through concerted interdisciplinary research that the complex problems that foment poverty can be addressed.

Political Activism and Advocacy. It is no longer possible to separate researchers' political stance from their work. There has been much questioning of the possibility of value-free science in the past 40 years, too much to go into here. The gist of the argument is that supposed value-free science is really a sort of value convergence, in which all meaning is assimilated into the dominant political thinking of the time. Opposing thinking is ignored, or considered an unwarranted intrusion into "neutral" research. A more candid approach is for the researcher to declare his or her position. There are many well-known social and natural scientists, such as Noam Chomsky and Pierre Bourdieu, who have openly assumed political stances. For community social psychologists, such commitments become even more relevant. It is often necessary, in working to ameliorate poverty-related issues, to take a stance on such questions such as international debt, environmental practices, human rights, and so forth. All this is related to participation in grassroots reform projects, facilitation of citizen participation, and the promotion and facilitation of active political debate.

Of special interest at the beginning of the twenty-first century is the avoidance of violence and war. This is an important social and political issue. Violence and war are probably the greatest producers of poverty and misery in the world. Community social psychologists and other social scientists can help facilitate debates, and look for mechanisms for reducing intergroup tensions, for creating compromises, and for problematizing extreme positions that lead to intolerance.

References

Altamir, O. (1992). *Extent of poverty in Latin America*. Washington, DC: International Bank for Reconstruction and Development: Report Summaries.

Amorós, P., & Ayerbe, P. (2000). *Intervención educativa en inadaptación social*. Madrid: Síntesis.

Bermúdez (2002). *An intervention in the El Caruto peasant community*. Caracas: Universidad de Venezuela.

Bessis, S. (March, 1995). *From social exclusion to social cohesion: Toward a policy agenda. The Roskilde Symposium, University of Roskilde, Denmark*.

BID & PNUD (1993). *Reforma social y pobreza. Hacia una agenda integrada de desarrollo. Trabajos del Foro sobre Reforma Social y Pobreza*. Banco Interamericano de Desarrollo and Programa de las Naciones Unidas para el Desarrollo. Internet document http://www.metabase.net/docs/funde/00363html.

Boltvinik, J, (1995). La pobreza en América Latina. Análisis crítico de tres estudios. En Sistema Económico Latinoamericano (SELA) (Co-ord.) *Una mirada hacia el siglo XXI* (pp. 80–115). Caracas: Nueva Sociedad. Comisión Económica para América Latina y el Caribe (CEPAL) (2001). Comunicado de Prensa. http://cepal.org/cgibin/getProd.asp?xml=/prensa/noticias/comunicados/9/7939/P7939.xml&xsl=/prensa/tpl/p6f.xsl.

Cronick, K. (1988) La psico-ecología: Un modelo para intervenciones en comunidades. En M. L. Platone (Co-ord.), *Dinámica de grupos: Método y aplicación. Fascículo 5 de AVEPSO*, 57–66.

Cronick, K. (1992). El uso de sesiones de cambio planificado en la psicología comunitaria. *Boletin de AVEPSO, 14*(2) 2–13.

Cronick, K. (2000). *Los borrachitos de siempre: Un análisis retórico y heremenéutico de la intención*. Central University of Venezuela. Unpublished doctoral thesis.

Derber, C. (2000). *Corporation nation. How corporations are taking over our lives and what we can do about it*. New York, NY: St Martin's Press.

España, L. P. (2001). Un mal posible de superar. En L. Ugalde, L. P. España, M. Riutort, L. Zambrano Sequín, B. Mommer, O. Bello, J. C. Guevara, M. J. González, M. de Viana (Co-ords.), *Pobreza: Un mal posible de superar,* Vol. 1, (pp. 8–14). Caracas: Universidad Católica Andrés Bello.

Fernie, K. (2000). Poverty, disadvantage and exclusion. Profile 2000. www.trp.dundee.ac.ut/research/geddes/monitor/profile-99.htm#intro

Freire, P. (1972). *Pedagogy of the oppressed*. New York, NY: Herder & Herder.

Freire, P. (1976). *La educación como práctica de la libertad*. México DF: Siglo XXI.

Furman University Mathematical Quotation Server. Internet document, http://math.furman.edu/~mwoodard/mqs/mquot.shtml

Gergen, K. (1999). *An invitation to social construction*. Thousands Oaks, CA: Sage.

Greenwood, D. J., & Levin, M. (2000). Reconstructing the relationships between universities and society through action research. In N. Denzin & Y. Lincoln (Eds.), *Handbook of qualitative research* (pp. 85–106). Thousands Oaks, CA: Sage.

Guba, E., & Lincoln, Y. (1994). Competing paradigms in qualitative research. In N. Denzin & Y. Lincoln (Eds.), *Handbook of qualitative research* (pp. 105–117). Thousands Oaks, CA: Sage.

Lewis, O. (1979). *Los hijos de Sánchez*. México, DF: Fondo de Cultura Económica.

McMillan, B., Florin, P., Stevenson, J., Kerman, B., & Mitchell, R. (1995). Empowerment praxis in community coalition. *American Journal of Community Psychology, 23*, 5, 699–727.

McMillan, D. W., & Chavis, D. M. (1986). Sense of community: A definition and theory. *Journal of Community Psychology, 4*, 6–23.

McMillan, D. (1996). Sense of community. *Journal of Community Psychology, 24*(4), 315–325.

Miller, Z. L. (1986). Self-fulfillment and decline of civic territorial community. *Journal of Community Psychology, 14*(4), 353–364.

Montero, M. (1983). La psicologia comunitaria y el cambio social. En búsqueda de una teoría. Paper presented at Taller Seminario sobre Psicología Comunitaria, Universidad Incca, Bogota.

Rahman, M. (1985). The theory and practice of participatory action research. In O. Fals Borda (Ed.), *The challenge of social change* (pp. 107–132). Beverly Hills, CA: Sage

Rappaport, J. (1987). Terms of empowerment/exemplar of prevention: Toward a theory for community psychology. *American Journal of community Psychology, 15*, 121–147.

Rawls, J. (1999). *A theory of justice.* Boston, MA: Harvard University Press.

Runciman, W. G. (1966). *Relative deprivation and social justice.* London: Routledge and Kegan Paul.

Sánchez, E., Cronick, K., & Wiesenfeld, E. (1988). Psychosocial variables in articipation: A case study. In D. Canter, M. Kramping & D. Stea (Eds.), *New Directions in Environmental Participation* vol. 3, (pp. 1–17). Aldershot: Avebury.

Sarason, S. B. (1974). *The psychological sense of community: prospects for a community psychology.* San Francisco, CA: Jossey-Bass.

Sarason, S. B. (1986). Commentary. The emergence of a conceptual center. *Journal of Community Psychology, 14*, 405–407.

Seligman M. E. P. (1975). *Helplessness: On depression, development and death.* San Francisco: Freeman.

Serrano-García, I. López, M., & Rivera-Medina, E. (1987). Toward a social community psychology. *Journal of Community Psychology, 15*, 431–446.

Strauss, A., & Corbin, J. (1990). *Basics of qualitative research: Grounded theory procedures and techniques.* Newbury Park, CA: Sage.

Torres, O. (1997). *Intervención psicosocial comunitaria en el Servicio de Nefrología del Hospital Universitario de Caracas.* Central University of Venezuela. Unpublished Manuscript.

Townsend, P. (1979). *Poverty in the United Kingdom: A survey of the household resources and standards of living.* Berkeley, CA: University of California Press.

Valentine, C. F. (1991). *The Ernst and Young guide to expanding in the global market.* New York, NY: Wiley.

Wiesenfeld, E. (1994). Critical theory and constructionist: Toward an integration of paradigms. *Interamerican Journal of Psychology, 28*(2), pp. 251–264.

Wiesenfeld, E. (1997). Lejos del equilibrio: Comunidad, diversidad y complejidad. En E. Wiesenfeld (Co-ord.), *El horizonte de la transformación: Acción y reflexión desde la psicología social comunitaria. Fascículo 8 de AVEPSO,* 7–22.

Willig, C. (1999). Beyond appearances: A critical realist approach to social constructionist work. In D. J. Nightingale & J. Cromby (Eds.), *Social constructionist psychology: A critical analysis of theory and practice* (pp. 37–51). Buckingham: Open University Press.

Chapter 8

Poverty and Prejudice

Anthony F. Lemieux and Felicia Pratto

The realities of poverty are striking, but certainly not uncommon. Malnourished children with distended stomachs, small and crowded dwellings without running water, and people walking among heavily armed military personnel are but a few of these stark images. Promises of economic development have yet to materialize for the vast majority of the world's citizens, despite an unprecedented growth in the global economy (Isbister, 2001, p. 3).

Poverty does not persist because there is a scarcity of resources,[1] nor does poverty exist because some societies have inefficient economic systems, lack natural resources, or because poor people lack ambition. Poverty is a product of human social relationships because social relationships determine how people distribute resources. In fact, social aspects of relationships set the structure for economic exchanges. The way that people assign and distribute things of value depends on both how integrated or segregated their relationships are and how powerful they are in relation to one another (Prilleltensky, this volume). In this chapter, we will show that how much or how little people value others in relation to themselves is a fundamental cause of poverty, and that basic aspects of social relations, including prejudice, power, violence, and inter-group dominance, work together in the creation and maintenance of poverty.

We define poverty as a lack of access to resources necessary to meet basic human needs. Like many others, we recognize the following as such needs:

---

[1] Indeed, a small proportion of the world's military budget could feed and provide heath care to everyone throughout the world. In the 1990s fully 3% of the world total production was spent on military production (Isbister, 2001). Additionally, war (e.g., assembling and maintaining armies, development and production of weapons) is estimated to cost 180 times more than peaceful efforts including education, healthcare, and food (Sloan, 1999).

nutrition, health care, shelter, clothing, sanitation facilities, and clean water. Because we are social psychologists, we also know that people have fundamental social and psychological needs: to belong (e.g., Baumeister & Leary, 1995), to have valued social identities (e.g., Tajfel & Turner, 1986), and to grow, develop, and realize their potential (e.g., Maslow, 1954; Rogers, 1951). Poverty can be created by limiting people's access to the means of meeting these basic needs, i.e., by depriving people of education, by fomenting prejudice and violence, and by restricting certain freedoms (e.g., meeting and assembly).

Throughout the world, economically poor people have a great likelihood of suffering from poor health, inadequate education, malnutrition, disrupted family and community life, fewer options, marginalized identities, and exploitation, all of which may be interspersed with fear of violence and warfare (e.g., Isbister, 2001, p. 17). Such hardships indicate that basic human needs are not met, and are thus taken as the chief indicators of poverty (e.g., Prilleltensky, this volume). Whereas people who have some value (e.g., arable land, marketable skills, training, health, education, prestige) may trade it for other forms of value (e.g., food, income, goods, services), people who have little value not only suffer its lack, but also have little to offer in trade relations with others. This is the fundamental reason that forms of poverty (e.g., economic, prestige, health) tend to be compounded in some people, while forms of wealth are compounded in others. Hypothetically, exchanges can redistribute value among people, but when resources are distributed unequally to begin with, those exchanges are unlikely to create egalitarian relationships or to result in a more even distribution of value. In the remainder of this chapter, we elaborate on some of the social barriers that can prevent people from distributing value evenly in social exchanges. Finally, we use this analysis to suggest methods of reducing global poverty.

Poverty and Prejudice

Western media are replete with negative images of poor people (Bullock, Wyche, & Williams, 2001). It is also the case that middle-class people the world over blame poverty on character deficits of poor people (Furnham, this volume). In many cultures, there is overt bigotry against the poor and against low-power groups who are associated with poverty (e.g., untouchables in India; gypsies in Europe; Indigenous peoples in much of the world). Therefore, poverty is potentially stigmatizing because stereotypes of and prejudice against people who have features associated with poverty (e.g., lack of hygiene, illness and disease, hard manual labor, lack of education) are both common (Cozzarelli, Wilkinson, & Tagler, 2001). Prejudice against other groups who are needy (e.g., children, women – especially pregnant women, people who are ill, handicapped people) is also common (e.g., Glick & Fiske, 2001).

These studies suggest that well-off people may become prejudiced against poor or otherwise disadvantaged others (e.g., those who are needy) as a way of distancing themselves psychologically (Lott & Bullock, 2001; Lott, 2002). Such prejudice serves as a barrier that helps to prevent powerful people from entering into close relationships with members of stigmatized groups or needy others. By sustaining segregation between rich and poor, prejudice against "the poor" prevents the exchange of resources between them. Segregation also prevents the development of inter-group empathy, and thus sustains group-based prejudice.

Prejudice against the poor also increases the likelihood that exchanges that do occur will maintain inequalities, because prejudice can reduce the value of both poor people themselves and what they have to offer. For example, both demeaning stereotypes that dehumanize, and envious prejudice that implies that others are undeserving, help legitimize discrimination against and exploitation of others. Poor people are demeaned and said to be undeserving for having to work at "undesirable" jobs most commonly performed by marginalized groups (e.g., agricultural labor, cleaning, care of children or the sick). However essential it is, work that is performed by poor people is often so undervalued that it is paid very little or not at all. As a result, the range of opportunities that are available to poor people is extremely limited and produces little in the way of economic returns and advancement. Thus, the double-bind of prejudice against the poor leads to both restricted options and ultimately to restricted power.

Poverty and Power

Poverty is also a symptom of power inequalities. Since Marx and Engels (1846), social scientists have been accustomed to thinking of power as control over the means of production of value, which can include both production of exchangeable material (e.g., food, manufactured goods, energy) and the social determination of what is valued through ideology. But this description of power can be augmented with the contemporary insight that power is not just something one holds, but rather something one has or does not have in relation to others (Foucault, 1980). Thibault and Kelley's interdependence theory (1959; Kelley & Thibault, 1978) elaborates how material control translates into social power.

People may exchange particular resources for other resources they want or need so long as they have access to both resources and to social networks in which resources can be exchanged. In such exchange relationships, there are four basic sources of power. First is *freedom from need*. Those who are able to meet their own basic needs and still have resources left over (surplus) are in an enviable, high-power position of being able to enter into exchange relationships with others without risking becoming needy through such exchanges. This is one reason why such exchanges may turn out to the advantage of the least needy party.

Surplus leads directly to another form of power: *freedom not to enter relationships*. If a party has what it needs without exchanging with others, then that party is free not to enter any exchange relationships with others. Ironically, then, the poor who have less to offer to others are more compelled to enter into exchange relationships with them. Those with surplus to exchange, having more freedom not to enter particular relationships, also then have more *freedom to set the price for exchange*, or the price for entering into a relationship. This third form of power can translate into both greater control over the conditions of the negotiation or relationship and greater ability to set the price of the thing to be exchanged.

Finally, because those with surplus have less need to be in exchange relationships, they also have more *freedom to exit* relationships than others. Leaving such relationships or threatening to leave them is a means of exerting power. Having less freedom to exit a relationship also has the potential to increase the price that one party is willing to pay to maintain an exchange relationship with another. Therefore, those who have no choice but to remain in a relationship are increasingly vulnerable to being exploited.

It is well known that control over scarce resources engenders more freedom to set the price of exchange, but from both the Marxist and interdependence theory perspectives, power is also influenced by how exchangeable resources are. Clearly, those in possession of highly exchangeable resources, such as those that are widely desired (e.g., food, petroleum), widely recognized as having value (e.g., gold), or highly portable (e.g., US dollars), have more freedom to enter exchange relationships. Conversely, if a resource is desirable but cannot be exchanged for other resources that meet basic needs, it has relatively little value, and possession of that resource does little or nothing to increase the freedom to enter exchange relationships. More starkly, one cannot eat gold, drink petroleum, or use coffee beans to cure pneumonia. If one does not have means to exchange these resources, controlling them is of no benefit, and actually may result in poverty.

The potential for exchange of positive value is not the only means by which power between individuals or between groups is enacted. Violence is a form of destructive power, and the threat of violence is an exercise of power that is potentially separate from resource control. Dominant groups are especially likely to use violence against subordinates, especially when subordinates have used violence. Moreover, dominant groups often escape sanction for overuse and abuses of violence (see Sidanius & Pratto, 1999, Chapter 8, for a review).

But, despite their efforts, more powerful groups do not hold a monopoly on violence. Indeed subordinates commit violence against other subordinates more than they do against dominants (see Jackman, 2001; Sidanius & Pratto, 1999, Chapter 9) because organizational arrangements such as segregation fence dominants off from contact with subordinates and because subordinates' behavior is closely monitored and severely restricted. In addition, people who are relatively powerless in other ways (e.g., in terms of respectability, politically, economically) may use violence to attempt to increase their power relative to others. Violence has been an important tool in instigating many liberation movements. And although the use of violence is sometimes effective in serving as a catalyst for change, it always carries a heavy price for both perpetrators and victims. Acts of violence committed by subordinates are disproportionately and harshly punished by dominants. A clear and tragic example of this disproportionality of violence is evidenced in the current violence between Israel and Palestine. Between September 2000 and March 15, 2002, 1,184 Palestinians as compared to 343 Israelis were killed (Omestad & Derfner, 2002). Additionally, when subordinates use violence, dominants brand them as dangerous and irresponsible. Thus, the use of violence may undermine liberation movements by delegitimizing them, and also by demonizing and vilifying subordinates. Demonization and vilification of subordinates provides powerful justification for further violence and coercion by dominants.

Group Membership

Though interdependence theory and Marxism emphasize resource control, we assert that material resources and commodities are far from people's only source of value. Of central importance to our analysis of group prejudice is social dominance theory (SDT). This theory centrally asserts that humans have a basic tendency to form group-based social hierarchies. A fundamental principle of SDT is that one's social identity and membership in socially recognized groups is itself either a resource or a cost, having either positive or negative value. Because cross-gender group divisions can take myriad forms (e.g., religious, race, nationality, ethnicity, colonial status), but are consistently associated with both power and status, we refer to such group distinctions in general as "arbitrary-set." Therefore, membership in (or exclusion from) arbitrary-set groups, where one group is dominant over others, is in large part what defines the extent to which one has value and access to resources necessary to meet needs.

Social Dominance Theory: An Integrative Approach to Power and Prejudice

Thus far, we have shown that poverty is linked to group membership, linked to group power, and linked to prejudice and other group-relevant ideologies. As such, social dominance theory (Sidanius & Pratto, 1999) is a useful tool for understanding poverty because it addresses how resource control, violence, and ideologies sustain group-based dominance.[2] Central to our analysis are several of the basic conditions that set the stage for the emergence and sustenance of systems of group-based hierarchy. Firstly, surplus is one cornerstone of power differentials. In fact, all societies with economic surpluses are structured as group-based hierarchies that are based upon membership in (or exclusion from) arbitrary-set groups (Sidanius & Pratto, 1999). Secondly, within these societies, individuals have different levels of social dominance orientation (SDO), which we describe as their desire for non-egalitarian, hierarchical relationships between social groups, and their overall tendency to view inter-group relations as a zero-sum game. Thirdly, we saw that group-based prejudice and other ideologies (e.g., capitalism) not only help segregate people into groups, but they justify discriminatory inter-group behavior. The social relationships that form (or are avoided) as a result of membership in arbitrary-set groups, individual differences in SDO, and group-based prejudice and related ideologies are the cornerstones of social and structural inequality. Social dominance theory views ideologies as legitimizing myths that offer reasons and justifications for methods of assigning and distributing value, even those that are grossly unequal (Sidanius & Pratto, 1999; Sidanius, Levin, Federico, & Pratto, 2001). As predicted by social dominance theory, such social ideologies have been shown to incite individuals to discriminate against the needy (Pratto, Tatar, & Conway-Lanz, 1999; Pratto, Sidanius, Stallworth, & Malle, 1994) and to legitimize discrimination by social institutions (e.g., Pratto, Stallworth, & Conway-Lanz, 1998). Because they are so strongly linked to culture, the worldviews and practices that define who people are, ideologies set up the faultlines for inter-group conflict that are triggered under social and economic stress.

    Social dominance theory also provides two more insights about ideology and group power. Firstly, members of dominant groups have more opportunity not just to control value, but to *define* what positive value is. Secondly, and not surprisingly, dominant groups do so in ways that advantage their own groups, even when propounding ideologies that are not ostensibly linked to group membership (e.g., meritocracy or capitalism; see Pratto, 1999). This is fundamentally why dominant groups seem not only powerful but also legitimate. As a corollary, dominant groups also have the power to define negative value and to determine what behavior should be punished, and the form of that punishment (e.g., military action, economic sanctions).

Contemporary Examples

    Thus far we have detailed a theoretical position that identifies poverty as a function of prejudice, power, violence, and inter-group dominance. To illustrate

---

[2] For a detailed discussion of social dominance theory and how it differs from other social psychological theories of inter-group relations (including social identity theory and realistic group conflict theory), see Sidanius & Pratto, 1999.

these key theoretical elements and the utility of understanding poverty in this way, we will consider several examples.

When Power Inequities Provoke Prejudice and Inter-group Violence: The Example of Rwanda

By as early as the 1960s, Rwanda was a nation with deep and long-standing rivalries – faultlines – between different groups in its population. In particular, Belgian colonialist practices had contributed to the formation and maintenance of an arbitrary set distinction (based largely on social class) in which Tutsis were advantaged over Hutus.[3] During the late 1980s and early 1990s, Rwanda had undergone massive political and economic restructuring, including currency devaluation, a significant increase in inflation rates, and the setting of price limits on its coffee exports (Melvern, 2000; Uvin, 1998). The ability to grow and produce coffee was originally something that Rwandans had that was of value to international markets. In this case, members of dominant groups (International Monetary Fund, World Bank, those in charge of overseeing the International Coffee Agreement and setting prices, and other government officials) defined the parameters of exchange relationships and placed substantial limits on the demands for products of the Rwandans (in this case, the subordinate group) and by extension, determined the value of their resources. Suddenly, the value of their coffee crops was greatly diminished, and many Rwandans found themselves in positions of tremendous disadvantage, having little or no ability to enter into exchange relationships that were at all favorable to them (e.g., Chossudovsky, 1997).

In terms of interdependence theory, Rwandans found themselves in the greatly compromised position of having to face the freeze and/or lowering of coffee prices, despite their best efforts to control the supply and thus the surplus. As a result of the devaluation of one of their primary resources, and the economic instability that accompanied this time of upheaval, the government of Rwanda (and thus its citizens) had little choice but to accept World Bank intervention. This intervention brought numerous terms and conditions that ultimately led to the devaluation of Rwandan currency and an increase in inflation rates that left many Rwandans without the ability to meet their basic needs, particularly the purchase of food. The faultlines (based on arbitrary-set distinctions) between the Hutus and Tutsis were triggered as the Rwandan economy underwent restructuring based on mandates imposed by the World Bank (Chossudovsky, 1997; Melvern, 2000).

In considering this sequence of events, it is important to note that as the prices paid to Rwandan coffee farmers were frozen or drastically lowered, the demand for coffee in the USA and around the world was increasing. Thus, the motivation to lower prices of Rwandan coffee was largely to increase the profitability

---

[3] For a more detailed discussion of Belgium's role and the emergence of Hutu-Tutsi rivalry, see Des Forges (1999), Keane (1995), Khan (2000), & Melvern (2000).

of larger coffee companies and distributors. As a result, those with economic interests in coffee production realized impressive profits while at the same time, a
nation that had been a significant contributor to the world's coffee economy was all
but completely destroyed (e.g., Madeley, 1999; 2000). The consequences of this
series of events included economic disruption, political disruption, inter-group violence, and ultimately genocide.[4] The power struggle during this period included
extreme violence in which an estimated 500,000 to 1,000,000 Tutsis were brutally
murdered (Isbister, 2001, p. 130). Thus, the exercise of power within exchange relationships, coupled with inter-group prejudice, has potentially massively harmful
consequences.

Developing Dependency and Making No Alternative a Good One: The Case of Somalia

Somalia provides another example of how changes in the economy and agricultural production of a "developing" nation that were designed to meet foreign
and industrial export demands had disastrous consequences. The probability of
drought and low crop yields had long been a realistic threat to the people of
Somalia. While the climate supported a fair amount of agriculture, it was quite
unpredictable. The people and farmers of Somalia knew this, and in the past had
met this potential threat with preparedness – in the form of maintaining adequate
stores of food. However, the 1990s saw a change in that preparedness that had
terrible consequences.

Before Somalia became involved in the business of agriculture intended for
export, enough of the population grew crops so that the general population would
have enough to eat, even in times of low crop yields, without having to become
dependent on foreign food supplies (particularly grain). However, as agriculture,
industry, and the basis of the Somali economy changed, so did the use of land.
What was once a relatively self-sustaining economy (at least in terms of its agricultural production and food supply) had become increasingly focused on developing
agricultural products for export. As a result of this shift in land usage, and as fewer
and less locally useful crops were grown, the impact of drought became too great,
which led to famine and violence. Though the 1992 United States military intervention in Somalia was purportedly intended to stop the use of violence, terror,
starvation, and brutality of warring factions within Somalia, with the ultimate goal
of ending the starvation of the Somali people, the result was still quite negative

---

[4] Our synopsis of the factors that precipitated the Rwandan genocide are meant to serve as examples
and to provide a cursory discussion. For a more detailed analysis of the political, economic, and
historical factors of the Rwandan genocide, see Destexhe (1995), Des Forges (1999), Keane (1995),
Khan (2000), Malkki (1995), Melvern (2000), & Uvin (1998). For a discussion of social psychological
factors that precipitate genocide see Staub (1989).

(e.g., Isbister, 2001, p. 207). Somalians suffered tremendously as they were relegated to the subordinate and powerless position of having to accept and depend on foreign intervention. They were displaced, victimized, and severely damaged (Chossudovsky, 1997). As was the case in Rwanda, the violence in Somalia left the population susceptible to hunger and malnutrition (e.g., Madeley, 2000).

Considering inter-group prejudice, the dynamism of power as suggested by both the social dominance approach and interdependence theory, and the use of violence, as three sources of social control, we can understand that as one of the poorest countries in the world, Somalia became a haven for groups committing acts of violence against the richest nations in the world (e.g., the Western industrialized nations). The Somali people had neither the power nor means to resist the occupation of wealthy and heavily armed groups. They were also unable to leave, and some Somalians may have even benefited (at least temporarily) by allying themselves with these powerful others.

Somalia's experiences illustrate an important implication of our theory for reducing and preventing poverty: societies need to prioritize meeting their own basic needs independently. Societies that are meeting at least some of their basic needs (especially food production) and who refuse to trade that resource for potentially more valuable items that must be exchanged with more powerful others (e.g., production of commodities valued by rich nations or foreign aid) have the advantage of independence. This independence makes them less vulnerable to the instability that is often the result of inequitable international trade relationships in which one group is dominant over others, the internal violence that often accompanies resource inequalities within a society, foreign military intervention, and the economic upheaval that results when the availability of goods locally is determined by decisions and actions of far-distant, dominant others who will not suffer from that upheaval (see McKibben, 2001 for a related discussion of choice of food crops in Bangladesh).

Dissecting the Components of Power: An Examination of Globalization

At this point in the chapter, we will explicitly examine the relation between power differences and globalization. As we detailed earlier in our consideration of exchange theory, these forms of power include the ability to set the price for exchange, to choose from a range of alternatives, the freedom to avoid involvement in a relationship that does not maximize one's advantage, and the freedom to exit a relationship.

Multinational and transnational corporations (TNCs), by their very definition, have interests in several countries, and are faced with a multiplicity of obligations and tasks: the task of meeting the needs of their employees (an income), shareholders (revenue), and ultimately their customers (goods and services). TNCs are also in the position of having to work within (or work to change) the parameters, rules, and laws, that are set by the various governments in whose countries they operate. Indeed, they have many masters to serve (for a detailed discussion of TNCs, see Madeley, 1999; Kozul-Wright, 1995).

As is commonly the case in business, TNCs have the expressed goals of making money for their shareholders by maintaining profitability and market expansion and domination. To this end, TNCs are able to obtain space, materials, and labor, from a number of prospective countries. By having a range of potential countries (read: exchange relationships) to choose from, and thus a wide range of potential alternatives, TNCs have greater power. They also have the ability to avoid entering into exchange relationships that are not maximally advantageous to them. In addition, TNCs often have the ability to set the price for exchange in those relationships that they do choose to enter (e.g., Isbister, 2001; Kozul-Wright, 1995). As a result, developing nations will make numerous concessions (including relaxing of labor laws and standards, environmental protection standards, and taxes) to win the "privilege" of becoming involved in an exchange relationship with a TNC. This trend has been dubbed the "race to the bottom" (e.g., Bhagwati, 2002; Sengenberger & Wilkinson, 1995).

In many cases, when a TNC settles in a particular country or region it draws its labor pool from the population. As the TNC experiences growth, the occupational profile and geographic distribution of the population necessarily changes as increasing numbers of people earn a salary from their employment with the corporation. This change may have many ramifications. People who gain employment with TNCs are often those who used to grow the food or make the clothes that they and many others in their community consumed. With employment, the people work for a salary that allows (and also forces) them to purchase food, clothes, and a number of other things that had previously been unavailable to them. For instance, many who take manufacturing jobs with the TNCs relocate from rural to urban areas (Isbister, 2001). In this instance, all involved seem to be benefiting from the arrangement, at least on the surface, and at least for the time being. However, the patter of migration to meet the demand to fill these jobs has been linked to increases is poverty rates in urban areas. To understand why this might be the case, let us consider the impact of exit freedom.

If the leadership of a TNC becomes dissatisfied in its relationship with the government or people of a country, the TNC has a much greater ability to exit that relationship. Its resources and power enable it to relocate. As we had detailed earlier, the freedom to exit a relationship is a critical component of power. By exiting a relationship in which others have grown dependent upon their employment with the TNC, it is exercising a tremendous degree of power in a way that will necessarily have negative consequences for those involved in the relationship. As a result, those who were employed by that TNC, and who depended on it for the income that they used to feed, clothe, educate, and house themselves and their families are harmed.

Presently, there is little that compels TNCs with tremendous resource and political influence from relocating from country to country based on the most advantageous conditions for their bottom line. The cost of labor, materials, taxes, and transportation all factor into corporations decisions to establish production and/or distribution centers in a country. Therefore, in order to keep the production (and jobs) in a country, governments are potentially engaged in a conflict of trying to balance their own interests (e.g., keeping the population employed, keeping a stream of tax and trade revenue) with the interests of the corporation (e.g., lowering taxes, reducing trade barriers, loosening of employment and workers rights' laws). So while the very presence of a corporation might mean that a greater percentage of the population has employment, it does not necessarily mean that the government (and infrastructure) of the country is enjoying a comparable benefit in this relationship. New and greater forms of poverty may even be the result of this increase in power asymmetry between a TNC and a population. It would be foolhardy for anyone to accept globalization as a panacea for global poverty.

Human Solutions to the Problem of Global Poverty: What Our Analysis Suggests About Alleviating and Eliminating poverty

As our discussion of poverty primarily focused on three features, namely prejudice, power, and inter-group dominance, we will now consider ways in which meaningful and sustainable change can be brought to bear on these basic aspects of human social relationships.

Prejudice Reduction

Social psychologists who have been concerned with developing effective methods of minimizing prejudice and its harmful consequences have developed several models that can be applied to the effort to eradicate poverty at both local and global levels. First, fundamental economic changes, and changes in power relations, must not trigger group faultlines through any form of threat, whether that threat is realistic, symbolic, or stems from uncertainty. If there is the perception of conflict based on scarcity of resources (either real or perceived), the efforts to invoke change will only serve to heighten the perception of group conflict and could have grave consequences, as was the case in Rwanda. Second, as was originally specified in realistic group conflict theory (Sherif, 1936, 1966), it may be helpful for separate groups to recognize a superordinate goal. Recognition of a superordinate goal will provide groups with a reason to cooperate and work together, rather than to compete. A superordinate goal will allow group members to share in the benefits of success and to develop more positive inter-group attitudes and positive interdependence. Having a superordinate goal could also reduce the "zero-sum" game mentality that is often involved in inter-group relations and which leads to inter-group discrimination and mistrust. Finally, working toward a superordinate goal may lead to a re-definition of in-groups and out-groups, and can ultimately have positive impact on the very nature of exchange relationships.

The common in-group identity model (Gaertner, Dovidio, & Bachman, 1996) posits that in order for prejudice reduction between groups to be lasting and meaningful, the groups must necessarily shift their boundaries. Again, this is difficult, but there are a number of causes that potentially affect all of Earth's inhabitants. To get dominant groups interested in better relations with the poor, issues of international interdependence such as global health (Hertzman, 2001) and the environment (Oskamp, 2000), can be cast in ways that foster the redefinition of group identities, thus potentially serving as catalysts for change in the definition of group identities. This redefinition can ultimately have significant positive impact on social relationships, and also on the assignment of value within those relationships.

Determining Value and the Redistribution of Power

In line with our theoretical position and our discussion of globalization, curtailing exit freedoms is an essential step in addressing this fundamental problem of power inequities. A tenable and enforceable international agreement could potentially lead to a redistribution of power and sustainable development by limiting the exit freedoms of advantaged groups. Resolutions and rules that limit exit freedoms will certainly be viewed with rancor by exactly those corporations and businesses that are the most likely to change their centers of operation and leave people in a difficult situation. Another means of limiting exit freedoms is the establishment of a universal minimum standard for wages, which would prevent TNCs from leaving one country to pay lower wages in another.

Another aspect of building shared power is by increasing commitment to sustainable economic development, rather than short-term aid in the form of food, loans, and military support. While these short-term remedies may be necessary at times, and are often mandated by the immediacy of the current situation, it is imperative that efforts are made to develop public works projects and infrastructure that stays in the country, and thus add value. By adding value in the forms of arable land, marketable skills, training, health, education, prestige, food, income, goods, and services, the freedom to enter some exchange relationships and the freedom to avoid others is greatly increased. Though the idea of developing infrastructure and self-sustaining economies seems to enjoy a substantial degree of popularity, it rarely occurs. In fact, it appears that there remains a lack of prioritization based on needs and goals that are identified as primary by the particular communities, states, and nations that are receiving aid (Sanchez, Cronick, & Wiesenfeld, this volume; Spink, this volume).

Developing Value in the Form of Appreciating Social Identities

Another method of change is to increase recognition of the humanness of the poor. It is all too often the case that the plight of the poor either goes unrecognized or is peculiarized as having little or nothing to do with the "non-poor." By recognizing that poor people have legitimate needs, wants and desires, and that they too are valuable members of the human community, members of dominant groups ready themselves to enter into exchange relationships with the poor on equitable terms. As Lott (2002) points out, the practice of psychologically distancing oneself from the poor is particularly problematic. It is likely that this process is amplified as we take a global perspective on poverty. However, recognition that problems caused by poverty are severe, widespread, and in need of immediate attention is becoming increasingly prevalent. As prioritizing peoples' basic needs becomes an important agenda, we move that much closer toward a greater recognition of the humanity, and value, of those who are poor.

Where Can We Go from Here?

Recently, US President George W. Bush stated that one of the key components of his so-called "war on terrorism" is the eradication of poverty on a global level (Ross, 2002). Our analysis does imply that the violence of terrorism and the violence of poverty are causally linked by power inequalities, but the manner in which the war on poverty is waged is a key issue. President Bush stated that nations cannot expect to get "development money" without strings of "political liberty, respect for human rights and adherence to the rule of law" attached (Ross, 2002, p. 3). In his statement, President Bush also mentioned the importance of "free trade" as part of this process. We have argued that free trade and globalization are also potentially complicit in the development and maintenance of global poverty, as they provide advantage to those with greater power.

Throughout this chapter we have argued that poverty is a complex problem that has more to do with human social relationships than it has to do with scarcity of resources. Thus, in terms of its causes, poverty is indeed largely a social and political problem. To meet the challenge of eliminating poverty, it needs to be addressed as such. In this chapter we have shown that a number of social factors including prejudice, power, and social dominance, are central in the creation and maintenance of poverty, particularly poverty on a global scale. We do not claim that there are not some important economic principles and historical sequelae at work in global poverty. But we do claim that even those "economic" decisions and "historical" events are social in nature. The good news that we offer is the fact that human social behavior is clearly a significant contributing factor to global poverty. Social psychologists, among others, have a long history of studying and changing social behavior, and working toward practical solutions to problems. If social behavior can be changed, and poverty is at least partially caused by social behavior, then it too can be changed.

References

Baumeister, R., & Leary. M. (1995). The need to belong: Desire for interpersonal attachments as a fundamental human motivation. *Psychological Bulletin, 117*, 497– 529.

Bhagwati, J. (2002). *Free trade today.* Princeton: Princeton University Press.

Bullock, H. E., Wyche, K. F., &Williams, W.R. (2001). Media images of the poor. *Journal of Social Issues, 57*, 229– 246.

Chossudovsky, M. (1997). *The globalization of poverty: Impacts of IMF and world bank reforms.* London: Zed Books.

Cozarelli, C., Wilkinson, A. V., & Tagler, M. J. (2001). Attitudes toward the poor and attributions for poverty. *Journal of Social Issues, 57*, 207–228.

Des Forges, A. (1999). *"Leave none to tell the story": Genocide in Rwanda.* New York, NY: Human Rights Watch.

Destexhe, A. (1995). *Rwanda and genocide* (A. Marschner, Trans.). New York, NY: New York University Press. (Original work published 1994).

Foucault, M. (1980). *Power/knowledge: Selected interviews and other writings.* Selected by C. Gordon, translated by C. Gordon. New York, NY: Pantheon Books.

Gaertner, S. L., Dovidio, J. F., & Bachman, B. A. (1996). Revisiting the contact hypothesis: The induction of a common in-group identity. *International Journal of Intercultural Relations, 20*, 271–209.

Glick, P. & Fiske, S. (2001). Ambivalent stereotypes as legitimizing ideologies: Differentiating paternalistic and envious prejudice. In J. T. Jost & B. Major (Eds.), *The psychology of legitimacy: Emerging perspectives on ideology, justice, and inter-group relations* (pp. 278–306). New York, NY: Cambridge University Press.

Hertzman, C. (2001). Health and human society. [Electronic version]. *American Scientist, 89.*

Isbister, J. (2001). *Promises not kept: The betrayal of social change in the third world* (5th ed.). Bloomfield, CT: Kumarian Press.

Jackman, M. R. (2001). License to kill: Violence and legitimacy in expropriative social relations. In J. T. Jost & B. Major (Eds.), *The psychology of legitimacy: Emerging perspectives on ideology, justice, and inter-group relations* (pp. 437–467). New York, NY: Cambridge University Press.

Keane, F. (1995). *Season of blood: A Rwandan journey.* New York: Viking.

Kelley, H. H., & Thibault, J. W. (1978). *Interpersonal relationships.* New York, NY: Wiley.

Khan, S. M. (2000). *The shallow graves of Rwanda.* London: I. B. Tauris Publishers.

Kozul-Wright, R. (1995). Trans-national corporations and the nation state. In J. Michie & J. G. Smith (Eds.), *Managing the global economy.* (pp. 135–171). New York, NY: Oxford University Press.

Lott. B. (2002). Cognitive and behavioral distancing from the poor. *American Psychologist, 57*, 100–110.

Lott, B., & Bullock, H. E. (2001). Who are the poor? *Journal of Social Issues, 57,* 189–206.

Madeley, J. (1999). *Big business, poor peoples: The impact of transnational corporations on the world's poor.* New York, NY: Zed Books.

Madeley, J. (2000). *Hungry for trade.* London: Zed Books.

Malkki, L. (1995). *Purity and exile: Violence, memory, and national cosmology among Hutu refugees in Tanzania.* Chicago: University of Chicago Press.

Marx, K. & Engels, F. (1846/1970). *The German ideology.* New York, NY: International Publishers.

Maslow, A. H. (1954). *Motivation and personality.* New York, NY: Harper.

McKibben, B. (2001). An alternative to progress. *Mother Jones,* May/June, 78–83, 115.

Melvern, L. R. (2000). *A people betrayed: The role of the west in Rwanda's genocide.* London: Zed Books.

Omestad, T., & Derfner, L. (2002, March 25). Mideast: Any way out? *US News and World Report, 132,* 12–15.

Oskamp, S. (2000). Psychological contributions to achieving an ecologically sustainable future for humanity. *Journal of Social Issues, 56,* 373–390.

Pratto, F. (1999). The puzzle of continuing group inequality: Piecing together psychological, social, and cultural forces in social dominance theory. *Advances in Experimental Psychology, 31,* 191–263.

Pratto, F., Sidanius, J., Stallworth, L. M., & Malle, B. F. (1994). Social dominance orientation: A personality variable predicting social and political attitudes. *Journal of Personality and Social Psychology, 67,* 741–763.

Pratto, F., Stallworth, L. M., & Conway-Lanz, S. (1998). Social dominance orientation and the legitimization of policy. *Journal of Applied Social Psychology, 28,* 1853–1875.

Pratto, F., Tatar, D., & Conway-Lanz, S. (1999). Who gets what and why? Determinants of social allocations. *Political Psychology, 20,* 127–150.

Rogers, C. (1951). *Client-centered therapy.* Boston: Houghton-Mifflin.

Ross, S. (2002, March 23). Bush urges tying aid to reform: Calls for global poverty fight to prevent terrorism. *Boston Herald,* p. 3.

Sengenberger, W., & Wilkinson, F. (1995). Globalization and labor standards. In J. Michie & J. G. Smith (Eds.), *Managing the global economy* (pp. 135–171). New York, NY: Oxford University Press.

Sherif, M. (1936). *The psychology of social norms.* New York, NY: Harper & Brothers.

Sherif, M. (1966). *In common predicament: Social psychology of inter-group conflict and cooperation.* Boston: Houghton-Mifflin.

Sidanius, J., & Pratto, F. (1999). *Social dominance: An inter-group theory of social hierarchy and oppression.* New York, NY: Cambridge University Press.

Sidanius, J., Levin, S., Federico, C. M., & Pratto, F. (2001). Legitimizing ideologies: A social dominance approach. In J. T. Jost & B. Major (Eds.), *The psychology of legitimacy* (pp. 307–331). New York, NY: Cambridge University Press.

Sloan, D. (1999). Imperialism, malnutrition, and children: Capitalism eats its young. *Political Affairs, 78,* 21–24.

Staub, E. (1989). *The roots of evil: The origins of genocide and other group violence.* New York, NY: Cambridge University Press.

Tajfel, H., & Turner, J. (1986). The social identity theory of inter-group behavior. In S. Worchel & W. G. Austin (Eds.), *Psychology of inter-group relations* (pp. 7–24). Chicago, IL: Nelson Hall.

Thibault, J. W., & Kelley, H.H. (1959). *The social psychology of groups.* New York, NY: Wiley.

Uvin, P. (1998). *Aiding violence: The development enterprise in Rwanda.* West Hartford, CT: Kumarian Press.

Chapter 9
Poverty and Wealth

Adrian Furnham

As a discipline, psychology has not been afraid to cross boundaries and examine the phenomena that are central to other disciplines. Cross-cultural psychology examines issues of interest to anthropologists; clinical psychologists and psychiatrists are often interested in the same thing; while mathematical psychology could be seen almost as a branch of mathematics. Educational psychologists, counselling psychologists, military psychologists and medical psychologists are interested in behavior in settings occupied by other experts. The range of interests of psychologists seems almost unlimited. There is a psychology of the Chinese and the psychology of Christmas; there is the psychology of lying and of literature; a psychology of religion and race relations. Psychologists have also formed a close relationship with experts in the arts, medical, physical, and social sciences. The one curious exception however has been, until comparatively recently, economics. While both disciplines are particularly interested in decision making and to a lesser extent in things like gambling and unemployment, psychologists have paid little attention to the really big economic issues such as the causes and consequences of poverty and wealth.

More recently, psychologists have attempted to consider their role in the analysis of poverty (Bullock, Wyche & Williams, 2001; Cozzarelli, Wilkinson & Taylor, 2001). Harper (1991; this volume) believes much previous research has been laden with pathologizing, victim blaming and ethnocentric assumptions. Others have also argued that attempts to "psychologize" political and economic problems are both unproductive and immoral. Connolly (1985) has wondered if we need to develop theories and methodologies in psychology specifically for the "Third World" though, as yet, this remains to be done.

Over the past 20 years there has been more and more psychological interest in poverty-related topics, like the reasons why people get into debt (Webley & Nyhus, 2001) as well as how they cope with unemployment (Waters & Moore, 2001). But how, where, and why people become, and stay, poor, is still a neglected area of study by psychologists. There has however been steady, international interest in how ordinary people attribute or explain the causes of poverty in their society. This work has been largely inspired by attribution theory and is concerned with the structure and function of these explanations for ordinary individuals as well as individual difference determinants and correlates of the attributions. More recent research has tried to go beyond somewhat simplistic, replicative, attributional studies to look at affective reaction to stereotypic and media images of poverty. But what is perhaps most interesting is the extent to which this research endeavour has been cross-national with studies from American and Australia, Brazil and Britain, as well as India and the West Indies.

The Paucity of Psychological Research on Poverty

As a discipline, psychology has not contributed much to the poverty literature. Furnham and Lewis (1986) have noted the paucity of psychological research and theorizing into the causes and consequences of poverty. Some of the most important topics in poverty research have been almost totally neglected by psychologists. Important omissions are the definition, measurement, incidence, and characteristics of poverty; the life of the poor; the causes of remedies for poverty; and politics, social policy and poverty. Certainly, poverty is a comparative, economic concept that can rarely be isolated from more general questions of inequality. Because the definition of poverty is problematic, involving macro-economic or political factors, psychologists have been hesitant to study it. Furthermore, some have been convinced that any psychological analysis would erroneously focus on individuals and their behavior, rather than on economic and industrial organisations, and institutions.

There are many reasons why the obvious joke about psychological theories of poverty being poor theories in psychology are true. Poverty is a relative economic concept that is too broad and heterogeneous a concept for psychologists. There are quite distinct poverty groups such as the welfare poor, the marginal poor, and the working poor. Because of some relative and flexible cut-off point, they are all classified as "poor;" yet have little in common psychologically. That is, "the poor" is not one unitary group. Secondly, poverty is almost always a consequence of (or at least a correlate of) some other variable, such as socio-economic class, or intelligence, etc., which psychologists are more experienced at measuring and theorising about than economists.

Thirdly, psychology is not used to analysing macro-sociological variables such as poverty, and has had neither the appropriate level of theoretical and conceptual analysis nor the most appropriate methodological tools, for analysing poverty. Psychological theories and variables have indeed been applied to the poor with a moderate degree of success, but they are of necessity never sufficient (and possibly not even necessary) to explain poverty, however it is defined. In this sense, poverty is an economic and sociological problem, not a psychological one. It is seen both by psychologists and others as the province of a different discipline.

Interestingly, content analysis of the media suggests that both television and the print media do little to contextualize poverty or explain its causes (Bullock et al., 2001). In this sense, the media may be a powerful contributor to lay understanding of poverty.

Psychologists are not as naïve or arrogant to suggest that poverty can be fully understood or eradicated by psychological factors alone, though many social and economic psychologists believe psychology does have a role in understanding, and even alleviating, poverty. "By concentrating on beliefs, expectations, values and motives, psychology is not asserting the pre-eminence of the behavioral over the economic, political or sociological factors, but merely suggesting that they too have an important role to play" (Furnham & Lewis, 1986, p. 81).

The theories in the area tend to be sociological, such as minority group theory, functional, or anthropological, such as subculture theory. The three theories – minority group, functional, and subcultural – though hotly debated, have contributed most to social psychological ideas and research. This has occurred mainly because each has specified various *behaviors* that are characteristic of, or describe, the poor, and may or may not be responsible for the cause and perpetuation of poverty. This is particularly true of the last theory that, because it appears to point out cognitive and behavioral universals in the poor, seemed highly crucial in stipulating psychological variables in causing poverty.

The sort of psychological variables that have been used to "explain" the causes and maintenance of poverty include:

1. *Need for achievement/independence.* The idea in this case is that having low needs for achievement (socialized in childhood) leads to lack of activity, initiative, risk taking and hence less education, poorer employment prospects and the lifestyle and culture of poverty.

2. *Locus of control.* People who believe that most life events are consequent upon their actions (behavior, personality) are said to have an "expectancy of internal control." People who believe events in their lives to be controlled by luck, chance, powerful others, or powers beyond their control or comprehension, have an "external local of control." Numerous studies have shown that poor, ethnic-minority, lower socio-economic, and other deprived groups, had greater external local of control beliefs than "normal" groups. However, as in so much of this research, it is unclear whether these beliefs are a cause or consequence of poverty. What is most likely is that

there is a bi-directional causality, and a spiralling effect, whereby poverty leads to external control beliefs, which in turn help to maintain and increase poverty. Gurin and Gurin (1970) have reviewed the not inconsiderable research on beliefs about expectation and poverty. They conclude:

> Perhaps the overall impression from the expectancy literature we have reviewed is one of complexity, contradiction, and tentativeness of our knowledge in this area . . . Success experience and reality changes in opportunities probably can be used to raise the expectancies on low expectancy people. Second studies consistently stress that this will be done under conditions where a person feels that the successes come from his own skill and competence. The literature on internal and external control indicates that effects of success and failure are not very reliable when a person feels they do not depend on his own actions (pp. 7–9).

3. *Just world beliefs.* People tend to believe either, that the world is just and that people get what they deserve, or not. The just world is orderly, predictable fair. If it is so then "victims" of poverty are (justly) the architects of their own condition.

    People who hold just world beliefs tend to blame the victim for his or her fate irrespective of the factors causing the problem. Thus the "non-poor" with just world beliefs see "the poor" as lazy and undeserving. Furthermore, if the poor themselves have just world beliefs (which is a cultural norm: Lerner, 1980) they would tend to derogate themselves with the probably consequence that they lose face and develop a poor self-concept. But the direction of causality between just world beliefs and poverty is not clear. Certainly, beliefs about justice appear to be consistent and powerful determinants on belief about poverty, and perhaps more importantly support for welfare programmes aimed at reducing poverty and inequality.

4. *Self-concept.* Most studies have hypothesized that people from disadvantaged groups (the disabled, the poor, ethnic minorities) will have more negative self-concepts than the general population because of a number of factors – defence against anxiety, admission of inadequacy, reference groups.

    Thus work on the relationship between school children's self-concepts and their manifest behavior perceptions and academic performance shows that successful students are typically characterized by self-confidence, self-acceptance and stable feelings of adequacy, personal competence and personal regard, while unsuccessful students tend to have feelings of uncertainty, low self-regard, self-derogatory attitudes and strong inferiority feelings. The research points strongly to a circular or feedback process that may be generalized to explain poverty.

Issues of Causality

There is no shortage of social science findings that have demonstrated that "the poor" hold different beliefs and behave rather differently from "the non-poor." But the establishment of a relationship between poverty and various behaviors is of little importance if it cannot explain how specific economic conditions produce which psychological phenomena that may account for the maintenance of the psychological condition.

Conspicuously missing from the psychological literature is both clear evidence of causality (as opposed to correlation) and also some description of process. That is, it is important to know where, when, and how, psychological variables are essentially the cause or consequence of poverty; or, indeed, whether they are mediating, moderating, or epiphenomenal variables.

There are those, mainly social psychologists, who believe that the individual level of analysis pursued by so many psychologists is inappropriate. Whilst there are the hard-core unemployed and those individuals who, despite considerable help, remain in poverty, many acknowledge that poverty is a social, and of course, an economic issue. Perhaps as a consequence of this recognition, social psychologists have turned their attention to attributions for poverty. That is, how the poor themselves and the non-poor, *perceive* the causes of economic affairs. This is important because it assumes that these attributions actually systematically affect salient behavior like voting, charitable donations, even tax evasion, by the non-poor, and specific behaviors of the poor themselves.

Ideology and Explaining Poverty

Ideological beliefs are clearly linked to beliefs about the causes of poverty and how to cure it. These are perhaps most clearly seen in welfare ideologies. Furnham (2000) has noted that ideologies of welfare can be identified, though all have certain characteristics. They tend to be relatively coherent (with internal logic and consistency), pervasive and extensive (widely shared). They also tend to be intensive, in the sense that holders tend to be committed to them. They are widely discussed on the media, particularly in times of election, economic crises, and general changes in the economy. Poverty is most often discussed in terms of welfare. Alcock (1996) has argued that ideologies of welfare are linked to the politics of welfare. Thus, on the extreme left are Marxists and socialists, who believe that the state should be the exclusive or major provider of welfare to help the poor. On the right however are anti-collectivists and liberals, who believe that individuals should be free to provide (or not) for their own and others' welfare to prevent poverty. Between these two extremes are Fabians, social democrats, "reluctant liberals," and others in new social movements (feminist, green), who are the results of a more pluralistic society. It is possible to distinguish different groups:

1. *The New Right.* These are neo-liberals who are pro-market and anti-state and who believe that state intervention leads to market dysfunction. They were particularly popular in the mid-1980s. The welfare state is seen to be economically, ideologically, and politically undesirable in practice, and unworkable in theory. Tax, for welfare and anti-poverty schemes, they believe, reduces private motivation and investment. Welfare, they argue, leads to a dependency culture and the poverty trap. They do not trust state politicians and bureaucrats to understand, target, or provide appropriate services, or the means to raise the capital. They argue that poverty arises from personal sloth, poor money management, or incompetence; or because state policies have actually created conditions that cause and perpetuate rather than cure poverty. Indeed, many assume it is as much political ideologies that cause poverty, as it is individual behavior.

2. *The middle/muddle way.* Various different believers in this camp are committed to the collective provision of welfare (through social services) and the planning of economic development through state channels. Most people in the middle position see some sort of partnership between "the market" and the state that may, in fact, help the ultimate growth of the market economy. This is a pragmatic, mixed economy approach, because social needs are recognized to be a public responsibility, as is private investment and economic growth. They believe that poverty has many causes, and that the state has an obligation to help – particularly "the deserving poor". They tend to be pragmatic and rather distrustful of ideology.

3. *Democratic Socialism.* This is a more interventionist perspective that aims at a gradual reform of the predominantly capitalist market economy. There is consistent stress on "social justice." This is pursued through redistributive tax and benefits policies. Democratic socialists aim at the universal and comprehensive provision of health and education. They believe that poverty is primarily the result of inequality of opportunity; or of subtler forms of exploitation, which need to be dealt with by careful, consistent, and constant legislation.

4. *Marxism.* This is the classic state socialist position where all ownership and means of production (and welfare) is in the hands of the people, and there is therefore no need for central state control. Marxists argue that any welfare provision, within a capitalist society, provides paradoxically both protection and control. It legitimizes and protects capitalists (as well as welfare recipients) and is, therefore, contradictory and inherently unstable. Marxists believe that in a Marxist state poverty does not, indeed cannot, exist. Being materialists, they command a great deal of the state resources, ensuring equality of output, if not input, to individuals.

5. *New Radical.* Whether their radicalism is based on gender, sex, race or disability, or issues such as environmentalism and nuclear disarmament, the people in the 'new social movements' are sensitive to very different social and economic forces. They often place themselves outside traditional debates about welfare and inequality, which focus on the relative values of the state or market forces. Taxes, restrictions, and provisions are aimed at radically different groups, given the values and priorities of the different groups. New Radicals are often "single-issue" people, and if the issue is poverty, they may be very radical in their attempts to cure it. Typically, they take a very international perspective.

These political camps are articulated through politicians, by economists, and by pundits. Most lay people are less "internally consistent" in their beliefs. They may support different camps simultaneously, and, to the trained philosophical eye, hold completely contradictory views. But these attributions are important. They affect how people vote; and whether they are likely to contribute to charity; and even their patterns of migration. This may account for the interest in the topic over a 30-year period. People in different societies are exposed to quite different views depending on state control of the media. Further, they are exposed not only to images of the rich and poor, but both groups in actuality. It is no surprise, therefore, that attributions for poverty differ consistently between national, cultural, and subcultural groups, and that this has been the focus of psychological research in the area.

Attributions for Poverty

There are explicit, coherent theories for the causes of poverty found in a variety of disciplines (economics, sociology, political science, psychology). There is also a fairly considerable literature on lay, or everyday, explanations for poverty and other economic conditions like wealth (Furnham, 1982a). This literature dates back over 50 years, but remains a topic of considerable interest (Cozzarelli, Wilkinson & Tayler, 2001). One of the first recorded surveys on this topic took place nearly 60 years ago. Just after World War II, an Opinion Research Survey in America asked a representative sample, "Why are some of the people always poor?" Relatively few people mentioned economic, political, or structural factors, such as employment conditions or educational differences. Most people spoke in fact of lack of effort and initiative, money mismanagement, weak character, and related causes (Allen, 1970).

Thirty years later, in a seminal study, Feagin asked over 1,000 Americans to rate the importance of 11 reasons why some people were poor in America (1975). He then categorized these explanations into three groups: *Individualist* (which places responsibility for poverty on the behavior of poor people); *Structural* (which places responsibility on external society and economic forces); and *Fatalistic* (which places responsibility on luck and fate).

Feagin's data showed various socio-religious, racial, regional, age, income and educational differences. Groups with the largest concentrations of persons giving high priority to individualistic explanations were: White Protestants and Catholics; Residents of the south and north-central regions; The over-50 age group; The middle-income group; Groups with middle levels of education. In contrast, the groups with the largest proportions ranking high on structuralism were: Black Protestants and Jews; The under-30 age group; The low-income group; The less well-educated.

Feagin argued that as long as Americans tend to individualize their economic and social problems, attempts at redistributive reform are impossible. Individualistic views reflect "false consciousness and mesh well with establishment attempts to maintain the status quo, whereas structural interpretations lend themselves to attempts at counter ideologies and at structural reforms in this society" (1975, p. 126). Later Feagin also notes: "The ideology of individuals seems to be a persisting constraint on the development and implementation of new public policies for aiding the poor. The relationship of American views of the poor and government action toward the poor is an intimate and reciprocal one, going back several centuries. Indeed, it is difficult to separate the two" (p. 164).

Furnham and Lewis (1986) listed five reasons why Feagin's study was, in retrospect, very important. Firstly, his a priori classification of explanations into three groups has received fairly considerable backing from factor analytic studies. Secondly, his study has been replicated in a range of countries on each continent. Thirdly, the variables that apparently discriminated between explanations for poverty (e.g., religion, age, education) have proved equally discriminatory in other studies. The variables that have shown most discriminatory power with regard to beliefs about poverty have been income and social class, age, rural/urban background, education, ideological beliefs, religion, and – to a lesser extent – sex. Fourthly, Feagin found that explanations for poverty are systematically linked to attitudes to welfare, suggesting that people hold coherent theories about both the causes of and cures for poverty. Consequently, his work inspired a great deal of further work in the field.

Feagin's (1975) a priori classification of explanations into three groups has received considerable backing from factor analytic studies in a range of countries, including India (Singh & Vasudeva, 1977), Israel (Rim, 1984), Britain (Furnham, 1982a, 1982b, 1982c) and Australia (Feather, 1974), as well as Canada (Guimond, Begin & Palmer, 1989), Turkey (Morcol, 1999), Brazil (Carr, Taef, de Riberio & MacLachlan, 1998) and Malaŵi (Campbell, Carr & MacLachlan, 2001). Table 9.1 attempts a comprehensive listing of salient studies done since Feagin's pioneering work.

Feagin found that explanations for poverty are systematically linked to attitudes toward welfare. This suggests that people hold coherent theories about both the causes of, and cures for, poverty; as well as how to "deal" with it. Indeed, there is a related literature on attitudes to welfare.

At the simplest level, it is obvious that left-wing people (and post-materialists), are more inclined to attribute poverty to social causes, whereas the right wing are more likely to blame the victims. Over 20 years ago, at the beginning of the Thatcher revolution in Great Britain, Furnham (1982c) found that Conservative (right-wing) voters placed more importance on individualist explanations for poverty than Labour (left-wing) voters. These, in turn, found societal explanations more important than Conservatives. Fatalistic explanations showed no difference between the groups, and were not rated as important in explaining poverty.

At the same time, in India, Pandy, Sinha, Prakash, and Tripathi (1982) found, as predicted, that those who were politically neutral and right-wingers attributed poverty more to individual habits and ability (as well as fate) than the left-wing activists. These Left-wing activists, in turn, attributed poverty in India more to government policies, and to the economic dominance of a few in their society. Williamson (1974) has proposed an ideological self-interest theory, which predicts a negative correlation between socio-economic status and perceived motivation of, and support for, the poor. This has, over the years, received considerable support.

Similar research has been carried out in developing countries over each decade. For instance, Payne and Furnham (1985) investigated national differences in the West Indies. Adolescents from Barbados and Dominica judged societal explanations to be primarily responsible for the causes and persistence of poverty in the Caribbean. However, when there were national differences, Barbadians were far more concerned with social inequalities and injustices than their Dominican counterparts. This was despite the fact that Dominica is the poorer and less well-developed of the two islands. Thus, poorer people may be apt to blame themselves for their own poverty. Payne and Furnham suggested that this tendency might be due to the fact that Barbados has a more informative media, and that economic inequalities are more exposed. Thus, cultural differences, in social representations about socio-economic issues, may be closely linked to media discussions about those issues. More recent cross-cultural comparisons between Australia versus Brazil (Carr et al., 1998); Canada versus the Philippines (Hine & Montiel, 1999); and Australia versus Malaŵi (Campbell et al., 2001) have supported classic attribution theory explanations (Harper, this volume).

Furnham (1982b) argued that, as different groups in a society are differentially likely to experience poverty, various explanations and social representations become salient in explaining these differences. This may also be true of different historic periods. Huber and Form (1973) asked a sample of Americans why they thought people were on social security during the Great Depression. Only 4% cited individualistic explanations. Yet, when asked why people had taken social security during the previous six years, 54% cited individualist reasons. Furnham (1982b) asked his subjects to imagine a poor person from one of four groups: Black/White;

Table 9.1. Table Showing Studies Specifically Looking at Attributions for Poverty

Author	Country	Participants	Findings
1. Feagin (1972)	USA	1017 Adults	There seemed to be three classes of explanation for poverty (individualistic, structural, fatalistic). Preference for explanations were shown to be related to age, education, income, religion and race.
2. Feather (1974)	Australia	667 Adults	Australians were less likely than Americans to blame the poor. Once again, attributions for poverty were linked to age, sex, education, occupational status, income and religion.
3. Singh & Vasudeva (1977)	India	Punjabi students	Societal explanations for poverty were judged to be most important by persons of lower educational attainment and income. There were very few differences between Hindus and Sikhs' attributions.
4. Furnham (1982a)	Great Britain	202 Adults	Confirmed Feagin's three-factor structure. Also found right-wing voters more likely to give individualistic explanations while left-wing voters give structural explanations.
5. Furnham (1982b)	Great Britain	90 School children (50 public and 40 private school)	Public (fee-paying) schoolboys estimated the income of the poor higher than comprehensive schoolboys. Public schoolboys found individualist explanations for poverty more important while comprehensive schoolboys found societal explanations more important.
6. Furnham (1982c)	India	72 Students at University of Bombay	Different religious groups (Christian, Hindu, Moslem, Parsi) tended to offer different explanations. Compared to British data the Indians seemed less individualistic and more fatalistic.
7. Pandy, Sinha, Prakash, Tripathi (1982)	India	30 left-wing; 30 right-wing students	Left-wing activists attributed poverty significantly more to governmental policies and economic dominance of a few, but less to self than fate, compared to right-wing activists.
8. Rim (1984)	Israel	137 Students in Haifa	Looked at personality, intelligence and ethnic group differences in explanations. Less intelligent people and neurotic extraverts gave more individualistic explanations. Western Jews, women and people from smaller families tended to give fatalistic explanations.

9. Payne & Furnham (1985)	Barbados, Dominica	354 Barbadian school children, 149 Dominican school children	Barbadians rated societal and fatalist explanations for poverty higher than did Dominicans. Prevailing conditions in the respective countries clearly influenced perceptions of the causes of poverty.
10. Guimond, Begin, & Palmer, (1989)	Canada	675 students	Social Science students attributed more to situational and less to dispositional factors than science of administration students. Unemployed people, more than social science students, blamed the poor and the unemployed themselves.
11. Harper, Wagstaff, Newton, & Harrison (1990)	Great Britain	138 people (1/3 students)	An 18-item scale investigating the causes of "Third World" poverty found four factors: blame the poor (dispositional), blame "Third World" governments, blame Nature, and blame exploitation. People who believed in a just world tended to favor the dispositional attributions.
12. Zucker & Weiner, (1993)	USA	112 students	Subjects rated the attributions of cause of poverty as well as of controllability, blame, affects of pity and anger. Conservatism correlates positively with a belief in individualistic causes of poverty, controllability; blame and negatively with societal causes, pity, and intention to help.
13. Morcol (1997)	Turkey	550 Adults in Ankara	Factor analysis confirms Feagin's three categories. Income, gender, age, and education were important determinants of explanations for poverty.
14. Carr, Taef, de Ribeiro & MacLachlan (1998)	Australia, Brazil	50 blue collar Australians, 50 blue collar Brazilians	Brazilians, more than Australians, invoked corruption as a cause of "Third World" poverty but the two groups did not differ in their attributions to nature or the poor themselves.
15. Bullock (1999)	USA	124 middle class; 124 welfare recipients	Welfare recipients were more likely to make structural attributions for poverty and more likely to regard welfare requests as dishonest and signifying idleness.

(continued)

Table 9.1. (continued)

Author	Country	Participants	Findings
16. Flanagan & Tucker (1999)	USA	434 teenagers	Higher maternal education and wealth of home district were related to attributions of poverty (and unemployment themselves), and to societal (rather than independent) causes. Those who endorsed individual causes believed all Americans enjoyed equal opportunities, and welfare led to dependency. They were also more committed to materialist goods.
17. Hine & Montiel (1999)	Canada, Philippines	Anti-poverty activists and non-poverty activists in the two countries	Poverty attributions fell into five dimensions: exploitation, characterological weaknesses of the poor, natural causes, conflict and poor government. Canadians attributed poverty more to "Third world" governments and characterological weaknesses and less to nature and conflict than Filipinos.
18. Bonn, Earle, Lea, Lea & Webley (1999)	South Africa	225 children aged 7–14 years	Open interviews showed the most common attributions for poverty were: unemployment, God's will, unequal distribution of money, lack of education, personal characteristics. Knowledge about poverty was clearly influenced by social environment.
19. Campbell, Carr & MacLachlan (2001)	Australia, Malaŵi	100 Australians, 98 Malaŵians	Australians were more likely than Malaŵians to attribute poverty to dispositional rather than situational factors. Australian situational/structural attributions were associated with frequency of monetary donation behavior.
20. Cozzarelli, Wilkinson & Taylor (2001)	USA	209 American students	Using a different measure about the characteristics of the poor they favor three factors labelling external, internal, and cultural attributions. Many factors were related to poverty attributions including participants' socio-demographic backgrounds as well as their beliefs in a work ethic, and a just world.

middle/working class; and then explain why they were poor. Explanations that were salient for one target group were not necessarily so for another. Although there was considerable agreement on the causes of poverty among those groups most susceptible to it, people began to differ radically in the causes of poverty ascribed to groups not usually thought of as poor. Thus, as well as the "deserving and undeserving" poor, there may be the "typical and untypical poor." These are people who *start* life in poverty, versus those who *fall into* poverty. Attributions for the causes of poverty differ once these finer but still important distinctions are made.

In two Canadian studies, Guimond, Begin and Palmer (1989) showed that socialisation into a particular subculture leads quite clearly to the development of person-versus-system-blame ideologies. An employed sample blamed the poor and the unemployed significantly more for the condition than did social science students. Thus, the ideological perspective of social groups exerted pressure on members' cognitive/thinking processes. They learned to see the world according to the beliefs and values of their own particular social groups. Thus, attributions for poverty are partly a function of the world views of particular subgroups in any culture linked by race, religion, language, and social status.

Wilson (1990) found beliefs about poverty were affected by exposure to public begging or panhandling. The more often that people on the streets were accosted by beggars, the more likely they were to regard poverty as a function of personal choice – though these findings have been challenged by Link et al. (1995). Certainly however, most big Western cities now have many explicit mendicants, whose begging makes people think more about the causes and cure of poverty.

Zucker and Weiner (1993) tested an attribution hypothesis about poverty that personal (political) ideology relates to attributions of cause and thence effect and finally, the likelihood of offering help. It was assumed that conservative and just world beliefs (together and separately) are likely to lead to individualistic attributions for the cause of poverty (high personal responsibility) and therefore, anger with the poor and little chance of help being offered. Equally, liberal political beliefs are likely to be associated with societal/structural explanations for the causes of responsibility (low personal responsibility), and the consequent emotion of pity, and thence support for welfare and personal help. Support for welfare for the poor was more directly linked with attributes of responsibility and political ideology than emotional reactions to the poor. The reaction of pity seems to lead to personal help, whereas perceptions of responsibility are more clearly related to welfare attitudes.

Once again, it is attribution theory that has informed the academic literature in this area. Morcoel's (1997) recent study in Turkey confirmed many of Feagin's American findings, including the threefold explanatory structure. Interestingly, in this fast developing country at the bridge of Asia and Europe, all the income groups favored structural explanations – the poor, more tangible, and the non-poor, more abstract. Poorer people, as ever, favored more fatalistic explanations for poverty in their country:

One can conclude that the tendency among Turks to use structural explanations contrasts with the consistently individualistic explanations among US residents, and is similar to the tendencies found in earlier studies among French-speaking Canadians, Italians, French, Barbadians, and Dominicans. Unlike the individualistic (internal) attributions nurtured by the dominant values in the USA, the Turkish structural (external) attributions have been influenced by a different set of dominant values, that has emphasized for centuries that the state and society are the main sources of power and influence in one's life (p. 736).

Recent studies by Carr and colleagues (Campbell et al., 2001; Carr & MacLachlan, 1998) not only confirm the actor-observer, rich-poor attribution error, in comparing groups from different cultures. They have taken the ideas further. They found "First World" students (Australians') belief in giving aid was inversely related to the extent to which they blamed the poor in developing countries for their poverty. They developed the "Donor Bias" hypothesis, which relates willingness to donate to personal attributions. They stress the role of television coverage in shaping attributions. The more sensational, dramatic, and negative the stories about "Third World" poverty (and in particular, the more talk of victims and the greater the emphasis on hardship over context), the more the poor are held responsible for their own plight. However, when war, exploitation and natural disaster are mentioned, people will tend to favor situational attributions.

Table 9.1 shows the results of 20 studies on the attribution of poverty, conducted over a 30-year period. Indeed, there seems to be an increase, rather than a decrease, in interest in the area. It is probably true to say that studies that have focused on the structural content of lay attributions, have broadly supported Feagin's (1995) threefold classification, though content analysis tends to yield more than three factors (Bonn, Earle, Lea & Webley, 1999; Hine & Montiel, 1999). Whilst the number of individual difference correlates of attributions appears to have increased, most studies have confirmed earlier work with regard both to strictly demographic factors and also belief systems (Cozzarelli, Wilkinson & Taylor, 2001). However the most recent studies by Carr and colleagues (Carr et al., 1998; Campbell et al., 2001) have extended the cross-cultural literature, to demonstrate how personal, national, and socio-economic conditions, shape attributions for poverty.

These studies have also looked at beliefs about the beliefs and behaviors of poor people, that may help explain their poverty. Feagin (1975) pointed out that figures available at that time indicated that the public were wrong about, or at least, vastly overestimated, the amount of people lying about or having illegitimate children to increase their social security payments. Similarly, Goodwin (1973) found that the middle class tended to underestimate the work values (ethic) and life aspirations held by the poor. Indeed, a considerable amount of psychological (Allen,

1970) and sociological (Davidson & Gantz, 1974) research has demonstrated few differences in attitudes, beliefs and values between the poor and those not so badly off. Goodwin (1973) did a path analysis on the relationship between education, age, the work ethic and the perceived motivation of, and support for aid to, the poor. Those who believed in the work ethic believed the poor to be badly motivated and did not want to support them. Goodwin thus concluded that the work ethic is a fundamental element in popular ideology, and that its change could lead to numerous important results. However, the work ethic is blamed for many issues, and there are as many lamenting as rejoicing in its demise (Furnham, 1990).

Certainly, psychologists have been interested in how particular value systems, associated not so much with politics as with work (the Protestant Work Ethic), and with justice (just world beliefs), shape not only attribution for poverty, but also willingness to actually help the poor (see final section).

Attributions about Social Security, Welfare, and the Alleviation of Poverty

Psychometric studies on attributions about welfare and related issues have attempted to find their underlying dimensions. Both *content analysis* of newspapers and *factor analysis* of questionnaires have shown that there are general beliefs about welfare. Using a content analysis, Golding and Middleton (1983) found four clear factors which they called *prodigality* (being to do with wasteful spending patterns, financial ineptitude, imprudent breeding habits and sheer fecklessness or lack of motivation of the poor on welfare), *injustice* (exploitation or unfair distribution of financial rewards), *bad luck* (cycle of deprivation thesis) and individualistic *fatalism* (sheer unpredictable, undeserved personal, as opposed to structural, misfortune).

Using a different methodology, Furnham (1983) looked at people's attitudes toward (unemployed) people receiving unemployment benefits. A factor analysis of the 12-item questionnaire revealed three clearly interpretable factors which indicated that attitudes centred around the difficulty of coping with the amount of benefit provided; beliefs about people being dishonest about their needs and abusing benefit payments; and the loss of self-esteem and stigma associated with being on social security. The results showed that, in Britain, as in America, people not on social security tend to have more negative attitudes toward those that are, although they may appreciate some of the problems of the unemployed on social security.

Furnham (1985) later replicated the above study but found four clearly interpretable dimensions underlying attitudes to social requests. In all the factor analytic (empirical or conceptual) work, similar factors arise with regard to attitudes to those on social security. These are: dishonesty/idleness/prodigality – referring

Table 9.2. Items Making Up the Four Attitudinal Factors

Dishonesty and idleness
There are too many people receiving social security who should be working.
Many people getting social security are not honest about their needs.
Many women getting social security are having illegitimate babies to increase the money they get.
A lot of people are moving to this country from other countries just to get the social security here.
Too many people on social security spend their money on drink.
There is no reason why a person who is able to work should receive social security.
Having a social security system only encourages idleness.
All people on social security should be expected to do various social duties to pay for their benefits.

Difficulty
Generally speaking, we are spending too little on social security programmes in this country.
One of the main troubles with social security is that it doesn't give people enough money to get along.
A country's compassion and humanitarianism can be judged by its social security payments.
There is no reason why a person on social security should be spied upon by the authorities.
Social security is a right, not a privilege.

Stigma/Shame
People are often ashamed of being on social security.
Many people in this country who are entitled to social security are too proud to claim it.
Nobody can possibly enjoy living on social security for any period of time.
There would be fewer people on social security if jobs were easier to find.

Need
Most people on social security who can work try to find jobs so they can support themselves.
Many of the people on social security have very little talent, ability and intelligence.
There will be a greater, rather than a lesser, need for a good social security system in the future.

to the *undeserving nature* of the recipients; difficulty/poverty – referring to the *economic deprivation* of those attempting to cope on the amount of benefit provided; and stigma (shame)/self-esteem – referring to the *social consequences* of being the recipients of "charity" (see Table 9.2).

Furnham and Rose (1987) argued that the rise of the welfare state, particularly in Western Europe, and recent high levels of unemployment in many industrialized countries, has seen the emergence of what may be called the "welfare ethic." This belief system (rather than an ethic) is based on the idea of a "cunning claimant of welfare." This person believes that because welfare is so easy to obtain (and to some extent, one's right), they should enjoy the good life (without work) by living off payments received from the welfare system. People who do this have become known, somewhat pejoratively, as "super scroungers." In other words, "the laxness, excessive generosity, inefficiency and vulnerability to exploitation of the welfare system" makes it open to less-than-honest people (Golding & Middleton, 1983, p. 109). As has been shown, many people *not* on welfare payments believe that those who *are*, are both idle and dishonest. Although there is considerable research to show that this view is misplaced, there is anecdotal evidence of people who thrive on welfare and espouse the welfare ethic. In that the welfare ethic tends to despise and avoid work, one may expect it to be negatively correlated with the Protestant Work Ethic, but positively correlated with the leisure and wealth ethics.

The welfare ethic is significantly and negatively associated with the work ethic, but positively correlated with wealth and leisure. However, an important distinction not made in the above scale refers to the extent to which people wish to exploit and extend welfare payments to themselves, and others, by legal means; and the extent to which they abuse the system by illegal practices. Furthermore, it should be particularly instructive to look at the differences in attitudes between countries that have relatively high versus low or no levels of welfare payments. It is expected that social representations about welfare will be directly related to national welfare policy.

In an American telephone survey of 1,507 people concerning their reactions to the homeless, Link et al. (1995) identified four clear factors: *Emotional responsiveness* (anger, compassion about the plight of the homeless); a *lack of empathy with the situation of the homeless* (self-inflicted, irresponsibility); a *link between homelessness and deviant characteristics* (addictions, delinquency, recidivism); and *endorsements of restrictions on homeless people* (no "panhandling" in particular places). Interestingly, Link et al. (1995) showed that exposure to the homeless was clearly related to attitudes about them. They believe that although the homeless are stigmatized, there is little evidence that the American public have lost their compassion or are unwilling to support policies to help the homeless begging on the streets.

Considerable research remains to be done on the distribution, structure and correlates of perceptions of people on welfare. Considerably less research has been done on the perceptions of social inequality in society (Lewis, Webley & Furnham, 1995). Perhaps the most interesting of all, however, are longitudinal replication studies showing how social representations change over time as a function of structural changes in society.

Studies on general attitudes to welfare/social security or indeed studies on the homeless in the West have naturally led on to an interest in studies on how to help people in other countries (Furnham, 1996). There is growing interest in the psychology of overseas. This includes helping aid organisations in fund-raising activities to try both the to influence and understand fund-raising activity. Clearly, how poor people are portrayed influences attributions for the causes of poverty that, in turn, influences the likelihood of donations (Carr, Mc Auliffe & MacLachlan, 1998).

There are, interestingly, both short- and long-term effects of media portrayals and aid agency advertisements. In the short term there is the question of whether involving certain emotions like guilt or pity will have any impact on donations. But perhaps more importantly, there are the long-term effects of trying to target those known groups whose individualistic explanations for poverty make them less likely to personally give aid or vote for it. As Feagin found nearly 30 years ago, attitudes to an explanation for poverty are logically related to attitudes to welfare, public aid, and, inevitably, to overseas aid (1975). Personal ideology, based on attributions, affects how people vote, as well as their personal donations; which can have very dramatic effects on both rich and poor countries alike.

Conclusion

Informed by Attribution Theory, psychologists have examined how people explain poverty. Their findings have been cross-nationally and temporally robust across countries and time, providing support for the fundamental and ultimate attribution error. What has been less discussed is the *function* of those beliefs. To a larger extent, these may be considered within the literature of Just World Theory (Furnham, 2002). It is argued that victim blaming (in this sense, the past) helps people maintain their beliefs that we live in a stable, just, and predictable world. If the world is just, poor people must be personally and morally responsible for their fate; and in turn, must be architects of their own recovery. Yet these attributes could also be seen as a coping strategy. They are associated with instrumentalism, rather than fatalism; optimism rather than depression; stability rather than instability. "Politically incorrect" attributes for the poverty of others seem stress reducing for many individuals. This, in part, explains why the attributes are so difficult to *change*.

The research in this area has produced a number of robust findings. Firstly, despite differences over time and national groups, the evidence does suggest that everyday explanations for poverty do appear to fit the threefold theory, although it is true that people's theories are not always internally coherent. They do appear both stable and functional. Their correlations with age, education, religion, etc. suggest they have a similar etiology. Because of these associations, they may prove very difficult to change.

Secondly, these attributions are logically related to other economic beliefs like the causes of wealth, and of unemployment. That is, that lay attributions are all part of an individual's lay politico-economic ideology. Beliefs about the causes and consequences are related. As above, the relations tend to be more psychological than purely logical.

Thirdly, and perhaps most importantly, though still awaiting more research, these attributions are related to behavior: whether one votes, and for whom; which newspapers are read and which television channels are watched; the extent of personal charitable donations and which charities are chosen to receive these; the disposition to do voluntary work of any kind; even where one chooses to take a vacation.

Our understanding of the causes and consequences of poverty is thus much more than social psychologists "doing some applied attribution theory research." Understanding poverty attributions is equally important for the poor and the non-poor alike. This is because these attributions are fundamentally implicated in the actual causes, and alleviation, of poverty worldwide.

References

Alcock, P. (1996). *Social policy in Britain: Themes and issues.* London: Macmillan.

Allen, V. (1970). *Psychological factors in poverty.* Chicago: Markham.

Alston, J., & Dean, K. (1972). Socio-economic factors associated with attitudes toward welfare recipients and the cause of poverty. *Social Services Review, 46,* 13–23.

Bagguley, P. & Mann, K. (1992). Idle thieving bastards? Scholarly representations of the "underclass." *Work, Employment and Society, 6,* 133–126.

Blasi. G. (1990). Social policy and social science research on homelessness. *Journal of Social Issues, 46,* 207–219.

Bonn, M., Earle, S., Lea, D., Lea, S., & Webley, P. (1999). South African children's views of wealth, poverty, inequality and unemployment. *Journal of Economic Psychology, 20,* 593–612.

Bullock, H. (1999). Attributions for poverty: A comparison of middle-class and welfare recipient attitudes. *Journal of Applied Social Psychology, 29,* 2059–2082.

Bullock, H., Wyche, K. and Williams, W. (2001). Media images of the poor. *Journal of Social Issues, 59,* 229–246.

Carr, Mc Auliffe, E., & MacLachlan, M. (1998). *Psychology of aid.* London: Routledge.

Carr, S. C., & MacLachlan, M. (1998). Actors, observers, and attributions for Third World poverty: Contrasting perspectives from Malawi and Australia. *Journal of Social Psychology, 138,* 189–202.

Carr, S. C., Taef, H., de Ribeiro, R., & MacLachlan, M. (1998). Attributions for "Third World" poverty: Contextual factors in Australia and Brazil. *Psychology and Developing Societies, 10,* 103–114.

Connolly, K. (1985). Can there be a psychology for the "Third World"? *Bulletin of the British Psychological Society, 38,* 249–257.

Cozzarelli, C., Wilkinson, A., & Taylor, M. (2001). Attitudes toward the poor and attributions for poverty. *Journal of Social Issues, 59,* 207–227.

Davidson, C., & Gantz, C. (1974). Are the poor different? A comparison of work behavior and attitudes among the urban and non-poor. *Social Problems, 22,* 229–245.

Feagin, J. (1975). *Subordinating the poor.* Englewood Cliffs, NJ: Prentice.

Feather, N. (1974). Explanations of poverty in Australia and American samples: The person society and fate? *Australian Journal of Psychology, 26,* 119–126.

Flanagan, C., & Tucker, C. (1999). Adolescents' explanations for political issues: Concordance with their views of self and society. *Development Psychology, 35,* 1190–1201.

Furnham, A. (1982a). Why are the poor always with us? Explanation for poverty in Britain. *British Journal of Social Psychology, 21,* 311–322.

Furnham, A. (1982b). The perception of poverty among adolescents. *Journal of Adolescence, 5,* 135–147.

Furnham, A. (1982c). Explaining poverty in India. *Psychologia, 25,* 236–243.

Furnham, A. (1983). Attitudes toward the unemployed receiving social security recipients. *British Journal of Social Psychology, 24,* 19–27.

Furnham, A. (1985). The determinants of attitudes toward social security recipients. *British Journal of Social Psychology, 24,* 19–27.

Furnham, A. (1990). *The Protestant Work Ethic.* London : Routledge.

Furnham, A. (1996). Attributions for increase in urban homelessness. *Journal of Social Behavior and Personality, 11,* 189–200.

Furnham, A., & Procter, E. (1989). Belief in a just world. *British Journal of Social Psychology, 28*, 365–384.

Furnham, A., & Lewis, A. (1986). *The economic mind.* Sussex: Wheatsheaf.

Furnham, A., & Rose, M. (1987). Alternative ethics: The relationship between the wealth, welfare, work and leisure ethic. *Human Relations, 40*, 561–574.

Furnham, A. (2001). Social representations of welfare and economic inequality. In C. Roland-Levy, E. Kirchler, E. Penz., & C. Gray (Eds). *Everyday representations of the Economy* (pp. 113–136). Vienna: Duv.

Furnham, A. (2002). Belief in a just world: Research progress over the past decade. *Personality and Individual Differences*, (in press).

Golding, P., & Middleton, S. (1983). *Images of welfare: Press and public attitudes to poverty.* Oxford: Martin Robertson.

Goodwin, L. (1973). Middle-class misperceptions of the high life, aspirations and strong work ethic held by the welfare poor. *American Journal of Ortho-psychiatry, 43*, 554–564.

Guimond, S., Begin, G., & Palmer, S. (1989). Education and cause attributions: The development of "person-blame" and "system-blame" ideology. *Social Psychology Quarterly, 52*, 126–140.

Gurin, G., & Gurin, G. (1970). Expectancy Theory in the study of poverty. *Journal of Social Issues, 26*, 83–104.

Harper, F. (1991). The role of psychology in the analysis of poverty. *Psychology and Developing Societies, 3*, 193–201.

Harper, D., Wagstaff, G., Newton, J., & Harrison, K. (1990). Lay cause perceptions of poverty and the Just World Theory. *Social Behavior and Personality, 18*, 235–238.

Hine, D., & Montiel, C. (1999). Poverty in developing nations: Cultural attributional analysis. *European Journal of Social Psychology, 29*, 943–959.

Huber, J., & Form, W. (1973). *Income and ideology. An analysis of the American political formula.* New York, NY: Free Press.

Jaspars, J., & Fraser, C. (1984). Attitudes and social representations. In R. Farr & S. Moscovici (Eds.), *Social Representations* (pp. 101–123). Cambridge: Cambridge University Press.

Lea, S., Tarpy, I. R., & Webley, P. (1989). *The Individual in the Economy.* Cambridge, UK: Cambridge University Press.

Lee, B., Jones, S., & Lewis, D. (1990). Public beliefs about the causes of homelessness. *Social Forces, 69*, 253–265.

Lerner, M. (1980). *The belief in a just world.* New York, NY: Plenum.

Lewis, A., Webley, P., & Furnham, A. (1995). *The New Economic Mind.* Brighton: Wheatsheaf.

Link, B., Schwartz, S., Moore, R., Phelan, J., Struening, E., Stueve, A., & Colten, M. (1995). Public knowledge, attitudes and beliefs about homeless people: Evidence for compassion fatigue. *American Journal of Community Psychology, 23*, 533–555.

McFadyen, R. (1998). Attitudes toward the unemployed. *Human Relations, 51*, 179–199.

Morcoel, G. (1997). Lay explanations for poverty in Turkey and their determinants. *Journal of Social Psychology, 13*, 728–738.

Mowbray, C., Bybee, D., & Cohen, E. (1993). Describing the homeless mentally ill. *American Journal of Community Psychology, 21*, 67–93.

Pandy, T., Sinha, T., Prakash, A., & Tripathi, R. (1982). Right-left political ideology and attributions of the causes of poverty. *European Journal of Social Psychology, 12*, 327–331.

Payne, M., & Furnham, A. (1985). Explaining the causes of poverty in the West Indies: A cross-cultural comparison. *Journal of Economic Psychology, 6*, 215–229.

Rim, Y. (1984). Explanation of poverty and personality aspects. *Personality and Individual Differences, 5*, 123–124.

Singh, S., & Vasudeva, P. (1977). A factorial study of the perceived reasons for poverty. *Asian Journal of Psychology and Education, 2*, 51–56.

Waters, L., & Moore, K. (2001). Coping with economic deprivation during unemployment. *Journal of Economic Psychology, 22*, 461–482.

Webley, P. & Nyhus, E. (2001). Life cycle and dispositional routes into problem debt. *British Journal of Psychology, 92*, 423–446.

Williamson, J. (1974). Beliefs about the motivation of the poor and attitudes toward poverty. *Social Problems, 18*, 634–648.

Wilson, G. (1990). Exposure to panhandling and beliefs about poverty causation. *Social Science Research, 76*, 14–17.

Zucker, G., & Weiner, B. (1993). Conservatism and perceptions of poverty: An attributional analysis. *Journal of Applied Social Psychology, 23*, 925–943.

Chapter 10
Poverty and Discourse

David J. Harper

One would like on the part of the psychologist a reversal of allegiance so that he [sic] endeavors to bring about a change in people who control the material resources of the world... Mehryar (1984, p. 166)

The Poverty of Psychology

Over 30 years ago Arthur Pearl wrote a chapter entitled "The poverty of psychology." In this, work, he commented that "psychologists as a group, along with other social scientists, have been guilty of refusing to accept the challenges that poverty presents to a society of unparalleled affluence" (Pearl, 1970, p. 348). Has the discipline learned? I will argue that it has not. In an earlier article, I argued that one of the reasons that the field had not contributed well to the fight against poverty was because of its overreliance on attribution theory, which was not adequate to the task (Harper, 1996). In that article I suggested that a *discursive* approach might avoid some of these problems. Whilst still arguing that research into poverty explanations needs to draw on a broader range of theoretical frameworks, I want to suggest now that research has not only been (1) methodologically inadequate, by using questionnaire measures and correlation designs, but also (2) politically unaware, by focusing mainly on students or the general public (see also, Aus-Thai Project Team, this volume). From (1) and (2), I will develop a critique of the attribution paradigm. Next, I will sketch out research questions suggested by one alternative, that of *critical discursive psychology*. One implication of such an approach is that research needs to focus on different target groups.

Methodological Inadequacy

Individualism (Instead of Collectivism).   A pervasive individualism characterises much of the poverty-explanation literature. There are different varieties of
individualism, but in this literature it is the "individual as explainer" who is the unit
of analysis. This means that organisational explanations are not examined. As a result a whole area of potential research materials such as government press releases,
ministerial statements, political manifestos, multinational corporation strategies,
and annual reports, are ignored. Thus, political and ethical ideologies implicit, for
example, in the just world theory literature (Conservatism, Liberalism, Socialism,
Equity) are reduced to individualistic concepts of attribution style (Furnham &
Procter, 1989). In one sense however, this individualism is a false one since most
of the studies compare statistical "group" means rather than individual scores in
an attempt to define abstract factors.

Rigidity (Instead of Flexibility).   Another problem with attribution accounts
is that they assume the existence of underlying attribution structures that remain
stable over time and across situations. Even research studies like those in Heaven
(1994) and in Muncer and Gillen (1995), which attempt to examine the complexity
of explanations, still rest on an essentially stable abstract causal network. Yet even
slight changes in the wording and context of paper-and-pencil questions can lead
to great differences in participant responses (Schuman & Presser, 1981). Adrian
Furnham (this volume) is a major contributor to the literature on this topic. He has
noted that explanations for poverty may be used variably according to which poor
"target group" is specified (Furnham, 1982; Furnham & Procter, 1989).

Mono-causal (Instead of Pluralistic).   People not only use different explanations for different target groups; they also use different explanations in different
contexts. A factor analysis conducted by Harper et al. (1990) found that many of the
items of the CTWPQ (Causes of Third World Poverty Questionnaire), for example
those relating to "natural" causes like climate, loaded on a number of factors. From
Table 10.1, we can see that whilst this might suggest merely that these items lack
discrimination, another possibility is that "natural" explanations for poverty have
the flexibility to be used together with victim-blaming and other types of explanations. Indeed a number of studies have found that participants draw on both individualistic and structural explanations for poverty, even though they are orthogonal
factors (Hunt, 1996). Verkuyten (1998) noted how single-cause explanations that
are typically studied in attribution research were used by only 7% of participants.
    One reason for the focus on these structures is psychologists' attachment to
questionnaire measures. The archetypal "explanations of poverty" study utilizes
Feagin's classic (1972) scale (described in Furnham, this volume), plus a selection
of measures of social psychological constructs, usually the Just World Scale, and

Table 10.1. Overall Means and Standard Deviations for Items of the Causes of "Third World" Poverty Questionnaire (CTWPQ, from Harper et al., 1990)

There is poverty in Third World countries because:[a]	Mean	(SD)
1. The people of such countries keep having too many children[b]	3.20	(1.25)
2. Of fate[b]	2.32	(1.01)
3. Their governments are corrupt[c]	3.64	(0.94)
4. Of the regional climate	3.76	(0.92)
5. Their governments are inefficient[c]	3.82	(0.82)
6. Of laziness and a lack of effort in the population of such countries[b]	2.18	(1.02)
7. Their land is not suitable for agriculture[d]	3.42	(1.02)
8. Other countries exploit the Third World[e]	3.81	(1.16)
9. Of disease in Third World countries	3.56	(0.96)
10. Their governments spend too much money on arms[c]	3.64	(1.04)
11. Of war	3.60	(0.96)
12. Of the world economy and banking systems being loaded against the poor[e]	3.57	(1.11)
13. Pests and insects destroy crops	3.64	(0.78)
14. The population of such countries make no attempt at self-improvement[b]	2.55	(1.09)
15. Of a lack of intelligence among the people there[b]	2.85	(1.26)
16. Of a lack of thrift and proper management of resources by the people there[b]	3.09	(1.15)
17. The people there are not willing to change old ways and customs[b]	3.24	(1.00)
18. Of a lack of ability among the people of such countries[b]	2.41	(1.13)

[a] Strongly agree = 5, strongly disagree = 1
[b] Items loading uniquely and significantly on "Blame the poor" factor
[c] Items loading uniquely and significantly on "Blame 'Third World' governments" factor
[d] Item loading uniquely and significantly on "Blame Nature" factor
[e] Items loading uniquely and significantly on "Blame exploitation" factor

measures of socio-demographic variables. Because of these methodological criticisms above, these studies have become self-perpetuating, with researchers seeking to replicate studies in different countries, in different groups of people, producing a morass of unsurprising, and occasionally un-interpretable, findings.

Political Naïveté

A final major problem with attribution poverty research is a startling lack of curiosity about what social function these kinds of explanations might have. Most studies find relationships between individual explanations and social psychological variables or demographic factors, but there is often little attempt to explain further. Lerner's (1980) account is motivational and largely individualistic, having recourse to a restricted range of relatively straightforward rational and non-rational motivational strategies. As some writers have noted, what is lacking in such accounts is a clear understanding of the role of ideology in structuring our views of the world. Explanations have ideological effects. Thus Finchilescu

(1991) has argued that the biasing of attributions and explanations constitutes a discriminatory practice. As Billig comments:

> To probe the ideological significance of these attributions one needs to go further than documenting their existence. One needs to discover how the explanation of one sort of social event fits into a wider pattern of explaining social events. (1988, p. 201)

Ironically, by ignoring such issues, traditional attribution research on poverty explanations has itself been politically and ideologically conservative in its theory and methodology. It has failed to deliver findings that might be of use in acting politically and socially, against poverty. One might ask of this research, what is the use of focusing 30 years of research on the explanations of individual members of the public, who have no control over world economic resources, as opposed to governments and transnational corporations, that *do*? In this respect, attribution research has made an ironic "fundamental attribution error" (Ross, 1977). It has focused on the explanations of individuals rather than systemic factors, and on those with little power to bring about actual change (Prilleltensky, this volume). Whilst most psychologists and other social scientists no longer engage in "blaming the victim" (Ryan, 1971), in the overt ways which Pearl (1970) documents, they continue to do so indirectly. They do so indirectly by conducting research on "the poor," which then gives credence to victim-blaming explanations (Wright, 1993), or by neglecting to do research on "the rich" (Furnham, this volume).

Toward Politically Useful Research into Explanations of Poverty: Alternative Theoretical Resources

An alternative approach to attribution theory draws from work in critical discursive psychology (Parker, 1997). Discourse theory can be useful, as it attends to how explanations are used, and what effects these explanations serve. Critical uses of discursive psychology, which attempt to avoid moral and political relativism, can attend to the inherently *contradictory* way in which explanations are used. According to Parker, explanations are "*constituted* within patterns of discourse that we cannot control" (1997, p. 290, emphasis in original). This means that in constructing explanations, cultural resources are drawn on. Discourse, and discursive positions, exist in a web of *power* relations (Prilleltensky, this volume). Thus, explanations do not just exist in a vacuum; they have political effects and functions (although they are not necessarily used intentionally).

Murray Edelman (1977, 1998) has written extensively about the meaning and functions of political language, especially as they occur in discussions about social problems like poverty. Edelman has suggested that there are three ways of explaining poverty. These are similar to Feagin's (1972) typology, outlined in Furnham (this volume). The existence of these different explanations, or "myths" as Edelman terms them, means that society can *live with its ambivalence*. For Edelman, these contradictions are a result of social relations: "Governmental rhetoric and action comprise an elaborate dialectical structure, reflecting the beliefs, tensions and ambivalences that flow from social inequality and conflicting interests" (1998, p. 134). According to Edelman, these myths work together in a mutually reinforcing way, and can have a wide range of effects because often one explanation implies other explanations and concomitant actions:

> To believe that the poor are basically responsible for their poverty is also to exonerate economic and political institutions from that responsibility and to legitimize the efforts of authorities to change the poor person's attitudes and behavior. (1998, p. 132)

What New Questions Might be Thrown Up by the Use of Alternative Theoretical Resources Like Critical Discursive Psychology?

Moving Away from an Assumption of Individual Explainers Giving Internally Consistent and Exclusive Explanations. Discourse analysts do not assume that individual explainers produce internally consistent accounts. Rather, there is an assumption of discursive variability. It is expected that people will use different explanations at different times. Parker (1997) argues that this variation points to contradictions inherent in culture. Edelman (1977, 1998) and Billig and colleagues (Billig et al., 1988) have argued that variation is common in talk about poverty. Iyengar (1990) notes that Lane's (1962) studies demonstrated that "ordinary people express considerable uncertainty, and even stress, when describing their political views and they often offer what appear to be contradictory positions on related issues" (1990, p. 20).

One of the problems with paper and pencil survey designs is that they lack the ability to examine the *dynamics* of explanations, for example, to see if people give different explanations at different times in ordinary conversation. From Table 10.1, we can see that some items from Harper et al.'s (1990) CTWPQ, including popular "natural" explanations, do not load uniquely and significantly on orthogonal factors. This suggests that some of the explanations may be used flexibly in association with others. Moreover, research consistently shows that people agree with many explanations for poverty. They often give both individualistic and structural accounts and they have access to broad cultural resources. Billig et al. note that often "contrary values are asserted, as the same people believe that the state should aid the poor and also that state aid is liable to undermine the moral worth of the poor" (1988, p. 41).

In this respect, some of the findings of traditional studies may be useful. It is likely for instance that the consistent finding of three broad explanations for poverty reflects a dominance of these explanations in national cultures. However, two broad problems have dogged much of the more traditional research: A search for orthogonal factors through the use of factor analysis; and the search for factors that lead to differential loadings on these orthogonal factors. Such a paradigm, and I write as someone who has contributed to that paradigm in the past, is likely to miss much of the complexity of how people account for poverty in an everyday context or, indeed, the meaning, effect, and function, of using a combination of explanations.

Building on Variability and Contradiction: Intervening to Produce Change. I have already noted that the attribution paradigm implicitly assumes the stability and consistency of explanations. If, instead, they are seen as dynamic and con-textual, psychologists might be less pessimistic about the possibility of *changing* them. Given that there is evidence that negative images and perceptions of those in poverty begin in childhood, interventions to change people's explanations are very important (Chafel, 1997). Is change *possible*? Two factors suggest that it is. Firstly, there is evidence that, over time, the numbers of people agreeing with simplistic individualistic explanations for poverty have decreased. For example, a survey by the Commission of the European Communities (1977) reported that Britain had the largest number of respondents blaming poverty on "laziness and lack of willpower" (43% compared to an EEC average of 25%). According to this study, Britain was below average in ascribing poverty to injustice in society and to luck, and nearer the average in blaming poverty on 'progress in the modern world.' By 1992, Gallup published a series of polls examining British explanations for domestic poverty, and found that a majority blamed environmental ("circumstances") rather than indi-vidualistic ("effort") factors (52% and 12%, respectively). As well, the percentage favoring individualistic explanations had decreased over recent years, although 34% agreed that poverty was due to both (Gallup/Social Surveys Ltd, 1992). Thus, fewer individualistic explanations were given at time one than at time two.

Changes from time one to time two are not invariably of course in a positive direction. A study two years after the above opinion poll survey by Gallup found that the ascription to individualist factors had risen by 3% to 15%, whilst the number ascribing poverty to "injustice in our society" had dropped by 10% to 42% (Gallup/Social Surveys Ltd, 1994). As with much of the poverty explanation literature, findings like this can be hard to interpret. One conclusion that can be drawn is that explanations are not impervious to attempts to change them. Of course, in such attempts, we must be vigilant that the change is not simply a move toward more subtle forms of victim blaming, but interventions can produce positive change. In one study for instance, Lopez, Gurin & Nagda (1998) investigated an educational intervention, for college students, on inter-group relations, that covered structural sources of racial or ethnic inequalities. They found that the course led to increases in structural (situational) thinking about racial or ethnic inequality, and that this generalized to other inequalities that had not been explicitly covered in the course, an effect enhanced by the use of active learning strategies.

A Shift in Focus from Individuals, to Organizations and Systems.   Of course, all theoretical frameworks can, to a greater or lesser extent, be invigorated by a political analysis of the problems they are investigating, and I would not want to argue that this is only the preserve of critical discursive work. Ignacio Martín-Baró (e.g., 1994)[1] for example, used opinion polling in a politically astute manner. But critical discursive psychology can also help to dissolve the artificial boundary between individuals-as-explainers and the institution-as-explainer. Individuals, governments and multi-nationals may use certain accounts in a similar way to warrant their conduct. An individual may not give to charity because, they say, the government should be giving money to that issue. Similarly a government may refuse foreign aid because, they argue, the national government is corrupt or inefficient. In the next section I therefore draw on work conducted within a variety of theoretical traditions, including attribution research, to argue that psychologists would do well to shift their focus from individual members of the general public, to the complex *system* that reproduces explanations of poverty. In this way, traditional research can be refocused and revitalized to make a more positive contribution toward poverty reduction.

Toward Politically Useful Research into Explanations of Poverty: Researching Systems Involved in Explaining, Maintaining and Addressing Poverty

There is a large range of institutions, agencies and systems involved in the network of those in a position to actually change inequality, and I will select a number here. These include the media; charities; government and politicians. They also include trans-governmental organizations, like the WTO (World Trade Organization), the World Bank, the IMF (International Monetary Fund), and the multinationals.

The Media

In a fascinating study, Iyengar (1990), has built on the work of others like Schuman & Presser (1981), to show that how a question is framed has a significant impact on participants' responses. Iyengar studied TV news broadcasts between 1981–86 about domestic poverty in the USA, and delineated two major categories. One of them described poverty primarily as a social or collective outcome (a thematic frame); the other described poverty in terms of particular victims (an episodic frame). Generally, episodic frame news stories outnumbered thematic

---

[1] Ignacio Martín-Baró was a Latin American social psychologist and Jesuit priest. He was assassinated by El Salvadorean government troops from the US-trained Atlacatl battalion on November 16 1989.

frame stories by two to one. In an initial experimental study, the participants' perceived responsibility for poverty was significantly influenced by the way the media framed the story. Thematic frame stories evoked more structural (situational) attributions, and episodic frame stories evoked more individualistic ones. Iyengar showed a selection of news stories illustrating thematic and episodic frames. The results reinforced the original finding, that beliefs about causal responsibility depended on *how poverty was framed*. In the episodic frame, Iyengar's sample of White middle-class American participants made different causal attributions about both causal responsibility and treatment responsibility (what should be done to prevent recurrence), depending on the characteristics of the poor person:

> When the poor person was White, causal and treatment responsibility for poverty were predominantly societal; when the poor person was Black, causal and treatment responsibility were more individual ... The particular combination of race, gender, age and marital status (e.g., Black adult single mothers) was particularly evocative of individual responsibility ... In this sense, the most 'realistic' individual-victim frame has the most inhibiting effect on societal conceptions of responsibility. (Iyengar, 1990, p. 35)

From this, Iyengar suggests that the finding of rates of individualistic explanations of poverty may be due not only to dominant cultural values (individualism) but also to "news coverage of poverty in which images of poor people predominate" (1990, p. 29). Such research applies equally to coverage of poverty in the so-called "developing world," which I shall refer to as the South. The news media are the major source of information on poverty for the general public. A recent report by the Third World and Environment Broadcasting Project noted that 82% of Britons relied on television as their main source of information on the South (Christian Aid News, 1995; see also Department for International Development, 2000, and Voluntary Service Overseas, 2002). They are also groups where the use of images and explanations are used to great effect, and they are, I will argue, greatly influenced by a variety of commercial and other interests.

With some notable exceptions, most coverage of poverty in the South, by the press and broadcasters, tends to focus less on any links between the North's wealth and the South's poverty. Instead, they concentrate on poor individuals, the climate, or corruption and inefficiency in national governments of the South. When political issues are focused on (as in the case of the Ethiopian war), no questions are asked about who the financial backers or arms-suppliers might be, nor what the history of the conflict is. If questions about these issues are raised, it is often only in terms of local politics (episodic), and not links with "First World" agencies or governments (thematic). The effect of such coverage is that famine becomes seen as something that "just happens," often immediately (episodic, individualistic), and is not connected to political processes.

What then are the interests involved in media discourse? One obvious interest is the need for media managements to avoid "political" topics, in order to maintain stable revenue (e.g., from advertisers). However, this cannot be a full explanation, since there is also evidence that "news-worthiness" and dramatic entertainment value are powerful influences on what gets broadcast and what does not (Golding & Middleton, 1982). One report indicates that 90% of all television news and current affairs reports, on issues in the countries of the South, focus on conflict and disaster (Christian Aid News, 1995). Sorenson (1991) has argued that there are a number of political interests and ideological influences on the way the mass media portray Southern poverty. In his analysis of media discourse on famine, in the Horn of Africa, he has shown how a number of entertainment, media, and political interests, were served by particular ways of explaining and portraying the famine. For example, a slow onset to the Ethiopian famine was depicted as sudden and related only to food and famine itself. Reports did not discuss the conflict, nor offer a political analysis of it. Sorenson describes such an account as one of *naturalization*:[2]

> Naturalization ignores conditions of poverty, repression and conflict that allowed drought to be translated into famine. Reports explaining famine as natural disaster are reductionist, and overlook growing bodies of work that recognises multiple causation of famine. (Sorenson, 1991, p. 226)

Sorenson also described some of the tactics used by the news media, noting the use of "inoculation" where reports admitted either the extent of the famine or some level of external causation, before going on to blame famine mainly on internal factors (i.e., the actions of Ethiopians themselves). This helped conceal continuing structural inequities, and illustrates how contrasting accounts can be combined to serve particular rhetorical purposes. Responsibility was placed on African governments, whilst Western benefactors were positioned as benevolent. Sorenson links such discourses on poverty with wider discourses on Africa, with racist discourses, and with victim-blaming of Africans who are often implicitly positioned in the media as "ignorant" and "primitive." The use of racist and colonialist views of Africans as "inferior," and "other"; as "primitive," "noble savages"; and as needing "to be converted"; has a long history (Mudimbe, 1988; Parker, 1992; Brookes, 1995).

Although written media texts might provide researchers with useful materials, the media's use of images is also potentially useful. Interpretations similar to Sorenson's on media text could, no doubt, be applied to media images. A British TV

---

[2] I would agree with Twose (1984) who argues that, for example, Britain's winter is as bad as "Third World" climactic extremes with the difference that Britain is economically able to meet the demands of the winter whilst countries of the South often cannot. Solomon Inquai has commented that "hunger is about politics, not the weather" (Oxfam, 1985).

documentary "Hard Times," broadcast over ten years ago (Beatrix Campbell, journalist in Channel 4 (UK) Television, 1991), explored how domestic poverty was portrayed in documentaries, dramas, and news items in the media. Hard Times reported that often very simple images of poor people were used, and that the media orchestrated artificial and stereotyped situations for the cameras, so that portrayals of poverty fitted public and media expectations and perceptions:

> What you do is find the worst possible example you can think of somebody who's poor rather than that you find examples that exemplify ordinary, typical, everyday poverty. (Beatrix Campbell, journalist)

Research like Sorenson's reveals how *the media are explainers too*. Can anything be *done* about such coverage? Certainly one option is to intervene to put pressure for accountability on the news and entertainment media, to adopt and adhere to ethical Codes of Conduct. An interesting intervention in the field of learning disability is reported by Jones & Eayrs (1996). They monitored coverage of learning disability in two British local newspapers, noting: The total number of articles published on learning disability; the use of quotations by people with learning disabilities; the percentage of articles including photographs portraying people with learning disabilities as active participants; and the percentage of articles about fundraising for charities associated with learning disability. At the end of a six-month monitoring project, they made a different intervention to each newspaper. One was sent a letter summarising the findings of the monitoring exercise, enclosing a copy of guidelines on the portrayal of disability produced by a disability campaigning group. The other newspaper was sent these but was also visited by a person with learning disability, who explained the findings of the monitoring exercise and made a number of recommendations for future coverage.

The results in the six months after the intervention were very interesting. The first newspaper, whose coverage of learning disability had been small, had a much-reduced coverage of learning disability. The second newspaper too had a slightly reduced coverage, but had also included accompanying photographs, that portrayed people with learning disabilities as *active*. Although such findings were focused on local rather than national newspapers, and so need to be tested further, they do suggest that some change is possible. Jones and Eayrs comment that their study suggests that media presentation can be changed, and that 'the best advocates for change are the individual stakeholders involved' (1996, p. 78).

A study by Voluntary Service Overseas (2002) found that members of the public were bewildered when presented with information which ran counter to dominant media images and angry at the press and broadcasters for not conveying this complexity. It was argued that the public needed both context for, and an emotional connection with, those portrayed in reports about the South.

Charities

Another major network where explanations of poverty circulate is in material produced by poverty charities. Here, I will focus on those charitable non-governmental organisations providing aid for the South. Carr, McAuliffe & MacLachlan (1998) have addressed general issues about the psychology of aid, but I want to examine the promotional and campaigning material used by such charities. Some research suggests that, like the media, charities are guided by similar interests (to both raise money and consciousness, often in dramatic ways) and by some different ones (challenging the economic status quo), whilst being limited and constrained by other discourses (legal and political). How are these competing interests managed in charity discourse?

Most of the non-structural explanations for poverty in the South, used in the Harper et al. (1990) study, have been disputed (Haru, 1984; Mehryar, 1984; Oxfam, 1991b; Twose, 1984). Instead, Oxfam (1991b) describes the major causes of poverty as: conflict; the debt crisis; declining prices of commodities like tea; inadequate aid; consumption of resources by the North; environmental damage; and lack of accountable government. One might also add unfair trading policies to this list. An attribution theorist, adopting a naïvely realist point of view, might try to compare individuals' attributions with the "real" causes of poverty, and speculate why there was a difference – education or political preference perhaps. Another line of inquiry, however, is to examine the interests and the constraints on charity discourse.

In an article examining challenges facing Oxfam, Brazier (1992) noted that the charity existed in a difficult political atmosphere. He recalled an instance when Oxfam had been reported to the Charity Commission in the United Kingdom. This complaint had been lodged through a Conservative Member of Parliament (or MP). The MP felt that an Oxfam campaign about poverty, in Southern Africa, had been politically biased. The campaign material had drawn links between the continuing poverty of that region and South Africa's pre-1994 policy of apartheid. The effect of the investigation, by the Charity Commission, was that Oxfam had to withdraw its campaigning material. Oxfam also had to undertake not to be 'politically biased' in future. This demonstrated as well that explanations of poverty, and the information on which they rest, exist in an ideological and political context. Charities are not 'free' to choose what explanations of poverty they promote in their materials. They are instead constrained by legal and political discourses and this, in turn, constrains the cultural availability of certain explanations.

One effect of charities attempting to offer certain explanations for poverty is to be accused of being *overtly* politically motivated. As the Brazilian Archbishop Helder Camara has commented, "When I give food to the poor, they call me a saint. When I ask why the poor have no food, they call me a Communist." A constraint on charity discourse then is the need for accounts to appear to be, overtly, politically disinterested. An effect of this is that such explanations do not challenge the dominant discourses available, in culture, for explaining poverty. The choice between particular explanations, at particular moments, is not just an individual one based on age, gender, political preference, and so on. Rather, it is crucially social, taking place in an arena of competing political and ideological interests.

Another influence on the kinds of explanations for poverty, given by charities, is whether they are aiming to (a) raise money or (b) raise awareness about the causes of poverty. This kind of dilemma is common to many charities, and has proved to be an interesting area for research (Eayrs & Ellis, 1990; Stockdale & Farr, 1987; Barnett & Hammond, 1999). Aid agencies have increasingly realised that the kind of images that raise funds often devalue the people portrayed, and fail to address crucial issues (van der Gaag, 1992). However, as one advertising executive involved in charity work has noted, "If my brief is to make people put their hands in their pocket and come up with some money, then one has to – it's quite right to use fairly dramatic techniques in doing that" (Simon Sherwood of advertising company Lowe, Howard-Spink in Channel 4 Television, 1991). Feagin (1972) links this concern to social and government policy. If respondents saw poverty as being due to the poor, they were antagonistic to welfare payments. Thus, agencies may feel that, in order to raise funds, they need to portray the poor as helpless and powerless (Billig et al., 1988).

There are particular dynamics involved in giving to charity (Radley & Kennedy, 1992). Burman (1994a, 1994b, 1994c) has argued that charity appeals for children in the South draw on a number of elements. These include a restricted range of ways of relating rich and poor peoples (in the form of funding or sponsorship to helpless recipients); little scope for reflection on the causes of these circumstances, or whether they are portrayed accurately; and the use of dominant models of child development. Such discursive strategies have particular effects, and can be seen as serving certain interests. These can be purely pragmatic for charities "raising money," but they can also be ideological, as in "policing" the relationship between rich and poor, so that the poor are eternally positioned beneath the rich in a hierarchy of social dominance (Lemieux & Pratto, this volume).

As with the South Africa campaign, Aid agencies' campaigns using such strategies have had the effect of attracting criticism about their use of images. This has generated a call both for more positive images of Southern peoples, and an emphasis on education rather than fund-raising (Lyne, 1990). As a result of these pressures, Oxfam has published both a statement of policy about the use of images (Oxfam, 1991a) and a training and educational package, examining the effects of images (Oxfam, 1992). However, such changes in advertising policy are taking place in a more difficult economic context for overseas aid charities. They are often being overtaken in revenue terms by 'conservation' and other charities 'closer to home,' and with dilemmas about to what extent to link with anti-globalisation protests and Drop the Debt, Jubilee 2000, and Fair Trade campaigns.

As the Oxfam report suggests, an educational discourse has become increasingly prominent in aid agency literature (Gill, 1988). But what might the effects of such a change of discourse be? Eayrs and Ellis (1990) are equivocal in their investigation of the effects of charity advertising. Although their study focused on the portrayal of people with learning disabilities, implications can be drawn about charity advertising for other marginalized groups. They argued that more normalising approaches have a cost. They may encourage people to feel there are no difficulties to be faced. So agencies should aim at encouraging people to have direct contact with people with learning disabilities, in order to overcome prejudice. Eayrs and Ellis also suggested a more pragmatic strategy, involving the use of positive images in promotional campaigns, which some evidence suggests may elicit donations *anyway*; even if they are not directly requested (Barnett & Hammond, 1999; Stockdale & Farr, 1987). However, work by Barnett & Hammond (1999) suggests that definitions about what constitutes a "positive" image may be contested by both disabled and by non-disabled people.

Government and Politicians

It is a little disappointing that, in a recent literature search of research examining explanations of poverty, of all the groups studied, I could find only one study whose sample involved a group with real access to power. Beck, Whitley and Wolk (1999) investigated the perceptions of poverty of members of the Georgia General Assembly, in the USA. This research was conducted at a time when there was debate about legislative change in US welfare policy, with the ending of Aid to Families with Dependent Children (AFDC), and a shift to Temporary Assistance to Needy Families (TANF). TANF was a program emphasizing personal responsibility for, and more individualistic solutions to, poverty. Building on Feagin's (1972) finding linking causal explanations of poverty with views of welfare, Beck et al. asked the legislators to rate ten causes of poverty. The top three explanations were individualistic. There were no differences in agreement with individualistic explanations as a result of political party, ethnicity, or gender. However, significant differences were found in relation to structural explanations: "Democrats, People of color, and women viewed discrimination and low wages as more important causes of poverty than their counterparts" (Beck et al., 1999, p. 96). Interestingly these explanations mapped onto views about welfare reform. Those preferring structural explanations favored AFDC, and those preferring individualistic explanations favored TANF. Beck et al. then developed a useful analysis of these data, suggesting that legislative change was, in part, driven by frustration with AFDC rather than by wholehearted support for TANF.

Campaigns should therefore seek to place individualistic explanations in a structural context, for example by explaining "lack of thrift" with reference to the day-to-day costs of living in poverty, for example the cost of housing as a percentage of income. As well, anti-poverty researchers and campaigners should gather detailed relevant information to rebut common myths, for example comparing the number of "help wanted" job offer signs with the numbers of those unemployed. Beck et al. argue that campaigners need to take into account what issues legislators are likely to see as most salient, for example, data from their constituencies. There is a need for much more research like this on legislators. Yet they too are only one system in the network, and it is to the wider world economic context that I will turn next.

Networks of Financial Power: The WTO, The World Bank, The IMF, and The Multinationals

Both Mehryar (1984) and Haru (1984) have argued that an accurate perception of the origins and perpetuation of poverty leads anyone to focus at the macro level, rather than at the micro level to which psychologists are more accustomed. This macro level constitutes the world economic system, where national governments, that tie aid to trade agreements and manage some of the debt of the South, are increasingly being superseded by trans-national organizations: the IMF; the World Bank; and multinational corporations. These organizations also include banks that, with the World Bank, hold most of the debt of the South.

Does this lead inevitably to the conclusion that psychology has no part to play? Mehryar (1984), for example, has suggested that psychology may simply be irrelevant: "To claim that psychology and other social sciences, singly or in combination, can solve these problems will amount to no more than wishful thinking" (Mehryar, 1984, p. 165). A turn to examining the world economic system can sometimes descend into conspiratorial thinking but, as Eco (1986) observes, there is no need for a conspiracy theory account when one considers that international capital is moved between these networks in accordance with the interests of the different organizations embedded within them. The link between the explanations of events, and the interests served by those explanations, can be seen very clearly when oil companies protest against explanations of global warming. Change can come from ensuring that anti-social actions currently in their interest do not always remain so.[3]

It would indeed be absurd to suggest that political problems can be solved through the social sciences alone. However, this is not to say that psychology has no part to play (Harper, 1991). It can be useful to examine some of the language and

---

[3] For example, one proposal to address the problems associated with currency speculation (the destabilizing of national economies and the triggering of currency devaluations and economic crises which deepen poverty, boost national debt and increase unemployment and hunger) is to introduce a "Tobin Tax" of 0.25% on it which could earn $250 billion a year which could be used to introduce basic health care, nutrition, education, clean water and sanitation for the poor across the world. For more information go to: www.tobintax.org

processes involved in policy formation and decision making. For example, the journalist John Pilger has noted that,

> The new order is beset by euphemisms, which can often mean the opposite of the new jargon term. Liberalization – more commonly known as the 'free trade' agenda – sounds reasonable in itself. Much of the language used to describe it suggests that it is a positive trend: the removal of "restrictions," "barriers" and "obstacles" to what should be "free" trade. These throw up a smoke screen. The important question: "Free" for whom? (Carlton Television (2001, p. 3))

Psychologists can also offer useful analyses of the organizational processes responsible for the creation of poverty. Although there is little psychological research on such institutional influences, there is an organizational psychology literature. Limitations of space do not permit a review of this area. However, a glimpse of the usefulness of an organizational psychology perspective can be gained from an appraisal of a discrete area of research on the decision-making processes involved in British nuclear weapons during the Cold War.

McLean (1986), in her paper on nuclear decision making, gives an example of what an organizational analysis might entail: The uncovering of lines of decision making; the position of key individuals in that process; the collection of biographical and other information on those individuals. She draws a number of conclusions that are relevant to this discussion:

1. That there is a process of "decision shaping" carried out by administrators in committees rather than by politicians. Thus discussions take place out of the public eye, but under the influence of powerful groups.
2. That the options presented to those in senior positions (in this case politicians) are limited. Thus, no one person in a system is solely responsible for decisions. Decisions are difficult to change, and are resistant to influences external to the system. In addition, those who wish to influence decisions are confused about where to aim their intervention.
3. That decision shapers do not want to feel personally responsible. This point is brought out more fully in Hamwee's (1986) research on dialogue between peace groups and decision makers. Hamwee notes that the latter deny responsibility for their decisions, and goes on to state:

[The decision maker] takes daily and detailed responsibility for one minuscule part of a giant worldwide process ... He [sic] concentrates, as he [sic] has to, on the technical task, and can only talk about it in technical language. To talk in the (peace) groups' language would be to abandon all the assumptions behind all that he [sic] knows and does. (Hamwee, 1986, p. 6).

Similarly, Hamwee et al's (1990) study details the assumptions implicit in Cold War bureaucracies whilst the contributors to McLean's (1986b) volume provide an analysis of the organizational and assumptive structures in nuclear weapons decision-making around the world. It is likely that decision makers in economic and governmental institutions, responsible for the maintenance of poverty, exist in organizational structures which could be analysed in similar ways and any attempt to influence these decision-making systems needs to take account of these kinds of processes and contexts. Moreover, those institutions, whilst largely unaccountable, can be influenced by external pressure. Such interventions need to be well targeted – witness the recent liberalization by international drug companies of AIDS medicines after concerted international pressure. Targeted interventions like this expose the differences between political rhetoric and actual practice, as campaigns surrounding the debt crisis are now seeking to do.

Future Directions

There is a need for future psychological research, into poverty explanations, to draw on a wider range of theoretical frameworks. This chapter has suggested the critical discursive approach as one model to use. I have also suggested that research should focus on those who *are* in positions to effect change more than on ordinary members of the public, who are not. This might provide a more adequate understanding of political explanations, and also extend research beyond merely individualistic accounts, to include the texts and images both produced by individuals and organisations, and in which those individuals and organisations are themselves located. It is to be hoped that future research, by de-mystifying explanations of poverty and exploring their ideological foundations in social context, will be more useful, practically and politically. In this way, psychology may become better positioned to contribute toward *conscientización* in the fight against poverty (Martín-Baró, 1994).

References

Barnett, J. & Hammond, S. (1999). Representing disability in charity promotions. *Journal of Community & Applied Social Psychology, 9*, 309–314.
Beck, E., L., Whitley, D. M., & Wolk, J. L. (1999). Legislators' perceptions about poverty: Views from the Georgia General Assembly. *Journal of Sociology & Social Welfare, 26*, 87–104.
Billig, M. (1988). Methodology and scholarship in understanding ideological explanation. In C. Antaki (Ed.), *Analysing everyday explanation: A casebook of method* (pp. 199–215). London: Sage.
Billig, M., Condor, S., Edwards, D., Gane, M., Middleton, D., & Radley, A. R. (1988). *Ideological dilemmas*. London: Sage.
Brazier, C. (1992). Changing charity, *New Internationalist, February*, 4–7.
Brookes, H. J. (1995). Suit, tie and a touch of juju – the ideological construction of Africa: A critical discourse analysis of news on Africa in the British press. *Discourse & Society, 6*, 461–494.
Burman, E. (1994a). Poor children: Charity appeals and ideologies of childhood. *Changes, 12*, 29–36.
Burman, E. (1994b). Development phallacies: Psychology, gender and childhood. *Agenda: A Journal about Women and Gender, 22*, 11–20.

Burman, E. (1994c). Innocents abroad: Western fantasies of childhood and the iconography of emergencies. *Disasters: The Journal of Disaster Studies and Management, 18*, 238–253.

Carlton Television (UK). (2001). *The new rulers of the world* (programme booklet). Birmingham, UK: Carlton Television.

Carr, S., Mc Auliffe, E., & MacLachlan, M. (1998). *Psychology of Aid*. London: Routledge.

Chafel, J. A. (1997). Societal images of poverty: Child and adult beliefs. *Youth & Society, 28*, 432–463.

Channel 4 (UK) Television. (1991). *Hard times: How the media portrays poverty*. The Media Show, 17 March.

Christian Aid News. (1995). "Third World" losing out on TV. *Christian Aid News, 87* (April/June), 2.

Commission of the European Communities. (1977). *The perception of poverty in Europe*. Brussels: EEC.

Department for International Development. (2000). *Viewing the world: A study of British Television coverage of developing countries*. London: DfID (www.dfid.gov.uk).

Eayrs, C. B., & Ellis, N. (1990). Charity advertising: For or against people with a mental handicap? *British Journal of Social Psychology, 29*, 349–360.

Eco, U. (1986). Striking at the heart of the State. In *Travels in Hyperreality* (pp. 113–118). London: Pan.

Edelman, M. (1977). *Political language: Words that succeed and policies that fail*. Florida: Academic Press.

Edelman, M. (1998). Language, myths and rhetoric. *Society, 35*, 131–139.

Feagin, J. R. (1972). Poverty: We still believe that God helps those who help themselves. *Psychology Today, November*, 101–129.

Finchilescu, G. (1991). Social cognition and attributions. In D. Foster & J Louw-Potgieter (Eds.), *Social Psychology in South Africa: An Introduction* (pp. 207–233). Cape Town: Lexicon.

Furnham, A. (1982). Why are the poor always with us? Explanations for poverty in Britain. *British Journal of Social Psychology, 21*, 311–322.

Furnham, A., & Procter, E. (1989). Belief in a just world: Review and critique of the individual difference literature. *British Journal of Social Psychology, 28*, 365–384.

Gallup/Social Surveys Ltd. (1992). Social trends. *Gallup Political & Economic Index, Report 384 (August)*, 30.

Gallup/Social Surveys Ltd. (1994). Social trends. *Gallup Political & Economic Index, Report 404 (April)*, 26.

Gill, P. (1988). Conclusion: Helping is not enough. In R. Poulton & M. Harris (Eds.), *Putting people first: Voluntary organizations and "Third World" organizations*. London: MacMillan Education.

Golding, P., & Middleton, S. (1982). *Images of welfare: Press and public attitudes to poverty*. Oxford, UK: Martin Robertson.

Hamwee, J. (1986, December). *Dialogue with decision makers*. Paper presented at the London conference of the British Psychological Society, London, UK.

Hamwee, J., Miall, H., & Elworthy, S. (1990). The assumptions of British nuclear weapons decision-makers. *Journal of Peace Research, 27*, 359–372.

Harper, D. (1991). The role of psychology in the analysis of poverty: Some suggestions. *Psychology and Developing Societies, 3*, 193–201.

Harper, D. J. (1996). Accounting for poverty: From attribution to discourse. *Journal of Community & Applied Social Psychology, 6*, 249–265.

Harper, D. J., Wagstaff, G. F., Newton, J. T., & Harrison, K. R. (1990). Lay causal perceptions of "Third World" poverty and the Just World Theory. *Social Behavior & Personality, 18*, 235–238.

Haru, T. T. (1984). Moral obligation and conceptions of world hunger: On the need to justify correct action. *Journal of Applied Behavioral Science, 20*, 363–382.

Heaven, P. C. L. (1994). The perceived causal structure of poverty: A network analysis approach. *British Journal of Social Psychology, 33*, 259–271.

Hunt, M. O. (1996). The individual, society or both? A comparison of Black, Latino and White beliefs about the causes of poverty. *Social Forces, 75*, 293–322.

Iyengar, S. (1990). Framing responsibility for political issues: The case of poverty. *Political Behavior, 12*, 19–40.

Jones, S. P., & Eayrs, C. B. (1996). Newspaper portrayal of disability: An intervention study. *British Journal of Learning Disabilities, 24*, 77–79.

Lane, R. E. (1962). *Political Ideology: Why the Common Man Believes What He Does.* New York, NY: Free Press.

Lerner, M. (1980).*The belief in a just world: A fundamental delusion.* New York, NY: Plenum Press.

Lopez, G. E., Gurin, P., & Nagda, B. A. (1998). Education and understanding structural causes for group inequalities. *Political Psychology, 19*, 305–329.

Lyne, D. (1990). Tapping into and turning on the public's emotions. *The Guardian,* 12 December.

Martín-Baró, I. (1994). *Writings for a liberation psychology.* London: Harvard University Press.

McLean, S. (1986a, December). *How nuclear decisions are made.* Paper presented at the London conference of the British Psychological Society, London, UK.

McLean, S. (1986b). *How nuclear weapons decisions are made.* Basingstoke, UK: MacMillan.

Mehryar, A. H. (1984). The role of psychology in national development: Wishful thinking and reality. *International Journal of Psychology, 19*, 159–167.

Mudimbe, V. Y. (1988). *The invention of Africa: Gnosis, philosophy, and the order of knowledge.* London: James Currey.

Muncer, S., & Gillen, K. (1995, April). *The perceived causes of poverty: A question of politics.* Paper presented at Annual Conference of the British Psychological Society, University of Warwick, UK.

Oxfam. (1985). *The News Behind the News.* Oxford, UK: Oxfam.

Oxfam. (1991a). *Oxfam and images.* Oxford, UK: Oxfam.

Oxfam. (1991b). *The Oxfam report.* Oxford, UK: Oxfam.

Oxfam. (1992). *How does the world look to you? An activity pack on the use and interpretation of images.* Oxford, UK: Oxfam.

Parker, I. (1992). Psychology, racism and the Third World: Five hundred years of resistance. *Changes, 10*, 323–326.

Parker, I. (1997). Discursive psychology. In D. Fox & I. Prillitensky (Eds.), *Critical Psychology: An Introduction* (pp. 284–298). London: Sage.

Pearl, A. (1970). The poverty of psychology: An indictment. In V. L. Allen (Ed.), *Psychological factors in poverty* (pp. 348–364). Chicago, IL: Markham.

Radley, A. & Kennedy, M. (1992). Reflections upon charitable giving: A comparison of individuals from business, "manual" and professional backgrounds. *Journal of Community & Applied Social Psychology, 2*, 113–129.

Ross, L. (1977). The intuitive psychologist and his shortcomings: Distortions in the attribution process. In L. Berkowitz (Ed.), *Advances in experimental social psychology, 10*, 173–220. New York, NY: Academic Press.

Rubin, Z., & Peplau, A. (1975). Who believes in a just world? *Journal of Social Issues, 31*, 65–89.

Ryan, W. (1971). *Blaming the victim.* New York, NY: Pantheon.

Schuman, H., & Presser, S. (1981). *Questions and answers in attitude surveys: Experiments on question form, wording and context.* New York, NY: Academic Press.

Sorenson, J. (1991). Mass media and discourse on famine in the Horn of Africa. *Discourse & Society, 2*, 223–242.

Stockdale, J. E., & Farr, R. M. (1987, December). *Social representation of handicap in poster campaigns.* Paper presented at British Psychological Society London Conference.

Twose, N. (1984). *Cultivating hunger: An Oxfam study of food, power and poverty.* Oxford, UK: Oxfam.

Van der Gaag, N. (1992). Every picture sells a story. *Oxfam News, Autumn*, 7.
Voluntary Service Overseas. (2002). The Live Aid legacy: The developing world through British eyes –
    A research report. London: VSO (www.vso.org.uk).
Verkuyten, M. (1998). Self-categorization and the explanation of ethnic discrimination. *Journal of
    Community & Applied Social Psychology, 8*, 395–407.
Wright, S. E. (1993). Presidential address. Blaming the victim, blaming society or blaming the
    discipline: Fixing responsibility for poverty and homelessness. *Sociological Quarterly, 34*, 1–16.

Chapter 11

Poverty and Economic Crisis

The Aus-Thai Project Team

Floyd H. Bolitho, Stuart C. Carr, Wiladlak Chuawanlee,
Yutthana Chaijukul, Oraphin Choochom, Pachongchit Intasuwan,
Nopawan Jotibun, Ian P. Purcell, Dusadee Yolao

Conceptual Analysis

During the last decade or so, the term "economic crisis" has become part of the global lexicon. In an economic sense, this term refers to relatively macroeconomic outcomes such as rapidly falling stock market prices, plunging currency devaluations, widespread bankruptcies, and mass unemployment (Eiamlapa-Quinn, 1998). In process terms, economic crisis is technically a reflection of the increasingly fragile interconnectedness of national and regional economies in a new global order (Kato, 2000). This fragility is estimated to be especially acute for the poor who live in developing countries (World Bank Group, 2001a). Indeed for a majority of people the world over, the most salient feature of economic crisis is probably its capacity for plunging millions of people into abject poverty. During the 1997–98 economic crisis in South East Asia for instance, over fifty million people in Indonesia were pushed below the poverty line, and some forty million Indonesians were left without enough basic food to eat (Soesastro, 1998). This chapter uses behavioral science to focus on the everyday meanings of catastrophes like these (World Bank, 2000). In essence, we argue that developing a better understanding of how people think and feel about economic crisis – its lay psychology – will improve human abilities to manage it, and therefore combat poverty within the global community (Aus-Thai Project Team, 1998, 1999, 2001, 2002).

Economic Issues are Social Issues

At first glance, *economic* crisis is an inherently economic *issue*, intertwined with globalisation, and so determined by global economics (Gates, 1998). From this perspective, economic crisis is clearly caused by – and to that extent needs to be managed through controlling – a number of "hard," macro, and structural factors. These might include for example austere budget cuts, high interest rates, and strict monetarist policies (Khor, 1998). Viewed exclusively against backdrops such as these, there appears to be little space for the softer social sciences like psychology, with its focus on the micro processes of human behavior, to make any significant practical or indeed theoretical inroads (*The Economist*, 2001). In this chapter, we take a step back from this naturally important economic perspective, to consider also micro-level perceptions of economic factors. In particular, we focus on how communicating these, both within and between community and organisational groups affected by crisis, will increase motivation to combat downward spirals into poverty. These inherently human processes – perception, communication, and motivation – have had their significance for development increasingly recognised by economists since the days of Adam Smith (Sen, 1999).

Emerging Psychological Research

Ironically perhaps, psychology has been slower to recognise a role in development for these same kinds of processes (Carr, Mc Auliffe, & MacLachlan, 1998). In the past decade or so, however, the sharp advent of economic crisis has prompted a steep increase in the number of development-related studies listed in PsycInfo (2001, use search term, "economic crisis"). This rapidly growing body of publications (close to 100, to-date) has three discernible and interrelated underlying themes. Firstly, through the poverty they create, economic crises impact negatively on human health and well-being, both physical (e.g., Ajuwon & Shokunbi, 1997) and mental (e.g., Brenner & Lipeb, 1993; Kloep, 1995). Often these downturns start in the workplace (Hoon & Lim, 2001), where they stem from perceived job *insecurity* (Apisakkul, 2000; Manzano, Llorca, Salmero, & Montejo, 1995). That insecurity, secondly, is facilitated by increased centralization of management and the sense of *disempowerment* that this brings (Prechel, 1994). This disempowerment further spills over into community settings (Woelk, 1992), fuelling downward spirals in self-esteem and social identity (Montero, 1996).

Prejudices in potential donors and investors too, thirdly, contribute to this depressive cycle, by *restricting opportunities* for disadvantaged communities to control their development, according to an agenda that is determined internally and locally. Within the International Monetary Fund (IMF) for example, a former chief economic advisor describes a "cookie-cutter" approach to compiling country reports, in which they are drafted using the "search and replace" button to substitute one country name for another (Stiglitz, 2000). In another example, schemata for the event "economic crisis" varied substantially from one general (donor) public to the next. Swiss observers emphasised managing bankruptcies, whereas Italians stressed instead inflation (Savadori, Nicotra, Rumiati, & Tamborini, 2001).

These three themes of insecurity, disempowerment, and restricted opportunity, that we have just seen underlie the emerging psychological literature on crisis, bear directly on the major concerns for development out of poverty identified in the latest World Bank Report (2001). According to this central document – which it is argued provides a blueprint for future initiatives against poverty globally – genuine "development" consists not just of economic production, but also crucial "human factors." These human factors form three new "pillars" of development. Those pillars in brief are: (1) having a sense of *security*; (2) feeling *empowered* with sufficient voice to address prejudice and discrimination; and, (3) sensing the *opportunity* to develop economic assets (Sen, this volume). Since these are precisely the underlying themes that we have just identified in the emerging psychological literature, the psychology of economic crisis evidently has a contribution to make to the current zeitgeist in development studies and practice.

A Process

Over and above this conformity however, our initial glance at the psychological literature also suggests an innovative psychosocial pathway for development to follow, namely through intra- and inter-community communication (UNDP, 2000). Communicating as we have seen is a human process, which in this case entails first and foremost sharing perceptions (views) about the crisis within the community directly affected by it. We already know that community surveys, for instance, are effective superordinate goals for putting otherwise alienated individuals into contact with one another, creating social support networks, and galvanising a community to re-take control of its own destiny (Carr, in press; Moskalewicz & Swiatkiewicz, 2000; Moreira, this volume; Sánchez, Cronick, & Wiesenfeld, this volume). Such repossession of identity, and regaining of control, is likely to reduce insecurity (World Bank, 2001). Secondly, the results of those surveys can be communicated to local community based organizations, national governments, and overseas donors or investors. This effectively empowers local community with voices to articulate for themselves what they need; rather what outsider observers think they want. This is how community survey data operates in parts of marginalised Indigenous Australia, and as well is consistent with recent community development programs initiated within Thailand (Teeravekin, 1998). By such processes, thirdly, these local communities create better *opportunities* to develop in the direction dictated by their own needs rather than the misperceptions of outside decision makers (Harper, this volume). Mehryar (1984) has made essentially the same point about a need to address biases amongst the various general publics in developed economies, who are asked to assist development efforts through taxes and personal donations (also, Carr et al., 1998).

A Theoretical Framework

Clues to what precisely these pre-existing biases might be are contained, in psychology, within attribution theory (Weiner, 1991). *Attributions* (e.g., "poverty is due to laziness," or "crisis is due to international exploitation") are simply the perceived causes of behavior, events, and life circumstances, such as poverty and living in the midst of an economic crisis. Attribution *theory*, including its theoretical application to (a) poverty-reduction initiatives, has been described and discussed at length in previous chapters within this volume. The details of this theory's relevance to (b) managing economic crisis, too, have been articulated in detail elsewhere (Aus-Thai Project Team, 1998). The essence of both of these applications however is that outside "observers" are liable to develop overly *dispositional*, trait-based and victim-blaming explanations for both (a) and (b) (Ross, 1977). This bias is especially noticeable when compared to insider, or "actor" counterparts, who have had more direct experience of the event itself (Furnham, this volume). These "players," according to the theory, will tend to perceive the same event (poverty, crisis) in more structural terms (Harper, this volume).

As this analysis suggests, much of the error in the difference between actors and observers lies with the observers (Carr et al., 1998, Chapter 2). Their tendency to blame the victim in cases of poverty is widely termed the "fundamental attribution error" (Ross, 1977; Harper, this volume). There are several quite understandable reasons for this error. They include, for instance, a lack of background knowledge about the actual life circumstances of the actors; a natural tendency for observers to focus on people rather than less visible causes of events (like the structural causes of crisis); and rising global individualism, which by definition entails attributing human conditions to individual characteristics rather than structural factors. Added to this confluence of cognitive factors are emotional realities like guilt, and the acute sense of powerlessness that comes from being reminded daily that one lives in the privileged sector of sharply stratified, "hourglass" economies (Carr, 2000). Such guilt (and insecurity of its own) is exacerbated by continuous and sensationalised media images that inadvertently motivate viewers to *rationalise* their inescapable privilege the only way they know how – *psychologically*. Thus the poor are poor "because they deserve to be," "because they are lazy," or "because they are corrupt and inept."

This "push down" process is not quite as crude as the above-imagined verbalisations make out (Harper, this volume). For example, rationalisations like this must in fact be substantially subconscious; otherwise their self-deception cannot logically work. Such tactics would also help to sustain development models in which the poor are implicitly not entrusted to manage their own development (Carr, this volume). One reflection of such a process would be if development "solutions" tended to be imposed from the outside, and to be structural rather than human in kind (Harper, this volume). Of course, this tendency is precisely why the World Bank and others like the Nobel prize-winning Laureate Professor Sen (this volume) have been arguing for a radical change in the way that the world thinks about poverty and crisis.

Psychologically speaking, however, there is a very clear "up" side to the idea that many of the prejudices against the poor are largely implicit. Their very implicitness creates a significant potential for observer consciousness, and mindfulness, to be *raised* (Gergen, 1994). That, in fact, is where attribution theory starts to derive a practical edge. It suggests that what may be sufficient to reduce fundamental attribution errors, such as the negative stereotypes described above, is to engineer a *change* of perspective – from observer to actor. This idea (of presenting actor views to observers) is not a new one in development studies. Perspective changes resembling these have already been advocated by UNICEF, in its program for students, "Education for Development" (Fountain, 1995). With respect to educating populations of adults, as Harper (this volume) points out, their consciousness can be raised by affording greater communicative voice to key stakeholders in the recovery process, the crisis-affected poor themselves. This very line of reasoning has just in fact provided the rationale for the global study, *Voices of the Poor*, which is described in detail elsewhere in this volume. As we have seen, that study provided a core impetus to the 2001 blueprint for attacking poverty (World Bank, 2001).

How, Exactly, Does This Perspective Sharing Work?

In the case of economic crisis, we can perhaps imagine the impact, on sceptical observers, of hearing directly from actors living in economic crisis about any personal sacrifices they have perceived as necessary for fighting the crisis, like job-sharing, for instance (Aus-Thai Project Team, 2002). Personal sacrifices of precisely this kind actually happened within the Thai civil service during the economic crisis of 1997–98 (Aus-Thai Project Team, 1999). In principle we agree with Harper (this volume), messages *conveying* local perceptions like this, to outside observers, could be communicated quite widely, to a whole range of relevant audiences and stakeholder groups. These could include, for instance, the various local, regional, and overseas donor publics; non-government organizations (NGOs) at home and abroad; policy makers; and potential business investors.

Such a give-and-take of alternative perspectives, on supposedly the same phenomena, is known in skills acquisition as "perspective sharing" (Carr, in press). Typically, this perspective sharing raises mindfulness about personal biases, like negative fundamental attribution errors. To see how that effect can occur with regard to crisis, imagine that a member of the donor public, an aid organization, a policy maker, or a prospective investor, is labouring under an implicit negative stereotype, in which the people directly affected by economic crisis are justifiably victims of their own corruption. Misperceptions like this were arguably encouraged in certain sections of the Australian press during the 1997–98 crisis in South East Asia (Carr, in press). Yet the readers of these disparaging media reports might have been surprised to learn that the poor themselves shared this perception of their own politicians (Aus-Thai Project Team, 2002). Under such conditions, relatively undifferentiated illusions about "corruption in Asia" (this kind of generalisation is known in attribution theory as an "out-group homogeneity effect" and an "ultimate attribution error" might have been more difficult to maintain (for details of these biases in aid and development settings, see Carr et al., 1998).

Encountering gentle but potentially profound nudges, that *contradict* the stereotype, is similar to what ethnographers call encountering "rich points" (Walsh, 1997). These rich points occur through experiencing very different perspectives from one's own, and can be sufficiently powerful to enable even so-called "experts" to rethink their existing assumptions, preconceptions, and apperceptions about other groups.

The same line of communication, again enhancing mindfulness, can flow in the opposite direction, i.e., from observers to actors. If, for example, actor groups directly affected by economic crisis become aware, through perspective sharing, that potential investors in their development perceive them, say, because of negative influences by the media, to be corrupted, or lazy, or too lacking in intelligence to ever really benefit from assistance and investment, then they can give themselves permission, and so empower themselves, to speak out against the stereotype. An example of precisely this occurred in Thailand, after striking workers were portrayed, in the national media, as pawns of agitator "rascals" (Eiamlapa-Quinn, 1998). According to Eiamlapa-Quinn, local NGOs reacted to this by publishing on behalf of the workers an open letter *rebutting* the negative stereotypes about them. This is an example of what the 1999 Human Development Report means, when it points out that communication networks involving relatively small players, like NGOs, can and do motivate wider support for marginal communities, among both donor publics and larger aid and development organizations (see, for example, UNDP, 2000, p. 5).

To sum up, there are at least two major ways in which perspective sharing can improve the prospects for development out of economic crisis. Firstly, initially demoralized and insecure actors may become less disposed to depressively blame their situation on factors beyond their own control. Secondly, perspective sharing may help to free local communities of any inherently disempowering stereotypes held by outside observers and decision makers. This would be a healthy contrast to their usual attempts to impose a solution on the crisis from the outside, just because the poor are implicitly stereotyped as incapable of managing their own development. Thirdly, therefore, perspective sharing enhances the opportunity for communities to take charge of and control their own development from within.

A Measure

None of this theoretical process can be put into motion, however, unless we begin to develop a *measure* of how the various stakeholder communities and organizations perceive economic crisis in the first place. Next, therefore, we concentrate on illustrating how a research team might go about constructing such a measure. Much of the material for this discussion is drawn from research conducted by the Aus-Thai Project Team (1999; for details, in press). Their initial work in this area has focused on attributions for the 1997–98 economic crisis in South East Asia. Although that particular economic crisis was by any standards a major event in its category, the argument we advance here is intended to be more process-based than outcome-oriented. We are not directly interested in analysing the specifics of 1997–98, however significant those events were at the time, and possibly still remain.

Preparatory Groundwork

Two Countries. A first step in this inherently collaborative task was to find locations in which there were clearly a wealth of both insider and outside stakeholder groups. In the wake of the Asian economic crisis of 1997–98, Thailand and Australia were prime candidates for cluster sampling. For example, prior to the crisis there had been good trade links between the two countries, whilst after the crisis many Australians were expatriated to work in the financial sectors (principally banking) in Bangkok (Australian Department of Foreign Affairs and Trade, 1999). Clearly then, both Thailand *and* Australia were major stakeholders in the 1997–98 crisis. On this basis, we decided to form an investigative team of university-based researchers and practitioners, from the two countries. Mutual capacity-building partnerships precisely like this have been explicitly recommended for human development research projects generally (Streeten, 2000).

Two Cities. Our samples, we decided, would be drawn from two strategically located cities within these countries. First and foremost, it was felt that Bangkok was a particularly apt location for the project because it had been right at the heart of the crisis, and was thus a prime site for sampling actor perceptions. Darwin, meanwhile, is popularly regarded as Australia's "gateway to Asia," as it forms a geographical nexus that is critical for regional trade links and development assistance between Australia and its Asian neighbours. Thus, as sites for measuring mutually informative sets of attributions, between actors and observers regarding crisis in South East Asia, Darwin and Bangkok could not be bettered.

Deriving an Item Pool

We considered it imperative to establish as wide a base as possible for the initial item pool that would eventually constitute our measuring instrument. Our concern during this phase was to avoid building any cultural or discipline biases whatsoever into our emerging measurement instrument. Any mistakes made at the beginning of this phase would become progressively compounded as the project developed. In order to minimise that unacceptable risk, our approach to item pool assembly became multidirectional.

Direction 1: Literature Searches Across the Social Sciences. Various literatures, both in psychology and other social sciences, principally economics, sociology, and social work, were scanned for the perceived causes of economic crisis. These attributions ranged from relatively technical (e.g., "faulty financial policy") to distinctively human (e.g., "lack of intelligence"). We also scanned both learned journals and widely read newspapers and magazine periodicals. Given our arguments about the media above, these more populist channels of information about the crisis were certain to have provided significant input to people's schemata for contemplating economic crisis as a whole. This was especially the case inside Thailand, where the press (as we have partly seen above) commented frequently and extensively on the crisis. Throughout this phase of the project therefore, we worked hard to respect the balance between publications in English and publications in Thai.

Out of this exercise there emerged a consensus within the team, that the most parsimonious lay model of the causes of crisis, which might underlie lay perceptions of economic crisis, was three-dimensional. It (the typical lay schema) would probably contain two interrelated and largely structural perspectives, economic causes of crisis and poor governance, and one largely human (or dispositional) category of attribution (Aus-Thai Project Team, 1999). This type of division between economic, political, and human factors is hardly a contentious view (Aus-Thai Project Team, 2002). Exemplar items reflecting each of these classic dimensions can be found in Appendix A (Aus-Thai Project Team, 1999). In particular, items 1–26 in Appendix A can be considered representative of the more structural categories, while the remaining items reflect a more human, disposition-focused category of attribution. Thus, based on careful consideration of relevant literatures accessible to the academic and lay publics across our respective countries of origin, we felt that we had derived an *a priori* model that could now be empirically tested.

Direction: Scan the Psychometric Literature. There is an emerging tendency in the psychological literature on economic crisis, to look back at previous economic depressions, and to view the poverty that they created as casting some psychological light on present day economic turbulence. Those early forms of crisis span, for instance, nineteenth-century Western Europe (Hildebrandt, 1994), 1930s North America (Elder, 1999), 1970s Australasia (Shirley, 1993), and 1980s Latin America (Filho & Neder, 2001). These essentially historical perspectives on contemporary economic crisis prompted us to take something of an historical tack ourselves. In particular, we were prompted to examine past literature on attributions for poverty, to help us generate items germane to today's economic turbulence.

Most of this past literature has adopted a psychometric, factorial approach to measuring attributions for poverty (Furnham, this volume). The predominant psychometric device for measuring attributions for poverty is called the "Causes of Third World Poverty Questionnaire," or CTWPQ (Harper, Wagstaff, Newton, & Harrison, 1990). The CTWPQ was particularly appropriate to our intercultural concerns, because it was one of the few instruments that had focused on poverty both domestically *and* internationally. In addition, the instrument had already had its underlying dimensions, or "factor structure," tested across a diverse range of social, cultural, and economic settings. These settings have included for instance East Africa (Carr & MacLachlan, 1998), Latin America (Carr, Taef, de Ribeiro, & MacLachlan, 1998), and, more recently, Australia (Campbell, Carr, & MacLachlan, 2001). To the extent that the underlying structure of the CTWPQ had in fact shown itself to replicate across these diverse contexts, its items were potentially robust enough to travel reasonably well across countries as diverse as Australia and Thailand (Gergen, 1973).

The CTWPQ comprises four factors that range from clearly situational to clearly dispositional. At one extreme, a respondent can blame international poverty on Nature, for example, "There is Third World poverty because their land is not suitable for agriculture." This factor however is not self-evidently linked to economic crisis. A second factor in the CTWPQ deals with international exploitation, for example, "because the world economy and banking system are loaded against the poor." A third factor in the CTWPQ reflects government ineptitude and corruption, for example, "Their governments are inefficient," and "Their governments are corrupt"). These latter factors, and hence their constituent items, were considered relevant to attributions about economic crisis, particularly since they reflected the governance dimension of our a priori schema. Questions derived from these factors, and their respective items, were therefore included in our initial item pool. Fourthly, a remaining factor in the CTWPQ is uniquely human in focus, being termed by Harper et al., "blame the poor," for example, "because of lack of effort." Items from this factor too are clearly relevant to any measure of attributions for crisis, and so they were included also in our initial item pool.

Direction 3: Cross-cultural Consultations

The purpose of these consultations has been outlined above. Partly because of the tyranny of distance (even despite joint access to the Internet); and partly because it was an inherently complex and sensitive task; the consultations took an entire year to complete (they took place throughout 1999). This length of time was needed to co-ordinate a series of face-to-face meetings in Bangkok. What we were especially trying to do in this crucial part of the research process was ensure that each item in the initial surviving pool was culturally and contextually appropriate biculturally, both to Australians and to Thais. The rationale for investing heavily in this iterative process was that we were "decentering" the emergent survey form from any particular cultural or contextual (observer versus actor) bias (above; Aus-Thai Project Team, 1999). This iterative process included extensive translation and back-translation to ensure item and construct equivalence across the two settings (Brislin, 1970); the questionnaire would also eventually be administered in English in Australia and Thai in Thailand).

This recursive and iterative process finally produced an initial pool of 59 items, each of which was given a 6-point scale (Unclear [0] – Strongly Disagree [1] – Disagree [2] – Undecided [3] – Agree [4] – Strongly Agree [5]). We negotiated a separate "Unclear" option in anticipation of relatively high %ages of people (particularly in Australia) who would not understand items on this topic, as distinct from understanding them but still being "Undecided" on whether to agree or disagree (after, Walther, 1993). This is an example of the kind of methodological issue that future psychosocial studies of economic crisis may need to consider carefully. Economic crisis is still for most people a relatively technical, not-well-understood concept. Indeed, that is precisely why studying people's *perceptions* is important.

During the latter part of 1999, we pilot tested this 59-item questionnaire in Darwin and Bangkok, through a combination of street interviews in shopping malls and interviews over the telephone. These were conducted in each case at weekends using systematic sampling. Those pilot tests indicated that a 59-item pool was too long to retain respondents' interest. In Darwin, particularly, we obtained a high number of refusals, and particularly so among blue-collar workers. Because of this high refusal rate, and a not dissimilar outcome in Bangkok, we decided to utilise a raffle incentive in the subsequent main study, as well as to focus, mainly in the Australian sample, on relatively well-educated, white-collar workers. In many respects, of course, these people are also potential donors and decision makers with respect to offshore events like economic crisis (Harper, this volume).

During the early part of 2000, a meeting was arranged in Bangkok at which the Thai and Australian members of the team discussed, negotiated, and finalised an abbreviated and psychometrically improved version of the item pool, based on the pilot studies. This improved pool contained 39 items, and was produced following the deletion of items that were either redundant, ambiguous (operationally defined as more than 25% of the sample responding "Unclear" to an item); or were uncorrelated with the rest of the items in the pool (and so having little to do with what the scale as a whole was measuring). Although there is always some arbitrariness in such "rules," it was felt that we would have had more arbitrariness *without* them in this highly exploratory situation (Aus-Thai Project Team, 2002).

Perhaps the most significant general "issue" that arose during the course of our cross-cultural discussions, as a team, was defining the overall ambit of the project itself. For our Australian members, whose circumstances clearly made them more like observers than actors in crisis itself, the project was preliminary "research," albeit with an eventual social function. Our Thai members, however, lived inside the crisis zone itself, and were closer to being actors in it, or "insiders" as they preferred to be called. For our Thai members therefore, the project had more social significance, and a wider ambit. These slightly differing foci and expectations, for the project as a whole, were creative influences on the course we eventually undertook. They resulted in a healthy middle ground or way for us to follow. As stated above, this "middle way" became (1) outlining the theoretical building blocks of communication networks against crisis and (2) assembling the rudiments of a structured instrument for measuring attributions for economic crisis, for eventual use in (1).

Choosing the Participants

In Darwin.   These consisted of 250 citizens of Australia's northernmost capital city, with a population of approximately 70,000 people (Australian Bureau of Statistics, 1997). Based on the pilot considerations outlined above, this was a social network rather than probability sample. The participants were contacted through acquaintances and everyday contact with the researchers rather than through the use of population lists and random number tables (Aus-Thai Project Team, 2002). The final sample gathered in this way consisted of a section of Darwin society that was equally balanced with respect to gender, and predominantly from white-collar occupations (above).

Only a small minority of this Australian sample reported having been themselves directly affected by economic crisis. This established that our Australian sample, as anticipated, were largely actors rather than observers. When the Darwin respondents were asked which crisis they had in mind as they completed the questionnaire, a majority of them reported either no country in particular or some combination of countries. Only a small minority of respondents indicated that they were thinking in particular about the 1997–98 crisis when they completed the questionnaire. Thus, for many of the Australians, economic crises had become more of a general situation rather than a specific event. Because of this generality, and general focus compared to our Thai participants (who we firmly anticipated would focus on crisis in our home country), any statistically confirmed similarities in the structure of attributions (basically the three dimensions proposed in our a priori model) would give us evidence of robustness in that pattern of findings as a whole (Aus-Thai Project Team, 2002). The logic here is classical in social psychology, namely that greater similarity over widely diverse settings is evidence for robustness of the model in question (Gergen, above); actually, this logic is applied right throughout psychological science).

When asked whose job it is to remedy economic crisis, and among those respondents who identified only one responsible agent, the modal attribution was (good) government. This governance factor was endorsed by almost one in four of the participants. Yet at the same time however, almost all of the remainder of the participants, and a clear majority (two-thirds) of the sample as a whole, reported that a combination of government, business, *and* individuals in the community, was responsible for remedying economic crisis. Overall therefore, among the observers that comprised this sample, both structural *and* human factors were perceived to be important factors in managing economic crisis.

In Bangkok.   Our Thai sample, of 400 individuals, was drawn in the same manner as the Australian group. Again it was balanced by gender, and predominantly white collar (for details, Aus-Thai Project Team, 2002). The modal occupational category was government official, which was a relevant sector to have represented (Harper, this volume). As anticipated above, this sample had its attention focused squarely on the economic crisis in Thailand. This had directly affected almost everyone in the sample. Despite these clear *differences* with the Australian sample however, a clear majority of our Thai participants (again two-thirds) *similarly* reported that the responsibility for managing recovery out of crisis should be shared, between government, business, and individuals in the community.

Exploring this attribution on human responsibility more closely, more than one in four of the Thai sample placed the responsibility for remedying the crisis exclusively onto individuals within the community. Consistent with this, responses for perceived causes of crisis, too, consistently fell on the "agree" side of the response scale (Aus-Thai Project Team, in press). Clearly therefore, our "insider" respondents were not just off-loading responsibility and blame for economic crisis onto outside agencies. This finding is broadly consistent with a community development initiative in Thailand at the time, the *Oh Boh Toh* Program (above). In addition however, it is also the kind of finding that might prove surprising to initially sceptical Western donor audiences (rationale above).

Handling the Data

In deciding what to do with the *twin sets* of perceptual (attribution) data, we deliberately decided *not* to extend (a) our cross-cultural consultations about items into (b) cross-cultural comparisons with them (Aus-Thai Project Team, 2001). There were a number of reasons for this reticence (for detailed examples, see Carr, Purcell, & Marsella, 2002). Chief among them however, was a commitment to an approach that was thoroughly decentralised (Aus-Thai Project Team, 1998;

1999; 2001). The Aus-Thai Project Team basically decided to conduct separate, equally weighted tests of the robustness in our *a priori* three-dimensional model of attributions, across radically diverse cultural settings (above; Gergen, 1973). According to Gergen's logic, the more *different* a second test population is from a first, and the more similar the pattern of results across the two studies and settings, the more confident researchers can be in the generality of the model they have independently tested (Aus-Thai Project Team, 2002).

In Darwin. During the initial screening of raw data, a problem that other researchers of economic crisis may face emerged. It became apparent, as anticipated, that we had a high proportion of "Unclear" and "Undecided" responses. For each of the 39 items, we therefore examined the percentages of respondents using the two categories. Across the 39 items, there was a high degree of correlation between these percentages, which suggested that the two response categories were being used interchangeably. Hence we gave each response category the conventional scale value of "3" (for further details, Aus-Thai Project Team, 2002). As an added precaution, we eliminated any item which had yielded 25% or more of responses in either the "Unclear" or "Undecided" category, and as well any item for which the combined total of "Unclear" and "Undecided" responses was 45% of the sample or greater. These objective procedures helped eliminate any items about which there was excessive uncertainty and perhaps misunderstanding (or excessive "noise"). As a final precautionary form of objective item screening, we again eliminated any item that did not correlate well with the (corrected) total score for the scale as a whole.

Our next step was to conduct an exploratory factor analysis, based on principle components, of the surviving items. This was intended as a first empirical check on the 3D a priori measurement model derived from existing literatures. This exploratory factor analysis showed that a three-factor solution, conforming to the three factors of economic, governance, and human (above), explained a reasonable 50% of the variance (for more details of this analysis, Aus-Thai Project Team, 2002). In order however to conduct a more rigorous check on this tri-dimensional structure, confirmatory factor analysis too was carried out. This more rigorous and conservative analysis revealed that the data were a moderately good fit to the (three-factor) model. Two of the latent factors, economic and governance, were also, as expected, closely intercorrelated. Thus, we tentatively concluded, subject to a confirmation of the same underlying structure with the Thai sample, that we were on a right path to developing a coherent attribution measure.

In Bangkok. As we learned above, almost all of the Thai participants reported that they had been personally affected by economic crisis. Consistent with that level of direct experience (and personal relevance), our Thai respondents very seldom used the response category "Unclear." For this group therefore, and in contrast to their Australian counterparts, we were not obliged to collapse the categories "Unclear" and "Uncertain." This is an example to would-be researchers of how different groups sometimes use the same scale differently, and how data are thus best analysed independently from each other (for expanded discussion of other, more serious scale positioning effects, see Bond, 1988; Carr, Munro, & Bishop, 1995; Carr et al., 2002).

The same objective decision criteria for retaining versus rejecting items were applied in this sample as with the Australian group. The application of these decision rules resulted in the retention of 27 items from the original pool of 39. An exploratory factor analysis, conducted on these retained items, was again indicative of three major underlying factors. When, for example, a scree diagram was plotted, there was a clear levelling-off beyond a third factor. This three-factor solution again explained a reasonable (and similar) proportion of the total variance (45%). Applying confirmatory factor analysis, as recommended in such situations (Carr et al., 1995), there was again high interfactorial correlation between the economic and governance factors. These collectively in turn, again, remained distinct from attributions involving a human factor. Although the various statistics summarising goodness-of-fit between data and model were still only moderately satisfactory, the overall level of convergence in the findings, between the samples, was sufficient to conclude that we had the beginnings of a meaningfully structured item pool (Aus-Thai Project Team, 2002; Grimm, 1993).

In the Thai sample, there were 17 participants who reported that they had not themselves been directly affected by economic crisis. With a view to developing attribution theory in this type of context, we ran a check on whether the extent to which these relatively immune (and thus "observer-like") participants differed in their level of endorsement of each of the three major types of perceived cause of economic crisis. Compared to their actor counterparts, those Thai participants who responded that they had not been directly affected by the economic crisis were significantly less likely to endorse *each of the three* causes of crisis. The comparison groups here were lopsided in *n*, so caution is required, but the finding is nonetheless contrary to attribution theory, which predicts a tailing away of dispositional attributions among actors. Instead of this however, direct experience of economic crisis was consistently associated with a more emphatic pluralism in the perceived causes of economic crisis.

Discussion

The original question in this project was whether it is truly possible to use attributions about crisis as informational building blocks for the construction of a communication *process* to help motivate development out of crisis. We believe that psychology offers a cogent theoretical case that this process can and should be undertaken, and that it goes beyond the current level of thinking in development studies, by suggesting a tangible way for this process to proceed. The basic specific *outcome* in the project was sketching out the kind of measure and constituent items that future investigators of economic crisis might draw from as they explore attributions in their particular setting. Every economic crisis, as well as having features in common, also has unique aspects to its causes and solutions (World Bank Group, 2000). As we learned during the course of this project, having this kind of item pool to draw from saves applied researchers precious time. These savings, especially in relatively fast-moving events like economic crisis, are crucial to avoid the damning criticism that psychological science is like journalism in slow motion (Gergen, 1994).

Our preliminary and modest first investigations suggest that there are at least three salient dimensions to the thoughts and feelings of various stakeholder groups, as they attempt to make sense out of an economic crisis. These dimensions are both macro (economic, governance) and micro (or human). Although our statistics for goodness of fit between data and model were not perfect, probably because of the inherently noisy nature of lay understandings of crisis to-date, they are substantive enough to keep road testing and refining the model (Grimm, 1993). To the extent that these same three factors emerge in those tests, we gain more *confidence* in the model. As well, such tests allow for the possibility of discovering additionally salient perceptions, for example non-material spiritual attributions about crisis (Aus-Thai Project Team, 2002). These have already been found to be salient concerns among Indigenous attributions for poverty, for example among the poor in Brazil and Indonesia (Carr et al., 1998).

In addition to these possibilities, we ourselves have also become more aware of possible limitations, and need for accommodation, in attribution theory. Classical attribution theory predicts that actors should have been *less* blaming of the human factor (Nisbett & Ross, 1980). However, our Thai participants with relatively direct experience of crisis (compared to their Thai observer counterparts) were significantly *more* likely than their observer counterparts to blame the human factor. One possible "explanation" for this apparent discrepancy is based on values, that Thais in the sample tended towards a "modesty bias," in which blame is comparatively readily taken on board and not simply self-servingly off-loaded onto structural factors (Kashima & Triandis, 1986). According to this interpretation, the small minority who felt unaffected by the crisis might have been relatively individualistic (individualists do not show a modesty bias; and for evidence that individualism rises with relative wealth, see Hofstede & Bond, 1988; Marshall, 1997). Thus, the link between values and attributions would seem to be a fertile area for future research. This research could for example examine the influence of values at personal, cultural, and cross-contextual (actor versus observer) levels (for more detailed critical discussion of attribution theory and development, see Harper, this volume)).

The same need for fresh research applies also to linking attributions directly to behavior. A prime example of this potential linkage is overseas investment behavior by regional entrepreneurs (Ivory, this volume). Creating opportunities for small business has been identified as a major opportunity for human development (World Bank Group, 2001b). Across North Australia for instance, in the wake of the 1997–98 crisis in South East Asia, the Australian Department of Foreign Affairs and Trade was actively attempting to promote investor confidence in Thailand (1999). Such initiatives might have gained significant momentum from the kinds of perspective sharing outlined in this chapter, by actually persuading more entrepreneurs to invest and reinvest in the region. In the literature on attributions for poverty, we already know that outside observers whose perspective becomes more structural are likely to behave more pro-socially (Campbell et al., 2001). The new challenge however is to ascertain whether this finding *generalizes* to a key twenty-first century issue – motivating pro-social behavior during an *economic crisis*.

Conclusion

This chapter has outlined a unique process of communication, within and between actor and observer groups regarding economic crisis. Among the building blocks in this communication process are attributions. To capture these attributions, we have developed and provided the beginnings of a measure of the perceived causes of economic crisis. This measure, in a rudimentary way, has shown itself to be relatively robust and internally coherent over a number of diverse groups with a stake in economic recovery. As well as economic and political factors, its internal structure respects attributions that are uniquely human. Communicating these has the potential to empower and motivate human development out of crisis, and to that extent engages psychology with the issue of global poverty.

Appendix 11.A.

We represent the Northern Territory University, Darwin/Srinakharinwirot University in Bangkok, Thailand. We are conducting an international study, in Southeast Asia and Australia, to try and discover the views that people hold about the current economic climate of the region. Our findings may eventually help us to better manage the many community projects across the region. If you are over 18, we would like to borrow a few minutes of your time to assist us to gather some information. You have been selected at random. We are not asking for names. Whatever you tell us will be completely confidential. If you decide to complete and return this questionnaire, in the sealed envelope provided, we will assume that you have given us your permission to proceed.

In your opinion, how have each of the following contributed to the economic crisis in Southeast Asia? Circling "Unclear" means that you lack information about, or cannot understand the question. Please feel absolutely free to circle this option – many of us do not know a lot about economic crisis! Please also feel free to use the "Undecided" option, if you have information about the issue and the question is clear, but you haven't made up your mind. "SD" stands for "*Strongly Disagree*," "D" means "*Disagree*," "A" = "*Agree*," & "SA" = "*Strongly "Agree*."

1.	Government corruption	Unclear	SD	D	Undecided	A	SA
2.	Incompetent politicians	Unclear	SD	D	Undecided	A	SA
3.	Frequent changes of government (e.g., discontinuity in financial policy)	Unclear	SD	D	Undecided	A	SA
4.	Government allowed excessive imports of luxury goods	Unclear	SD	D	Undecided	A	SA
5.	Government promoted industrial sector more than agricultural one	Unclear	SD	D	Undecided	A	SA
6.	Government gave insufficient information on financial investment	Unclear	SD	D	Undecided	A	SA
7.	Ineffective financial & fiscal management by the government	Unclear	SD	D	Undecided	A	SA
8.	Inept government leadership	Unclear	SD	D	Undecided	A	SA
9.	Overreliance on the government	Unclear	SD	D	Undecided	A	SA
10.	Faulty financial policy	Unclear	SD	D	Undecided	A	SA
11.	Improper protection of financial institutions by the government	Unclear	SD	D	Undecided	A	SA
12.	Government laxity in supervising financial institutions	Unclear	SD	D	Undecided	A	SA
13.	Poor economic management by the government	Unclear	SD	D	Undecided	A	SA
14.	Political unrest	Unclear	SD	D	Undecided	A	SA
15.	Vulnerability of financial institutions	Unclear	SD	D	Undecided	A	SA
16.	Over-borrowing from overseas	Unclear	SD	D	Undecided	A	SA
17.	Collapse of bubble economy (unreal stock and land prices)	Unclear	SD	D	Undecided	A	SA
18.	Banking liberalization	Unclear	SD	D	Undecided	A	SA
19.	Fixed exchange rate	Unclear	SD	D	Undecided	A	SA
20.	High rate of non-performing loans	Unclear	SD	D	Undecided	A	SA
21.	Domestic economic recession	Unclear	SD	D	Undecided	A	SA
22.	High youth unemployment	Unclear	SD	D	Undecided	A	SA
23.	Attacks on local currency from overseas	Unclear	SD	D	Undecided	A	SA
24.	Stock market speculation	Unclear	SD	D	Undecided	A	SA

(continued)

25.	Global competition	Unclear	SD	D	Undecided	A	SA
26.	Over-lending by banks	Unclear	SD	D	Undecided	A	SA
27.	Inexperienced executives	Unclear	SD	D	Undecided	A	SA
28.	Incapable staff	Unclear	SD	D	Undecided	A	SA
29.	Patronage system	Unclear	SD	D	Undecided	A	SA
30.	Lack of intelligence	Unclear	SD	D	Undecided	A	SA
31.	Lack of motivation	Unclear	SD	D	Undecided	A	SA
32.	Lack of education	Unclear	SD	D	Undecided	A	SA
33.	Loose morals	Unclear	SD	D	Undecided	A	SA
34.	Lack of understanding of the production process	Unclear	SD	D	Undecided	A	SA
35.	Lack of discipline	Unclear	SD	D	Undecided	A	SA
36.	Lack of social responsibility	Unclear	SD	D	Undecided	A	SA
37.	Use of child labor	Unclear	SD	D	Undecided	A	SA
38.	Neglect of traditional values	Unclear	SD	D	Undecided	A	SA
39.	Fate	Unclear	SD	D	Undecided	A	SA
OTHER? (please specify)		Unclear	SD	D	Undecided	A	SA

40. Was there a particular country or country in your mind as you answered the above questions? Yes/No If "yes," which was it/were they?

41. Have you yourself been affected by economic crisis? No/Yes. If so, please explain how?

42. Whose job is it to remedy the crisis? Individuals in the community/government/business/other . . . . . . (circle more than one, if appropriate)

Acknowledgments

We thank Gillian Long for her invaluable input during earlier stages of this project; Jodette Fox, Fiona Greatorex, and Michelle Roger, for their extensive and professional research assistance; The Northern Territory University, Australia, for an internal project grant; and the Behavioral Science Research Institute, Srinnakharinwirot University, Thailand, for its largesse in supporting this project in a multitude of ways.

References

Ajuwon, A. J., & Shokunbi, W. (1997). Women and the risk of HIV infection in Nigeria: Implications for control programs. *International Quarterly of Community Health Education, 16*, 107–120.

Apisakkul, A. (2000). Job insecurity: A study of white-collar workers in Thailand. *Dissertation Abstracts International: Humanities and Social Sciences, 60*, 4081.

Aus-Thai Project Team. (1998). Managing economic crisis: A psychosocial approach. *Development Bulletin, 46*, 53–56.

Aus-Thai Project Team. (1999, June). *Complementary perspectives on economic crisis from Bangkok, Thailand, and Darwin, Northern Territory, Australia.* XXVII Interamerican Congress of Psychology, Caracas, Venezuela.

Aus-Thai Project Team. (2001, July). *Perception of economic crisis: A cross-contextual study.* Asian Association of Social Psychology 4th Annual Conference: Asian Social Psychology in the 21st century. Melbourne, Australia.

Aus-Thai Project Team. (2002). *Managing economic crisis: A human factors approach. Psychology and Developing Societies, in press.*

Australian Bureau of Statistics. (1997). *Census of population and housing: Counts by age and sex for selected areas: Northern Territory* (Catalogue No. 20187). Canberra: Australian Government Publishing Services.

Australian Department of Foreign Affairs and Trade (1999, November). *Ambassador to Thailand's talk,* Centre for South East Asian Studies, Darwin, Australia.

Bond, M. H. (1988). Finding universal dimensions of individual variation in multicultural studies of values: The Rokeach and Chinese Value Surveys. *Journal of Personality and Social Psychology, 55*, 1009–1015.

Brenner, G. A., & Lipeb, M. (1993). The lottery player in Cameroon: An exploratory study. *Journal of Gambling Studies, 9*, 185–190.

Brislin, R. W. (1970). Back-translation for cross-cultural research. *Journal of Cross-Cultural Psychology, 1*, 185–216.

Campbell, D., Carr, S. C., & MacLachlan, M. (2001). Attributing "Third World" poverty in Australia and Malawi: A case of Donor Bias? *Journal of Applied Social Psychology, 31*, 409–430.

Carr, S. C. (2000). Privilege, proximity, and privation: Eternal triangle for development? *Psychology and Developing Societies, 12*, 167–176.

Carr, S. C. (in press). *Social psychology: Context, communication, and culture.* Sydney, Australia: John Wiley & Sons.

Carr, S. C., Mc Auliffe, E., & Maclachlan, M. (1998). *Psychology of aid.* London: Routledge.

Carr, S. C., & MacLachlan, M. (1998). Actors, observers, and attributions for "Third World" poverty: Contrasting perspectives from Malawi and Australia. *Journal of Social Psychology, 138*, 189–202.

Carr, S. C., Munro, D., & Bishop, G. D. (1995). Attitude assessment in non-Western countries: Critical modifications to Likert scaling. *Psychologia: An International Journal of Psychology in the Orient, 39*, 55–59.

Carr, S. C., Purcell, I. P., & Marsella, A. J. (in press). Researching intercultural relations: Towards a middle way? *The Asian Psychologist.*

Carr, S. C., Taef, H., de Ribeiro, R., & MacLachlan, M. (1998). Attributions for "Third World" poverty: Contextual factors in Australia and Brazil. *Psychology and Developing Societies, 10*, 103–114.

Eiamlapa-Quinn, R. (1998). Social impacts of the Thai economic crisis. *Development Bulletin, 46*, 39–42.

Elder, G. H., Jr. (1999). *Children of the Great Depression: Social change in life experience* (25th anniversary edition). Boulder, CO: Westview Press.

Filho, G. C., & Neder, G. (2001). Social and historical approaches regarding street children in Rio de Janeiro (Brazil) in the context of transition to democracy. *Childhood: A Global Journal of Child Research, 8*, 11–29.

Fountain, S. (1995). *Education for development.* London: Hodder & Stoughton/ UNICEF.

Gates, C. L. (1998). The East Asia crisis: Causes and dynamics. *Development Bulletin, 46*, 7–10.

Gergen, K. J. (1973). Social psychology as history. *Journal of Personality and Social Psychology, 26*, 309–320.

224   The Aus-Thai Project Team

Gergen, K. J. (1994). *Toward transformation in social knowledge* (2nd ed.). London: Sage.
Grimm, L. G. (1993). *Statistical applications for the behavioral sciences.* New York, NY: John Wiley & Sons.
Harper, D. J., Wagstaff, G. F., Newton, J. T., & Harrison, K. R. (1990). Lay causal perceptions of "Third World" poverty and the Just World Theory. *Social Behavior and Personality, 18,* 235–238.
Hildebrandt, H. (1994). Mental disorders and economic crisis: A study on the development of admission into the psychiatric hospitals of Prussia between 1876 and 1906. *Social Psychiatry and Psychiatric Epidemiology, 29,* 190–196.
Hofstede, G., & Bond, M. H. (1988). The Confucius connection: From cultural roots to economic growth. *Organisational Dynamics, 16,* 4–21.
Hoon, L. S., & Lim, V. K. G. (2001). Attitudes towards money and work: Implications for Asian management style following the economic crisis. *Journal of Managerial Psychology, 16,* 159–172.
Kashima, Y., & Triandis, H. C. (1986). The self-serving bias in attributions as a coping strategy: A cross-cultural study. *Journal of Cross-Cultural Psychology, 17,* 83–97.
Kato, T. (2000). Lessons from the Asian crisis. *Journal of Human Development, 1,* 165–168.
Khor, M. (1998). Rethinking IMF policy in the wake of the Asian economic crisis. *Development Bulletin, 46,* 11–13.
Kloep, M. (1995). Concurrent and predictive correlates of girls' depression and antisocial behavior under conditions of economic crisis and value change: The case of Albania. *Journal of Adolescence, 18,* 445–458.
Manzano, J. M., Llorca, G., Salamero, C., & Montejo. A. L. (1995). Influence of unemployment on mental health. *Psiquis, 16,* 41–47.
Marshall, R. (1997). Variances in levels of individualism across two cultures and three social classes. *Journal of Cross-Cultural Psychology, 28,* 490–495.
Mehryar, A. H. (1984). The role of psychology in national development: Wishful thinking and reality. *International Journal of Psychology, 19,* 159–167.
Montero, M. (1996). Negative social identity and socio-economic crisis: A socio-psychological study. *Revista Interamericana de Psicologia, 30,* 43–58.
Moskalewicz, J. & Swiatkiewicz, G. (2000). Malczyce, Poland: A multi-faceted community action project in Eastern Europe in a time of rapid economic change. *Substance Use and Misuse, 35,* 189–202.
Nisbett, R. E., & Ross, L. (1980). *Human inference: Strategies and shortcomings of social judgments.* Englewood Cliffs, NJ: Prentice-Hall.
Prechel, H. (1994). Economic crisis and the centralisation of control over the managerial process: Corporate restructuring and neo-Fordist decision-making. *American Sociological Review, 59,* 723–745.
Ross, L. (1977). The intuitive psychologist and his shortcomings: Distortions in the attribution process. *Advances in Experimental Social Psychology, 10,* 174–221.
Savadori, L., Nicotra, E., Rumiati, R., & Tamborini, R. (2001). Mental representation of economic crisis in Italian and Swiss samples. *Swiss Journal of Psychology, 60,* 11–14.
Sen, A. (1999). *Development as freedom.* Oxford, UK: Oxford University Press.
Shirley, I. (1993). The culture of violence. *Community Mental Health in New Zealand, 7,* 3–9.
Soesastro, H. (1998). The social impact of the economic crisis in Indonesia. *Development Bulletin, 46,* 24–26.
Stiglitz, J. (2000). What I learned at the world economic forum: The Insider. *The New Republic Online, April 17,* 1–10.
Streeten, P. (2000). Looking ahead: Areas of future research in human development. *Journal of Human Development, 1,* 25–48.

Teeravekin, L. (1998, November). *Decentralisation and community development.* Keynote address, National Community Development Policy Conference, Bangkok, Thailand.

The Economist. (2001). East Asia's slump. *The Economist* (Global Agenda). November 23rd.

UNDP. (2000). *Human Development Report 1999.* London: UNDP (United Nations Development Programme).

Walsh, M. (1997). *Cross-cultural communication problems in Aboriginal Australia.* Darwin, Australia: The Australian National University North Australia Research Unit.

Walther, J. B. (1993). Impression development in computer-mediated interaction. *Western Journal of Communication, 57,* 381–398.

Weiner, B. (1991). Metaphors in motivation and attribution. *American Psychologist, 46,* 921–930.

Woelk, G. B. (1992). Cultural and structural influences in the creation of and participation in community health programmes. *Social Science and Medicine, 35,* 419–424.

World Bank. (2000, February). *Knowledge creation and management in global enterprises.* Conference on the generation and application of knowledge, gained through research, to development, Washington, DC, USA.

World Bank. (2001). *World Development Report 2000/2001: Attacking poverty.* Washington, DC: World Bank.

World Bank Group. (2001a). *Global economic prospects and the developing countries 1998/99: Beyond financial crisis.* Washington, DC: World Bank.

World Bank Group. (2001b). *World Bank Review of Small Business Activities, 2001.* http://www.ifc.org.

Part III
Opportunity

Chapter 12

Poverty and Youth

Carola Eyber and Alastair Ager

Armed conflict and the mass displacement it can produce brings with it specific dynamics that impact on the experiences of poverty, on issues of psychosocial well-being, and on ways in which forced migrants confront the difficulties they face. This chapter focuses on the interrelationship between displacement, poverty and psychological factors in order to gain insight into the daily challenges in the lives of refugees and the internally displaced.[1]

Participatory research was conducted with young displaced people in Angola in the year 2000. The chapter begins with a critical discussion of some of the main concepts employed in this investigation, namely poverty, displacement and youth/adolescence. There follows a brief description of the Angolan context, including an outline of the political, social and economic consequences of the situation of war that lasted for more than 40 years. This is followed by a presentation of some of the salient aspects of the lives of displaced youths, namely their thoughts and feelings about areas such as work, schooling, and leisure activities. The impact of the continuing conflict and the resulting suffering and distress is discussed, and the connections to psychosocial well-being and health and illness are highlighted.

A capacity-centered approach to poverty is adopted in the chapter, demonstrated in the final section that concentrates on the agency, resilience and creativity displayed by the youths in their attempts to cope with the difficult situations in which they find themselves. Social, personal, religious, cultural and political

---

[1] According to UNHCR, refugees are defined as forced migrants who have crossed the border of a country because of persecution or threat to physical safety. Internally displaced people (IDPs) are defined as those who have been displaced within the borders of a country.

strategies of coping are presented, emphasising not only the diversity of coping methods displayed by the youths, but also their capacities "as active managers of complex asset portfolios" (Moser, 1998 in Jones and Nelson, 1999, p. 14).

Poverty

Conceptualisations of poverty have increasingly emphasized the fact that poverty cannot be understood in relation to economic wealth or the possession of material assets alone (Jones & Nelson, 1999). Poverty is the result of disparate factors that include social, cultural, economic, political, psychological and ecological aspects (Ochoa, 2001; O'Gorman, 1992). Definitions should thus reflect the multidimensional nature of poverty and need to include issues such as quality of life, survival, resilience, justice and equity.

Narayan (2000), in his research into how poor people themselves define poverty, suggests that the notion of social exclusion is central to their experiences. Poverty is seen as a lack of resources that prevents participation in the normal life of a community, for example the inability to reciprocate with gifts and to perform important cultural rituals and festivities. This may lead to marginalization and exclusion from social networks when the poor are compelled to violate social norms as they do not have the means to observe them. Scholars such as Lewis (1965; 1968) and Allen (1970) who have concerned themselves with identifying some of the psychological factors involved in experiences of poverty, emphasise the fact that the experience of poverty is characterized by feelings of marginality and dependence which may lead to shame, resentment and anger. The lack of voice and power leaves the poor vulnerable to rudeness, humiliation and inhuman treatment with very little recourse to address such occurrences, expressed in the following quote by a person from Latvia: "Poverty is humiliation, the sense of being dependent, and of being forced to accept rudeness, insults, and indifference when we seek help" (Narayan, 2000, p. 30).

Attitudes toward the poor impact on the psychological dimensions of poverty. Generally, the poorest of the poor are considered to be people devastated by misery and incapable of transcending their own situation, still less capable of contributing to the development of their country (Ochoa, 2001). They appear before the rest of society as people without an identity of their own and as deficient in one way or the other, easily dismissed and ignored. Misconceptions about the poor include the idea that they are idle, a notion which Feuerstein (1997) dismisses as untrue; the poor work constantly to survive but receive little to show for it in return. The poor are often perceived as a threat to stability and as a burden to the economy of a country, yet are simultaneously considered powerless. They are "other" in an uncomfortable and disturbing way, and their views and opinions are usually not seriously considered.

The definition of poverty adopted in this chapter is taken from Ochoa (2001, p. 55) who defines poverty as social vulnerability resulting from the absence of one or more assured capacities which permit individuals and their families to carry out basic responsibilities and enjoy fundamental rights. Poverty is thus firmly linked to the concepts of justice and human rights, and the connection between poverty and vulnerability is made explicit. The definition also draws attention to the capacities of the poor to deal with the situations of hardship they confront.

In considering the efforts made by people to overcome poverty-related hardship, one needs to be aware, firstly, of the different types of poverty that exist and, secondly, of the variety of resources that are available or absent to specific groups of people, families or individuals. The majority of the Angolan youths who form the focus of this chapter were affected by extreme or absolute poverty, the most severe form of poverty which gravely compromises the ability of those affected by it to recover their capacities to participate in rights and responsibilities (Feuerstein, 1997). For some of the youths poverty came instantaneously when they were forced to leave their possessions behind in armed attacks; for others, poverty had been endemic for most of their lives as they and their families had experienced a series of disastrous events that prevented them from recovering from situations of absolute poverty. People possess different kinds of capital which may allow them to overcome losses in different areas: physical capital which includes ownership of land and assets; human capital in the form of health, education and labor; social capital derived from benefits of membership of a social group; and environmental capital comprising seasonal changes, food and water availability (Narayan, 2000). Coping strategies frequently involve the reinvestment of resources from one area of functioning to compensate for resource loss in another (Hobfoll, 1998). During armed conflict and displacement, however, this compensation is frequently not possible as will be discussed below.

Displacement: The Situation of the *Deslocados* in Angola

In this section we present the situation of the displaced in south-western Angola, outlining some of their common experiences, and highlighting how these affect the ways in which they live with and struggle against poverty.

Angola has been at war for over 40 years. The War of Independence started in 1961 and was aimed at ridding the country of the Portuguese colonial regime. Independence was achieved in 1975 but armed conflict continued between three political movements who all sought to obtain influence and power after the withdrawal of the colonial forces. With only brief interludes of peace, civil war has continued in the country since then, mainly between the government forces of the Movimento Popular de Libertação de Angola (MPLA) and the União Nacional para a Independencia Total de Angola (UNITA), led by Jonas Savimbi. In February 2002, following the death of Jonas Savimbi, a peace agreement was signed between UNITA and the government, giving renewed hope for an end to the violent conflict that has brought destruction to the country for almost four decades.

The effects of the war on the civilian population have been severe. Death and injury result not only from direct combat but also from the estimated 10 million land mines planted throughout the country; and from non-existent or inadequate health services available to those affected by illness and disease. The infrastructure has been seriously damaged and public services in the area of education are minimal. It is estimated that 70% of first-grade-aged children failed to enter school in the year 2000 due to lack of resources and facilities. Of the small proportion of those who do enter the educational system, two-thirds currently do not reach their fifth year of schooling (Norwegian Refugee Council (NRC), 2001).

The UNHCR considers approximately 2 million people to be internally displaced in Angola as a consequence of the war (NCR, 2001). *Deslocados*, the Portuguese term used to refer to the war-displaced, usually follow one of two settlement patterns: they may be settled in government-run centers on a transitory or permanent basis, or they may become self-settled in nearby towns or cities. The research on which this chapter is based was conducted in both situations in the province of Huila: amongst self-settled *deslocados* in the town of Lubango and its surrounding areas, and amongst government-settled *deslocados* in two IDP (internally displaced people) camps near Matala. The latter group of *deslocados* originated from the municipality of Ndongo in the north-eastern part of Huila province where they had been attacked in the middle of August 1999 by UNITA forces.[2] This resulted in a mass displacement of approximately 12,000–13,000 people who fled toward Matala. Their condition upon arrival was extremely poor as the flight had been long and exhausting and many people succumbed to illness and malnutrition. People arrived with no or few possessions, being entirely reliant on external assistance for essential items such as blankets, kitchen utensils and clothing.

Living conditions in the centers are difficult. Inadequate shelter from the harsh weather conditions and living in close proximity to neighbors who may be strangers to them, lead to physical illnesses and social problems (Andrade, 2001). Economic survival is a constant concern and high priority in both centers. The *deslocados* do not have access to farming land around the centres, and are thus deprived of their previous methods of subsistence through agriculture and animal husbandry. They are largely dependent on the food provisions of the World Food Program (WFP), consisting of 10 kg maize meal, 1.2 kg beans, 0.75 kg cooking oil and 0.15 kg salt per person per month, which sustain a person for

[2] The attack started at 3:00 am at night and the *deslocados* reported the brutality and viciousness with which this attack was carried out. Many people had already fled their own homes some months earlier, moving into the central village of Ndongo in order to avoid persistent attacks, and were thus displaced for the second, third or fourth time over a period of two years.

approximately for two weeks. Additional sources of income are sought through a combination of kinship exchange, petty-commodity production, collecting and selling firewood, and food and beverage preparation. Women also perform farm labor on the fields of local residents in exchange for food, usually paid in the form of maize. Despite these initiatives, people live in a state of acute poverty, unable to cope with disruptions to their survival strategies through illness or other events (OCHA, 2001).

The lives of the free-settled *deslocados* in the towns are stressful in different ways, the single most important factor for economic survival being whether or not the arriving *deslocados* have kinship networks in the town that they can draw on for initial support (Andrade, 2001). However, not even highly effective kinship networks can cope with the massive levels of displacement that have occurred in the provinces over the past 10 years, and host households quickly find themselves depleted if they are expected to cope with large numbers of additional people (United Nations Security Council, 2000). Creativity and desperation have led to many innovative survival strategies amongst the *deslocados* living in towns, including "green belt farming" in semi-urban neighborhoods, chicken, pig and goat farming in small backyards, and *negócio*: informal trading in anything from soft drinks and cigarettes to diamonds and weapons (van der Winden, 1996). Less conventional economic activities such as money changing, child care and carrying water are common ways in which people try to make a living. Urban environments may offer more chances of access to work, education and medical facilities than rural areas but many *deslocados* found it very difficult to survive in Lubango, the competition in the informal trading market already being strained to maximum capacity. Many work long hours in order to make enough for just one bread roll and a tea bag at the end of the day, living constantly and precariously on the brink of destitution.

While the vast majority of the Angolan population lives on the poverty line, the *deslocados* face additional problems. The first is that in terms of the different forms of capital outlined above, i.e., physical, social, human and environmental capital, the displaced have far fewer resources to draw on than other poor Angolans. Almost all of the *deslocados* flee without being able to take any assets with them, thus losing all their physical capital in one instant. The social capital of the *deslocados* is also affected as death, illness and separation during flight results in the disruption of extended family structures. The absence of family members may lead to a fragmentation of relationships as well as leave work roles unfilled which may be performed with difficulty by the remaining family members. The hardships that result from this are not always alleviated by neighbors or other "community members" who may be strangers to one another.

The second issue relates to the psychosocial effects of the *deslocados'* past experiences and present difficulties. Due to a lack of financial means, *deslocados* were often unable to perform the appropriate traditional ceremonies needed to deal with some of the spiritual problems brought about through warfare, killing, and witchcraft. Some of the *deslocados* required specific forms of traditional healing to help with illnesses related to distress (Eyber, 2001) and had difficulties locating local healers who could perform these treatments. In addition, feelings of being unwanted, unwelcome and regarded as a burden by local residents were a source of distress and sometimes fear for the displaced. Conflicts between *deslocados* and local residents over issues such as firewood collection and the distribution of food rations escalated into violent attacks in certain areas, and incidents of rape of women *deslocados* by local men were reported.

Thirdly, while civil society in general does not have much voice nor influence on the Angolan government, the *deslocados* are without doubt the most marginalized of all groups within the country. Of all the population, the *deslocados* have least opportunity to participate in affairs that affect their lives. This is evident in the way in which they are relocated to other areas by state ministries without consultation, and the ways in which they are treated in the everyday life by local residents. The feeling of powerlessness experienced by the poor is thus further exacerbated for the displaced who have little means of making their opinions heard or of telling their stories.

Youth

Youth are often overlooked in situations of forced migration, as humanitarian aid agencies concentrate their assistance on children and women, and vulnerable groups such as the disabled and orphans. Recently, attention has been drawn to the negative consequences that the exclusion of youths from political and economic agendas can have in post-conflict societies, and to the potential for creativity, agency and coping amongst this group of the population (see, for example, Women's Commission for Refugee Women and Children, 1999). Angola's age distribution is typical of many developing countries, with an estimated 45% under the age of 15 in 1993, and more than 50% under the age of 25 (OCHA, 2001). Young people thus make up a considerable proportion of the general population, as well as of the displaced. In this section we briefly discuss the way in which young people are perceived in Angola and what role they are accorded in society.

Within the discipline of psychology emphasis has often been placed on the notion of the universality of the adolescent experience, following theorists such as Anna Freud (Blos, 1967) and Erik Erikson (1968), to argue that all adolescents undergo similar experiences, irrespective of cultural, economic or social contexts (see for instance Offer, Ostrov, Howard, & Atkinson, 1988; Noller & Callan, 1991). Social constructionists on the other hand, have argued that the categories of adolescence, youth and adulthood are social and cultural constructions of particular phases in the life course rather than universal categories. All societies have ways of defining what constitutes adulthood and how one attains it, and these may be age-related or may be determined by physical, social and religious rites (La Fontaine, 1986). The concept of adolescence is not present in all societies and some scholars argue that it is a construction that does not apply in societies where childhood and adulthood are the only two defining phases of a human being's life cycle. A central argument of this perspective holds that young people cannot be considered in isolation from other social groups within communities and societies, and that social, cultural and political issues, rather than biological or intrapsychic processes, should be foregrounded (Scheper-Hughes & Sargent, 1998).

Amongst many ethnolinguistic groups in Angola the transition from childhood to adulthood is generally marked by initiation rites performed during puberty.[3] These rites are of utmost importance in the communities as they are accompanied by a change of status for the youths: one cannot be considered a man (or amongst some ethnic groups a woman) if one has not performed them (Milheiros, 1967). The adolescents who participated in this study, both in the town and in the IDP centres, saw initiation as an essential part of becoming an adult. After the rites the initiate is still considered a *jovem* (youth) as opposed to an *adulto* (adult) for some time. The concepts of *juventude* (youth) and *jovens* (youths) are commonly held notions in Angola that are in some ways unrelated to conventional definitions of adulthood. They include anyone who is no longer a child up to approximately 35 years of age, thus including young adults. Adogame (2001, p. 2) notes that in African societies the "youth age range is usually wide and somewhat elastic" where the term "youth" can indicate a particular position in society, for instance unmarried status, certain political views or specific lifestyles. Clear distinctions between a child and a youth, and between a youth and an adult are thus not necessarily easy to make in many social situations. In the research reported on here, participants ranged between the ages of 13 and 19, and they are referred to as "youths," rather than as "adolescents" in order to more closely reflect Angolan use of terms.

In Angola a recurrent theme in adults' conversations about youth is the issue of the increasing "unruliness" of young people who are disregarding the authority of the elders. This resonates with the age-old perception of youth as a "problem" (Griffin, 1993). In many countries, both developing and developed, youths are perceived as a threat, as was described by Robert Kaplan in an influential article on West African cities which was published in the *Atlantic Monthly*: "I saw young men everywhere – hordes of them . . . They are like loose molecules in a very unstable social fluid, a fluid that was clearly on the verge of igniting" (in Sommers, 2000, p. 68).

Kaplan, whom Richards (1996) describes as a proponent of the New Barbarism Theory, warns of the anarchic, volatile and irrational nature of African youth who are "criminally inclined young migrants." They have "spun off from a failing traditional society" and are dispirited, unskilled, undereducated and therefore potentially dangerous young men (Kaplan, 1993 in Richards, 1996, p. xv). The representation of African youths as barbarians has racist implications, but may

[3] The age at which these rites are performed may vary greatly (Mbiti, 1989).

also resonate with concerns and fear for economic and political control that the ruling elite within the countries have. The associations between jobless youths in cities and crime are made in many parts of Africa, for instance in South Africa (Ramphele, 1997). In particular, young displaced people who migrate to cities instead of remaining in designated camp areas, are perceived as being a destabilising factor, contributing to crime and insecurity, despite evidence to the contrary (Sommers, 2000). Angola is no exception to the phenomenon of young displaced migrants who crowd into urban areas where they are regarded as a danger and a major factor in crime.

Young people may act as catalysts of change in societies. Adogame (2001) points out that in modern African societies youth have been a constant source of criticism and protest against institutions and the social, economic and political boundaries of states:

> ... societies have a tendency to stigmatise those who represent such a threat to their symbolic orders. Thus, youth represent various forms of threat: new ideas, new ways of life, and independence of judgement. To identify and isolate the threat, societies place a kind of stigma on the person(s). (Adogame, 2001, p. 3)

Young Angolans are, for instance, critical of the traditional ways of resolving problems, as reflected in a statement by a displaced elder from the province of Huambo:

> Our problem now is that we, *os mais velhos* [the elders] here, are also fighting with life. We came here and invade the life of the locals and when we tell them this is not in our tradition, they don't take any notice of us. The young people say that our traditions are outdated. But the reason why we don't manage to resolve our problems is because of the war [CCF Report, 2000].

The core issues prioritized by young, displaced Angolans in articulating their needs and goals are considered in the following section.

The Lives of the Youths: Perspectives and Opinions

As part of our participatory research with displaced youths in Huila province (Eyber, 2001), youths completed exercises where they identified, ranked and discussed issues of concern to them. Youth never forms one homogenous group within a community but consist of various subgroups that may have different problems to varying degrees. The youths generally distinguished between girls and boys, *deslocados* and local residents, workers, *negociantes* (traders) and students, and used these as a basis for their discussions.

An issue of utmost importance to the youths was education and school-related problems and this was ranked as the most pressing issue. A lack of financial means to pay for educational materials and exam papers, as well as to meet the demands of teachers for "additional contributions" was the main hindrance preventing the youths from attending school. The behaviour of teachers was experienced as discouraging as teachers sometimes arrived late or drunk for classes, taught badly, beat and ridiculed the students. Poor facilities such as a lack of classrooms, desks, toilets, sportsgrounds, etc. were cited as other school-related problems.

As in many developing countries (Serpell, 1996), the youths were convinced that the best opportunity for their future development lies in obtaining as much formal education as possible. Formal education symbolises hope to the youths, an alternative to a lifestyle of poverty and hardship, and the possibility of personal achievement. Not being able to study, on the other hand, threatens future plans which include obtaining a job, a family and having a house. None of the youths who had dropped out of school had given up the desire and the hope to be able to return to education at some point in the future.

A further pressing issue of concern for the displaced youths was the lack of clothing and shoes. In the town, local youths make fun of the *deslocados* who are poor and often wear old, torn clothing. According to the youths, having appropriate clothing prevents one from being immediately identified as a *deslocado*, thus from being branded even more of an outsider, and helps facilitate integration into friendship groups. The youths also often outgrew their clothes quickly and were embarrassed about having to wear clothes that were too small for them. They no longer identified themselves as children and part of representing this was by dressing in a way that they perceived reflected their new status, for instance boys wanted to wear long trousers. Wearing shoes is particularly relevant in this respect, as children often do not have shoes whereas many adults in the towns have at least one pair. The youths were also concerned about looking attractive in order to find a girl/boyfriend. Looking good and wearing clean clothes was seen as an important factor in attracting the attention of a member of the opposite sex. And the difficulty in obtaining soap to wash their clothes was a problem for the youths in the IDP centres.

Narayan (2000) notes that clothing functions as a powerful social marker, particularly for youth and children. In reports from Armenia, Bangladesh and Georgia children who wear old, patched clothing are often cruelly taunted and may feel humiliated and unable to participate in a normal social life. The daily prospect of appearing dirty and poorly groomed in front of others prevents some poor children from attending school. Social exclusion from activities that others engage in makes it more difficult for the youths to cope with their present circumstances of displacement, expressed by one of the young *deslocados*:

It is important that you don't leave the things that others are doing. For example, a person has to be able to buy clothes, and so on and then things become easier [Diogo, 15, Lubango].

Experiences of War and Displacement

When the youths talked about their worries they seldom mentioned the war directly as a problem or a concern, nor the distressing experiences, such as the killings and attacks, to which they had been subjected. The war was, however, an ever-present feature of their lives, much as it was for adults, and one which they saw as being not only the direct cause of their own displacement and misery but also of general problems in the health and educational sectors of society.

For many of the youths the war had been continuing in their home areas for numerous years before the latest displacement to Lubango and Matala. The experience of pre-flight life in a war zone was described vividly:

> People don't sleep inside the houses. Sometimes, at night, when you are sleeping in the *capin* houses [huts made from grass and wood] you just hear other people screaming and you can't say or do anything. If they [UNITA soldiers attacking the village] hear your voice, they will take you and put you in the fire and kill you . . . At times the troops from MPLA and UNITA meet and they fight. The troops don't always die – it is the people who die. At times when UNITA leave, they leave mines in the countryside. At times they hide nearby in the countryside. They wait until you go to fetch your maize from your fields. And when you go there they catch you and cut your throat [Zacarias, 13, Lubango].

The youths recounted experiences which included sleeping in the bush before and after the attacks, seeing land mine accidents, bombings, rapes, people and houses being burnt, having possessions stolen, being beaten and witnessing people being maltreated and killed. Many youths talked of the hardship of flight during which they suffered severe hunger, illness, and exhaustion. Although they were now in relatively secure areas where they no longer feared attacks on a daily basis, ongoing distress was caused by worrying about family members and friends who had been left behind in the war zones, and receiving sporadic news of further attacks and deaths in their home areas. Not being able to communicate with family and friends was a constant problem for the youths and their families. A further disturbing issue frequently mentioned was the inability to perform appropriate funeral rites for a deceased family member.

One issue consistently mentioned by the youths in connection with the war was the loss of their homes and possessions. This signified a number of things to the youths: for many in Lubango it meant that they had lost the protection of their families and parents and had to fend for themselves. A large number of the youths had lost either a father or a mother in the war or had been sent out of the war zones on their own, and lived with relatives in the town or on the streets. They lived lives of extreme hardship and sometimes of neglect and abuse. Ngongo, an orphan whose mother had been killed in front of him three years ago, was one of the youths whose malnourished appearance testified to a life of poverty:

> I was only 12 years [when they killed my mother]. I was very sad and I was thinking how will I live. I am the oldest of the siblings and I need to take care of all of them . . . Here I live with the sister of my father. I feel very bad when I remember these things and I start to cry . . . If my mother had not died I would be living differently, I would be living well [Ngongo, 15, Lubango].

The loss of home and possessions also means a change in status for all *deslocados*, a fact that affected many youths strongly:

> When I lived with my father, he didn't let me do the kind of work I am doing here now. When I arrived here, I didn't manage to live like I did before. I have to do other things in order to get what I need [Sousa, 15, Lubango].

The loneliness and vulnerability that may result from not being part of an extended family or community is an important issue affecting the psychosocial well-being of the youths and their perceived ability to cope. Orphans frequently need to rely on the goodwill of others, a situation which many felt uncomfortable with. Feelings of homesickness and longing (*saudades*) for their home areas were common among the youths who associated a variety of aspects with home, including a sense of rootedness in the traditions and culture of their ethnolinguistic groups.

Illness presents a problem to the displaced youths as the costs of health care were an additional burden on their limited resources, and because illness may lead to a loss of livelihood and the inability to perform household work. Many youths who were supporting their families through casual work or informal trading could not afford to lose out on income. According to the youths, war causes health problems and they made clear links between their own state of health and the worries they had to contend with in their daily life. One boy expressed this in the following way: "I have a lot of headache and stomach ache because of thinking too much about not having money and a job" [Rui, 16, Lubango]. Apart from becoming frail and weak because of a lack of food, worrying and "thinking too much" can lead to a number of illnesses such as headaches, heart pain, and excessive tiredness:

> My health is not good because I think a lot. I am a *deslocado* without any family in Lubango. When I stay at home not doing anything, I think too much. Sometimes the others get up early to go to school or to work, some go to the market, and I stay behind thinking a lot with nothing to do. Because of that my health is not good, because if I had some money or some work I wouldn't have these bad *pensamentos* [thoughts, memories]. It's these *pensamentos* that provoke one to steal or to look in the rubbish on the streets. With the rubbish you catch even more illnesses [Ornelio, 17, Lubango].

What emerges from the statements of the youths is that they perceive a definite interrelationship between displacement, poverty and their psychosocial well-being. The youths, talking about what helps them to cope with the distressing experiences and memories of war, were unanimous in their opinion that one needs to have

Table 12.1. Key Themes: Concerns and Issues

Education
— lack of finances to pay for educational materials, exam papers and "additional contributions"
— behavior and attitudes of teachers
— inadequate school facilities

Lack of clothing and shoes
— social exclusion
— adult status
— relationship issues

Experiences of war and displacement
— hardship, hunger, violence, death
— loss of homes and possessions
— worry about relatives left behind
— unfulfilled burial obligations
— loneliness and vulnerability

Illness
— loss of income
— relationship between physical health and psychosocial well-being

condições [the right conditions] to establish a new life. This includes having some of the minimum material resources such as food, clothing and shelter. If life consists of a daily struggle to survive, it is a constant reminder of what one has lost:

> For me to forget is very difficult. Because the work here is very heavy. When you remember the past, you think: "If it wasn't for the war I wouldn't be doing this heavy work". I fetch firewood, sometimes many hours a day. I work from sunrise to sunset for very little money. How can I forget what happened? [Jeremias, 16, Lubango].

The relationship between impoverishment and mental health is complex, bi-directional and dynamic (Leon & Walt, 2001). Stresses such as social isolation, insecurity resulting from a higher exposure to violence and the devastating consequences of falling ill, and feelings such as low self-confidence and powerlessness may all constitute challenges to the psychosocial well-being of poor people. As demonstrated above, the displaced face additional challenges to dealing with the distress and suffering caused by war and forced migration. The next section addresses how young displaced Angolans cope with such difficulties.

Coping Strategies: Agency and Resilience

As noted earlier in the chapter, a capacity-centered approach to poverty is adopted in examining issues affecting the young *deslocados*. This implies a focus on poverty from the standpoint of the capacities demonstrated by those who live in poverty, thereby transcending those approaches that reduce poverty to a matter of material deprivation, and giving recognition to the resilience and creativity of poor people in struggling to transcend their situation. According to Ochoa (2001), such an approach permits us to assess to what extent we have knowledge about the daily efforts of the poor to emerge from their misery, and to question how we can support them in defence of the human rights they are frequently denied. The author suggests that we have a responsibility to recognise and accept the experiences, thoughts, wisdom and knowledge of people living in extreme poverty, rather than seeing them as passive subjects who have little to contribute.

Unlike the stereotype of disenfranchised and angry young men hanging around the streets looking for trouble (see Kaplan above), the vast majority of male youths with whom we worked had relatively structured lives that involved "juggling" many different daily commitments. Most boys and girls engaged in various activities such as educational, work and sports activities on regular bases and with a sense of seriousness and responsibility for what they do. A number of the boys in the town, for example, attend training sessions at a soccer field or basketball area early in the morning at 5:30 am, then moving on to their work and/or educational activities. The data show that the youths make decisions about their lifestyles and their futures, explore their options, contribute to their families' households, develop their own opinions and perspectives and live multifaceted lives.

Increasing attention has been paid to the active way in which children and youths confront and attempt to cope with adversity, emphasising that rather than being helpless victims, children draw on a number of resources and interpret, adjust to and change the situations in which they find themselves (Dawes & Donald, 1994; Hutchby & Moran-Ellis, 1998; James, Jenks, & Prout, 1998). Coping has been defined as "the cognitive and behavioural efforts to manage specific external or internal demands (and conflicts between them) that are appraised as taxing or exceeding the resources of a person" (Lazarus, 199, p. 112). Resilience can be understood as the capacity to transform oneself in a positive way after difficult events.

Social and Personal Strategies

The most common way in which the youths deal with feelings of distress related to the war and from their daily problems is to try and distract themselves. These findings correlate with studies conducted on coping strategies amongst Malawian students which found evidence to suggest that distraction is a commonly used coping strategy in times of stress (Ager & MacLachlan, 1998). Various methods of distraction were used by the displaced youths in this study, most involving being in the company of friends, talking to them, playing games, and "hanging out" at the market places. All the youths agreed that the worst thing that can happen when one feels overwhelmed by one's problems is that one stays alone brooding, as this will make the problems seem insurmountable:

> When one is alone, doing nothing, you remember these things. But when someone comes with a game, a person forgets [Rosa, 16, Matala].

> In my case, when someone comes to distract me I don't think anymore. That is better [Jeronimo, 18, Lubango].

Friends have the responsibility to help a person who is feeling sad and overwhelmed by his or her situation or by memories of the war by preventing him or her from staying at home alone. A good friend thus goes around to someone's house, persuades the person to join in some activity and gives advice along the following lines:

> Listen, my friend, don't think about this anymore. All of this will pass. Don't cry anymore. Let's go to the market so that you can stop thinking [Diogo, 16, Lubango].

> Don't think too much about this. If you think too much you will become sick. You have to have hope because things will get better [Ester, 15, Matala].

The fact that the youths supported each other through action and advice confirms what medical anthropologists have argued for a long time, namely that the vast majority of psychosocial and mental health problems are dealt with by friends, relatives and community members in the popular health care sector (Kleinman, 1978; Nichter, 1992; Rubel & Hass, 1996). Social distraction and lay advice as in the form above, are thus active ways in which youths, who are in similar situations and therefore have insight into what the distressed, sad person in going through, assist one another to cope with the difficulties they face.

Personal strategies include listening to music, watching television (if accessible), keeping busy, working and studying. Young people frequently mentioned listening and dancing to music as a way of making themselves feel better, and the music seemed to have personal as well as social meaning to them. Schlegel (2000) observes that young people in most parts of the world listen to music to pass time, to relieve boredom, tension, loneliness and as a stimulus for fantasy and imagination. From conversations with the youths this seems to apply in Huila as well, in addition to the fun and enjoyment that they derived from dancing:

> We like dancing so much. When I go home I play the music of Michael Jackson and we dance and we dance. You won't believe how well I can dance [Bernardo, 17, Lubango].

The youths described that they often feel as if they are in a different world when they are absorbed in the music, an experience that helped them forget their difficulties and become more hopeful.

The youths expressed overwhelmingly pessimistic sentiments about their future in Angola (see Eyber, 2001). Despite this, the youths mentioned hope and courage as two effects that emerge as a consequence of war. Living through such difficult circumstances as they had done required both of these qualities, and the majority of youths felt that they had these:

> We have hope that one day peace will come [Carlos, 14, Matala].
> Or that one day you will meet your family again [Julieta, 15, Matala].

> When we left our homes, we came here and we have some hope for the future [Veronica, 16, Lubango].

> When you are in the war, you need courage. Otherwise you can't survive [Maurício, 18, Lubango].

Hope and courage, two qualities that are not normally associated with war, attest to the fact that the youths face adversity with an expectation of and a desire for a more positive future ahead, including the advent of peace, reunification with family members and an improvement in their living conditions.

Religious and Traditional Practices

Going to church, praying and reading the Bible were also used by the youths as a means of coping with their problems. The majority of the youths in this study in both areas attend church on a Sunday. Most of the youths considered this a regular and accepted weekly activity in which they participate with other family members and which they enjoy:

> I like going to church and singing and praying [Mariana, 14, Lubango].

> In church to pray and worship with other people you already feel differently. People behave honestly. You can ask God to help you and stop doing the bad things [Gonçalves, 17, Matala].

When asked how this helped them with their problems the youths identified three aspects: firstly, it was a way in which to distract oneself from one's problems by thinking about something else; secondly, it involved asking God for assistance with the problems one was facing at the time, and, thirdly, one could receive consolation from one's faith which may in turn lead to accepting one's fate. One young woman who often went to church to pray when she remembered the death of her father, expressed this by saying:

> Every time I remember my father I cry. But no one knows when the Lord will call a person to Him. I have to accept this [Odeth, 18, Lubango].

In both Matala and Lubango subgroups of youths existed that distinguished themselves from the rest by describing themselves as *religiosos* [religious]. These youths participated more actively than others in church events such as youth groups, and tried to live their lives according to the particular doctrine of the churches to which they belonged. Independent charismatic churches in Angolan towns are increasingly attracting youths who are welcomed as valued members. The churches facilitate and encourage young people to take on responsibilities such as leading in prayer and conducting healing rituals, thus empowering youth who have little opportunity for participating in other spheres of civil society. In addition, the networks and connections established through these churches give the youths not only a sense of identity and community, but can also provide support and access to scarce resources (Sommers, 2000). While the latter issue was less salient for Angolan youths, the peer network from which they derived legitimacy was important for the young people. The social life of the *religiosos* often revolves around the church where there are daily activities and meetings thus providing a structure and consistency in a world that usually offers neither of these.

The youths frequently referred to aspects of the African traditional religions practised in their communities in conversations about what was troubling them or other members of their families, for instance not having been able to perform burial rites for a deceased relative. Great importance was attached to being able to show respect to the deceased as well as to preventing trouble with the spirits in the future; caused by unfulfilled obligations to the dead (see Eyber, 2001; Honwana, 1997; Reynolds, 1996). The youths also discussed at great lengths illnesses caused by witchcraft which were feared greatly by both groups in Matala and Lubango. Recourse for witchcraft-related illnesses could only be found by consulting a traditional healer and/ or a diviner. Traditional healers and diviners were also consulted for various other illnesses and problems related to distress (see Eyber, 2001, for detailed discussion). Most youths attend clan and family rituals for ancestral spirits and expressed the sentiment that they considered it important to participate in and have knowledge of these as they formed a salient aspect of their identity. When they become adults they would be required to perform these rituals that serve to protect their homestead and families from misfortune.

Political Strategies

In Angola youths have not been allowed to play an overtly political role in public life nor in civil society. Many youths below the age of 18 have been recruited, forcefully and voluntarily, by both sides in the conflict; and the mobilisation of children for participation in the war is an ongoing concern (Queiroz, 2001). Adolescence is commonly held to be a time when the lure of ideology is particularly strong (Cohn & Goodwin-Gill, 1994; Machel Study, 1996) and where there is a strong receptivity to socio-political learning and attitude formation (Finchilescu & Dawes, 1998). Some of the youths who participated in this study actively supported the government's public campaigns disseminating the MPLA's perspectives on the conflict. If youths supported UNITA they would not have expressed this openly at any point as they found themselves in government-held territories where expressions of support for the opposition were dangerous. Overall, however, the youths do not seem to make large-scale use of party membership or political affiliation as a strategy for coping with their difficulties.

During our participatory work with youths they debated the effects of feelings of hatred, anger and revenge toward those who had caused their displacement and who were responsible for the violence. The overwhelming majority said that anger was a bad way to respond to war because it causes more destruction:

> Sometimes with this anger you destroy even more. Because sometimes when someone comes and you see him you just want to hit him. At times with lots of thinking about what your parents had [and lost], you begin to hate and you want to destroy everything . . . And some of the children who have been in the war, when you play with them, they do the same things they have seen there . . . the gestures they make are to insult you [Filipe, 16, Lubango].

Some youths felt that one should not hate the "other side," because people sometimes had no choice about which side of the conflict they ended up on. In the IDP camps many youths said that although they and their families had suffered the consequences of UNITA attacks, they felt no anger or hatred toward UNITA. A few of the youths had brothers who had joined UNITA voluntarily, a choice many said they accepted. It is not possible to say how widespread these sentiments were, but they resonated with attitudes of adults in the community who at times suggested that whether one becomes part of the MPLA or part of UNITA depends more on the area in which one is born than on individual choice. This feeling was, of course, not shared by all. A few youths stated that they feel a lot of anger toward those who had caused their misery, and it seemed as if especially those who had witnessed a parent being killed expressed feelings of wanting to take revenge:

> Those who killed my father – I have a lot of anger toward them. Sometimes I have thoughts of revenge: if I catch them I would do some things to them. But this will be very difficult [Sousa, 15, Lubango].

Economic Strategies

The youths engage in a variety of income-generating and household activities in order to support themselves and their families. Since the majority of these activities take up large amounts of time in return for little income, many youths work full time, especially the boys. The type of work and household activities in which the youths engage differed between the town and camp settings, and for the two sexes. Girls in both areas perform household work such as washing clothes and dishes, fetching water, pounding maize, taking care of the younger children, cooking, and cleaning. The girls in the camps also participate in activities such as fetching firewood, working on the fields in return for food, and selling at the market place. Boys in both areas are responsible for fetching grass, helping construct or repair houses, cutting wood and doing *negócio* at the market places. In Lubango, boys are furthermore involved in hourly paid work such as carrying water and crates, and helping in the fields.

Not all of the activities described above involve direct financial gain, but all contribute to the overall functioning of households by maintaining the various work roles that form an essential part of these households. A large part of the work that children and young people do is not financially rewarded and is indeed often not considered to be part of the economic survival strategies of families by policy makers and child labor experts (Boyden, Ling, & Meyers, 1997). However, young people are involved in numerous "hidden" ways in income-generation, for instance through preparing the alcoholic beverages sold at the market places, working on the fields and fulfilling essential task such as child care and cooking, thus allowing adults to perform work in exchange for money.

In Lubango, young boys and men had become increasingly successfully involved in the informal trading sector and were sometimes the only source of income for a household. Adults reported that this disturbed traditional relations of authority between adults and youths as the latter could challenge the sole decision-making power of older family members. The youths were usually expected to hand over the money they earned to their parents but some participants in this study mentioned that they kept money aside for themselves or for their siblings.

The myth of poor people as "idle" and "passive" is easily refuted by looking at the activity diaries kept by the youths over a period of a week in which they recorded all their work, leisure and educational activities. The youths were indeed "active managers of complex asset portfolios" (Moser, 1998 in Jones & Nelson, 1999, p. 14), balancing a large number of activities and responsibilities under extremely difficult circumstances.

The reactions and perspectives described in this section and in other parts of this chapter can be viewed as coping strategies on behalf of youths who not only engage with but also transform the environments around them. Not all of these strategies are viewed positively by adults and perhaps not all can be seen as being constructive in the long term. Criminal activity, drug-taking and acts of violence were common among certain groups of youths in the displaced communities, especially in urban and peri-urban areas. While these are not a phenomena unique to communities affected by displacement, an association between these activities and poverty certainly exists (Geremek, 1994).

Conclusion

This chapter has emphasised the fact that the physical, material and social aspects of the lives of young displaced people are fundamentally intertwined with their emotional and psychological well-being. This has implications for both practitioners who seek to provide psychological assistance to young people affected by war as well as for development practice that aims to redress issues of poverty. Firstly, it implies that programs of assistance should not focus exclusively on either the psychosocial or the material dimensions but that holistic, comprehensive approaches to helping young displaced people need to be sought. Secondly, the youths themselves clearly understand the relationship between poverty and psychosocial well-being and were of the opinion that in order to help someone cope with their experiences of violence and displacement, the right *condições* need to be created: the person needs to be given access to a job, education or training; and they need to have material help that will prevent them from feeling socially excluded. The insights of the *deslocados* themselves are crucial in understanding what sort of assistance is most appropriate for the situations of extreme poverty in which they find themselves. The chapter concludes with some reflections and practical suggestions for working with young displaced people.

Youth-to-youth programs are ways of tapping into and enhancing the already existing networks of support amongst young people. A number of such programs have been running successfully in different parts of the world (Hawes & Scotchmer, 1993) by drawing on and facilitating the special characteristics that young people bring with them, such as creativity, energy, and the potential for being agents of change. The youths in this study displayed varied and often mature problem-solving skills, suggesting the need to take seriously the critical capacity of the youths to engage with issues in constructive ways. A vitally important issue is the area of peace building and conflict resolution which could be incorporated into a number of different initiatives with displaced youth, for instance in educational, vocational, health and recreational activities.

Consideration needs to be given to the different groups of adolescents and their varying coping strategies as well as their needs and concerns. Boys and girls make use of different types of resources to varying degrees, for example girls were generally more involved in church-related activities and boys engaged more regularly in physical and sports activities. These differences between the sexes reflect the lifestyles and strategies of both girls and boys. In addition, attention should also be paid to the differences and similarities between displaced and local youths in the towns, in order to see if they identify themselves as distinct groups with particular sets of problems, or whether they share the majority of concerns. Careful thought must also be given to how to assist different groups without singling them out for preferential treatment, an issue which could lead to further conflict as has been noted in other situations of poverty involving forced migrants.

Programs aimed at improving the situation of youth should not only be oriented toward the young people themselves but needs to incorporate other groups from the community as well. Conflict between the generations is likely to increase as more and more displaced youths are forced to fend for themselves in urban areas. In addition, adult perceptions of adolescents as criminals and as a problem to society need to be addressed in various forms, for example through advocacy on behalf of organisations for the involvement of youth in the reconstruction of societies and communities in post-emergency situations. Sommers (2000) suggests that "understanding and addressing connections between perceptions of... [youths] as criminals during and after wars and their role in the construction or obstruction of peace is a critical component of peace building" (p. 86).

The standard response of the Angolan government to youths has been repressive and, while this is by no means unique to Angola, it illustrates the extent of their marginalisation in civil society. Prospects of enduring peace in post-war Angola will in part depend on whether or not the country continues to exclude over 50% of its population from participating in its civil society.

Attempts to eradicate extreme poverty and forge a more just and equitable society depend necessarily on developing a new awareness of misery, highlighting its human dimensions and overcoming reductionist emphases that conceive of poverty as a simple problem of material deprivation. Much of this can be learnt from young displaced people themselves who assume responsibility in their struggle to re-establish lives for themselves and their communities.

References

Adogame, A. (2001). *Tomorrow's leaders of today: Youth empowerment and African new religious movements.* Paper presented at the conference Africa's Young Majority. Meanings, victims, actors. May 23–24 2001. Edinburgh: Centre for African Studies, University of Edinburgh.

Andrade, F. (2001). *A life of improvisation: Displaced people in Malanje and Benguela.* Development Workshop Occasional Paper No. 1. Luanda: Development Workshop.

Ager, A., & MacLachlan, M. (1998). Psychometric properties of the Coping Strategy Indicator (CSI) in a study of coping behaviour amongst Malawian students. *Psychology and Health, 13,* 399–409.

Allen, V. L. (1970). (Ed.). *Psychological factors in poverty.* Institute for Research on Poverty Monograph Series. New York, NY: Academic Press.

Blos, P. (1967). The second individuation process of adolescence. *The psychoanalytic study of the child, Vol. 22.* New York, NY: International Universities Press.

Boyden, J., Ling, B., & Myers, W. (1997). *What works for working children.* Stockholm: Rädda Barnen.

CCF Report (2000). *Diagnostico da Communidade de Lalula.* Lubango: CCF.

Cohn, I., & Goodwin-Gill, G. (1994). *Child soldiers: The role of children in armed conflicts.* Oxford: Clarendon Press.

Dawes, A., & Donald, D. (1994). *Childhood and adversity: Psychological perspectives from Southern African research*. Cape Town: David Philip.

Dixon, J., & Macarov, D (1998). (Eds.). *Poverty: A persistent global reality*. London: Routledge.

Erikson, E. (1968). *Identity: Youth and crisis*. New York, NY: Norton.

Eyber, C. (2001). *Alleviating psychosocial suffering: An analysis of aprpaoches to coping with war-related distress in Angola*. Unpublished doctoral dissertation, Queen Margaret University College, Edinburgh.

Feuerstein, M. (1997). *Poverty and health: Reaping a richer harvest*. London: MacMillan.

Finchilescu, G., & Dawes, A. (1998). Catapulted into democracy: South African adolescents' sociopolitical orientations following rapid social change. *Journal of Social Issues, 54*(3), 563–583.

Geremek, B. (1994). *Poverty. A history*. Oxford: Blackwell.

Griffin, C. (1993). *Representations of youth*. Cambridge: Polity Press.

Hawes, H., & Scotchmer, C. (1993). (Eds.). *Children for health*. London: Child-to-Child Trust in association with UNICEF.

Hobfoll, S. E. (1998). *Stress, culture, and community: The psychology and philosophy of stress*. New York: Plenum Press.

Honwana, A. (1997). Healing for peace: Traditional healers and post-war reconstruction in Southern Mozambique. *Peace and conflict: Journal of Peace Psychology, 3*(3), 293–305.

Hutchby, I., & Moran-Ellis, J. (1998). (Eds.). Children and social competence: Arenas of action. London and Washington: Falmer.

Jones, S. and Nelson, N. (1999). (Eds.). *Urban poverty in Africa. From understanding to alienation*. London: ITP.

James, A., Jenks, C., & Prout, A. (1998). *Theorising childhood*. Cambridge, UK: Polity Press.

Kleinman, A. (1978). Problems and prospects in comparative cross-cultural medical and psychiatric studies. In A. Kleinman, P. Kunstadter, E. Alexander & J. Gate, (Eds.), *Culture and healing in Asian societies: Anthropological, psychiatric and public health studies*. Cambridge, MA: Schenkman.

La Fontaine, J. (1986). An anthropological perspective on children in social worlds. In M. Richards & P. Light (Eds.), *Children of social worlds*. Cambridge: Polity Press.

Lazarus, R. S. (1991). *Emotion and adaptation*. New York, NY: Oxford University Press.

Leon, D. and Walt, G. (2001). (Eds.). *Poverty, inequality and health: An international perspective*. Oxford: Oxford University Press.

Lewis, O. (1965). *La vida: A Puerto Rican family in the culture of poverty – San Juan and New York*. London: Secker & Warbung.

Lewis, O. (1968). *A study of slum culture*. New York, NY: Random House.

Machel Study on the Impact of armed conflict on children (1996). Geneva: United Nations.

Mbiti, J. (1989). *African religions & philosophy* (2nd ed.). Oxford: Heinemann.

Milheiros, M. (1967). *Notas de etnografia Angolana*. (2.a Edição). Luanda: Instituto de Investigação Cientifica de Angola.

Narayan, D. (2000). *Voices of the poor: Can anyone hear us?* Washington, DC: Oxford University Press.

Nichter, M. (1992). *Anthropological approaches to the study of ethnomedicine*. Philadelphia: Gordon and breach Science Publishers.

Noller, P. & Callan, V. (1991). *The adolescent in the family*. New York, NY: Routledge.

Norwegian Refugee Council (2001). Global IDP database. Angola. Electronic document: http://*www.idpproject.org*.

(Office for the Co-ordination of Humanitarian Affairs) (2001). *Angola. Report on rapid assessment of critical needs*. Luanda: United Nations.

Ochoa, M. A. U. (2001). Poverty and human rights in the light of the philosophy and contributions of Father Joseph Wresinski. In W. Van Genugten & C. Perez-Bustillo (Eds.), *The poverty of rights. Human rights and the eradication of poverty*. London: Zed Books.

Offer, D., Ostrov, E., Howard, K., & Atkinson, R. (1988). *The teenage world: Adolescents' self-image in ten countries.* New York: Plenum Medical Books.

O'Gorman, F. (1992). *Charity and change: From Bandaid to Beacon.* Melbourne: World Vision Australia.

Queiroz, C. (2001). Pretending to return: Invisible children – demobilising in Angola. *The Health Exchange, February 2001,* 16–17.

Ramphele, M. A. (1997). Adolescents and violence: "Adults are cruel, they just beat, beat, beat". *Social Science and Medicine, 45*(8), 1189–1197.

Reynolds, P. (1996). *Traditional healers and childhood in Zimbabwe.* Athens, Ohio: University of Ohio Press.

Richards, P. (1996). *Fighting for the rain forest: War, youth and resources in Sierra Leone.* Oxford: James Currey.

Rubel, A., & Hass, M. (1996). Ethnomedicine. In C. F. Sargent & T. M. Johnson (Eds.), *Medical anthropology: Contemporary theory and method.* London: Praeger.

Scheper-Hughes, N., & Sargent, C. (1998). (Eds.). *Small wars: The cultural politics of childhood.* London: The University of California Press.

Schlegel, A. (2000). The global spread of adolescent culture. In L. Crockett and R. Silbereisen (Eds.), *Negotiating adolescence in times of social change.* Cambridge: Cambridge University Press.

Serpell, R. (1996). Cultural models of childhood in indigenous socialisation and formal schooling in Zambia. In C. P. Hwang, M. Lamb & I. Sigel (Eds.), *Images of childhood.* Mahwah, New Jersey: Lawrence Erlbaum.

Sommers, M. (2000). On the margins, in the mainstream: Urban refugees in Africa. In S. C. Lubkemann, L. Minear & T. G. Weiss. *Humanitarian action: Social science connections. Occasional Paper #37.* Providence, USA: The Thomas Watson Institute for International Studies.

Summerfield, D. (1999). Socio-cultural dimensions of war, conflict and displacement. In A. Ager, (Ed.), *Refugees: Perspectives on the experience of forced migration.* London: Pinter.

United Nations Security Council (UN SC) (2000). *Report of the Secretary-General of the United Nations Office in Angola.* Luanda: UN.

van der Winden, B. (1996). *A family of the musseque: Survival and development in postwar Angola.* Amsterdam: One World Action.

Women's Commission for Refugee Women and Children (2000). *Untapped potential: Adolescents affected by armed conflict. A review of programs and policies.* New York, NY: Women's Commission for Refugee Women and Children.

Chapter 13

Poverty and Enterprise

Bill Ivory

An Emergent Focus on Small Business

Across a range of social sciences, enterprise development (the development of small businesses) has been seen as one of the key elements for development out of poverty (Panda, 2000). In economics, for instance, enterprise developers (or entrepreneurs) have been viewed as key innovators in developing economies, because they create new products, means of production, markets, supplies, and forms of organisation (Schumpeter, 1934). In sociology, entrepreneurs are seen as the creators and co-ordinators of forms of social organisation, from the inception of the group, through its maintenance, to its expansion (Bhanushali, 1987). In psychology, enterprise development has been seen primarily as a function of the personality of the entrepreneur, and in particular as being dependent on the entrepreneur's level of Need for Achievement (nAch) (McClelland, 1987). However, the nAch approach has been criticized in the recent psychological literature on poverty, for its lack of attention to social context, and in particular for its inherent individualism (Carr, McAuliffe, & MacLachlan, 1998). In development studies, nAch has come under fire for failing to predict economic growth in a global setting (Lewis, 1991). Addressing each of these concerns simultaneously, this chapter describes an alternative approach to enterprise development that is as much anchored in traditional values as it is attuned to the global economy.

The Place of Small Business Development in Attacking Poverty

This approach is also geared to the emergent zeitgeist in development studies and practice. A recent World Development Report, for example, highlights a key role, in reducing poverty, for the creation of *opportunities*, such as those to develop small businesses and experience inclusion within the global economy instead of exclusion from it (World Bank, 2001). The World Bank has, for example, explicitly promoted small business networks as part of Women in Development (Viswanath, 1995). Giving advice about small business development is also one of the key roles provided by a range of non-government organizations, or NGOs (Burgess, 2001). Most importantly of all perhaps, many of the poor themselves *believe* in small business development as a means of empowering themselves out of economic insecurity, and so providing themselves and their families with a decent quality of (working) life (World Bank Group, 2001). This chapter brings that report to life with an updated review about an innovative enterprise development program currently running across the northern region of Indigenous Australia (Ivory, 1999).

A Brief Overview of Recent History

The significance of this program will not be fully appreciated without the international reader taking at least a cursory glance at some of the recent history of Indigenous Australia. Although Indigenous peoples have inhabited the continent for as much as 60,000 years (Gracey, 1998), most of the recorded history dates from the late eighteenth century, with the arrival of British colonists from Western Europe. Since that time, the Indigenous populations of Australia have survived epidemics of killer diseases, massacres, and attempted genocide (Dudgeon & Pickett, 2000; Trudgen, 2001; Wessells & Bretherton, 2000). The worst example of this occurred during the twentieth century, when between one in three and one in ten of Aboriginal children (those with sufficient "White blood") were forcibly removed from their Indigenous families and placed into homes or fostered out to non-Indigenous families (Human Rights and Equal Opportunities Commission, 1997). Many of those locations were the forerunners of today's Indigenous "communities" (Riley, 1998). These communities are precisely where some of the emergent enterprises described below are situated.

Poverty across Indigenous Australia

Despite the self-evident resilience amongst Indigenous peoples, poverty remains a significant social issue across the country. Health statistics for many Indigenous communities, for instance, are on a par with the "Third World," despite the relative affluence of Australia as a "developed" OECD country (O'Reilly, Carr, & Bolitho, 2002). In regard to economic development, unemployment amongst Indigenous groups is twice the national average (Australian Bureau of Statistics [ABS], 2001). Across Australia as a whole, it is estimated that at least half of

Australia's 400,000 Aboriginal and Torres Strait Islander population is dependent on some form of welfare (Carruthers, 2000). In the Northern Territory, which is home to the highest percentage nationally of Indigenous peoples (many of them living in remote communities), just 40% of Indigenous Territorians currently participate in the workforce, compared to 75% of other Territorians (ABS, 2001). This 40% includes people who are participating in Community Development and Employment Programs, or CDEP schemes, which are equivalent to relatively low-paid work-for-the-dole programs (O'Reilly, Carr & Bolitho, 2002). Such schemes ("painting rocks and . . . hanging off the rubbish truck") have been heavily criticized by some Aboriginal leaders as being just another plank in the demeaning welfare system (Pearson, 1999, p. 26). Pearson and other senior advocates for the Indigenous peoples of North Australia have been campaigning vigorously for an end to the "gammon" (or false, sick) economy, and welfare dependence, that welfare has created. The Cape York group for example has co-ordinated roundtable discussions between Indigenous leaders and federal ministers, with a view to determining new, and in particular more economically inclusive, directions for Indigenous people to take. This chapter describes one such initiative that has been running for several years now in the Northern Territory (Ivory, 1999).

A Northern Territory Model

The founding rationale of this program is that opportunities exist within the current political and economic climate to build on some of the concepts of traditional Aboriginal society, and create a working environment for enterprise development. A model or models are required not just for Aboriginal people to gain support from government or wider institutions, but for governments and other institutions to work to. Clark (1990) when referring to voluntary organisation grass roots development in Zimbabwe, argued that "projects will remain irrelevant to the majority of the needy unless [they are] used as beacons to light up pathways for others – notably the state – to pursue" (Clark, 1990, p. 65). Development in Aboriginal towns and communities needs to go beyond the stage of relief and welfare, to an era of more sustainable development. In that regard, it has been argued that developing sustainable systems and self-managing networks will require changes in both policies and institutions, across global, national, *and local* levels (Korten, 1990, p. 120). Changes are gradually occurring in terms of policies, however institutions active in the field need to become more positively interactive with their clients. The program for enterprise development described below is an example of this interactivity. In fact, it is being deliberately molded especially to involve such institutions, and their resources, in full interaction with their Indigenous clients.

Bill Ivory

Building on Traditional Values

Concepts associated with the conduct of good business, such as organisation, communication, and planning were evident within Indigenous societies during pre-contact days. Both traditional and contemporary Aboriginal society has elements of good planning. The Yolgnu of Arnhemland for example, when organizing a *bapurru* (funeral), not only have to choreograph the ceremony with organizing performers, fulfilling ritual obligations, body paintings, songs and the like. They also have to arrange for the movement of people (sometimes hundreds) from isolated locations, and then house and feed them over extended periods. This by any standards is a major exercise, which has to be very carefully co-ordinated by the senior people from various clans, and it could never take place without serious organisational, communicative, and planning capabilities.

More specifically, "economic" concepts of "doing business" may have been present in Australia long before Europeans arrived. Evidence suggests that Aboriginal people have been trading for thousands of years amongst themselves, and for centuries with neighbours to the north. Worsely (1955) refers to "economic activities" between the Arnhem Land Aborigines and the Macassarese. Rose (1987) also refers to a system of "payment in kind," with reference to economic activities in the Northern Australian region (Rose, 1987, p. 99). Berndt and Berndt noted that "bartering centers" were established across the entire region (1999, p. 494). In addition to the trade with the Macassans, there was also "traditional" trade and the "constant movement of goods" along routes that "criss-cross the whole Continent" (p. 128). Regional trade was also important, with each clan participating to keep their clan in a "credit position" (Aboriginal Resource and Development Services Incorporated, 1994, p. 9). These goods were predominantly implements associated with production, such as spear tips and grinding implements, but as well there were items associated with ritual and religious importance (Rose, 1987). One study has elaborated on the significance of *wubarr* (sweat) within Arnhem Land communities, as a culturally valued means of wealth accumulation (Aboriginal Resource and Development Services Incorporated, 1993). This study also explored the existence of *djugu-gurrupan* (contracts), in an economic sense, between various trading clans (1993). Importantly for the present program, the exchanges in this relationship were not "straightforward commercial transactions" in the true sense, but involved other factors such as "partnership," "social relationship," and the "prestige" obtained (Berndt & Berndt, 1999, p. 133).

The traditional trade of Arnhemland "collapsed," or at least was severely damaged, in about 1907, with the emergence of the pastoral industry and the deliberate blocking of Macassan trade by the South Australian Government. This consequently resulted in "massive internal conflict and turmoil" (Aboriginal Resource and Development Services Incorporated, 1994, p. 9). It could further be argued that the results were subsequently also felt in other parts of the Northern Territory and beyond, because a vital link in the traditional trade routes had been jealously broken by the colonial government of the day, in order to protect their own economic interests.

The breakdown of the Aboriginal economic system of trade with Asia was followed by a period, commencing during the 1930s, when Australian government policy was based on a premise of the need for "welfare." Assistance provided to Aboriginal groups was on a "communal," or "democratic" system. The formation of an "Incorporated Association" (with all the associated problems) was deemed necessary to acquiring project funding. It is significant to note that individuals and family groups were not fostered to the same degree as community projects. This approach has only recently begun to be challenged.

In March 1998, the Federal Minister for Aboriginal and Torres Strait Islander Affairs, Senator John Herron, delivered a discussion paper titled, "Removing the Welfare Shackles." The paper was intended as a reform initiative for Indigenous economic development, and coincided with similar development philosophies that were emerging in the States and Territories. The paper argued that a new focus away from "ongoing welfare dependency" would lead to better *opportunities*, and more effective and efficient *economic development* programs (Herron, 1998). Subsequently, the Aboriginal and Torres Strait Islander Commission (1998) argued that whilst the move away from welfarism was to be applauded, it should be done in conjunction *with the private sector*. It was also stated that constraining factors such as remoteness, resources, and skill deficiencies should be addressed as a matter of priority in future development initiatives.

A long-standing intent by government to encourage Indigenous income- generating businesses was evident by the numerous attempts in policy and programs over some 20 years to that end (Herron, 1998). By 1997, there was a range of financial, management service, training and employment assistance schemes available to Indigenous business proposals. At that time, field officers in the Northern Territory, such as the writer, were aware of an increasing demand among Aboriginal people to be more proactive in pulling themselves away from welfare dependency, by starting their own businesses. Despite this motivation however, people did not have the working knowledge or familiarity with the bureaucratic and institutional structures to take their initiative to the next step. Government servicing, plentiful though it was, was thus not meeting with the demand and opportunity latent within the community – at least in the Territory.

The chances of business success are stacked against many of the hopeful Aboriginal entrepreneurs. In mainstream Australian society, statistics indicate that the percentage of small businesses still operating after the initial five years is only about 35% (Australian Bureau of Statistics, 1996). Aboriginal entrepreneurs face additional obstacles. Access to capital funds is a difficult and arduous process. Whilst many of the groups may "own" land (about 42% of the Northern Territory is Indigenously owned whilst 10% is under claim) under the *Aboriginal Land Rights*

(NT) Act 1976, major institutions such as banks are reluctant to lend because of lack of security or collateral. This is mainly due to the perception in some quarters that the inalienable freehold title granted under the Aboriginal Land Rights (NT) Act 1976 has a communal nature about it. Hence the term sometimes heard in the Territory, "land-rich, money-poor." Government funding agencies such as ATSIC (the Aboriginal and Torres Strait Islander Commission) have established rigid bureaucratic procedures in response to persistent audit scrutiny. Joint partners are reluctant in some instances to invest into situations where they perceive there may be a third-party influence. Access to business advice and training is restricted in the "bush." Most government agencies do not provide a field or extension service. Others are reluctant to visit for a variety of reasons including remoteness and cost.

The writer's observations at the time suggested the services were not bearing fruit because of:

- a lack of Aboriginal ownership for developments – from conceptual stage onwards,
- reduced or inadequate field services by agencies with the services to offer,
- increasingly complex and burdensome application processes for government assistance,
- lack of information among Aboriginal people about what assistance was available and from whom,
- literacy-associated problems, and
- a "fund and forget" approach by staff-stressed agencies.

Development of a Pilot Study

By early 1997, there was a persistent demand for assistance from Territory Aboriginal people on governments, accompanied by a political pressure on the Northern Territory Government's Office of Aboriginal Development, to become active in promoting Aboriginal economic development. This provided an impetus for a series of pilot studies that would examine the requests to provide one-on-one assistance to individuals, groups or communities. One of the objectives was to positively identify some of the obstacles facing potential Aboriginal entrepreneurs. By identifying these factors, government might then be in a better position to tailor their support initiatives. Another objective was to demystify the enterprise process where possible, and thus allow better access by Aboriginal people wanting to set up their own businesses.

Evolution of a Process into a Program

What commenced as a pilot study across five projects had, by client demand, in just over three years, grown into a program servicing *over 100 business project proposals*. In that growth, and although there is still in many ways a long way to go, an effective systematic approach to enterprise project development has evolved. Although the approach has varied to a degree with each client's situation, assistance was generally provided in the following ways:

- facilitation of the business concept or idea,
- development of a business establishment flow chart (as a simple readable diagram on one sheet of paper),
- assistance with organizing business workshop training,
- advice on appropriate agencies to contact for assistance (eg. training),
- assistance in obtaining endorsement from community and traditional decision makers,
- assistance with obtaining permits and clearances,
- assistance with the organizing of a business plan, feasibility study or similar,
- assistance with the application for funding, and
- limited mentor support once the business was established.
- a holistic approach to the enterprise initiative because of issues such as education, lack of knowledge about career opportunities, and training needs.

In the delivery of this program to our growing number of clients, two key elements are respected. The first is to have as a foundation an "awareness" phase. As Hobbs (1998) recently argued when referring to the process of self-empowerment, there needs to be initially self-awareness and an understanding of "why I am poor, who controls my community," and what can be done to break out of the poverty cycle (Hobbs, 1998, p. 1). An integral part of this awareness stage is to let the client appreciate what is happening in the economic world, and especially so with regard to Aboriginal entrepreneurism. The above research by the Aboriginal Resource and Development Services Incorporated (1994) highlighted a need to understand the world view of Aboriginal groups. In addition, this research also advocated an educational awareness process to be introduced of *balanda* (non-Aboriginal) culture, and in particular the associated Western economic system.

A key element in the program is for the Aboriginal entrepreneur to be the decision maker, and to make informed decisions throughout each stage of development. These guiding principles apply right from the conceptual stage in terms of what types of businesses they want to get into, through to the operational stage. This "ownership" factor is paramount to the long-term success of each business, and to the self-esteem and personal development of the entrepreneur. By developing each project within the framework of a business flow chart, the ownership factor appears to grow and prosper. So does the awareness. This enables the entrepreneurs to keep their fingers on the pulse. If a key adviser to the project leaves, then they can inform the incoming adviser exactly where the project is, and what has to be done next. Ownership is also a strong weapon in the fight to clear a path through the bureaucratic maze. An example of such a flow chart is included in

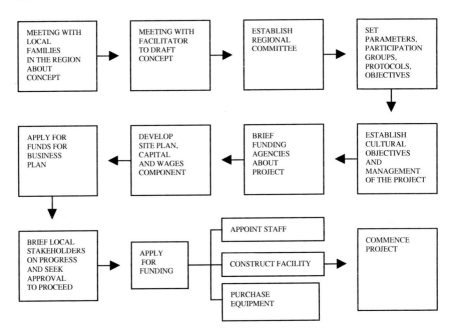

Figure 13.1. An exemplar flow chart for enterprise development

Figure 13.1. The process depicted in Figure 13.1 continues to evolve toward an ever more workable model of enterprise development.

Observations and Outcomes

An interesting dilemma was apparent with some clients in terms of what they wanted out of business. Most Aboriginal entrepreneurs do not necessarily wish to become a "Rupert Murdoch" (Australian Financial Review, 1999, p. 52). Their key objective in many cases is to get out of the "welfare system," obtain some independence, and ensure some sort of a future for their family. This raises questions about the definition of "success." Is success defined for instance as making a 20% profit margin? Or, is it a situation where a family living 250 kilometres out of Alice Springs, in a remote community (for instance), in marginal circumstances, is able to operate a limited business, and enjoy some element of pride and subsequent self-empowerment. In some instances, a business may be assisted to a degree by a Community Development Employment Program (CDEP) support scheme (above), and may take years to stand on its feet in terms of economic viability (Aboriginal and Torres Strait Islander Commission, 2000). However, if the business is nurtured and allowed to grow, then the long-term benefits are immeasurable. A crucial outcome in this respect, as previously mentioned, is the development of self-esteem (Aus-Thai Project Team, this volume).

This observation parallels that of other authors. Wismer and Pell (1981) refer to this as the difference between "social profit" and "economic profit." Research on some 50 Aboriginal businesses, found that 56% of owner/managers saw community and social development as a primary object of an enterprise, 38% saw community and commercial goals as equal in importance, and only 5% saw purely commercial goals as the primary objective (Byrnes, 1994).

An inescapable observation made within our program is that enterprise development is in demand, and that the program itself is having some impact for its clients. With over one hundred proposals undergoing development, these projects are extremely diverse in nature. They range for instance from an individual lawn-mowing service to a community-owned motel and roadhouse. They are also diverse in terms of location. Some are in the northern part of the Northern Territory, and others are in its central region. Some are in urban centers; others are kilometres out in the bushland. There are about 18 projects fully operating, which is almost double the number at the same point two years ago (Ivory, 1999). The remainder are in the development stages in Figure 13.1. A selection of these projects is given in Table 13.1.

A further observation is that this approach – particularly the development of a broad business flow chart (Figure 13.1), allows agents to clearly identify where they can provide assistance at the earliest stage of the proposals formulation. Some of these agency roles are mentoring, providing assistance with ideas and concepts, identifying funding and application opportunities, training, nurturing, and giving standard business advice. This program has also identified, for some agencies, a need to develop new assistance models. But to us, it has become clear that one of the critical elements to project success is the development of a business plan by the Aboriginal entrepreneurs themselves. Consistent with this, assistance under the program is only provided at the request of the client, and any development from then on is at their pace. If they wish to take five years to establish their business, then all well and good. If they wish to progress their initiative relatively quickly, then this too is respected.

This process allows for the determination, at some stage, of the economic feasibility of each project. The feasibility (or viability) testing exercise is worked through with the owner, and if a project clearly is non-viable, then the entrepreneur actually owns the decision on whether to proceed or not. After all, there is no sense in setting people up to fail. Out of this leeway, some of the entrepreneurs have ended up looking at another type of business that may be viable. Others have expressed contentment that at least their ideas were put to the test in a serious assessment.

Implications for Policy and Service Delivery

It has become obvious, in our program, that there are some key elements necessary for enterprise development initiatives to become successful. The entrepreneurs need to be keen and committed; if only to endure the negative responses they will

Table 13.1. Type and Structure of Enterprise Projects

Project No.	Type of Enterprise	Project Structure
1	CULTURAL TOURS	FAMILY GROUP
2	TOURIST WALKING AND CAMPING	COMMUNITY
3	MOBILE STORE	COMMUNITY
4	FISHING	COMMUNITY
5	FURNITURE & CANOE BUILDING	COMMUNITY
6	AUDIO SOUND	PARTNERSHIP
7	CATERING	INDIVIDUAL
8	BUTCHER SHOP	PARTNERSHIP
9	ELECTRICAL CONTRACTING	INDIVIDUAL
10	ARTEFACTS	COMMUNITY
11	FISHING TOURS	FAMILY
12	CAMPING GROUNDS	FAMILY
13	TOURISM VENTURE	FAMILY
14	FABRIC DESIGN	FAMILY
15	GRAPE FARM	COMMUNITY
16	MARKET GARDENS	COMMUNITY
17	ROAD HOUSESTORE	COMMUNITY
18	SAFARI CAMP	COMMUNITY
19	BUSINESS CENTER	COMMUNITY
20	KIOSK	FAMILY
21	FISHING	FAMILY
22	MOTEL COMPLEX	FAMILY
23	CULTURAL TOURS	FAMILY
24	CROCODILE FARM	FAMILY
25	CATTLE	JOINT VENTURE
26	TAKEAWAY SHOP	INDIVIDUAL
27	PACKAGED WATER	CORPORATION
28	MODELLING AGENCY	INDIVIDUAL
29	PASTORAL	INDIVIDUAL
30	PASTORAL	PARTNERSHIP
31	TRAILBIKE RIDING	INDIVIDUAL
32	BUSHWALKING	INDIVIDUAL
33	BOAT TOURS	INDIVIDUAL
34	PASTORAL W/RETAIL	COMPANY
35	POULTRY SUPPLIER	FAMILY
36	SERVICE STATION	COMMUNITY
37	TOURISM VENTURE	COMMUNITY
38	TOURISM VENTURE	CORPORATION
39	ABATTOIR	COMPANY
40	BUS SERVICE	FAMILY
41	ROADHOUSE	CORPORATION
42	ARTEFACT PRODUCTION	COMMUNITY
43	CATTLE AGISTMENT	COMMUNITY
44	TOURISM/ARTS VENTURE	FAMILY
45	GENERAL EXPERTISE	COMMUNITY
46	CHILDCARE CENTER	INDIVIDUAL
47	GRAVEL EXTRACTION	FAMILY

Table 13.1. (continued)

Project No.	Type of Enterprise	Project Structure
48	GRAVEL EXTRACTION	COMMUNITY
49	BUFFALO AGISTMENT	COMMUNITY
50	PRINTING SHOP	ORGANISATION
51	LAWNMOWING	INDIVIDUAL
52	ENVIRONMENT LEARNING CENTER	INDIVIDUAL
53	INDIGENOUS COSMETICS	INDIVIDUAL
54	CHILDCARE	COMMUNITY
55	FISHING TOURS	FAMILY
56	TREPANG HARVESTING	COMMUNITY
57	WHOLESALE	RESOURCE CENTER
58	HOTEL/ROADHOUSE	FAMILY
59	LEATHERWORK	COMMUNITY
60	BULK STORE	COMMUNITY
61	EMPLOYMENT AGENCY	INDIVIDUAL
62	PRODUCE DISTRIBUTOR	COMPANY
63	CATERING	PARTNERSHIP
64	ARTS & CULTURE (POETRY)	INDIVIDUAL
65	PARK ENTERPRISE DEVELOPMENT	BOARD OF MANAGEMENT
66	HORTICULTURE	CLAN GROUP
67	CAFÉ/GUEST HOUSE	COUNCIL
68	TOURIST DEVELOPMENT	CLAN GROUP
69	SHOP/CAMPING GROUND/TOURS	PARTNERSHIP
70	TELECOMMUNICATIONS	PARTNERSHIP
71	BUS SERVICE	ASSOCIATION

receive from many quarters. They also need to realise that it could be a long process before the business may be termed to be successful. But there also needs to be a serious consideration, by governments and the private sector, of how they can assist the process in a meaningful way. They need to examine how they can assist through the provision of appropriate training, business advice and planning, funding programs, and mentoring. They need to consider the role of the facilitator and the educator. They need to examine how their assistance programs, with all the associated "flash" media launches, can be successfully taken *from* the stage of a glossy brochure *to* people living in remote locations, under adverse conditions. There is a need to get rid of a lot of the red tape, and for agencies such as the banks to take a more proactive and interested approach. The long-term consequences of not addressing these issues, do not need to be spelt out.

Agencies play a role in the creation of "awareness," and to some degree that is happening. The Northern Territory Government's Office of Aboriginal Development, for example, is producing a newsletter that gives a view of the broader scene, and also focuses on issues associated with development, such as education. This newsletter also highlights specific "role model" projects that are either successful, or are in the process of being developed. In addition, the Northern Territory Department of Industries and Business is producing a booklet, entitled *Starting and Staying in Business,* specifically to complement the overall initiative. There are other initiatives also beginning to emerge across the Northern Territory. There is a training program that is now being funded by the Northern Territory Government, to take business planning to the "bush." Another development has been the establishment of an economic advisory group, consisting entirely of Aboriginal people who advise the responsible Northern Territory Minister. There is also a focus group of government departments and other agencies operating in the Territory. The role of this group is specifically to facilitate development and create a proactive environment for Aboriginal business development.

Another key initiative for Aboriginal business is a working group made up of representatives from Commonwealth agencies, including ATSIC, Northern Territory Departments, and, importantly, agencies such as the Land Councils, Indigenous Land Corporation, and an accounting firm, Deloites. Other members are invited as required. The role of this group is to co-ordinate assistance at the grass-roots level.

Some agencies are becoming interested and involved with the initiative. The Australian Taxation Office for example, has appointed a dedicated Remote Area Training Officer, who is now working in conjunction with the Office of Aboriginal Development's business workshops that are held in the outback. Overall therefore, the Office of Aboriginal Development is gradually changing its outlook, from one of regulation to one focusing more on knowledge dissemination and assistance.

Conclusion

The intent of the program in the first instance was to create a process that would simplify the world of business, and enable it to grow in the Aboriginal sector. The process continues to be refined through hard experience as well as through civil advice from all parties.

Another goal was to bring government funding programs and the like out of the "cold," and make them more accessible, particularly to those in the remote areas. Despite what appears to be a genuine spirit of co-operation at a middle manager level, this has proven a much more difficult task to accomplish.

A further aim was for field staff and mainstream agencies to be able to identify at what phase they can come in to assist business development. Some agencies, whilst indicating interest, still grapple with the logistics. The writer remains optimistic however that agencies will, following small-scale success stories, see the potential long-term benefits of Aboriginal participation in the economic sector, and become much more pro-active. The benefits for all could be both economic and social (O'Reilly et al., 2002).

The major encouraging outcome out of the whole process has been the attitude of Aboriginal people. They have taken on the concept of "business development" with a vengeance. However, at this stage there are limited resources available in terms of practical assistance, and perhaps their greatest allies in the long term will come from within their own wider community. The "beacons" described by Clark will have to come from the successful Aboriginal entrepreneurs of today. However, governments and the private sector have an important role to play in creating a proactive and nurturing environment for further economic development.

Overview

The projects described in this chapter are living examples of the revival of social identity. They illustrate that Indigenous people have passed well beyond both assimilation and isolationism (Tajfel, 1978). They demonstrate a process of thinking globally and acting locally, or "glocalization" (Hermans & Kempen, 1998). According to Noel Pearson (1999), such initiatives, in the context of small business development, are the sole sustainable antidote to welfare dependence and ongoing community poverty. Economic integration with the wider economic community is the way forward for Aboriginal people to break the cycle of poverty experienced since first contact (above; O'Reilly et al., 2002). In terms of the pillars for development in the World Bank Report, the key to this development is self-empowerment. As outlined earlier, economic activities have been thriving in, across, and outwards from Australia for a long time. The program outlined above is living proof that those traditions, today more than ever, have fitness for purpose in the global economy.

Postscript

The Labour Party came to power in July 2001 in the Territory after 26 years of conservative "Country Liberal Party" (CLP) governments. They dissolved the Office of Aboriginal Development and created the Department of Community Development, Sport and Recreation and Cultural Affairs. The emphasis of the new government is outlined in its policy document (Martin, 2001). This document is focused on "partnerships" and "regional and local decision making." The intention is to negotiate and fund "Regional Agreements." Such agreements will define "appropriate levels of self governance and arrangements for Indigenous participation." Indigenous groups (communities, regions) will be identified who wish to participate in "regional economic development initiatives," and Regional Agreements will be negotiated. The desired outcome is facilitated "economic development across all sectors of the economy."

I will now be involved with the Regional Agreements and my "hands-on" role has ceased. However, I believe that the model of development has now gained an impetus of its own. At the most recent meeting of the Aboriginal Economic Development Focus Group (made up of Commonwealth and NT Departments, Land Councils, private service providers, etc.) that is referred to in the paper, concern was expressed that the process of economic development could be jeopardised. However, our intent in the first place was to facilitate a model that they could all work to, and that it would end up having a life of its own. I think, and hope, that the awareness, expectations, and knowledge of the Indigenous entrepreneurs has been raised to such a level that they can begin to control the "movement" themselves in any case.

I am thus interpreting the changes, on a personal basis, to mean a change in involvement from developing a grass-roots model of enterprise/community development to a broader role in participating in regional economic and social development that incorporates all of the emerging Indigenous businesses/entrepreneurs/other players. There is the need for a model to be developed in the Northern Territory of pathways to successful regional arrangements.

Acknowledgments

I gratefully acknowledge the assistance of Mr John Gardiner from the Office of Aboriginal Development for his comments on an earlier draft of this article. Mr Ray Hempel from OAD commented on a later draft. Banambi Wunungmurra of Yirrkala gave advice on Yolngu language terms. Dr. Stuart Carr from the Northern Territory University also provided much appreciated advice and assistance. This chapter is an updated and expanded version of a paper that appeared in Volume 11 (1999) of the *South Pacific Journal of Psychology*. Whilst the philosophy behind the concept of economic development is very much supported by the Northern Territory Government, it should be noted that the opinions expressed in the chapter are those of the author.

References

Aboriginal Resource and Development Services Incorporated. (1993). *Information Paper Number 5*, ARDS Inc., Darwin, Australia.
Aboriginal Resource and Development Services Incorporated. (1994). *Cross-Cultural Awareness Education for Aboriginal People*. Consultancy for the NT Office of Aboriginal Development, ARDS Inc., Darwin, Australia.
Aboriginal and Torres Strait Islander Commission. (1998). *Getting on with Business: "Pursuing a partnership with the private sector. An ATSIC response to: 'Removing the welfare shackles.'"* ATSIC unpublished paper, Canberra, Australia.
Aboriginal and Torres Strait Islander Commission. [ATSIC] (2000). Ten years on: A top vote. *ATSIC News*, Feb. 2000
ABS (Australian Bureau of Statistics). (1996). *Small business statistics*. Canberra: Australian Government Publishing Services.

ABS (Australian Bureau of Statistics). (2001). http://www.abs.gov.au.

Australian Financial Review. (1999). Aboriginal people start flexing their economic muscle. *Australian Financial Review*, 1 November.

Berndt, R. M., & Berndt, C. H. (1999). *The world of the First Australians: Aboriginal traditional life, past and present*. Canberra, Australia: Aboriginal Studies Press.

Bhanaushali, S. G. (1987). *Entrepreneurship development*. Delhi, India: Himalaya Publishing House.

Burgess, R. (2001). Retiring youthfully. *New Zealand Herald, October 30*, E7.

Byrnes, J. W. (1994). *Aboriginal enterprise development in remote areas: Prospects, problems and potential strategies*. Darwin, Australia: Northern Territory University.

Carr, S. C., McAuliffe, E., & MacLachlan, M. (1998). *Psychology of aid*. London: Routledge.

Carruthers, F. (2000). Broken dreaming. *The Australian Magazine, September 16–17*, 20–25.

Clark, J. (1990). What are voluntary organisations, and where have they come from? *Democratizing development: The role of voluntary organisations*. Hartford, CT: Kumarian Press.

Dudgeon, P. & Pickett, H. (2000). Psychology and reconciliation: Australian perspectives. *Australian Psychologist, 35*, 82–87.

Gracey, M. (1998). Substance misuse in Indigenous Australian Australia. *Addiction Biology, 3*, 355–362.

Hermans, H. J. M., & Kempen H J. G. (1998). Moving cultures: The perilous problems of cultural dichotomies in a globalizing society. *American Psychologist, 53*, 1111–1120.

Herron, J. (1998). [Minister for Aboriginal and Torres Strait Islander Affairs]. *Removing the Welfare Shackles, A Discussion Paper on a Reform Initiative for Indigenous Economic Development*. Canberra, Australia: Australian Government Publishing Services.

Hobbs, J. (1998). Indigenous rights: What are we afraid of? *The Canberra Times,* 10 December.

Human Rights and Equal Opportunities Commission. (1997). *Bringing them home: National enquiry into the separation of Aboriginal and Torres Strait Islander children from their families*. Sydney, Australia: The Spinney Press.

Ivory, B. (1999). Enterprise development: A model for Aboriginal entrepreneurs. *South Pacific Journal of Psychology, 11*, 62–71.

Korten, D. (1990). From relief to people's movement. In *Getting to the 21st century: Voluntary action and the global agenda*. Hartford, CT: Kumarian Press.

Lewis, J. (1991). Re-evaluating the effect of nAch on economic growth. *World Development, 19*, 1269–1274.

Martin, C. (2001). *A framework for partnership with Indigenous Territorians: A new direction*. Darwin, NT Labour Platform: Aboriginal Affairs.

McClelland, D. C. (1987). Characteristics of successful entrepreneurs. *Journal of Creative Behavior, 21*, 219–233.

O'Reilly, B., Carr, S. C., & Bolitho, F. H. (2002). Glocalization of alcohol and drug services for Indigenous youth in the Northern Territory, Australia. In A. J. Marsella (Ed.), *Paradise lost, paradise found* (in press). Dordrecht, Netherlands: Kluwer-Plenum Press.

Panda, N. M. (2000). What brings entrepreneurial success in a developing region? *The Journal of Entrepreneurship, 9*, 199–212.

Pearson, N. (1999). *Our right to take responsibility*. Discussion paper for community and regional organisations. Cape York Peninsula: Cape York Council.

Riley, R. (1998). From exclusion to negotiation: Psychology in Aboriginal social justice. *In-Psych, 20*, 12–19.

Rose, F. G. G. (1987). *The traditional mode of production of the Australian Aborigines*. Sydney: Angus & Robertson Publishers.

Schumpeter, J. A. (1934). *The theory of economic development*. Cambridge, MA: Harvard University Press.

Tajfel, H. (1978). *Differentiation between social groups*. London: Academic Press.

Trudgen, R. (2001). *Why warriors lay down and die*. Darwin, Australia: Aboriginal Resource and Development Service.

Viswanath, V. (1995). *Building partnerships for poverty reduction: The participatory planning approach of the Women's Enterprise Management Training Outreach Program* (WEMTOP). Washington, DC: World Bank.

Wessells, M. G., & Bretherton, D. (2000). Psychological reconciliation: National and international perspectives. *Australian Psychologist, 35*, 100–108.

Wismer, S., & Pell, D. (1981). *Community profit: Community-based economic development in Canada,* Ottawa: Is Five Press.

World Bank. (2001). *World Development Report 2000/2001: Attacking poverty.* Washington, DC: World Bank Group.

World Bank Group. (2001). World Bank Group Review of small business activities 2001. http://www.ifc.org

Worsely, P. M. (1955). Early Asian Contacts with Australia. *Past and Present No.7.* Oxford: Oxford University Press.

Chapter 14

Poverty and Process Skills

Malcolm MacLachlan and Eilish Mc Auliffe

The model of Technical Assistance (TA) that has dominated the ethos of international aid for the last fifty years is increasingly becoming recognised as an inappropriate approach for helping people to develop out of poverty. Its overtones of paternalism, its focus on the hardware of aid (i.e. provision of equipment), and its lack of responsiveness to the needs of local communities has heralded a new age of local ownership and empowerment. International aid efforts are now less concerned with predetermining the *outcome* of projects and more concerned with establishing the proper *process* to build local capacity. Process skills, everybody seems to agree, are important. What is unclear, however, is what process skills *actually are*.

In this article we outline the theory of *incremental improvement* in a development context, and synthesise a set of *process skills* for development work. The Incremental Improvement Theory builds on diverse areas of psychology such as "small wins" and Field Theory. Our studies of critical incidents among psychology students working in refugee camps, refugees who themselves became refugee counsellors, nurses on emergency relief assignments and teachers on long-term development assistance, constitute a rich and diverse source of qualitative data. Having delineated the elusive process skills, we briefly consider the implications of these for future training and development.

International Aid

A comprehensive evaluation of international aid is beyond the scope of this chapter and our purpose here is simply to note the problematic nature of aid, both conceptually and in terms of its outcomes. While the idealistic basis of the "development" ethos is one source of criticism (Dore, 1994), a more pragmatic source is the failure of many development projects to achieve their stated goals. The Wapenhans (1993) evaluation, of 1,800 projects funded by the World Bank, stated that 37.5% of the projects completed in 1991 were failures. In another large-scale evaluation, of 212 USAID (United States Agency for International Development) projects, Kean, Turner, Wood and Wood (1988) concluded that only 11% of them had strong prospects for sustainability. More recently, in *The Reality of Aid*, Enge (2001) has argued that even though some aid is indeed effective in alleviating poverty, with poverty and inequality continuing to increase, we need fundamental changes in our approach to it.

In addition to the disappointing process and results of various projects (see also Cassen, 1994), there has been considerable criticism of macroeconomic interventions by the World Bank and International Monetary Fund (IMF). These multilateral organisations have made development loans contingent upon the adoption of Economic Structural Adjustment Programmes (ESAPs). Such programmes have sought to switch resources from public sector services into the private sector, with particular emphasis on enhancing export potential, establishing foreign markets, and earning "hard currency" (Campbell & Lexley, 1989). It is our contention that these powerful and influential institutions in the "development world" have highlighted issues that are macro, possibly at the expense of those that are more micro. The micro focus is at the core of identifying important process skills for developing *local* human resources.

Berg's (1993) UNDP report is perhaps the most influential critique of the era of technical assistance. This report condensed a "consensus diagnosis" focusing on four main problem areas: (1) weaknesses in the design, implementation and supervision of technical co-operation projects; (2) overreliance on the resident expatriate-counterpart model of technical co-operation; (3) the donor-driven nature of technical co-operation which has disempowered local communities; (4) poor incentives and working conditions in the public sector of recipient countries, with attendant low motivation and high turnover.

A good deal of the criticism concerning the effectiveness of technical co-operation has been directed at its "expert expatriate" component (Carr, Chipande & MacLachlan, 1998; MacLachlan, 1993) and its associated costliness, its substitution for, rather than development of local capabilities, and its demoralising role on the recipients of aid (Fahey et al., 2000).

Building Capacity

Although international aid for development is increasingly focusing on building *capacity* for development, rather than on specific outcomes, this is not without its problems. "Agencies that have taken capacity development seriously have likened the experience to opening up Pandora's box. Instead of the anticipated "treasures" – conceptual clarity, tried and tested instruments, and demonstrated impact – they find uncertainty about the concept and how to measure it, a confusing array of process and participatory techniques, and a wide gap between policy prescriptions and actual practice" (Bossuyt, 1995, p. 1). The idea of capacity building is particularly attractive to those who see lack of effective governance as being key. It is argued that such a deficiency results in institutions that are too weak or dysfunctional to guide collective action in a positive direction. Once again, however, this is clearly a top-down orientation, seeing the creation of appropriate structures as paramount. While *capacity building* may be the current buzzword, it is plagued by the lack of an agreed definition, disagreement as to whose capacity should be developed, by which means and under whose direction. We argue that it is the capacity of the poorest of the poor that should be directly "developed," rather than this supposedly being facilitated through a trickle-down aspiration. Again, it is at this person-to-person level, that identification of key process skills has much to offer. But can much come of such "small" thinking?

Community Psychology

"Community psychology concerns the relationships of the individual to communities and society. Through collaborative research and action, community psychologists seek to understand and to enhance quality of life for individuals, community, and society" (Dalton, Elias, & Wandersman, 2001, p. 5). This definition thus emphasises the *contextual setting* of *individual's relationship with their community* and how through *participation* their *quality of life* may be enhanced. Community psychology is an action-oriented approach that engages with issues of social, political and economic disadvantage and in which there has traditionally been a unity of values, research and action (Rappaport & Seidman, 2000). Most of our own research reported in this chapter is concerned with health and welfare, particularly of refugees, and it perhaps most strongly resonates with "community health psychology." Murray et al. (2001) characterise this emerging subdiscipline as endorsing values of caring, compassion and community; health promotion and prevention; countering oppression and facilitating empowerment; respecting diversity and seeking social justice. For us, one of the major benefits of the community approach is the implicit recognition of the possibility of "experts" *learning from* those they seek to assist, and then reflecting back this learning.

A Case Study: The Orangi Pilot Project

Orangi, a squatter district of Karachi, Pakistan, had been plagued by political riots, murderous drug Mafiosi, and corrupt officials. However, it is now recognised as a shining example of how urban squalor can be overcome to produce positive social change. This was achieved with very little help from either local or national government, or from foreign aid (Pearce, 1996; Carr, Mc Auliffe & MacLachlan, 1998). Previously residents of Orangi would empty their bucket latrines into the narrow laneways every four or five days. Typhoid, malaria, diarrhoea, dysentery and scabies were rampant, and the children played in filth. Akhter Hameed Akhan, a retired school teacher and sociologist, reasoned that because municipal authorities would never be able to provide appropriate sanitation for the poor of Orangi, and because foreign aid would not filter through to them, the community would have to solve the problem itself.

An important starting point for this project was the rejection of existing technical standards as being too exacting and inappropriate to this impoverished context. For example, basic septic tanks were installed between each latrine and sewer, so that only liquids reached the pipe, thus preventing them from becoming blocked and saving local streams from the worst pollution. New manhole covers were designed, smaller and simpler than conventional ones, and these could be produced in situ at one tenth of the price charged by outside contractors for conventional designs. There were no grants and no subsidised demonstration projects. Householders were simply encouraged to band together and install sewers at their own expense. United Nations consultants visiting the project in its early days found many faults with it; no targets, no surveys, no master plan. Orangi's sewer network was constructed in a piecemeal and incremental fashion. People living in the individual lanes organised themselves to construct their own sewer, starting with those nearest the main streams and working up the hillsides.

Following the development of better sewers, the Orangi Pilot Project focused on improving housing, education and health. Again the approach was to look at what already existed and how it could be developed, rather than imposing solutions from outside. The Orangi project received some funding to pay project staff, but it also turned down offers of funding to build or set up 'a project'. The ethos of the Orangi project was that people will look after something that they themselves have paid to develop. In addition, they recognised that subsidies can create conflicts within a community: If subsidies exist for some, then everybody will want one, and self-help may cease.

In Orangi, literacy rates have improved and are now twice the national average, sewage has been banished from the streets and health indices reflect dramatic improvements: in 1982 when the project began, infant mortality was 130 per 1000 live births, but by 1991, this had dropped to 37 per 1000. Orangi also compared very favourably with Thikri, another squatter settlement outside Karachi, with no sewers and little organised preventive health care. Nine times as many couples used family planning in Orangi as Thikri, rates of illness were half that found in Thikri, and spending on doctors was only one fifth of that in Thikri.

The Orangi success story started with sewage, and so it is interesting to note that the UN launched its own sewage scheme also in Orangi, in the early 1980s, based on a master plan and using conventional contractors. Pearce (1996) states that "with a bloated bureaucracy, poor workmanship and inadequate maintenance it collapsed within five years, with just 35 lanes served. By contrast over 15 years the Orangi Pilot Project, working through principles of 'pay-your-own-way self-help,' with modest materials, making small scale improvements, has installed 94,000 latrines, connected up to approximately 5,000 underground lane sewers and 400 secondary drains." Projects such as the Orangi Pilot Project give hope to the recipients of many failed development projects. They do this by emphasizing that communities who take charge of their own lives can determine their own future.

While there is much to be admired in the Orangi experience it also raises some awkward ideological issues. For instance, although an admittedly extreme position, one could argue that the self-help discourse is "victim blaming," in that those communities who do not take charge of their own lives have only themselves to blame. This of course could be an attractive message to those who wish to maintain an inequitable status quo in resource allocation, if they can point to examples where urban squalor can be overcome with little help from local or national government, or from foreign aid. Yet to identify examples of a community investing time, ownership – and indeed money – in providing solutions to its problems, is not to deny the critical importance of the social, political and economic context though which such conditions are created. Indeed community psychology *"concerns the relationships of the individual to communities and society."* The ingenuity, resourcefulness and motivation of individuals should not be "hijacked" by the need to reform the macroeconomic policy of the World Bank or International Monetary Fund, for instance. Furthermore, the increasingly problematic role of large multinational corporations, regarding the impact they have on the empowerment and welfare of communities, is also of great concern (MacLachlan, 2003). However, while reform of these institutions and multinationals may be a crucial aspect of community empowerment, so too is the role of individuals within those communities. As with so much else, we require *pluralism* in our approach to alleviating poverty. There will be no "one best fit" for all problems. Below we outline one perspective that grew out of an awareness of the difficulties that many aid projects run into – trying to do too much, too quickly.

Improving Incrementally

Development administration has been described as "a subject matter in search of a discipline" (Turner & Hulme, 1997). Drawing on an interdisciplinary range of concepts and analytical tools, it seeks to combine aspects of economics, engineering sociology and politics, anthropology and management. Psychology, with the exception of some aspects of organisational psychology, has had little influence. While it would be naive to think that psychology has all the answers, it is clear that its distinctive contribution has not been developed to its full potential (Carr &

MacLachlan, 1998; MacLachlan & Carr, 1994). Before examining how practical process skills have been derived from critical incident analysis, we develop a psychological perspective on development theory, one that supports the ultimate possible value of "thinking small."

For the last three decades the catchphrase of international aid has been "sustainable change" (e.g. Bossert, 1990; Brinkerhoff, & Goldsmith, 1992). We have previously argued that this is coming at the problems from the wrong perspective; not only is it focusing on outcomes rather than process, but it also implies focusing on achieving a fixed, rather than dynamic, state. This may in part be due to the fact that the process of development work often uses project management as its framework. Project management has its origins in the engineering and construction industry where typically the desired outcome is a stable entity, e.g. a building or physical infrastructure. Naturally enough when aid workers encounter a situation of human impoverishment, they don't just want to make a small difference, they want to make a big difference – they want change on a massive scale. However the scale of aid projects can be a bone of contention (Cassen, 1994), with donors (e.g., Dore, 1994), and host governments (e.g., Thomas, 1996) who may seek somewhat larger leaps forward than do host local communities and their representatives (e.g., Porter, Allen, & Thompson, 1991). This discrepancy exists despite evidence that it may often be more appropriate to pursue smaller-scale, "incremental improvements" (MacLachlan, 1996). Psychological changes often take longer than technological ones (Moghaddam, 1990). People will be able to adapt to change more easily when the scale of change is small. While this is a simple message, we also realise that it may be contrary to the inclinations of many involved in international aid. We therefore briefly review various sources of psychological evidence, which together suggest that often the best solutions to development problems involve setting smaller, more modest, goals in the short term, and slowly incrementing these developments to achieve more substantial change in the long run. The general principle that we develop here is that the *more* you change, the *less* you can sustain.

When it comes to the psychology of change, Field Theory has had enduring appeal since its original inception, 50 years ago (Lewin, 1952). An important feature of the theory is its explicit acknowledgement that stability reflects a dynamic of interacting forces, not simply a failure of something to happen. Rural peasant communities in many developing countries are sustained through a way of life that may have changed little over hundreds of years. Yet this does not mean that such communities are stagnant. If instead they are seen as a "successful" balancing act, between opposing forces, then the would-be "developer" must approach "community development" with a new set of questions. Instead of asking, "Why have these people not 'developed' more?", a better approach may be to ask, "Why has this situation continued to exist?" and "What forces are involved in maintaining the balance here?" These latter questions acknowledge the existence of an important dynamic prior to any "development initiative."

Leavitt, Dill, and Eyring (1973) in their systems model of change, assert that whilst change efforts may focus on any of four subsystems (structure, technology, people or task), intervention effects will be influenced by factors in each of the four subsystems. If development workers see communities as dynamic systems, then they will appreciate that any change introduced in one subsystem may result in unexpected changes in other subsystems. Typically, for example, development projects focus on changing the "task" or "technology" subsystems, but fail to allow for the inevitable changes that occur in the "people" subsystem. Large scale and unexpected changes in several sub-systems may well create instability in the system, or community, as a whole. Thus, the smaller the imbalance produced by change, the easier it should be to adapt to.

If the status quo represents a balance between opposing forces, it also represents a balance between those people who control the forces. Such a "balance of power" should not, of course, be taken as suggesting an egalitarian distribution of resources, instead "balance" here simply implies equilibrium. Various reasons for resisting change have been described by Bedeian (1980). These reasons include parochial self-interest, misunderstanding the reason for change, and a lack of trust in those who are trying to create change. Different people, with different values, evaluate change in different ways. Furthermore individuals differ in their ability to cope with change. To engage in a process of change necessarily creates a situation of risk. A willingness to accept risk varies from one person to another. There is some evidence that tolerance for risk taking also varies across cultures, with some cultures being described as "high uncertainty avoidance" cultures, and others being described as "low uncertainty avoidance" cultures (Hofstede, 2001). This may be especially relevant to the differing perspectives of foreign expatriate "developers" and local people. Any change involves a degree of risk and expatriate and local workers, due to their differing cultural backgrounds, may be most comfortable with different degrees of uncertainty. It is important that local people are allowed to work in ways that are challenging, yet not threatening, to them.

Weick (1984) has argued that people often define social problems in ways that overwhelm their ability to do anything about them. For instance, take the problem of poverty in sub-Saharan Africa. One construction of this problem is that developing countries are being encouraged, through structural adjustment programmes, to compete in a global market. These countries may have a market advantage in the supply of cheap labour. Because labour wages are low, people struggling to get by on a day-to-day basis are not able to save money, or invest their money in health, education or other services. Furthermore, competing in a global market means that you are vulnerable to changes in the market, anywhere in the world. Attempts to improve the standard of living in one developing country (for instance, by increasing the wages) may give another developing country an economic advantage (by making labour in that country relatively cheaper), thus taking the trade away from the country that increased the wages of its workers.

Scaling up the gravity of social problems also increases the importance of the issue at hand, and similarly the magnitude of the demands to cope with the situation. In such situations, Weick has argued, when perceived demands exceed perceived capacity to cope, stress, in the form of frustration, arousal and helplessness, ensues and these reactions result in poor performance and thus poor problem solving. Interestingly, the logic of "small wins" being preferable, has also been applied to technological innovations in the USA:

> A technological innovation is a big step forward in the useful arts. Small steps forward are not given this designation; they are just "minor improvements" in technology. But a succession of many minor improvements adds up to a big advance in technology . . . It is understandable . . . that we eulogize the great inventor, while overlooking the small improvers. Looking backward, however . . . it may well be true that the sum total of all minor improvements, each too small to be called an invention, has contributed to the increase in productivity more than the great inventions have. (Machlup, 1962, p. 164)

The same argument may be made for technological, or indeed any other form of improvement, in the less industrialized countries. International aid has too often focused on the size of the (perceived) gap to be bridged between "developed" and "developing" countries, and in doing so has overlooked the value of "small wins." Rather than bridging the gap, technological leaps may often *create* the gap. Many technological innovations in developing countries reach beyond the carrying capacity of the local economic, social and educational infrastructure. Their inability to subsequently "service" such innovations may demoralise local communities.

The notion of small wins has much in common with incremental improvements. Weick characterises a small win as "a concrete, complete, implemented outcome of moderate importance. By itself, one small win may seem unimportant. A series of wins at small but significant tasks, however, reveals a pattern that may attract allies, deter opponents, and lower resistance to subsequent proposals. Small wins are controllable opportunities that produce visible results . . . Once a small win has been accomplished, it forces a set [an attitude] in motion that favors another small win" [1984, p. 43]. If we accept the idea of aiming for "smaller wins," we then need to establish just how small can a "win" be, and still be meaningful?

As we have described elsewhere (Carr, Mc Auliffe & MacLachlan, 1998) clearly different contexts will require different levels, and indeed types, of input to create a change that is a noticeable difference, but not a daunting leap. So, for example, a small investment of resources in a drought situation may make a large difference, while the same size of investment in improving the hygiene facilities of a large town may make very little, or no, difference at all. Furthermore, not only the explicit psychosocial context, but also the choice of valued domains will be influenced by an array of cultural factors (MacLachlan, 1997, 2001), which will often emphasise different priorities for the "foreign" donors and local recipients of aid. It is clear that this local perspective – the consumer's perspective – must be given due recognition if the services and facilities to be developed are to be a meaningful part of local people's lives (Mc Auliffe, 1996a, b, 1998). Our contention is that small-scale improvements, at a local level, that genuinely respond to the wishes of local people, are best facilitated through *process skills*. Such skills focus more on *how* things are to be changed, rather than on achieving predetermined outcomes, often set well outside the local normative frame of reference. How can process skills be differentiated from more outcome-focused activities?

Identifying Process Skills

Over the past 10 years we have undertaken a number of studies of critical incidents with a variety of people working in emergency relief or development contexts. A consistent finding across these studies is that despite the contexts requiring different technical skills, a common set of process skills are required. In fact, such skills have repeatedly been rated as the most important skills to have – above and beyond technical skills. As the same method of identifying these skills has been used in each of our studies, we briefly describe it here.

Flanagan (1954) described " . . . a set of procedures for collecting direct observations of human behaviour in such a way as to facilitate their potential usefulness in solving practical problems and developing broad psychological principles. The Critical Incident Technique outlines procedures for collecting observed incidents having special significance and meeting systematically defined criteria" (p. 327). It is a technique for collecting incidents that the respondents feel have been critical to their experience of their job. The incidents are recorded and discussion of the incidents helps to elucidate a composite picture of job-related behaviour (see also Coghlan & Mc Auliffe, 2003).

The procedure used throughout our Critical Incident Techniques (CIT) studies (MacLachlan & Mc Auliffe, 1993; Kanyangale & MacLachlan, 1995; Raymond-McKay & MacLachlan, 2000; Cullinan & MacLachlan, in press) has been that after a brief introduction participants are told that "in this interview we are going to ask you to identify some incidents which have occurred during your assignment as a development worker [e.g. counsellor in a refugee camp]. These incidents should be 'critical incidents.' They should be events that have made a strong impact on you. A Critical Incident has a beginning and an end, and its outcome is relatively important to the objectives of your assignment."

Statement of Objectives

Each interviewee was asked to try and state 4–6 clear and unambiguous objectives of the work they performed while on assignment. "I would like you to state your own opinion as to the objectives of the job you performed [e.g. as a refugee counselor]. These may or may not coincide with the objectives of the organisation for whom you worked. I do not want to know how others have defined the aims of your work; I want to know your opinion, based on the experience you have gained actually doing the job." The majority of subjects wrote these objectives down. This process usually takes approximately five to ten minutes.

Recording of Critical Incidents

Interviewees were then asked to recollect two critical incidents (one positive and one negative) from their work. Critical incidents were defined as any event which had a strong impact on the person achieving their objectives. They were given two Critical Incident Record Sheets which were divided into two columns, one headed "Incident Details," the other "Abilities/Characteristics." Under the first heading on each sheet, interviewees were asked to write a brief account of the incident in question.

Probing of Critical Incidents

Following the recording of the critical incidents, interviewees were probed for further information and detail about each incident, in order to heighten recall and make the description as vivid as possible. Examples of questions used in probing are: "What led up to the incident?" "What were you thinking/ feeling?" "How did you attempt to deal with . . . ?"

Specifying of Job-related Attributes

Having obtained descriptions of each critical incident, interviewees were asked to consider them in turn. Taking it as an example of the sort of work required by their job, their task was to state what they would consider the abilities or characteristics required of a person in order to perform well in that job. For each incident, the replies were written in the second column on the corresponding record sheet.

Examples of Critical Incidents

To illustrate how the job-related skills were identified, and something of the character of the incidents described, we present summaries of two of the incidents (one positive and one negative). The first incident, categorised as negative by the interviewee, relates to the experience of a nurse in a refugee camp (from Raymond-McKay & MacLachlan, 2000). In this incident she was engaged in assessing the feeding and basic medical requirements of refugees, and prioritising assistance to those most in need, according to the standards set by the aid agency. Approximately 3,000 people per week would pass through the feeding centre. A six-month-old infant had been identified as being in urgent need of nutrition and to this end was provided with a gastro-nasal feeding tube. The mother subsequently removed the feeding tube and the infant died. It emerged that the mother had decided that available resources would best be given to her other children who had in her opinion a more realistic chance of surviving. The interviewee was shocked and distressed at first, but eventually came to terms, as best she could, with what turned out to be a not infrequent occurrence.

The principal skills identified here were the ability to respect the dignity, customs and traditions of others (specifically the tendency of the mothers to reject the puniest child in order to maximise the survival chances of the sturdier children), and the ability to recognise the limits of the job – especially in regard to the handing out of advice which has little relevance in a war-torn situation (evidenced by the mother's response to the aid worker's intervention to save the child). The remaining skills identified were related to how best to cope on a personal level with a survival ethos that is generally uncalled for in a stable Western environment. These included: being able to express one's emotions; developing and maintaining good interpersonal relationships with colleagues; being able to nourish oneself after a day's work without feeling guilty.

The second incident was identified as a positive critical incident by the respondent who was working as a nutrition teacher in a high school in the Solomon Islands (Cullinan & MacLachlan, 2003):

> She had identified lack of protein as a major problem in the local diet, after having educated herself thoroughly on indigenous foods. She felt that another source of protein (besides fish) that would be acceptable to the local people was needed. The (expatriate) headmaster insisted that milk was the way to go and refused to listen when she tried to explain that the people just would not drink milk – she had asked them about this. They had never drunk milk and the concept seemed disgusting to them. She felt that many projects fail because they ignore the people they are trying to help. She wanted to start a chicken program, but it was met with resistance (from the headmaster) at every step. When she finally got some chickens at the school, and wanted to teach the pupils how to rear and cook them, the headmaster insisted on selling them all. She recalled a long and heated meeting one morning with the headmaster, where she pleaded with him to let her try out the idea of giving the students a few chickens to bring home over the Christmas break. Eventually she persuaded him. The program was a great success. The students came back after the break knowing how to rear chickens, having also taught their families. Once they got the taste for chicken, they loved it.

This incident was described as a positive one because the respondent succeeded in her goal of identifying a new source of protein for the local diet, which would be acceptable and viable. Taking this incident as an example of the type of work her assignment required, the respondent identified a number of relevant skills/characteristics: knowledge of the local culture (*from* learning about local foods, and those which would not be compatible with local traditions); the ability to listen (*from* asking the local people about their diet and preferences before embarking on the project); and the ability to persevere despite barriers (*from* continuing despite opposition from the headmaster). The researchers further identified communication skills (*from* achieving her goal via lengthy discussion/persuasion with the headmaster); the ability to be flexible in problem solving with meagre resources (*from* recognising that many other options were not viable, either culturally or financially, and discovering the solution of rearing chickens); the restraint to not impose one's own values on others (*from* recognising that the obvious solution as far as the headmaster was concerned was not acceptable to people of this culture and background); knowledge of the success/failure of previous projects (*from* knowing that ignoring the needs/wishes of the local people previously had led to failed nutrition programmes).

Comparative Studies of Process Skills

Characteristically, in our studies, aid workers have identified a large and diverse range of objectives, and no one objective has been given by more than half of those actually doing the same work. This is despite participants often having had the same professional and pre-assignment-departure training, and working with the same client group and agency. Thus aid workers do not simply set out implementing the stated objectives of the agency which sent them, they evaluate the situation on their own terms – and no doubt in terms of their own personal coping resources and values – and derive personally meaningful goals. While it would be surprising if discrepancies in what workers saw as their overall objectives did not influence the cohesion of an agency's intervention programme, such variation need not necessarily be a bad thing, if it reflects variation in an individual's estimation of what they can achieve.

Table 14.1 synthesises the results from our four previous studies and groups them under thematic headings. These categories are necessarily overlapping and incomplete but can offer a guide to the sort of skills and characteristics identified by people actually involved in aid work. While some technical skills (e.g., classroom control for teachers, or putting up a drip for nurses) were mentioned, such skills were mentioned much less frequently than what we have referred to as *process skills*. Although it is beyond the scope of this chapter to discuss each of the attributes identified (the interested reader should refer to our original papers), we briefly outline some of the important issues.

From Table 14.1, the categories of *organisational, analytical and intercultural skills, self in relation to others*, and *attitudinal behaviors* cover a broad range

Table 14.1. Thematic Synthesis of Job-related Skills/Characteristics Derived from Four Studies of Critical Incidents Experienced by People Working in Development and Relief Contexts

Organizational Skills
Flexibility in problem solving
Ability to identify strengths and weaknesses in colleagues and clients
Openness to ask, advise and learn from others including locals
Awareness of influence of power relationships on interactions
Preparedness to hand over projects to local workers
Ability to achieve closure
Diplomacy/tact

Self in Relation to Others
Ability to communicate clearly and precisely
Readiness to compromise
Listening skills
Ability to create a sense of security and trust
Awareness of other's suspicions and fears
Ability to cope with being an outsider
Readiness to pass power on (not self-promoting)
Ability to establish a social support network in a new environment
Ability to establish rapport with local counterparts
Ability to deal with people on an individual/human basis, rather than at a merely functional level
Patience
Ability to express sympathy

Analytical skills (in relation to aid)
Willingness to question projects even in rigid/authoritarian organisations
Ability to continually challenge assumptions
Knowledge of previous projects' successes and failures
Ability to see things at a policy as well as practical level
Ability to detach from the situation one is involved in re critical analysis.
Flexibility/Adaptability
Clear definition of one's role (and its limits)
Tolerance of ambiguity
Ability to establish a role for oneself in an ambiguous situation
Non-dependence on praise/affirmation from others
Reflective rather than impulsive

Intercultural Skills
Local language skills
Awareness of own and local cultural perspectives
Tolerance of different views/ways of life
Ability to restrain from imposing one's own values on others (non-judgmental)

Attitudes/Behavior in Relation to Problems
Sense of humor
Ability to detach & relax off-duty
Assertiveness
Decisiveness
Tolerance

(continued)

Table 14.1. (continued)

Resourcefulness
Emotional resilience ("thick-skinned")
Perseverance in the face of difficulties/criticism
Realistic expectations of one's assignment
A refusal to take failures/setbacks personally
Easy-going/laid back
Ability to cope with stress
Ability to be a facilitator (versus a "doer" or decision maker)
Awareness that one cannot solve every problem, and the willingness to hand over to someone more
  experienced
Other Personal Skills/Attributes
Ability to live/spend time alone
Ability to endure difficult living conditions
Belief in God

of job-related skills and characteristics, not all of which will be necessary on any
one assignment. Nevertheless, it could be said that all the attributes cited here
would be desirable for any job anywhere. It is our view that while some of these
skills are clearly "universally" required, others are especially necessary in the sorts
of contexts where aid workers find themselves, and it is therefore these we concentrate on here. In terms of organisational skills, an awareness of the implicit power
relationship between the expatriate (donor) and local (recipient), and perhaps
related to this a demonstrated openness to learning from others, and the preparedness to hand over projects to local workers, are important job attributes. Regarding
the self in relation to others, the ability to create a sense of security and trust, an
awareness of others' suspicions and fears, an ability to cope with being an outsider,
to pass on power, and the ability to express sympathy are all key process skills.

Intercultural skills are perhaps some of the skills most strongly related to the
context of aid assignments and those identified in our studies – an awareness of
own and local perspectives, a tolerance of different ways, the ability to withhold
judgement – all require an ability to decenter from one's self as the basis for
making decisions. Such an ability is also important when it comes to stepping back
from a project and using analytical skills to question the aims and assumptions
of projects, to appreciate one's own role, the limitations of that role, and to work
with ambiguity, perhaps independently of others' support. Finally, the attitudinal
behaviors category includes a number of attributes that are probably closely related
to personality, such as an ability to detach from a situation and relax when off duty,
emotional resilience, and tolerance.

Across the many incidents we have studied, it is clear that often it is not the
"work itself" that people find most trying, but the *inter*personal and *intra*personal
context in which it occurs. It is how people manage their relationships with others
and how they "sort out" in their own head what is going on – in terms of natural

disasters, long-term deprivation, war affected children, or whatever – that is of prime importance for how well they are able to perform at their work. The interpersonal stresses we alluded to are often not just in relation to clients, but also (perhaps even mostly) to do with the "organisational politics" within and between agencies. Some may find it surprising that key process skills include "decisiveness", "assertiveness" and so on. However, in the contexts in which our respondents worked, an inability to make decisions, to persevere in the face of difficulties, or to be assertive (which of course is completely different from being aggressive) in following a course of action, would have often undermined the collaborative trust established between these workers and the communities they sought to help. Process skills are not then about being "soft," they are about an ability to follow through a course of action, that action being rooted in the expressed needs, and wants of the particular community.

Training and Development of Process Skills

The sorts of skills identified above are key when it comes to training people who are to undertake assignments in developing countries. They represent a valuable reservoir of field experiences – critical incidents – which people feel have had an important bearing on whether or not they were able to achieve their objectives. Fortunately, therefore, they do not simply represent skills and characteristics in the abstract. These critical incidents may be seen as a resource, in that they can be role-played and the requisite skills and characteristics shaped-up prior to assignees being placed in the field.

Critical incidents have been used in the related field of training in intercultural competence. "Success" in intercultural interactions can be thought of across four domains: (1) the positive feelings that people have about the development of intercultural relationships, (2) the reciprocation of these feelings from members of other cultural groups, (3) the efficient manner in which the task at hand is accomplished, and (4) minimal stress arising from intercultural misunderstandings and difficulties (Brislin, Cushner, Cherrie & Yong, 1986; Brislin, 1993). The relevance of such communication skills is obvious with increasing globalization of the market economy and migration creating even more diverse populations (Malatu & Berry, 2001). Communication style is key to understanding and managing such multiculturalism (Berry, 1991). However, it is important to realize that appreciation of the social, economic and political context in which relief and development work occurs, is probably as key to successful outcomes (and a "good process" may be a "good outcome"!), as are interpersonal skills. As is clear from Table 14.1 a good number of the skills identified are organisational skills grounded in particular contexts. Table 14.1 also identifies many other skills where the scope of the proven technique of critical incident training could be imaginatively expanded upon.

Something of a paradox in the use of such training techniques has been identified by Brislin (1993): "Interestingly, the *more* people develop intercultural relations, the more difficulties they are likely to have. Culturally influenced norms will be violated, conversational topics will be raised at the wrong time, polite comments to pass the time will be taken seriously, and so forth" (pp. 239–230, 1993). Brislin jokes that it is easy to avoid these mistakes by simply avoiding interactions with people from other cultural backgrounds! But there is a very important point here: even our training programmes must be more strongly focused on developing the right process, where people feel free to make mistakes – indeed, where they expect to make mistakes. It is thus at the very early stages of development work, before assignees even leave "home," that attention to developing process skills and improving incrementally can be worked on by feeding back field experiences from real-life critical incidents and incorporating their contextual complexities and frustrations.

Summary

International development work has historically focused on material resources and the technical expertise necessary to use them. Within the last decade emphasis has begun to shift away from "technical assistance" and towards an ethos of development facilitation and capacity building. It is now recognised that the establishment of the right kind of *process* is a prerequisite to successful development initiatives. However, while the rhetoric of "process skills" is now part of the nomenclature of international development, there is very little theoretical or empirical research identifying what process skills actually are and why they are so important. We outline a psychological framework, for understanding the importance of process skills – incremental improvement – and identify relevant process skills through a number of studies that have explored critical incidents in international development work. We argue that such approaches are only one, but an important, perspective in international development work.

References

Bedeian, A. G. (1980). Organization theory and analysis. Chicago, IL: The Dryden Press.
Berg, E. (1993). *Rethinking technical co-operation: Reform for capacity building in Africa.* New York, NY: Regional Bureau for Africa, United Nations Development Programme (UNDP) & Development Alternatives, Inc.
Berry, J. W. (1991). Understanding and managing multiculturalism. *Psychology & Developing Societies, 3,* 17–49.
Bossert, T. J. (1990). Can they get along without us? Sustainability of donor-supported health projects in Central America and Africa. *Social Sciences & Medicine, 30,* 1015–1023.

Bossuyt, J. (1995). Capacity building: How can donors do it better? *Policy Management Brief No. 5.* ECDPM, Maastricht.

Brinkworth, D. W., & Goldsmith, A. A. (1992). Promoting the sustainability of development institutions: A framework for strategy. *World Development, 20,* 369–383.

Brislin, R. (1993). *Understanding culture's influence on behavior.* Fort Worth, TX: Harcourt Brace.

Brislin, R., Cushner, C., Cherrie, C., & Yong, M. (1986). *Intercultural interactions: A practical guide.* Newbury Park, CA: Sage.

Campbell, B. K., & Lexley, J. (Eds.). (1989). *Structural adjustment in Africa.* London: Sage.

Carr, S. C., Mc Auliffe, E., & MacLachlan, M. (1998). *Psychology of aid.* London: Routledge.

Carr, S. C., Chipande, R., & MacLachlan, M. (1998). Expatriate aid salaries in Malaŵi: A doubly demotivating influence? *International Journal of Educational, 18,* 133–143.

Carr, S.C., & MacLachlan, M. (1998). Psychology in Developing Countries: Reassessing its impact. *Psychology and Developing Societies, 10*(1), 1–20.

Cassen, R. (1994). Does aid work? Oxford: Oxford University Press. *Development, 18,* 133–143.

Coghlan, D. & Mc Auliffe, E. (2003). *Changing healthcare organisations.* Dublin: Blackhall.

Cullinan, S., & MacLachlan, M. (2003) Critical incidents for Irish teachers on international development assignments. Unpublished paper.

Dalton, J. H., Elias, M. J., & Wandersman, A. (2001). *Community psychology: Linking individuals and communities.* Stamford, CT: Wadsworth Thompson Learning.

Dore, R. (1994). Why visiting sociologists fail. *World Development, 22,* 1425–1436.

Enge, E. (2001). *The Reality of Aid.* London: Earthscan.

Fahey, T., Gilsenan, F., Beggan, P., O'Driscoll, A., Greene, M., Wall, B., MacLachlan, M., & O'Brien, E. (2000). *Capacity building in the Irish bi-lateral aid programme: Report by The Irish Aid Advisory Committee Working Group on Capacity Building.* Dublin: Department of Foreign Affairs.

Flanagan, J. C. (1954). The critical incident technique. *Psychological Bulletin, 51,* 327–349.

Hofstede, G. (2001). *Culture's consequences: International differences in work-related values.* (2nd ed.). Thousand Oaks, CA: Sage.

Kanyangale, M., & MacLachlan, M. (1995). Critical incidents for refugee counselors: An investigation of indigenous resources. *Counseling Psychology Quarterly, 8*(1), 89–101.

Kealey, D. (1989). A study of cross-cultural effectiveness: Theoretical issues, practical implications. *International Journal of Intercultural Relations, 13,* 387–428.

Kealey, D. (1994). *Overseas screening and selection: A survey of current practice and future trends.* Toronto, Canada: Technical Co-operation Directorate, Canadian International Development Agency.

Kean, J., Turner, A., Wood, D. H., & Wood, J. M. (1988). Synthesis of aid evaluation reports: FY 1985 and FY 1986. *Evaluation Occasional Paper, 16.* Washington, DC: USAID.

Leavitt, H. G., Dill, W. R., & Eyring, H. B. (1973). *The organisational world: A systematic view of managers and management.* New York, NY: Harcourt, Brace Jovanovich.

Lewin, K. (1952). Group decisions and social change. In T. Newcomb & T. Hartley (Eds.), *Readings in social psychology* (pp. 197–211). New York, NY: Holt, Rhinehart & Wilson.

Mc Auliffe, E. (1996a). Closing Address. Conference on Poverty and Ill-health in Developing Countries: Learning from NGOs. WHO & Government of Ireland Co-sponsored Conference, Maynooth, Ireland, 12–14 June.

Mc Auliffe, E. (1996b). AIDS: The barriers to behavior change. In H. Grad, A. Blanco, & J. Georgas, (Eds.), *Key issues in cross-cultural psychology* (pp. 371–386). Lisse, The Netherlands: Swets & Zeitlinger.

Mc Auliffe, E. (1998). The consumer in health care. In E. Mc Auliffe & L. Joyce, (Eds.), *A healthier future? Key issues in health services management.* Dublin, Ireland: Institute of Public Administration.

Machlup, F. (1962). *The production and distribution of knowledge in the United States.* Princeton, NJ: Princeton University Press.

MacLachlan, M. (1993). Sustaining human resource development in Africa: The influence of expatriates. *Management Education and Development, 24*, 153–157.
MacLachlan, M. (1996). From sustainable change to incremental improvement: The psychology of community rehabilitation. In S. C. Carr & J. F. Schumaker (Eds.), *Psychology and the developing world* (pp. 26–37). Westport, CT: Praeger.
MacLachlan, M. (1997). *Culture and health.* Chichester, UK: John Wiley & Sons.
MacLachlan, M. (Ed.). (2001). *Cultivating health: Cultural perspectives on promoting health.* Chichester, UK: John Wiley & Sons.
MacLachlan, M. (in press). Culture, empowerment and health. In M. Murray (Ed.), *Critical health psychology.* London: Palgrave.
MacLachlan, M., & Carr, S. C. (1994). Pathways to a psychology for development: reconstituting, restating, refuting and realizing. *Psychology and Developing Societies, 6*(1), 21–28.
MacLachlan, M., & Mc Auliffe, E. (1993). Critical incidents for psychology students in a refugee camp: Implications for Counseling. *Counseling Psychology Quarterly, 6*(1), 3–11.
Moghaddam, F. M. (1990). Modulative and generative orientations in psychology: Implications for psychology in the three worlds. *Journal of Social Issues, 46*, 21–41.
Malatu, M. S., & Berry, J. W. (2001). Cultivating health through multiculturalism. In M. MacLachlan (Ed.), *Cultivating health: Cultural perspectives on promoting health.* Chichester, UK: Wiley.
Murray, M., Nelson, G., Poland, B, Matycka-Tyndale, Ferris, L., Cammeron, R., & Prkachin, K. (2001). *Training in community health psychology.* Report to Canadian Institutes of Health Research.
O'Dwyer, T., & Woodhouse, T. (1996). The motivations of Irish "Third World" development workers. *Irish Journal of Psychology, 17*, 23–34.
Pearce, F. (1996). Squatter take control. *New Scientist,* 1 June, 38–42.
Porter, D., Allen, B. & Thompson, G. (1991). *Development in practice: Paved with good intentions.* London: Routledge.
Rappaport, J., & Seidman, E. (2000). *Handbook of community psychology.* New York, NY: Kluwer Academic/Plenum Publishers.
Raymond-McKay, M., & MacLachlan, M. (2000). Critical incidents for emergency relief workers. *Development in Practice, 10*(5), 674–686.
Schiffman, H. R. (1982). *Sensation and perception.* New York, NY: John Wiley & Sons.
Thomas, A. (1996). What is development management? *Journal of International Development, 8*, 95–110.
Turner, M. & Hulme, D. (1997). *Governance, Administration and Development: Making the State Work.* London: Macmillan.
Wapenhans, W. (1993). *Effective implementation: Key to development impact.* Washington, DC: World Bank.
Weick, K. E. (1984). Small wins: Redefining the scale of social problems. *American Psychologist, 39*, 40–49.

Chapter 15

Poverty and Research

Stuart C. Carr and Stephen G. Atkins

This chapter argues that aid advertisements, designed to help relieve poverty, are creating social problems of their own. Not only are the global aid media unintentionally fuelling local backlashes, in the form of negative stereotypes about "the poor" (Carr, Mc Auliffe, & MacLachlan, 1998). They are also encouraging implicit versions of those stereotypes, i.e., the negative stereotypes themselves are *not available to consciousness*. As a result, they pass by unrecognised and unmanaged, whilst latent prejudice and social division continue to grow. The reasons *why* this counterintuitive and insidious "rebound effect" happens are found in classical social psychological theory on reactions to social pressure, as well as the latest research on social cognition and affect. This chapter integrates these strands into a compelling case for rethinking current practice in aid advertising.

Social psychological researchers too have a key part to play in this process, all the way from problem recognition to problem management. Timely and effective responses to crises like famine, for example, will only ever happen if marketing "pull" is accompanied by researcher "push." Yet laboratory researchers are not, currently, applying their increasingly relevant models of social cognition and affect to directly study global issues like poverty relief. This chapter argues that twenty-first century research techniques, in these twin domains of cognition and affect, can be harnessed to improve our ability to conduct emergency fund-raising campaigns in the near-term, whilst at the same time improving broader practices in social marketing over the long-term. With these twin goals in mind, we synthesise a range of emerging research techniques and paradigms, ending with a suggested research programme that is first and foremost a research response to global poverty.

To sum up therefore, this chapter is a "call to arms" to both sides – aid marketer and academic psychologist alike – to work more collaboratively in order to more effectively combat, and so help alleviate, global poverty. Specifically, the chapter aims to excite researchers about what might be the most powerful applications for their developing models and technologies, whilst at the same time stimulating interest among aid practitioners on the potential fruits of these new developments.

Background

From Feagin (1972) to Lott (2002), three decades of psychological research has focused on attributions for poverty (for a review, see Furnham, this volume). These attributions are important, because they alter willingness to aid the poor, whether by encouraging charitable donations (Cheung & Chan, 2000), or by encouraging political activism (Hine & Montiel, 1999). The mass media play a huge part in this process (Bullock, Wyche, & Williams, 2001). They fuel negative attributions about the poor; both through biased news coverage (Dorward, 1996) and, surprisingly perhaps, through aid agency advertisements appealing for donations (Carr, 2000; Fountain, 1995; Godwin, 1994; Harper, this volume). For example, aid advertisements may remind audiences of their own mortality (Schimel et al., 1999) and identity (Lowery, Hardin, & Sinclair, 2001), thereby activating prejudicial stereotypes in a self-serving role (Cozzarelli, Williamson, & Tagler, 2001). Stereotypes in fact are implied by every aspect of the current literature on attributions for poverty (Carr, 2002). Ironically however, at least three decades of literature directly focused on implicit processes and stereotyping, from Argyris and Schön (1974) to Stangor (2000), has been virtually ignored in aid-related attribution research (see also, Cohen, 2001). This chapter now bridges that schism, by reviewing key research studies in stereotyping, and exploring their implications for both (1) contemporary aid advertising and (2) developing civil society.

The Issue of Self-report

The parallel literature just identified arguably began in studies of organizations, where stereotyping is rife (Operario & Fiske, 2001). A prime example of this is the negative stereotyping of workers, as being lazy and unwilling to assume responsibility – a lay theory of worker motivation known as "Theory X" (McGregor, 1960). McGregor contrasted this Theory X with "Theory Y," which essentially advocates an opposite, positive stereotype of worker motivation. The first writers to translate these lay theories about worker motivation directly into stereotyping were Argyris and Schön (1974). They suggested that some managers can and do verbally espouse Theory Y, and yet tacitly adhere to Theory X (Anderson, 1997). What these managers say is not necessarily what they do (see also, Argyris & Schon, 1978; 1996). The relevance of this finding for the present chapter is that almost all research on attributions for poverty has relied on what people say about poverty, on paper-and-pencil questionnaires.

Self-contradiction between speech and action is still common in organizations today (Vecchio, Hearn, & Southey, 1997). It happens for instance when promises about worker empowerment are under-delivered with the same old Theory X model (Carr, 2002). One of the reasons for these under-deliveries, according to Carr, is globalisation. This prescribes compliance to the idea of "empowering" the laity, without really addressing vested local interests in maintaining the status quo (of relative privilege). Similar vested local interests might apply also in the case of empowering "the poor" (e.g., "charity begins at home").

Another facet of globalisation, again studied in management, is the cross-cultural sojourn (Kosmitzki, 1996). An integral part of these sojourns is, by definition, the cross-cultural encounter. When these occur, the presence of others who are visibly from another cultural or ethnic group socially facilitates, or primes, cultural stereotypes (Bochner & Perks, 1971; Kosmitzki, 1996) as well as defensive routines (Lowery, Hardin, & Sinclair, 2001). There are two ways in which this kind of process is relevant to anti-poverty advertising. Firstly, increased actual encounters with "the poor," for example on city streets or whilst on vacation in a "developing" country, will partly fuel the stereotyping process (Carr, 2000). Secondly, increased vicarious encounters with the poor, for example through aid advertisements that journey every night into their viewers' living rooms, will partly fuel the stereotyping process (Carr et al., 1998).

In a related vein, the management and organisational literature on stereotyping (outside of specific attributions for poverty) implies that today's aid advertisement viewers are not necessarily reliable witnesses to their own psychological processes (Smith, 2001). Self-report measures, as used in the literature on attributions for poverty, illuminate only part of the story about stereotyping.

The Issue of Political Correctness

To appreciate "why" many people espouse models that they do not necessarily use, we need to briefly review a trend observed in surveys of racist attitudes. This trend was first noticed in the late 1970s (see, for example, McConahay, Hardee, & Batts, 1981). Prior to that point, prejudiced attitudes had customarily been measured using direct statements about an out-group in question. Participants were simply asked to overtly agree or disagree with these statements. Classic examples of this relatively direct approach to measuring attitudes, and their underlying stereotypes, can be found in Bogardus (1925), Adorno, Frenkel-Brunswik, Levinson, and Sanford (1950), and Pettigrew (1979).

During the latter quarter of the twentieth century, this type of instrument began to indicate a drop in racist and prejudiced attitudes (Pedersen, Griffiths, Contos, Bishop, & Walker, 2000). As the trend continued, some researchers began to feel that it jarred a little too uncomfortably with actual levels of inter-group discrimination and violence, such as "ethnic cleansings" and "glass ceilings" and racially defined neighborhoods. This apparent inconsistency prompted authors like

McConahay et al., and more recently Pederson et al., to infer that what people were saying on attitude scales was probably in part a response to increased normative pressures to be "politically correct" when speaking about minority groups. Thus, underneath it all, people might be saying one thing whilst thinking and feeling something else.

To capture this discrepancy between saying and doing – between overt and implicit opinions – McConahay and colleagues coined a distinction now commonplace in the stereotyping literature. This is the distinction between "old-fashioned prejudice" and "modern racism." Old-fashioned prejudice, according to McConahay et al, was relatively uncomplicated and direct. People generally said what they thought. Modern racism, however, is very different. It reflects more of a mixture, between (a) denial that racism exists and (b) an advocacy that minority groups are given too many "special privileges" compared with the mainstream majority (McConahay, 1983). In this way, globalizing norms of "equality" and "empowerment" are supposedly used to justify the very inequalities they profess to oppose. They could be used, for example, to promote, not reduce, the gap between rich and poor. Compared to its earlier counterpart, therefore, stereotyping today is much more indirect, implicit, and elusive to counter-persuasion. In fact, it may not even show *up* on relatively direct measures of attributions for poverty (however – for a critical appraisal of the McConahay approach, see Redding, 2001).

The Issue of Self-deception

In order to confirm that this kind of stereotyping actually happens, we need to briefly review a key experimental paradigm from social psychology – the priming study (Fazio, Jackson, Dunston, & Williams, 1995). Priming means that experimental participants are first shown a picture of somebody who visibly comes from an ethnic minority group, where this minority group is presumably less affluent. This prime is assumed to be sufficient to activate any latent stereotype that the participant may hold. A split second later, so that there is no time for conscious resistance, a negative stimulus like the word "unattractive" is presented and the participant is asked to decide, as rapidly as possible, whether the word has a positive or negative meaning. The quicker the answer to this task, the more likely it is that the participant is actually thinking and feeling in negative stereotype mode just prior to the task, i.e., whilst still looking at the person from a minority out-group. In this way, stereotypes are no longer measured by verbal reports. In the newer tradition, away from the attributions-for-poverty paradigm, stereotypes, and stereotyping, are measured by *reaction time*.

As a baseline against which to gauge reaction times, Fazio et al. used response latencies when the priming stimulus was visibly a member of the in-group. Compared to this in-group priming study (as a baseline), when the prime visibly came from an out-group minority, reaction time was quicker. According to the logic above, this indicates that the participants were negatively stereotyping the out-group. As well, when the stimulus word at stage two was positive (e.g., "attractive"), this tendency reversed. Now, reaction time was quicker when the prime had been a member from an in-group. Thus, whilst in-groups were stereotyped positively, out-groups were stereotyped negatively.

Most interestingly of all, and despite behavioral signs that stereotyping was actually operating, many of the participants earnestly averred that they did *not* harbor stereotypes, either positive or negative, and neither did they wish to (also, Devine, 1996). In fact, the participants with the lower scores on a paper-and-pencil measure of prejudice were statistically more negative towards the out-group on a reaction time measure (Fazio et al., 1995, p. 1020). During a debriefing to the study, the participants were observed interacting with an actual member of the out-group. The participants with faster reaction times to the negative word at stage two of the experiment displayed more non-verbal indicators of prejudice (reduced smiling, increased distance, etc.) than their slower reaction time counterparts. Thus, what people said and what they did, and even what people believed and what they did, in terms of both reaction time and social interaction behaviour, were at odds with each other (Dovidio, Kawakami, Johnson, Johnson, & Howard, 1997).

The study by Fazio et al. was by no means a one-off. Since it was undertaken, the same pattern of findings has been replicated across a variety of difference issues and groups. These groups include for example gender, age, and – most relevant for this chapter – social class (Paul, 1998). Students from poorer backgrounds, for instance, are often automatically stereotyped as lacking intellectual ability, compared to their wealthier student counterparts (Croizet & Claire, 1998). Thus, relatively direct reasons are emerging, in the stereotypes literature itself, for believing that priming effects, and implicit stereotyping, apply to "the poor."

These studies as a whole have profound implications for the way we think about media audiences who are watching aid advertisements appealing for donations to help relieve poverty. In essence, they fundamentally challenge the rather comforting idea that many viewers have – namely that they are free from prejudice and discrimination against the poor. Instead, according to this research literature, those viewers could belong to any one of three basic audience segments:

1. Openly prejudiced population.
2. Openly *un*prejudiced population whose members, as well, show *no* signs of stereotyping the poor in priming tests. This is the group to which many of us like to think we belong – a population of "chronic egalitarians" (Moskowitz, Gollwitzer, Wasel, & Schaal, 1999). Chronic egalitarians apparently do not experience accelerated reaction times after being primed for heavily stereotyped groups, even though they may be equally knowledgeable about the contents of commonly held stereotypes.

3. In-between (1) and (2), overtly *un*prejudiced people whose reaction times would nonetheless still speed up if primed with an image representing "the poor." Within this category, some people will be (a) quite aware of, and even privately comfortable with, their stereotypes. They will simply "impression-manage" it in everyday life (Carr, 2002). Many others, however, will (b) be genuinely unaware that they harbor stereotypes about the poor. If they found themselves in a priming experiment however, their behavior would probably indicate implicit stereotyping. This would occur both during the task and afterwards, during social interaction with people in poverty. This is the group to which, according to a now substantial body of research, many (and maybe most) of the "non-poor" might unwittingly and unwillingly belong.

The Issue of Reactivity

The research just described has not yet directly explored the practical implications of the priming studies, for real social applications like *fund-raising to combat poverty*. As we have seen from previous chapters in this book, fund-raising campaigns tend to rely on high-pressure techniques to make the viewer feel guilty about the gap between their own affluence and the various relative deprivations experienced by the poor. Their thinly disguised chief campaign tactic is to create a perceived discrepancy between actual self (comparatively wealthy) and ideal self (equally wealthy). Hopefully, this will motivate viewers to *close* the gap by offering a donation of some kind (Higgins, 1987; Bizman, Yinon, & Krotman, 2001). What these advertisements do *not* configure, however, is any duality of conscious and implicit processes. In particular, they typically fail to consider the possibility that the best of intentions are often matched by an implicit reaction in another direction (above, Fazio et al., 1995).

To explore the implications of Fazio et al.'s findings in detail, we need to dig a little into the literature on reactions to high-pressure tactics prescribing pro-social behaviour. There are at least three interrelated branches of this wider literature to consider. These are Reactance Theory (Brehm, 1966), the Ironic Effect (Wegner, Schneider, Carter, & White, 1994), and the Rebound Effect (MacCrae, Bodenhausen, Galen, Milne, & Jetten, 1994). Linking each of these three ideas together is not just that they all discuss the probable reactions of people who are exposed to high-pressure admonitions to think, feel, or behave morally. Each of them, as well, deals, either indirectly or directly, with how the *implicit* part of our being responds to this kind of tactic.

Reactance Theory. The central tenet of Reactance Theory is that when people feel constrained into doing, believing, or feeling "Y" they may well end up doing, believing, or feeling, "not Y" (Brehm, 1966). According to Brehm, a sign saying, "Do not walk on the grass" (which has a mild moral undertone) will prompt a significant number of people to actually walk on the grass even though they would otherwise have stuck to the "right" pathway. Reactance is essentially an act of defiance, which cathartically reasserts an individual's right to choose. In an early experimental demonstration of this effect, arguments for a more communitarian society were either laced or not with explicit moral overtones, e.g., "You cannot believe otherwise" (Worchel & Brehm, 1970). Adding such entreaties increased the proportion of people changing their attitudes in the opposite direction, from 15% to 40%. As well, conversion to the speaker's point of view dropped from 67% to 50%. Reactance effects have been directly linked to charitable appeals, with calls for aid, and especially images of dependency, being linked to "boomerang effects" on the part of would-be donors (Brehm, 1973, p. 313). In this kind of "backlash" manner, therefore, "reactance can actually increase the attractiveness of the very opinions, attitudes, or alternatives a persuader seeks to discourage" (Wheeler, Deci, Reis, & Zuckerman, 1978, p. 160).

Warnings like this are surely relevant to many contemporary aid advertisements. Theirs' is a moral message par excellence. It is often deliberately designed to make us feel morally compelled to give assistance, through heavy admonishments that we "should" be helping (Harper, this volume). Their central tactic, as Harper has shown, is to quite deliberately "crank up the guilt factor," in order to solicit charitable donations. According to Reactance Theory however, this is likely to be experienced, at least in part, as a constraint on freedom to choose. To that extent, it will backfire; by encouraging both short-term reactance (switching the channel) and as well perhaps a long-term backlash. Instead of generating sympathy for the poor, this tactic will actually start to fuel disdain. Concepts like "compassion fatigue," stemming in part from the sheer volume of aid advertisements currently on air, would certainly suggest this possibility (Carr, 2002).

Reactance Theory is not very clear on whether this backlash from constraint is liable to be fully conscious or implicit. Nor is it terribly clear on whether reactance effects would apply directly to the stereotyping of relatively disadvantaged groups, like precisely "the poor." These two considerations fall mainly, and respectively, to what are termed *ironic effects and rebound effects.*

Ironic Effects.   The original *ironic effect* was illustrated through the writer Dostoyevski, who challenged his brother "not to think of a white bear." Strangely enough, the brother could not help *but* think of this white bear. The very effort of suppressing the thought of it actually, and ironically, made thinking about it unavoidable. Since Dostoyevski's original illustration, ironic effects like these have been demonstrated more widely, in for example laboratory demonstrations (Wegner et al., 1987). An everyday example of the ironic effect, familiar to many of us, is given by the innocent traveller waiting in line before filing in front of Customs officers. Some of these individuals may find themselves feeling increasingly more "shifty" and "guilty" the more they remind themselves that they are *not* so. The more they try to think about not looking guilty, the more "shifty" their behavior becomes – until they are eventually stopped by the suspicious customs and excise officer. Such effects are relevant to a range of compulsions, from signing credit card vouchers to committing acts that defy our conscious credos. In each contravention, it becomes an internal struggle to perform in exactly the way we are constrained to perform. The relevance of this internal struggle for aid organizations is that many aid advertisements are typically explicit, and to that extent constraining, invitations *not to stereotype*. They deliberately invite the viewer to think about the poor as individual human beings ("This individual is just like you! This group is just as human as yours!"). According to the stereotyping literature on ironic effects, admonitions like this *not to stereotype* will not work. Precisely because the viewer *wants* to agree with the advertisement's message, and so *not* stereotype the poor, the viewer will end up partly doing precisely that.

Worse than this, when Wegner et al.'s participants were finally told that they could freely express their thoughts about white bears, they did so at an "accelerated rate, mentioning it more often than if they had simply been asked to express the thought from the start" (1987, p. 8). These findings suggest that concerted attempts not to stereotype an out-group (like the out-group "the poor") even if they are initially *successful*, will, in time, result in some kind of backlash, or "rebound."

Rebound Effects. In a classic study of rebound effects, participants saw a photograph of a skinhead (minority out-group) and wrote a paragraph describing the person (Macrae et al., 1994). Half the participants were pre-warned that social perceptions can be prejudiced by stereotypes and were asked to try and avoid this kind of bias. The other half of the participants received no such moral message; their condition was minimally constraining. Once the paragraph was written, all the participants were shown a second picture to evaluate, using a similar type of written task. What this study found was that the moral admonition not to stereotype did reduce stereotyping in the short term, on the first task. However, this effect was not sustainable. By the time of the second task (constraint removed), there was a post-suppression rebound. The participants who had been previously constrained were now more likely to stereotype the out-group than their unconstrained counterparts. This included being more likely to sit apart from an actual member of the stereotyped out-group, in a pre-arranged meeting after the experiment ostensibly ended. Some of this rebound effect was undoubtedly due to self-consciousness. In a later study, simply seeing their own images in a laboratory-room mirror was sufficient to replicate these suppression-rebound effects (MacCrae, Bodenhausen, & Milne, 1998).

It might be objected at this point that skinheads are a group that most people would feel relatively okay about stereotyping. In other words, skinheads are not the kind of group that viewers would normally fret about stereotyping (Monteith,

Sherman, & Devine, 1998). If this were totally correct, we should not expect to see rebound effects when the out-group is less inherently objectionable, for example if they represent a minority ethnic group or gender, or "the poor." In a recent study testing the rebound hypothesis in precisely each of these domains, suppression and rebound effects were again replicated (Liberman & Förster, 2000). Interestingly, and consistent with the general idea of a hydraulic model (above), Liberman and Förster found that if participants were explicitly encouraged at stage II to "act out" a prejudiced attitude in their writings ("assume the perspective of a sexist person" [p. 194] and "you should not hesitate to write a racist story" [p. 195]), the previously observed rebound effect disappeared. Thus, being encouraged to express what has been suppressed was in the short-term cathartic (Monteither, Spicer, & Tooma, 1995). However, we can easily perhaps imagine such tactics being socially counterproductive in the long term (Liberman & Förster, 2000, p. 196).

It is helpful in comprehending the destructive or negative flavour of rebound effects by viewing the rebound-provoking experience from the perspective of the rebounder. For instance, it is reasonable for the rebounders, Macrae's participants, to experience the encouraged stereotype suppression as encouragement to forego a convenient or self-serving efficiency. Macrae's participants would normally have leaned on their stereotype for skinheads in writing that essay, because it was, in that case, a self-serving convenience. The stereotype made the task of writing an essay about the skinhead much more straightforward. But when the participants repressed stereotypical thinking, at Macrae's request, they were responding to a request to forego a self-serving convenience, in the interest of a higher moral stance. As a result however, their later behavior, as they sat further away from the skinhead's chair, suggested that Macrae's manipulation had caused them to give the negative aspects of the stereotype *more* credence. Stereotyping had become a motivator of their immediate behavior.

It is reasonable to expect relatively affluent television audiences to suffer similar consequences when viewing aid appeals. Given that these aid advertisements prime the stereotype, there would be no reason to suppress it in the first instance. The negative elements in the stereotype would be a self-serving convenience, making it easier for the viewer to avoid feeling guilty, or to avoid feeling obligated to send any kind of donation. However, the very context of the advertisement would then become salient as fast or almost as fast as the stereotype is primed. This context is now clearly requesting the viewer to stop thinking of these victims as lesser or less worthy beings. Instead, it is asking that viewers think of "the poor" as equals, i.e., as fellow human beings, with children who are as deserving of a shot at good health and nutrition as anyone else. In other words, the context within which the stereotype was primed is asking viewers to forego a self-serving convenience, in the interest of taking a higher moral stance. If this thinking is correct, such advertisements are expected to cause viewers to give the negative aspects of the stereotype *more* credence. This of course is the opposite of what most aid appeal producers intend.

To make the irony of this even more explicit, the reader might imagine two kinds of household, each of them containing television audiences or Internet users. Over the airwaves is broadcast a particular aid advertisement. During this time, one of the two types of household just happens to be viewing or using another channel – a channel devoid of the aid advertisement. According to the theory and evidence reviewed above, subsequent solicitations for aid donations, in temporal proximity to the advertisement being broadcast, would probably encounter more success in the household that had *not* experienced the advertisement. Aid advertising would be doing more harm than good!

To summarise the research evidence reviewed so far, relatively heavy-handed, high-pressure sales tactics, of the kind often used in aid advertisements, are likely to produce a *rebound effect*. As Macrae and others have pointed out, such reactances are largely implicit. Most of the participants in these kinds of studies will consciously and earnestly aver that they are not themselves prejudiced, and would not actually wish to be. Harboring stereotypes is not what they want to do, or where they want to be. It is only half the story of what they are and what they will do, when faced with yet another aid appeal. This means that the rebound and priming research are far from invalidating the attribution literature on poverty, most of which is based on the kinds of processes that are available to conscious awareness. But what the rebound literature *also* indicates is that there is more to potential donor behaviour than conscious intentions alone. Rebound effects are a force to be reckoned with, by any socially responsible – and indeed market-responsive – aid agency.

A Role for Neuropsychology

Relatively recent research (Vanman, Paul, Ito, & Miller, 1997), into affect-related neurophysiological manifestations of prejudicial reactance, suggests additional future research paths. Some researchers have argued that affect-based (i.e., emotion-based) measures are more likely to predict inter-group stereotyping of the poor (Vanman & Miller, 1993; Stangor, Sullivan, & Ford, 1991). Consistent with this, attitude theorists have in the past asserted that emotions predict behavior better than cognitive measures of opinions (Breckler & Wiggins, 1989; Zanna & Rempel, 1988). Arguments of this kind would seem to be particularly germane to advertisements for poverty relief, which explicitly rely on evoking viewers' higher emotions (Harper, this volume).

In general, between social cognition and social affect, the latter system is more dominant than the former in most situations (Epstein, 1994). The rational system is comparatively slow, because it operates primarily through the medium of language via evidence and logic. This is quite different from the affective-experiential system, which processes information automatically and swiftly. These notions, taken together, suggest that involuntary affective measures may be especially valid for assessing uncontrolled, automatic reactions to out-group members, such as disadvantaged groups. In one study for instance, psychophysiological measures of emotion were used to assess involuntary affective reactions to cross-racial targets or out-group members (Vanman et al, 1997). Specifically, Vanman et al. used facial electromyography (fEMG) to assess emotional reactions to varying, but very specific, social contexts or relationships. Facial EMG typically employs the simultaneous measure of multiple *emotion-expressing* surface muscles on the human face. The instrumentation detects differing levels of electro-physiological activity associated, typically, with muscles of the brow, the cheek, and the lower lip – all on one side of the face. Ideal locations for the facial EMG sensors have been developed and applied, with increasing certainty, over the past two decades (Petty & Cacioppo, 1984; Fridlund & Cacioppo, 1986; Tassinary, Cacioppo, Geen, & Thomas, 1989; Hess, Banse, & Kappas, 1995; Vanman et al., 1997; Winkielman & Cacioppo, 2001).

Conceivably, fEMG data can accurately reflect covert emotional states, even when a participant's face shows no overt expression (Cacioppo, Petty, Losch, & Kim, 1986; Fridlund, Schwartz, & Fowler, 1984; McHugo, Smith, & Lanzetta, 1982). More to the point however, fEMG is not afflicted in ways described earlier regarding self-report measures, such as socially desirable responding (Vanman et al, 1997). This is especially true when respondents believe that the face-mounted sensors are actually measuring something other than facial muscle activity (McHugo et al, 1982). Such mild (and temporary) deception turns out to be fairly easy to accomplish, especially when "dummy electrodes [are] placed on the back of the neck to divert attention from the face as the site of interest [and] additionally, heart rate is recorded" via multiple electrodes (Vanman et al., 1997, p. 946, parenthesis added). With further developments, such measures could be used to catalogue a reliable set of facial muscle-activity configurations, specifically reactions reflecting implicit emotions of pity, disdain, disgust, sadness, guilt, superiority, hate, fear, etc. The goal in taking such measures would be to triangulate and capture implicit effects, centering separately and sequentially on each discernible component of the advertisement, via multiple assessment modalities, from fEMG to reaction time and rebound effects in behavior. Given such a research program, it would become clearer which features of aid advertisements provoke desirable versus undesirable outcomes.

None of this information would come cheaply in financial terms. However, what are the social costs of avoiding such financial expenses? Relatively affluent society could choose to continue using advertisements that actually do more harm than good (Mehryar, 1984). Given the frightening trends across the past century, regarding the distribution of wealth, differential qualities of life, mortality rates, etc. (previous chapters, this volume), the status quo does not bode well for future human existence. Another option would be to stop using these advertisements altogether, but that too would probably be counter-productive. Overall therefore, instead of retreating to less complex and less expensive "quick fixes" (that may ultimately fail), and less invasive research methods, a more reasonable tack might be to look ahead to ever more sophisticated research.

This might well be found, for instance, in realms like functional magnetic resonance imaging (fMRI). Such technology is now increasingly used to identify brain regions, in some cases tightly circumscribed brain regions, that are activated as people discriminate between faces expressing anger versus faces expressing fear (Whalen, Shin, McInerney, Fischer, Wright, & Rauch, 2001). Another fMRI study – by Golby, Gabrieli, Chiao, & Eberhardt (2001) – found brain region activation differences associated with preferential memories for same-race faces compared to non-same-race faces. Another fMRI research program identified brain regions activated whilst the person was implicitly feeling disgust (Phillips, Marks et al., 2000). Another identified fMRI signatures for the perception of threatening versus non-threatening faces while simultaneously considering relevant individual differences in paranoia (Phillips, Williams et al., 1999). Fear, anger, disgust, paranoia, are emotions that are all potentially relevant to aid advertisements. They are response latencies that *should* concern aid psychology researchers. An ability in the future to predict subsequent behaviors, from studies of antecedent brain activity, may serve all of the stakeholders in aid advertisements generally.

The opportunities to engage in human behavioural fMRI and fEMG research are politically elusive, expensive, complex, and rare. But such opportunities cannot simply be passed by. Given the state of human societies, it seems clear to us that psychological science should be focused on fighting issues like poverty. In this way, laboratory research is integrated with, not alienated from, the more critical and discursive approaches outlined elsewhere in this volume. Together, these approaches can be integrated to focus on the same goal – combating poverty.

A Suggested Research Program

As yet, the theory of rebound is still in its infancy. We do not really know exactly why, for instance, rebound effects occur (Liberman & Förster, 2000). Nor do we really know how such effects will translate in the everyday life, in the long-term situation outside of laboratory walls. Most basically of all, from the point of view of the chapter and book as a whole, we do not (yet) have any research that directly tests the rebound hypothesis in a context of watching aid advertisements themselves. Accordingly, the precise practical implications of the priming and rebound literature have yet to be determined. In the interim however, and in anticipation of those issues being recognised as socially significant, Figure 15.1 outlines a set of practical questions to which we urgently need some relatively clear and concise answers.

Do aid advertisements, or series of them, encourage implicit stereotyping of the poor, as measured by reaction times and other forms of non-verbal behavior (including making donations)?

Can advertisements that contain even distressing images of poor *children* encourage implicit stereotyping and rebound effects (Florian & Mikulincer, 1998)?

Can lowering the pressure of sales tactics reduce these deleterious social impacts whilst still raising donations? Is there a point of maximum efficiency, in terms of both financial and social capital?

Do strategic initiatives like giving voice to disadvantaged groups (see Voices of the Poor, this volume) help to more effectively break the stereotype mold? This could be investigated for example by putting the same words into different mouths, ranging from the conventional "father-figure" or "mother-figure" aid worker, who is often in practice foregrounded in aid advertisements, to an actual "poor person" themselves.

What, precisely, are the *long*-term impacts of implicit stereotyping and rebound effects, on human social capital?

What do fEMG and fMRI tell us about how to design aid advertisements so as to minimise negative implicit stereotyping and maximise pro-social behaviour?

Figure 15.1. An integrated Applied Research program on implicit stereotyping/rebound effects in aid advertising

The world is not short of real social issues for psychology. From managing glass ceilings to designing affirmative action programmes; establishing harmonious co-worker relations to reducing rater bias; and implementing workplace surveillance to conducting integrity testing. The list of worthy topics for applied psychology is endless. Admirable as they are however, these (plus many other) behavioral challenges look like comparative luxuries, or even indulgences, against the backdrop of world poverty, and poverty relief. Viewed against this backdrop, they are very likely to be less than urgent. Thus whilst these admittedly significant issues bite, the truly pressing issues still remain. In Africa alone, 13 million more human beings are expected to die in this year's famine.

References

Adorno, T. W., Frenkel-Brunswik, E., Levinson, D. J., & Sanford, R. N. (1950). *The authoritarian personality*. New York, NY: Harper & Row.
Anderson, L. (1997). Argyris and Schön's theory on congruence and learning. http://www.scu.edu.au/schools.sawd/arr/argyris.html
Argyris, C., & Schön, D. A. (1974). *Theory in practice: Increasing professional effectiveness*. San Francisco, CA: Jossey-Bass.
Argyris, C., & Schön, D. A. (1978). *Organisational learning: A theory of action perspective*. Reading, MA: Addison-Wesley Publishing Company.
Argyris, C. & Schön, D. A. (1996). *Organisational Learning II: Theory, method, and practice*. Reading, MA: Addison-Wesley Longman.

Bizman, A., Yinon, Y., & Krotman, S. (2001). Group-based emotional distress: An extension of self-discrepancy theory. *Personality & Social Psychology Bulletin, 27*, 1291–1300.

Bochner, S., & Perks, R. W. (1971). National role evocation as a function of cross-national interaction. *Journal of Cross-Cultural Psychology, 2*, 157–164.

Bogardus, E. S. (1925).Measuring social distances. *Journal of Applied Sociology, Jan/Feb*, 216–226.

Breckler, S. J., & Wiggins, E. C. (1989). Affect versus evaluation in the structure of attitudes. *Journal of Experimental Social Psychology, 25*, 253–271.

Brehm, J. W. (1966). *A theory of psychological reactance.* New York, NY: Academic Press.

Brehm, J. W. (1973). Reactance and the unwillingness to help others. *Psychological Bulletin, 79*, 310–317.

Bullock, H. E., Wyche, K. F., & Williams, W. R. (2001). Media images of the poor. *Journal of Social Issues, 57*, 229–246.

Cacioppo, J. T., Petty, R. E., Losch, M. E., & Kim, H. S. (1986) Electromyographic activity over facila muscle regions can differentiate the valence and intensity of affective reactions. *Journal of Personality and Social Psychology, 50*, 260–268.

Carr, S. C. (2000). Privation, privilege, and proximity: "Eternal triangle" for development? *Psychology and Developing Societies, 12*, 167–176.

Carr, S. C. (2002). *Social psychology: Context, communication, and culture.* Brisbane, Australia: John Wiley & Sons.

Carr, S. C., Mc Auliffe, E., & MacLachlan, M. (1998). *Psychology of aid.* London: Routledge.

Cheung, C. K., & Chan, C. M. (2000). Social-cognitive factors of donating money to charity, with special attention to an international relief organization. *Evaluation & program Planning, 23*, 241–253.

Cohen, S. (2001). *States of denial.* Boston, MA: Blackwell Publishing.

Cozzarelli, C., Wilkinson, A. V., & Tagler, M. J. (2001). Attitudes toward the Poor and attributions for poverty. *Journal of Social Issues, 57*, 207–227.

Croizet, J. C., & Claire, T. (1998). Extending the concept of stereotype and threat to social class: The intellectual under-performance of students from low socio-economic backgrounds. *Personality & Social Psychology Bulletin, 24*, 588–594.

Devine, P. G. (1996). Breaking the prejudice habit. *Psychological Science Agenda, Jan/Feb*, 10–11.

Dorward, D. (1996). Africa and development in the 21st century. *Development Bulletin, 37*, 4–7.

Dovidio, J. F., Kawakami, K., Johnson, C., Johnson, B., & Howard, A. (1997). On the nature of prejudice: Automatic and controlled processes. *Journal of Experimental Social Psychology, 33*, 510–540.

Epstein, S. (1994). Integration of the cognitive and the psychodynamic unconscious. *American Psychologist, 49*, 709–724.

Fazio, R. H., Jackson, J. R., Dunton, B. C., & Williams, C. J. (1995). Variability in automatic activiation as an unobtrusive measure of racial attitudes: A bona fide pipeline? *Journal of Personality and Social Psychology, 69*, 1013–1027.

Feagin, J. R. (1972). Poverty: We still believe God helps those who help themselves. *Psychology Today, 6*, 101–129.

Florian, V., and Mikulincer, M. (1998). Terror management in childhood: Does death conceptualisation moderate the effects of mortality salience on acceptance of similar and different others? *Personality & Social Psychology Bulletin, 24*, 1104–1112.

Fountain, S. (1995). *Education for development.* London: Hodder & Stoughton/UNICEF.

Fridlund, A. J., & Cacioppo, J. T. (1986). Guidelines for human electromyographic research. *Psychophysiology, 23*, 567–589.

Fridlund, A. J., Schwartz, G. E., & Fowler, S. C. (1984). Pattern recognition of self-reported emotional state from multiple-site facial EMG activity during affective imagery. *Psychophysiology, 21*, 622–637.

Godwin, N. (1994). A distorted view: Myths and images of developing countries. *Development Bulletin, 30,* 46–48.

Golby, A. J., Gabrieli, J. D., Chiao, J. Y.; and Eberhardt, J. L. (2001). Differential responses in the fusiform region to same-race and other-race faces. *Nature Neuroscience, 4*(8), 845–850.

Hess, U., Banse, R., & Kappas, A. (1995). The intensity of facial expression is determined by underlying affective state and social situation. *Journal of Personality & Social Psychology, 69*(2), 280–288.

Higgins, E. T. (1987). Self-discrepancy theory: What patterns of self-beliefs cause people to suffer? *Advances in Experimental Social Psychology, 22,* 93–136.

Hine, D. W., & Montiel, C. J. (1999). Poverty in developing nations: A cross-cultural attributional analysis. *European Journal of Social Psychology, 29,* 943–959.

Kosmitzki, C. (1996). The reaffirmation of cultural identity in cross-cultural encounters. *Personality & Social Psychology Bulletin, 22,* 238–248.

Liberman, N., & Förster, J. (2000). Expression after suppression: A motivational explanation of post-suppressional rebound. *Journal of Personality and Social Psychology, 79,* 190–203.

Lott, B. (2002). Cognitive and behavioral distancing from the poor. *American Psychologist, 57,* 100–110.

Lowery, B. S., Hardin, C. D., and Sinclair, S. (2001). Social influence effects on automatic racial prejudice. *Journal of Personality and Social Psychology, 81,* 842–855.

McConahay, J. B. (1983). Modern racism and modern discourse: The effects of race, racial attitudes, and context on simulated hiring decisions. *Personality & Social Psychology Bulletin, 9,* 551–558.

McConahay, J. B., Hardee, B. B., & Batts, Y. (1981). Has racism declined in America? It depends on who is asking and what is asked. *Journal of Conflict Resolution, 25,* 563–579.

MacCrae, C. N., Bodenhausen, G. V., & Milne, A. B. (1998). Saying No to unwanted thoughts: Self-focus and the regulation of mental life. *Journal of Personality and Social Psychology, 74,* 578–589.

MacCrae, C. N., Bodenhausen, G. V., Milne, A. B., & Jetten, J. (1994). Out of mind but back in sight: Stereotypes on the rebound. *Journal of Personality and Social Psychology, 67,* 808–817.

McGregor, D. (1960). *The human side of enterprise.* New York, NY: McGraw-Hill.

McHugo, G. J., Smith, C. A., & Lanzetta, J. T. (1982). The structure of self-reports of emotional responses to film segments. *Motivation & Emotion, 6,* 365–385.

Mehryar, A. H. (1984). The role of psychology in national development: Wishful thinking and reality. *International Journal of Psychology, 19,* 159–167.

Monteith, M. J., Sherman, J. W., & Devine, P. G. (1998). Suppression as a stereotype control strategy. *Personality & Social Psychology Review, 2,* 63–82.

Monteith, M. J., Spicer, C. V., & Tooman, J. D. (1998). Consequences of stereotype suppression: Stereotypes on and not on the rebound. *Journal of Experimental Social Psychology, 34,* 355–377.

Moskowitz, G., Gollwitzer, P., Wasel, W., & Schaal, B. (1999). Preconscious control of stereotype activation through chronic egalitarian goals. *Journal of Personality & Social Psychology, 77*(1), 167–184.

Operario, D., & Fiske, S. T. (2001). Causes and consequences of stereotyping in organizations. In M. London (Ed.), *How people evaluate others in organizations* (pp. 45–62). Mahwah, NJ: Lawrence-Erlbaum Associates, Inc.

Paul, A. M. (1998). Where bias begins: The truth about stereotypes. *Psychology Today, May/June,* 52, 55–82.

Pedersen, A, Griffiths, B., Contos, N., Bishop, B., & Walker, I. (2000). Attitudes toward Aboriginal Australians in city and country settings. *Australian Psychologist, 35,* 109–117.

Pettigrew, T. F. (1979). The ultimate attribution error: Extending Allport's cognitive analysis of prejudice. *Personality and Social Psychology Bulletin, 5,* 461–476.

Petty, R. E., & Cacioppo, J. T. (1984). The effects of involvement on reponses to argument quantity and quality: Central and peripheral routes to persuasion. *Journal of Personality and Social Psychology, 46,* 69–81.

Phillips, M. L., Marks, I. M., Senior, C., Lythgoe, D., O'Dwyer, A-M., Meehan, O., Williams, S. C. R., Brammer, M. J., Bullmore, E. T., & McGuire, P. K. (2000). A differential neural response in obsessive-compulsive disorder patients with washing compared with checking symptoms to disgust. *Psychological Medicine, 30*(5), 1037–1050.

Phillips, M. L., Williams, L., Senior, C., Bullmore, E. T., Brammer, M. J., Andrew, C., Williams, S. C. R., & David, A. S. (1999). A differential neural response to threatening and on-threatening negative facial expressions in paranoid and non-paranoid schizophrenics. *Psychiatry Research: Neuroimaging. 92*(1), 11–31.

Redding, R. E. (2001). Sociopolitical diversity in psychology: The case for pluralism. *American Psychologist, 56*(3), 205–215.

Schimel, J., Simon, L., Greenberg, J., Pyszcynski, T., Solomon, S., Waxmonsky, J., & Arndt, J. (1999). Stereotypes and terror management: Evidence that mortality salience enhances stereotypic thinking and preferences. *Journal of Personality and Social Psychology, 77,* 905–926.

Smith, M. K. (2001). Chris Argyris: Theories of action, double-loop learning and organizational learning. In *The Encyclopedia of informal education.* http://www.infed.org/thinkers/argyris.htm

Stangor, C. (Ed.). (2000). *Stereotypes and prejudice: Essential readings.* Philadelphia, PA: Psychology Press/Taylor & Francis.

Stangor, C., Sullivan, L. A., & Ford, T. E. (1991). Affective and cognitive determinants of prejudice. *Social Cognition, 9,* 359–380.

Tassinary, L. G., Cacioppo, J. T., Geen, J. T., & Thomas, R. (1989). A psychometric study of surface electrode placements for facial electromyographic recording: I. The brow and cheek muscle regions. *Psychophysiology, 26,* 1–16.

Vanman, E. J., & Miller, N. (1993). Applications of emotion theory and research to stereotyping and iner-group relations. In D. M. Mackie & D. L. Hamilton (Eds.), *Affect, cognition and stereotyping: Interactive processes in group perception* (pp. 213–238). New York: Academic Press.

Vanman, E. J., Paul, B. Y., Ito, T. A., & Miller, N. (1997). The modern face of prejudice and structural features that moderate the effect of co-operation on affect. *Journal of Personality and Social Psychology, 73,* 941–959.

Vecchio, R. P., Hearn, G., & Southey, G. (1997). *Organizational behavior.* Marrickville, Australia: Harcourt, Brace, & Company.

Wegner, D. M., Schneider, D. J., Carter, S. R., & White, T. L. (1987). Paradoxical effects of thought suppression. *Journal of Personality and Social Psychology, 53,* 5–13.

Whalen, P. J., Shin, L. M., McInerney, S. C., Fischer, H., Wright, C., & Rauch, S. L. (2001). A functional MRI scan of human amygdala responses to facial expressions of fear versus anger. *Emotion, 1,* 70–83.

Wheeler, L., Deci, E. L., Reis, H. T., & Zuckerman, M. (1978). *Interpersonal influence* (2nd ed.). Sydney, Australia: Allyn & Bacon.

Winkielman, P., & Cacioppo, J. T. (2001) Mind at ease puts a smile on the face: Psychophysiological evidence that processing facilitation elicits positive affect. *Journal of Personality and Social Psychology, 81*(6), 989–1000.

Worchel, S., & Brehm, J. W. (1970). Effects of threats to attitudinal freedom as a function of agreement with the communicator. *Journal of Personality and Social Psychology, 14,* 18–22.

Zanna, M. P., & Rempel, J. K. (1988). Attitudes: A new look at an old concept. In D. Bar-Tal & A. W. Kruglanski (Eds.), *The social psychology of knowledge* (pp. 315–334). Cambridge, MA: Cambridge University Press.

Chapter 16

Poverty and Psychology: A Call to Arms

Tod S. Sloan

The United Nations Development Programme (2000) estimates that 1.2 billion people have income or consumption levels of less that US$ 1 a day. A second billion people are living on less than $ 2 a day. These low income and consumption levels are directly associated with hunger, inadequate shelter, poor working conditions, illiteracy, poor health care, and vulnerability to natural disasters and human rights violations. Economists debate whether the gap between rich and poor has been increasing over the past few decades, because the situation of certain social sectors in some countries has improved significantly (Wade, 2001; Butler, 2000). Unfortunately, although many people have been lifted out of poverty by economic growth, population growth in low-income countries has kept the overall number of people living in poverty about the same (UNDP, 2000).

Given the sheer numbers of people in the world who are affected by poverty, it is striking how few psychologists in high-income countries are engaged directly in doing something about it. If parallel neglect were occurring in medicine, for example, doctors would ignore serious diseases affecting one-third of the world's population while treating the minor ills of a few million people living near their own neighborhoods. The likely response to this analogy would be that psychologists could do little to reduce global poverty. Given contemporary modes of psychological training and practice, this may be true, but it need not be so. One aim of this chapter is to demonstrate that the profession of psychology, if it is to claim any ethical justification for its existence, both can and should transform its practices in order to be part of the global effort to eradicate poverty. Given the recent American Psychological Association Resolution on Poverty and Socio-economic

Status (2000) within the USA – the center of the "psy" industry – and the fact
that the conditions of poverty are in many ways worse in regions outside of the
USA, the first step toward this transformation is a simple shift to a *global* frame of
reference. This implies recognition of the common humanity of all human beings
and the fact that our lives are now thoroughly interdependent. The second step
is to review avenues of approach where the skills associated with psychological
training can be either directly applied or expanded through further training. Acting
in a concerted manner on the basis of global awareness, psychologists could have
a significant impact on the world's ability to achieve the United Nations' goal of
reducing by half the proportion of people living in extreme poverty between 1990
and 2015.

A Broader Concept of Poverty

The multidimensional nature of poverty reflected in the chapters in this volume has become clearer with each decade of development work since the 1950s. In
light of this, the World Bank, in its *World Development Report 2000/2001*, recently
expanded the traditional definition of poverty as *material deprivation combined
with low achievements in education and health* to include *vulnerability, exposure
to risk, and lack of power to influence debate, decision making, and the allocation
of resources*. These additional dimensions of poverty reflect a new emphasis on the
centrality of *freedom* as a foundation for socio-economic development. This vision is articulated powerfully by the winner of the 1998 Nobel Prize in Economics,
Amartya Sen (1999). Strategies for eradicating poverty are changing accordingly
and now place major emphasis on dimensions of poverty related to the sphere of
civil, political and socio-economic rights.

Psychologists have, of course, previously expressed concern about global
social problems, particularly about peace and human rights issues, but also regarding potential roles for psychology in relation to national development (Rosenzweig, 1988; Moghaddam, 1990; Sloan, 1990; Carr & Schumaker, 1996; Anderson
& Christie, 2001). Further, certain subdisciplines within Anglophone and Latin
American psychology such as community psychology (Sanchez, 1996; Montero,
1998; Maton, 2000) and social-organizational psychology (Carr & Schumaker,
1996; Wittig & Bettencourt, 1996), have developed concepts, methods and practices that are relevant to this task, but only scattered individuals have taken the
step to become engaged with the concrete realities of global poverty (Serpell,
1997/1998).

The scope and degree of engagement that is now necessary has been described
and advocated by Marsella (1998) as *global-community psychology*. The project of
global-community psychology would be a "superordinate or meta-psychology concerned with understanding, assessing, and addressing the individual and collective

psychological consequences of global events and forces by encouraging and using multicultural, multidisciplinary, multisectoral, and multinational knowledge, methods, and interventions" (Marsella, 1998, p. 1284). This project would also reflect central concerns of the various forms of *critical psychology* and *liberation psychology* emerging around the world, particularly in Europe, Latin America, and Oceania. These approaches have been working out the ethical, epistemological, and methodological frameworks that will be necessary to catalyze and inform the participation of psychologists in the eradication of global poverty. I have become convinced that psychology will only be able to contribute to the eradication of poverty if it is able to transform itself radically as a discipline. Otherwise, psychology risks operating as a neo-colonial technocratic process of domination. Critical perspectives on psychology are pointing the way for the necessary transformation.

Shifting the Frame: Emerging Critical Psychologies

If professional training in psychology included major emphases on social responsibility in a global era, there would be no need for a shift in our frame of reference, but reviews of the impact of psychology on "Third World" development demonstrate that we have not come very far (Serpell, 1997/1998). If we had already made significant progress, we would already orient the majority of our efforts toward solving the most pressing psychosocial problems of humanity in the most direct and effective ways possible. Sensing this gap between psychology's potential and its action, proponents of critical psychology perspectives have urged a major rethinking of our primary activities as psychologists (Fox & Prilleltensky, 1997; Sloan, 2000; Prilleltensky & Nelson, in press). Critical psychology is actually a set of diverse theoretical perspectives that have recently joined forces to organize conferences and publish journals such as the *International Journal of Critical Psychology* and the *Annual Review of Critical Psychology*. The various approaches have in common a dedication to the reduction of suffering attributable to exploitation and oppression. This core concern leads to a claim that the individualism inherent in most psychological interventions seriously restricts their effectiveness as solutions to social problems. In fact, individualism generally serves an ideological function by attributing problems to personal defects rather than to the failures of social systems (Prilleltensky, 1994; 2001). The unjust status quo is thus reinforced. For example, it has been argued that the dominant cognitivist paradigm of the last two decades reinforces individualist ideology and therefore maintains social inequality in Western society (Sampson, 1981).

Some critical perspectives emphasize the ways in which all psychological practices and the scientific discourses that justify them are inseparable from power relations. These views are usually inspired by the French philosopher Michel Foucault or other post-structuralist social theory (Henriques, Hollway, Urwin,

Venn & Walkerdine, 1984; Rose, 1996). Other critical psychologies focus on the effects of economic exploitation, political oppression, or ideological forces that pacify citizens. These tend to draw on Marxist or neo-Marxist theory (Tolman, 1994; Sloan, 1996). Feminism has also been an important impetus for critical psychology, particularly for its critique of patriarchy, but also for its emphasis on methods that attend to the diversity of subjective experience and give voice to participants in research (Hollway, 1989).

In Latin America, liberation theology and Freire's (1980, 1970/1994) method of conscientization as a basis for literacy work and community organizing with oppressed communities have inspired the development of a social psychology of liberation that engages directly in collective action with poor people and brings social science resources such as survey methods and action research to bear in the process of social change. The work of the assassinated social psychologist and priest Ignacio Martín-Baró in El Salvador has been a rallying point for this approach (Martín-Baró, 1983, 1994; Montero, 1994, 1998; Dobles, 2000). Many aspects of Latin American political psychology are also directly relevant to poverty work (Montero, 1989).

Recent syntheses that draw on the common values and insights of several of these traditions have put critical psychology on the map as an important intellectual movement in international psychology (Parker & Spears, 1996; Fox & Prilleltensky, 1997; Holdstock, 2000; Prilleltensky & Nelson, in press).

With regard to strategies for producing change, critical psychologists would not deny that interventions aiming to change behavior at the level of the individual may actually succeed in doing that. They insist, however, that individual-level approaches often tend to reinforce the societal status quo by helping individuals adapt to organizational and institutional frameworks, while failing to challenge systematic injustice, inequity, and oppression affecting the quality of individual and collective life (Prilleltensky, 1994). Solutions for individuals may only appear to be solutions because a narrow socio-cultural lens is being used to assess well-being.

To counter individualism, approaches focusing on altering larger macroso-cial, systemic, ecological, structural, or environmental factors are often proposed. Behaviorist schemes for altering social behavior by manipulating environmental reinforcers of desired action are widely known. Such approaches may also be successful in reducing the incidence of problematic behaviors, but can be either shortsighted, have unanticipated consequences, or entail non-democratic political arrangements. Proponents of critical psychology insist on deep democratic processes for achieving ends that groups choose for themselves.

What is missing in both individualistic and macrosystem approaches is the awareness that both these levels, in the final account, are *mediated* by social, ideological, and cultural relations at the institutional, organizational, and community levels (Sloan, 1997; Spink, in press). The "individual" and the "system" are actually abstractions that can only be separated analytically from the dynamic process of history and social action. When one comprehends social reality in its dialectical multidimensionality, attempts to produce behavior change through instrumental intervention problematic.

Critical psychology approaches often build on related ecological perspectives that are popular in community psychology (Maton, 2000). Ecological models attend to the interactions between the multiple levels – individual, family, community, society and culture – in which humans live out their lives. Ecological perspectives in psychology, however, have tended to ignore power structures at the macrosocial level that control political, economic, and ideological processes in ways that seriously constrain life possibilities at the individual, family, institutional, and community levels. The macrosocial sphere is too often understood as lingering in the background, too large and distant to be concerned with, as one addresses individual or family problems. Rather than aiming to engineer social programs at the community level to change individual outcomes, critical psychology perspectives advocate working with citizens to challenge macrosocial power relations as they are manifested in local spheres. Thus, what differentiates a critical perspective from a general ecological perspective is its focus on social injustice embedded in the everyday operations of a social order in both the material and ideological spheres.

What, then, are the implications of critical psychology for the contribution of psychologists to the eradication of global poverty? To answer this, we turn first to a brief review of current thinking on economic development.

The Failure of a Strategy

A rare convergence is emerging between the official policies of global financial institutions and the wisdom of community-level poverty workers. For over 50 years, the former, in particular the International Monetary Fund and the World Bank, have imposed economic development strategies based on formulas that had sustained economic growth in Western industrial democracies. These formulas add up to what is known as structural adjustment, which includes the following measures: elimination of subsidies for basic goods, devaluation of national currency to stimulate exports, reduction of state support for social services and education, and higher interest rates to attract foreign investment. Structural adjustment policies have often succeeded in stopping hyperinflation and reducing government budget deficits, but their negative impact on the poor, especially women and children, has been well documented (Anderson & Cavanagh, 2000). Even if employed, the poor in low-income societies rely on low prices for food staples and medicine. Structural adjustment undermines these supports and exposes the poor people to higher prices that are rarely matched by higher pay. Some of the most devastating effects of structural adjustment stem from the exposure of weak national economies to price fluctuations in the global marketplace. Structural adjustment also paves the way for the free movement of capital across borders. As speculative capital in Asia or Africa abandons one market for another, what is noted as a minor drop in the value of individual stock portfolios in the USA can be experienced as unemployment and hunger for the poor in Indonesia or Kenya (Friedman, 2000).

Structural adjustment aimed to increase employment and individual income by providing optimal conditions for investment in production of commodities for export markets. From the beginning, this strategy has been challenged by people who work on the streets and in villages with the most marginalized and impoverished groups. They have insisted that poverty is not only a matter of cash income, but is rather an expression of an ongoing confluence of social structure, group process, community history, and political decisions. Solutions are therefore unlikely to emerge from purely macroeconomic strategies, and especially not when these require cutting support for nutrition, education, health care, and social services. In fact, when new employment opportunities are available primarily in or near major urban centers in the "Third World," rural poverty is aggravated.

Some of the limitations of structural adjustment have been duly noted, even in the institutions that first propagated these policies (World Bank, 2000), and more comprehensive development strategies have been proposed. These recognize that the work of eradicating poverty will necessarily be multidimensional and will attend to the social, cultural, environmental, and political dimensions of poverty, as well as the economic.

Human Rights and Human Development

The reconceptualization of poverty as deeply multifaceted is reflected in the new global consensus that is emerging around the idea that economic development, if its effects are to reach the poor, must be accompanied by real advances in the exercise of basic human rights. In the *Human Development Report 2000,* the United Nations Development Programme (UNDP) articulates this new linkage as follows:

> Poverty eradication is a major human rights challenge of the twenty-first century. A decent standard of living, adequate nutrition, health care, education, decent work and protection against calamities are not just development goals – they are also human rights. (p. 8)

The UNDP report then explains that the struggle must continue in seven major areas if the long unfinished agenda for human rights and human development is to be achieved. All of these areas depend on poverty eradication in a direct manner:

- freedom from discrimination – for equality,
- freedom from want – for decent standard of living,
- freedom to develop and realize one's human potential,
- freedom from fear – with no threats to personal security,
- freedom from injustice,
- freedom of participation, speech, and association, and
- freedom for decent work – without exploitation (UNDP, 2000, p. 31)

Realizing these freedoms at the practical level, the UNDP report continues, implies certain policy priorities for human rights and development. In particular, states and international institutions must ensure the civil and political rights of the poor and the organizations that represent them. When such rights are protected, non-governmental organizations (NGOs), the media, and labor organizations, in particular, can open new spaces for the voices of poor people. Advances in realizing economic and social rights will depend on increased public spending on education and enforcing labor standards, which in turn will catalyze the exercise of civil and political rights.

Similar policy priorities stem from the World Bank's *World Development Report 2000/2001: Attacking Poverty*. Besides promoting opportunity for poor people by building their assets and reducing their vulnerability to illness, violence, and disasters, the World Bank also urges the facilitation of empowerment by "making state institutions more accountable and responsive to poor people, strengthening the participation of poor people in political processes and local decision making, and removing the social barriers that result from distinctions of gender, ethnicity, race and social status." (p. 33)

The importance of the full range of human rights – from political to social and economic rights – in poverty eradication is highlighted by *Voices of the Poor,* a massive study based on interviews with over 40,000 poor men and women in 50 countries (Narayan, Patel, Schafft, Rademacher, & Koch-Schulte, 2000; Narayan, Chambers, Shah, & Petesch, 2000). The interviews revealed that low incomes are only the beginning of the everyday misery of the poor. The interviewees reported being subjected to maltreatment and violence, bureaucratic neglect and corruption, inefficient non-profit agencies, degraded environmental conditions, frequent ill health, and stigmatization. The situations of the poor were found to be quite diverse, but the study nevertheless came to these general conclusions: (1) poverty is multidimensional; (2) the state has been largely ineffective in reaching the poor; (3) the role of non-governmental organizations (NGOs) in the lives of the poor is limited, forcing the poor to depend primarily on their own informal networks; (4) households are crumbling under the stress of poverty, and (5) the social fabric – poor people's only "insurance" – is unraveling. (Narayan, Patel et al., 2000, p. 4)

Among the dimensions freshly documented as central to the multidimensionality of poverty are psychological ones such as powerlessness, voicelessness, shame, and humiliation as well as their manifestations in alcoholism, domestic violence, and depression. Gender-based power inequities are repeatedly noted by *Voices of the Poor* authors as factors in all aspects of poverty. The psychological perspective, in combination with awareness of the failure of government programs and the limitations of NGO projects, opens the door for consideration of extensive psychosocial community-level interventions with input from professionals with training in the human sciences.

At every turn, proposed strategies for change emerging from the Voices of the Poor study echo the need for attention to psychosocial aspects of poverty *in conjunction with* the economic, legal, and organizational. Specifically, the authors recommend starting with poor people's realities, investing in the organizational capacity of the poor, changing social norms, and supporting "development entrepreneurs," individuals who are leading the way in providing solutions to their communities' problems (Narayan, Patel et al., 2000). At every turn, the eradication of poverty implies that norms must be changed, consciousness must be raised, organizations must be improved, and community assets must be mobilized. Consider the shift in thinking that is occurring when the World Bank, an institution that has primarily focused on macroeconomic strategies, publishes a major study that concludes with the following sort of comment: "To bring about large-scale change will require the power of both individual and institutional action, but attention has first to be given to the personal over the institutional" (Narayan, Patel et al., 2000, p. 279). Even if this does not reflect official World Bank policy, it nevertheless serves as a wake-up call for psychologists who may have assumed that their sphere of expertise was irrelevant to the global poor. We now turn, therefore, to examine avenues of action that are open to psychologists.

Paths of Engagement

Psychologists can become engaged in the eradication of global poverty along many different paths, as the authors in this volume testify. The paths mentioned here are neither exhaustive nor prescriptive. They are intended to illustrate some of the current types of work that can be done. Each of these paths initially appears fairly straightforward, but from the standpoints of prior development experiences as well as those of critical and liberation psychologies, numerous pitfalls must be avoided. The pitfalls in each of these paths may be serious enough to make one consider less problematic routes, but such decisions will have to be taken by individuals and organizations according to their understandings of what will make the greatest contribution.

Community Development.   Applications of methods developed in the fields of community psychology and organizational behavior are among the more direct ways of making a difference for the global poor. Strategic planning, needs assessments, program evaluation, and leadership training can be utilized to improve literacy programs, vocational and entrepreneurship training, prevention programs, non-profit and public management skills, schools, environmental conditions, and health and human services delivery. Not all of this work needs to be done directly in developing societies. Many of the organizations that sponsor development projects are based in high-income countries and many aspects of the work, such as research, fund-raising, and inter-organizational collaboration, can be effected without extensive travel or language skills.

A few of the possibly problematic aspects of community development work are the imposition of Western models of appropriate organizational behavior, failure to develop local leadership or enhance local skills in the process of consulting, neglect of national or regional political and economic structures that mediate local community processes, and ignorance of gender issues affecting organizational development (Carr & Schumaker, 1996; Enarson & Morrow, 1998; Mohan & Stokke, 2000; Cooke & Kothari, 2001; Raven, 2001). Furthermore, many of the most effective community organizations are rather informal "people's organizations" with scarce resources that cannot be devoted to paying for Western-style strategic planning or program evaluation (Spink, in press).

Advocacy for Marginalized Groups. Work that is more directly political, but still very relevant to psychologists' skills, can be done by supporting advocacy and mobilization for groups that are marginalized and therefore experience powerlessness and voicelessness (Montero, 1998). Among the poor, women, children, the elderly, and people with disabilities are often the most vulnerable and the least heard. New political settings will need to be opened up for the effective practice of democracy by these groups (Barker, 1999). An interesting idea that emerges in this context is that work with poor people with mental illnesses might involve building their citizenship skills (Moreira, in press; Prilleltensky, 2001). In work along these lines, possible pitfalls include acting on the basis of limited understanding of local political culture and power structures, putting vulnerable people at risk unnecessarily, and raising unrealistic expectations. These pitfalls can be avoided in part by building effective collaborations with interdisciplinary teams of professionals based in the regions where the work is being done.

Human Rights Work. Emerging leaders among the poor need to know that international outrage will be expressed toward their governments if their civil rights are not respected. Human rights work in support of such leaders is essential to ensure that the few who stand up to speak for the social and economic rights of thousands may continue to do so safely. Given the central role women play in the material survival of their families, leaders struggling for gender equity are of particular importance at this historical juncture (UNDP, 2000; World Bank, 2001). Psychologists can make important contributions in the emerging field of mental health and human rights (Lykes & Liem, 1990), but can also have an impact by becoming familiar with general human rights issues and working to improve conditions for those who are leading local struggles for social change (Van Genugten & Perez-Bustillo, 2001).

Humanitarian Assistance and Trauma Intervention. In communities torn by ethnopolitical and other forms of civil war, post-conflict programs for trauma intervention, reintegration, community building, and reconciliation can prepare the foundations for eventual economic development and poverty prevention. Similarly, humanitarian assistance following natural disasters can be organized in a manner that leaves communities less vulnerable to similar disasters and paves the way for sustainable development. In all such situations, political naïvete and cultural assumptions about gender roles may become major obstacles to assistance that is helpful over the long run (Enarson & Morrow, 1998).

Conflict Resolution: Building Cultures of Peace. A major factor contributing to poverty in certain regions is expenditure on arms and the disruption of normal production by war and other conflict. Psychologists have developed numerous methods for the prevention and resolution of conflict, some of which have already proven effective in negotiating truces and peace agreements. Methods for building cultures of peace need to be implemented widely not only to prevent bloodshed but to solidify social bases for community development and economic well-being (Anderson & Christie, 2001). Important work is also being done with indigenous peoples in previously colonized regions. These projects try to build bases for empowerment and full participation of indigenous people, a process that implies a sort of disempowerment for the colonizers (Drew, Sonn, Bishop & Contos, 2000).

Social Marketing. Most organizations working to eradicate global poverty require funding. Although some advertising strategies designed to raise money for development projects have been criticized for using images of starving children to manipulate emotions, the fact remains that resources from the North will need to be transferred to the South either through charitable donations by foundations and individuals or by governments, intergovernmental organizations, and international financial bodies. Awareness of, and concern for, the conditions of the global poor must be raised much more effectively both to increase giving and to shape national foreign aid policies. Psychologists can work in many capacities in these efforts, from consulting on advertising to analyzing flaws in foreign aid systems (Carr, this issue).

Labor Solidarity. International solidarity among workers' organizations is particularly important in the era of corporate globalization. Corporations have repeatedly relocated plants to other countries when labor begins to organize for better wages or working conditions (Brecher, Costello, & Smith, 2000). Only international co-operation between workers' organizations will halt this trend (Wright, 2000). In this sphere, psychologists can improve effectiveness of unions through support for democratization, improved communications, research, and advocacy. Work with labor organizations will also be necessary to generate support for the ecologically sustainable modes of production that must be developed quickly in order to preserve life on this planet (Oskamp, 2000; Raven, 2001).

Appropriate Global Psychology. For psychologists who are unable to shift energies in any of the above directions that involve direct engagement, other options are available. These options may even turn out to make more of a difference in the long run. Historically, involvement in "international psychology" has meant fostering international exchange between psychologists, collaboration in cross-cultural research, and indirectly laying the groundwork for the exportation of Western scientific psychology to regions of the world where psychology as a discipline was still in its early stages. These international efforts have set the stage for consideration of the importance of indigenous psychologies as well as concerns about the appropriateness of employing psychological methods and practices in non-Western societies (Moghaddam, 1990; Sloan, 1996).

Some cross-cultural psychologists and most critical psychology advocates argue that the individualizing, depoliticizing, and objectifying tendencies in scientific psychological practices are potentially so destructive of cultural processes in non-Western societies that extensive international dialogues should occur before further exportation and importation of scientific psychology is sponsored (Sloan, 1990, 1996; Moghaddam, 1996). One can imagine that such dialogues might lead to significant changes in both "First World" and "Third World" graduate psychology training programs. Programs might start requiring, for example, advanced language expertise, relevant interdisciplinary studies in anthropology, economics, and political science, and training in participatory research methods.

Global Citizenship

The professional training and education of psychologists certainly does not discourage active global citizenship, but neither does the discipline do much to equip psychologists for such engagement. In fact, it would be fair to say that psychological studies have a general depoliticizing effect. This stems from the combination of individualizing and asocial assumptions about behavior at the level of theory, lack of support for interdisciplinary studies in, for example, history, political science, anthropology and sociology, gender/ethnic studies, and minimal institutional recognition for engaged citizenship as a form of service.

The confluence of global social movements of the early twenty-first century provide a great opportunity for psychologists to engage constructively with processes that will affect the fate of the world's poor. A "globalization from below" is developing on the basis of new collaborations between the movements for peace, for responsible trade policies, for the rights of workers, women, children, and people with disabilities, for ecologically sustainable economies, and against racism and homophobia (Brecher, Costello, & Smith, 2000). These global movements aim to foster policies and related institutional arrangements that respond to the declining power of nation-states and establish new political spaces that take into account the world's poor people (Hardt & Negri, 2000). Psychologists who are not participating in some manner in support of these movements may be, in the final analysis, part of the problem. The path of non-engagement, of neutral scientific scholarship, or local applied work simply affirms the status quo with its egregious disparities of wealth and power.

Acknowledgments

I am grateful to Jill Norman at the University of Tulsa for her assistance in gathering information for this article. Bernardo Jimenez, Virginia Moreira, and Stuart Carr made useful suggestions in response to earlier versions.

References

American Psychological Association (2000). Resolution on poverty and socio-economic status. www.apa.org/pi/urban/povres.html
Anderson, S., & Cavanagh, J. (2000). *Field guide to the global economy.* New York: New Press.
Anderson, A., & Christie, D. (2001). Some contributions of psychology to policies promoting cultures of peace. *Peace and Conflict: The Journal of Peace Pyschology, 7*(2), 173–185.
Barker, J. (1999). *Street-level democracy: Political settings at the margins of global power.* West Hartford, CT: Kumarian.
Brecher, J., Costello, T., & Smith, B. (2000). *Globalization from below: The power of solidarity.* Cambridge, MA: South End Press.
Butler, C. (2000). Inequality, global change and the sustainability of civilization. *Global Change and Human Health, 1*(2), 156–172.
Carr, S., & Schumaker, J. (Eds.). (1996). *Psychology and the developing world.* Westport, CT: Praeger.
Cooke, B., & Kothari, U. (2001). *Participation: The new tyranny?* London: Zed Books.
Dobles, I. (2000). A Central American voice. In T. Sloan (Ed.), *Critical psychology: Voices for change* (pp. 125–135). London: Macmillan.
Drew, N., Sonn, C., Bishop, B., & Contos, N. (2000). "Is doing good just enough?" Enabling practice in enabling discipline. In T. Sloan (Ed.), *Critical psychology: Voices for change* (pp. 171–183). London: Macmillan.
Enarson, E., & Morrow, B. (Eds.). (1998). *The gendered terrain of disaster.* Westport, CT: Praeger.
Fox, D., & Prilleltensky, I. (Eds.). (1997). *Critical psychology: An introduction.* Thousand Oaks, CA: Sage.

Freire, P. (1980). Conscientização: Teoria e pratica da liberaçao [Conscientization: Theory and practice of liberation]. Sao Paolo: Moraes.

Freire, P. (1970/1994). *Pedagogy of the oppressed.* (Rev. ed.). New York, NY: Continuum. Original edition 1970.

Friedman, T. (2000). *The Lexus and the olive tree: Understanding globalization.* New York, NY: Anchor.

Hardt, M., & Negri, A. (2000) *Empire.* Cambridge, MA: Harvard University Press.

Henriques, J., Hollway, W., Urwin, C., Venn, C., & Walkerdine, V. (1984). *Changing the subject: Psychology, social regulation and subjectivity.* London: Methuen.

Holdstock, T. L. (2000). *Re-examining psychology: Critical perspectives and African insights.* London: Routledge.

Hollway, W. (1989). *Subjectivity and method in psychology: Gender, meaning, and science.* London: Sage.

Lykes, M. B., & Liem, R. (1990). Human rights and mental health in the United States: Lessons from Latin America. *Journal of Social Issues, 46*(3), 151–165.

Martín-Baró, I. (1983). *Accion y ideologia: Psicologia social desde Centroamerica.* El Salvador: UCA Editores.

Marsella, A. J. (1998). Toward a "global-community psychology": Meeting the needs of a changing world. *American Psychologist, 53,* 1282–1291.

Martín-Baró, I. (1994). *Writings for a liberation psychology.* Cambridge, MA: Harvard University Press.

Maton, K. (2000). Making a difference: The social ecology of social transformation. *American Journal of Community Psychology, 28*(1), 25–57.

Moghaddam, F. (1990). Modulative and generative orientations in psychology: Implications for psychology in the three worlds. *Journal of Social Issues, 46*(3), 21–21.

Moghaddam, F. (1996). Training for developing-world psychologists: Can it be better than the psychology? In S. Carr & J. Schumaker (Eds.), *Psychology and the developing world* (pp. 49–59). Westport, CT: Praeger.

Mohan, G., & Stokke, K. (2000). Participatory development and empowerment: The dangers of localism. *Third World Quarterly, 21*(2), 247–268.

Montero, M. (Ed.). (1987). *Psicología política latinoamericana.* Caracas: Panapo.

Montero, M. (1994). Consciousness-raising, conversion, and de-ideologization in community psychosocial work. *Journal of Community Psychology, 22*(1), 3–11.

Montero, M. (1998). Psychosocial community work as an alternative mode of political action (The construction and critical transformation of society). *Community, Work, and Family, 1*(1), 65–78.

Moreira, V. (In press). Psychopathology and poverty. In S. Carr and T. Sloan, (Eds.), *Poverty, wealth, and community development.* New York, NY: Kluwer.

Narayan, D., Patel, R., Schafft, K., Rademacher, A. & Koch-Schulte, S. (2000). *Voices of the poor: Can anyone hear us?* New York, NY: Oxford University Press.

Narayan, D., Chambers, R., Shah, M., & Petesch, P. (2000). *Voices of the poor: Crying out for change.* New York, NY: Oxford University Press.

Oskamp, S. (2000). A sustainable future for humanity? How can psychology help? *American Psychologist, 55,* 496–508.

Parker, I., & Spears, R. (1996). *Psychology and society: Radical theory and practice.* London: Pluto Press.

Prilleltensky, I. (1994). *The morals and political of psychology: Psychology and the status quo.* Albany, NY: SUNY Press.

Prilleltensky, I. (2001). Cultural assumptions, social justice, and mental health: Challenging the status quo. In J. Schumaker and T. Ward (Eds.), *Cultural cognition and psychopathology* (pp. 251–265). Westport, CT: Praeger.

Prilleltensky, I., & Nelson, G. (In press). *Doing psychology critically.* London: Macmillan.

Raven, J. (2001). Psychologists and sustainability. American Psychologist, 56, 455–457.

Rose, N. (1996). *Inventing our selves: Psychology, power, and personhood.* Cambridge: Cambridge University Press.

Rosenzweig, M. (1988). Psychology and the United Nations Human Rights Efforts. *American Psychologist, 43*(2), 79–86.

Sampson, E. E. (1981). Cognitive psychology as ideology. *American Psychologist, 36,* 730–743.

Sanchez, E. (1996). The Latin American experience in community social psychology. In S. Carr & J. Schumaker (Eds.), *Psychology and the developing world* (pp. 118–129). Westport, CT: Praeger.

Sen, A. (1999). *Development as freedom.* New York, NY: Anchor.

Serpell, R. (1997/1998). The impact of psychology on "Third World" development. *African Social Research,* Nos. 39–40, 1–18.

Sloan, T. (1990). Psychology for the "Third World"? *Journal of Social Issues, 46*(3), 1–20.

Sloan, T. (1996). Psychological research methods in developing countries. In S. Carr & J. Schumaker (Eds.), *Psychology and the developing world* (pp. 33–45). New York, NY: Praeger.

Sloan, T. (1997). *Damaged life: The crisis of the modern psyche.* New York, NY: Routledge.

Sloan, T. (Ed). (2000). *Critical psychology: Voices for change.* New York, NY: St. Martin's Press.

Spink, P. (In press). The place of psychology within poverty and the recovery of channel theory. In S. Carr & T. Sloan (Eds.), *Poverty, wealth, and community development.* New York, NY: Kluwer.

Tolman, C. (1994). *Psychology, society, and subjectivity: An introduction to German critical psychology.* London: Routledge.

United Nations Development Programme. (2000). *Human development report 2000.* New York, NY: Oxford University Press.

Van Genugten, W., & Perez-Bustillo, C. (Eds.). (2001). *The poverty of rights: Human rights and the eradication of poverty.* London: Zed Books.

Wade, R. (2001). Winners and losers. *The Economist,* April 28.

Wittig, M. and Bettencourt, B. (Eds.) (1996). Social psychological perspectives on grassroots organizing. *Journal of Social Issues, 52*(1). [Entire issue].

World Bank. (2000). *World development report 2000/2001: Attacking poverty.* http://www.worldbank.org/poverty/wdrpoverty/report/index/htm.

World Bank (2001). *Engendering development – through gender equality in rights, resources, and voice.* New York, NY: Oxford University Press. Wright, E. O. (2000). Class compromise, globalization, and technological change. In D. Kalb, M. van der Land, R. Staring, B. van Steenbergen, & N. Wilterdink (Eds.), *The ends of globalization: Bringing society back in* (pp. 87–106). Lanham, MD: Rowman & Littlefield.

Index